OXFORD HISTORICAL MONOGRAPHS

EDITORS

Model Mothers

Jewish Mothers and Maternity Provision in East London, 1870–1939

LARA V. MARKS

CLARENDON PRESS · OXFORD
1994

Oxford University Press, Walton Street, Oxford OX2 6DP
Oxford New York Toronto
Delhi Bombay Calcutta Madras Karachi
Kuala Lumpur Singapore Hong Kong Tokyo
Nairobi Dar es Salaam Cape Town
Melbourne Auckland Madrid
and associated companies in
Berlin Ibadan

Oxford is a trade mark of Oxford University Press

Published in the United States
by Oxford University Press Inc., New York

British Library Cataloguing in Publication Data
Data available

Library of Congress Cataloging in Publication Data
Marks, Lara, 1963–
Model mothers : Jewish mothers and maternity provision in East
London, 1870–1939 / Lara V. Marks.
p. cm.—(Oxford historical monographs)
Includes bibliographical references.
1. Jewish women—Health and hygiene—England—London. 2. Maternal
health services—England—London. 3. Maternal and infant welfare—
England—London. 4. Jewish women—Services for—England—London.
5. Infant health services—England—London. 6. Infants—Health and
hygiene—England—London. I. Title. II. Series.
RG964.G72E545 1994
362.1'982'00899240421—dc20 93–37962
ISBN 0–19–820454–X

1 3 5 7 9 10 8 6 4 2

Typeset by Graphicraft Typesetters Ltd., Hong Kong
Printed in Great Britain
on acid-free paper by
Biddles Ltd.
Guildford and King's Lynn

This book is dedicated to my parents and grandparents, whose own experience and history of immigration inspired me to write this book

Preface and Acknowledgements

THIS book started as a doctoral thesis submitted to the University of Oxford in 1990. Like all books it has had a long and varied history. While this book was partly inspired by my own family background which has been one of continual immigration, it has also been greatly influenced by the current debates concerning women's experience of childbirth and the problems ethnic minorities face today in access to healthcare provision. Only in the final stages of writing the book, however, did I really understand the significance of this research, when, crippled with back-pain from too many hours spent on the computer, I was forced to turn for relief to an acupuncturist who had no English, speaking only Chinese. Unfortunately the acupuncturist could not cure the pain, but the difficulties I experienced in communicating with her and the cultural barriers I encountered revealed to me what it must have been like for many of the Jewish mothers I had been studying. Indeed I began to understand the acute problems that can arise from a health professional not understanding a patient's language or culture and the ways in which this can intensify physical as well as mental suffering.

No words can express the gratitude I feel for all those who have helped and encouraged me over the past few years in preparing this book. The book could not have been written without the continual support and encouragement of my parents and brother, whose interest and help made the work immeasurably easier. Similarly, this book would never have materialized had it not been for the steadfast patience and enormous encouragement given to me by Irvine Loudon and Anne Summers who not only supervised my doctoral dissertation but have continued to be bulwarks of support. Great appreciation also goes to Richard Smith as sub-editor, whose constant advice and reassurance were vital in the preparation of the final manuscript. Warm thanks go to Marion Aptroot, without whom the final proof-reading of the manuscript could not have been completed. Much gratitude is also owed to Humaira Ahmed for her skill and stamina in helping me draw up the tables and for sustaining me when my computer abilities failed me. I am grateful to Edward Oliver for producing such wonderful maps. Special thanks go to Lisa Hilder and Enid Henessey for all their patience and help in the statistical side of the book. I am greatly indebted to Graham Mooney for supplying crucial statistics for infant mortality in the sub-wards of East London. This book would not have been the same without the support of Hilary Marland, who not only taught me invaluable editing skills when we were co-editing another book, but who has continually given me advice and encouragement. Appreciation goes to Helen Nicholls and John Clute for their help in the final stages of finishing the manuscript. Other personal debts, too numerous to mention, are owed to friends, most particularly to Sandra den Otter and Maridowa Williams.

I would also like to thank Pat Thane, Liz Peretz, Mathew Thomson, Tony Kushner, and Bill Williams for their support and useful suggestions on parts of the thesis and the final manuscript. In preparing both the book and the thesis academic help was given freely by Gerry Black, Rickie Burman, Claire Collins, Gretchen Condran, Felix Driver, Judith Emanuel, David Feldman, Eilidh Garrett, Anne Hardy, Ellen Kramarow, John Mohan, Roger Lee, Jane Lewis, Margaret Pelling, Frank Prochaska, Diana Rau, Gillian Rose, Ellen Ross, Humphrey Southall, Michael Steinlauf, Charles Webster, Paul Weindling, Jerry White, and Naomi Williams. In addition to their support I learnt a great deal from discussions at seminars at the Wellcome Unit in Oxford and at the Institute for Historical Research, as well as from those who attended papers I presented at various seminars and conferences. The work could not have been completed without the support of the academic and secretarial staff at the following: the Wellcome Unit in Oxford; Wolfson College, Oxford; and the Geography Department at Queen Mary and Westfield College, London University. I have learnt a great deal in teaching a course on the history of childbirth, both through my co-worker Geoff Wycurz and through my medical students, Tammy Angel, Gill McFarlane, Chris McLean, and Theresa Patton whose oral history interviews reinvigorated my own research.

This book was largely supported by a Research Assistantship funded by the Wellcome Trust for my doctoral dissertation. I am grateful to Wolfson College for their financial assistance in the early stages of the thesis and for their research awards. Part of the book has also benefited greatly from another research project I am presently completing with the help of the Leverhulme Trust. Gratitude goes to the Nuffield Foundation whose sponsorship of another pilot project to the USA also provided material for this book.

Research for this thesis was made immeasurably easier by the knowledge and kindness of the staff at the Anglo-Jewish Archives and Mocatta

Library, the Bodleian Library, the British Library, the British Library of Political and Social Science, Cambridge University Library, the Greater London Records Office, the Jewish Welfare Board, the London School of Hygiene and Tropical Medicine, the Library of Congress Archive, the London Museum of Jewish Life, Manchester Jewish Museum, Mayfield Convent, the Public Records Office, Mrs C. Rantzen, St Bartholomew's Hospital Archives, The Royal London Hospital Archives, the Tower Hamlets Local History Library and Archive, and the Westminster Diocese Archive. I am deeply grateful to Claire Daunton, who as the archivist at The Royal London Hospital Archives provided some important leads when I started my research. Warm appreciation also goes to all the people I interviewed for the research, whose memories brought the project alive and added a rich texture to my work.

Contents

List of Figures

List of Maps

List of Tables

Abbreviations

AJA	Anglo-Jewish Archives
Am. Hist. Rev.	*American Historical Review*
Am. J. Nursing	*American Journal of Nursing*
Am. J. Obstet. and Diseases for Women and Children	*American Journal of Obstetrics and Diseases for Women and Children*
Am. J. Publ. Health	*American Journal of Public Health*
Am. J. Stud. Rev.	*American Jewish Studies Review*
Am. J. Sociol.	*American Journal of Sociology*
Ann. Eug.	*Annals of the Eugenics*
AR	Annual Report
BL	British Library
Bodl.	Bodleian Library, Oxford
Br. J. Obstet. & Gynaecol.	*British Journal of Obstetrics and Gynaecology*
BLPES	British Library of Political and Economic Sciences
Br. Med. J.	*British Medical Journal*
Bull. Hist. Med.	*Bulletin of the History of Medicine*
CLMH	City of London Maternity Hospital
CRO	Chief Rabbi's Office Archive (also known as United Synagogue's Archive)
CMB	Central Midwives Board
Econ. Hist. Rev.	*Economic History Review*
EEMH	East End Maternity Home
ELA	*East London Advertiser*
ELNS	East London Nursing Society
ELO	*East London Observer*
Epidemiol. Rev.	*Epidemiological Review*
Eur. J. Popul.	*European Journal of Population*
Fem. Stud.	*Feminist Studies*
Gender and Hist.	*Gender and History*
GLRO	Greater London Record Office
HCSC	House of Commons Select Committee
Hist.	*History*
Hist. J.	*Historical Journal*

Hist. Research	*Historical Research*
Hist. Workshop J.	*History Workshop Journal*
IMR	Infant Mortality Rate
Internat. Migration Rev.	*International Migration Review*
Irish Hist. Stud.	*Irish Historical Studies*
JAPGW	Jewish Association for the Protection of Girls and Women
JBG	Jewish Board of Guardians
JC	*Jewish Chronicle*
JMH	Jewish Maternity Home
Jewish Soc. Stud.	*Jewish Social Studies*
Jewish J. Sociol.	*Jewish Journal of Sociology*
Jewish Stud. Rev.	*Jewish Studies Review*
JWB	Jewish Welfare Board Archive
J. Am. Hist.	*Journal of American History*
J. Am. Med. Ass.	*Journal of the American Medical Association*
J. Biosoc. Sci.	*Journal of Biosocial Science*
J. Br. Stud.	*Journal of British Studies*
J. Contemp. Hist.	*Journal of Contemporary History*
J. Eur. Econ. Hist.	*Journal of European Economic History*
J. Hist. Geog.	*Journal of Historical Geography*
J. Hist. Med.	*Journal of the History of Medicine and Allied Sciences*
J. Interdisc. Hist.	*Journal of Interdisciplinary History*
J. Roy. Stat. Soc.	*Journal of the Royal Statistical Society*
J. Sanitary Institute	*Journal of the Sanitary Institute*
J. Soc. Hist.	*Journal of Social History*
J. Soc. Pol.	*Journal of Social Policy*
J. Stat. Soc.	*Journal of the Statistical Society*
J. Urban Hist.	*Journal of Urban History*
LCC	London County Council
LGB	Local Government Board
Loc. Popul. Stud.	*Local Population Studies*
LH	London Hospital (Archive)
Lond. Hosp. Illust.	*London Hospital Illustrated*
Lond. Med. Gaz.	*London Medical Gazette*
LSPCJ	London Society for Promoting Christianity Amongst the Jews
MCW	Maternity and Child Welfare
Med. Hist.	*Medical History*

Med. Offr.	Medical Officer
MH	Ministry of Health
MMR	Maternal Mortality Rate
MOH	Medical Officer of Health
Mocatta	Mocatta Library, University College, London University (Most of this collection has now been moved to Parkes Library, Southampton University)
NSP	Nursing Sisters of the Poor (Little Sisters of the Assumption)
Oral Hist.	Oral History
Popul. Stud.	Population Studies
PP	Parliamentary Papers
PMJ	Parochial Mission to the Jews
P&P	Past and Present
PRO	Public Record Office
Publ. Health	Public Health
Recusant Hist.	Recusant History
RC	Royal Commission
RMC	Royal Maternity Charity
St Bart's	St Bartholomew's Hospital Archive
SA	Salvation Army Archive
SAMH	Salvation Army Mothers' Hospital
Sanitary Rec.	Sanitary Record
SP	Special Papers
SRHS	Sick Room Helps Society
Soc. Hist. Med.	Social History of Medicine
Soc. Serv. Rev.	Social Services Review
SBGNA	Stepney and Bethnal Green Nursing Association
SHCJ	Society for the Holy Child of Jesus
THL	Tower Hamlets Local History Library and Archive
Trans. Internat. Med. Cong.	Transactions of the International Medical Congress
Trans. Obstet. Soc.	Transactions of the Obstetrical Society
Twentieth Cent. Br. Hist.	Twentieth Century British History
UCH	University College Hospital
Vict. Stud.	Victorian Studies
Women's Internat. Forum	Women's International Forum

Introduction

In the care of their children the Jewish mothers are a pattern to their Gentile neighbours in the East End. Go and visit the schools in the East End and see the Jewish children. They stand out in marked contrast to other children for brightness and healthy appearance. That is only due to the Jewish mothers.[1]

SUCH visions of Jewish women as good mothers with robust children were portrayed by many medical practitioners, voluntary workers, and statesmen in late nineteenth-century England. Much of their praise focused on the good care Jewish mothers took of their families and in particular of their infants. Indeed, Jewish mothers were presented as models to other mothers. They were not only seen to be scrupulous in the attention they paid to household chores, but were also lauded for ceasing to work early in pregnancy, and for their good breast-feeding habits. The remarkably low rates of mortality among Jewish infants in East London and elsewhere were also attributed to the exemplary care Jewish mothers took of their babies.

While it is impossible to measure the extent to which Jewish mothers were as perfect as contemporaries in the late nineteenth century suggested, their remarks reflect the importance attached to motherhood both in the Jewish community and in the outside world during this period. This has not only shaped the roles Jewish women have been expected to play, but also the way in which their history has been written. Much of the image of the Jewish woman has been influenced by traditional Judaism which asserts that a woman's prime responsibility is to her family and home. Thus women are exempt from all religious tasks which have to be performed at a certain time of day. Women are not counted in *minyans* (the quorum of ten needed for communal prayer) and cannot lead communal prayers.[2] Similarly Jewish women have usually been prevented from reciting the blessings over the Torah,[3] reading from the Torah scroll, or studying sacred texts. Traditionally, therefore, women have been

[1] Mr J. Prag, member of the St Pancras Health and Insanitary Areas Committee, evidence to *RC Alien Immigration*, PP 1903 IX Pt. II (henceforth PP 1903 IX), Minutes of Evidence, Q17877.

[2] R. Biale, *Women and Jewish Law: An Exploration of Women's Issues in Halakhic Sources* (New York, 1984), 21–4. [3] The five books of Moses, or the Pentateuch.

restricted from participating in religious and communal decision-making, areas which have been primarily reserved for men.[4] Instead, a woman's worth has been measured by her ability to be a good mother. Her role as a good wife and mother has been viewed as the key to the survival of the Jewish family and community.[5]

The stereotype of Jewish women has not only been influenced by the roles prescribed by traditional Judaism, but also by the social concerns of British contemporaries. Arriving at a time of great fear about the future strength of the British nation, the East European Jewish immigrants were often the focus of the social and political debates of the late nineteenth century. At the heart of these discussions was the perceived physical and military deterioration of the British empire.[6] Much of the anxiety focused on the diminishing birth rate, persistently high infant mortality, and the failure of many recruits to pass the fitness tests needed to join the army for the South African War (1899–1902). For many social reformers and politicians 'good motherhood' was seen as the answer to the high infant mortality and physical deterioration. Attention concentrated on the need to educate 'ignorant' and 'feckless' mothers in proper infant management. This, it was argued, would reduce infant mortality and secure the health of future generations. To this aim health-visiting and schools for mothers were established on an unprecedented level. Drawing on nineteenth-century notions of 'good motherhood' many of these activities were moulded around middle-class ideals of domesticity and the family unit.[7] The Jewish mother and her virtues symbolized the solutions to

[4] P. Hyman, 'The Other Half: Women in the Jewish Tradition', and S. Berman, 'The Status of Women in Halakhic Judaism', in E. Koltun, *The Jewish Woman: New Perspectives* (New York, 1976); L. Gordon Kuzmack, *Woman's Cause: The Jewish Woman's Movement in England and the United States, 1881–1933* (Columbus, Oh., 1990), 4–5.

[5] See e.g. R. Yellin, 'A Philosophy of Jewish Masculinity: One Interpretation', *Conservative Judaism*, 32/2 (1979), 93, and M. Meiselman, *Jewish Woman in Jewish Law* (New York, 1978), 16, both cited in S. Herschel (ed.), *On Being a Jewish Feminist* (New York, 1985), xviii.

[6] This can be seen in the evidence given to the *House of Lords Select Committee on Sweating System*, PP SP 1888 XX; PP 1889 XIII, XIV; PP 1890 XVI; *House of Commons Select Committee on Alien Immigration*, PP 1888 XI; PP 1889 X; and *RC Alien Immigration*, PP 1903. An interesting analysis of the way in which perceptions of alien immigration impinged on more general discussions concerning social and political questions of physical deterioration, unemployment, high rents, and poverty in Britain appears in D. Feldman, 'The Importance of Being English: Jewish Immigration and the Decay of Liberal England', in D. Feldman and G. Stedman Jones (eds.), *Metropolis London: Histories and Representations Since 1800* (London, 1989).

[7] For more detail on the connections between the fears of racial degeneration and the South African War and how these affected issues of infant mortality and maternal and infant welfare see A. Davin, 'Imperialism and Motherhood', *Hist. Workshop J.* 5 (1978), 89–96; C. Dyhouse, 'Working-Class Mothers and Infant Mortality in England, 1895–1914', *J.*

infant mortality which forbade women from working outside the home, and promoted domesticity, good cooking skills, and, above all, lengthy breast-feeding.[8]

In reality, of course, not all Jewish women conformed to the idealized notions of motherhood. This was particularly the case for unmarried Jewish mothers and deserted wives whose presence did not accord with the ideal nuclear family model proposed by the Jewish community or the outside world.[9] Even more strongly contrasting with the idealized vision of the Jewish mother, however, was the Jewish prostitute. Indeed, it is no exaggeration to say that in the late nineteenth century, when not being praised for motherhood, Jewish women were being cursed for prostitution, reflecting the major anxieties of these years. While the Jewish mother represented the merits of the Jewish community and what influence mothers could have on the British nation, the Jewish prostitute symbolized the social evils which were undermining the strength of the family and the empire.[10] This was not only a view held in the outside world but also among many established Anglo-Jews who saw any Jewish involvement in prostitution as a threat to their own respectability as well as an incitement to anti-Semitism. As the German-Jewish feminist Bertha Pappenheim expressed it, 'If we admit the existence of the traffic our enemies decry us, if we deny it, they say we are trying to conceal it.'[11] The image of the Jewish prostitute coincided with the other negative popular visions of the East European Jew being painted during these

---

Soc. Hist. 12 (1979), 248–67; J. Lewis, *The Politics of Motherhood: Child and Maternal Welfare in England 1900–1939* (London, 1980); P. Thane, 'Genre et protection sociale: La Protection maternelle et infantile en Grande-Bretagne, 1860–1918', *Genèses*, 6 (1991), 73–97.

[8] *RC Alien Immigration*, PP 1903 IX, Dr Shirley Murphy, Q3960, p. 203; see also Qs17877, 17899, 18311; S. Rosenbaum, 'A Contribution to the Study of Vital and Other Statistics of the Jews in the UK', *J. Roy. Stat. Soc.* 68 (1905), table 17, p. 528. *Report of the Interdepartmental Committee on Physical Deterioration*, PP 1904 XXXII, Minutes of Evidence, Q1608.

[9] For more information on the experience of unmarried Jewish mothers see L. Marks, ' "Luckless Waifs and Strays of Humanity": Irish and Jewish Immigrant Unwed Mothers in London, 1870–1939', *Twentieth Cent. Br. Hist.* 3/2 (1992), 113–37.

[10] For the general fears concerning prostitution see J. Walkowitz, *Prostitution and Victorian Society* (Cambridge, 1981). For more information on Jewish involvement in prostitution see E. J. Bristow, *Prostitution and Prejudice* (Oxford, 1983); L. P. Gartner, 'Anglo-Jewry and the Jewish International Traffic in Prostitution, 1885–1914', *Am. Jewish Stud. Rev.* 7–8 (1982–3), 129–78; L. Marks, 'The Experience of Jewish Prostitutes and Jewish Women in the East End of London at the Turn of the Century', *Jewish Quarterly*, 34/2 (1987), 6–10, and 'Race, Class and Gender: The Experience of Jewish Prostitutes and Other Jewish Women in the East End of London at the Turn of the Century', in J. Grant (ed.), *Silent Voices* (forthcoming).

[11] Cited in E. J. Bristow, *Vice and Vigilance* (Dublin, 1977), 180.

years. This was most clearly seen in the debates around the Aliens Act of 1905, which portrayed the Jewish immigrant not only as immoral, but also as sickly, weak, and the carrier of disease.[12]

One of the themes of this book is the extent to which such stereotypes allotted to Jewish women, particularly that of the model mother, reflected the reality of Jewish women's experience of childbirth and motherhood in East London in the years 1870–1939. Despite the exaltation of Jewish mothers in both the Jewish community and the outside world, this is a subject which has hitherto received relatively little attention by historians. *Model Mothers* brings together subjects which have to date remained separate and draws on sources from a variety of disciplines and fields. A vast literature exists on the history of maternal and infant welfare and immigration in Britain, but few historians have attempted to unite these issues.

Much of the research on the Jews in Britain has focused on the social, economic, and political background of their migration and settlement without referring to the experience of women in detail or understanding the importance of gender.[13] This contrasts with the literature in America, where a large number of books have combined the issue of ethnicity with gender. One reason for the abundance of such work in the United States and not in Britain is related to the different emphasis that has been put on ethnicity in each country. This has not only affected the experience of the immigrants and their children but also the history that has been written of them. In the United States, where immigrants have constituted a large part of the population, ethnicity has been regarded as a dominant part of American culture and something to be respected. By contrast, in

[12] *JC*, 8 Oct. 1897, p. 18; 6 Oct. 1901, p. 18; C. Holmes, *Anti-Semitism in British Society* (London, 1979), 40.

[13] Works which have examined the economic, social, and political background of the Jewish community include L. P. Gartner, *The Jewish Immigrant in England, 1870–1914* (London, 1960; 1973); B. Williams, *The Making of Manchester Jewry, 1740–1875* (Manchester, 1976; 1985); J. White, *The Rothschild Buildings: Life in an East End Tenement Block, 1887–1920* (London, 1980); D. Feldman, 'Immigrants and Workers, Englishmen and Jews: The Immigrant to the East End of London, 1880–1906', Ph.D. thesis (Cambridge, 1985); D. Cesarani (ed.), *The Making of Modern Anglo-Jewry* (Oxford 1990), and V. D. Lipman, *A History of the Jews in Britain since 1858* (Leicester, 1990). The last two books have good bibliographic references and an overview of the literature on Jewish immigrants, but that of Lipman makes no reference to gender. For a fuller critique of the absence of research on gender and Jewish women and the importance of such research see L. Marks, 'Carers and Servers of the Jewish Community: The Marginalized Heritage of Jewish Women in Britain', in T. Kushner (ed.), *The Jewish Heritage in British History* (London, 1992); and M. A. Kaplan, 'Gender and Jewish History in Imperial Germany', in J. Frankel and S. J. Zipperstein (eds.), *Assimilation and Community: The Jews in Nineteenth-Century Europe* (Cambridge, 1992).

Britain, the immigrant population has been smaller, and the pressures for immigrants to forget their ethnic identity and conform to precepts set by the English majority have been much greater. This has meant that the research on Jews in Britain has tended to emphasize the ways in which they came to be part of the British nation and not to distinguish them as a separate group which was important in its own right.[14]

Ethnicity features more prominently in American primary documents than in British ones. Records from hospitals and other welfare institutions, for instance, regularly recorded the ethnic identity of their patients alongside their social and economic circumstances.[15] Thus the American interest in ethnicity has given historians a rich source to work from as well as a greater ability to pursue research in this area. Some American historians have confused the importance of ethnicity with class and at times glorified ethnicity. None the less the stress laid on ethnicity in the United States has enabled historians to explore its importance in a greater diversity of areas, including that of gender, than those in Britain.[16]

In Britain, class rather than ethnic identity has been more prominent in people's consciousness. This has not only affected people's own perceptions of themselves and their views of their position in British society, but has also influenced historical research on Jewish immigration. Much of the focus of this research has been on areas perceived to be important for understanding class tensions and struggles in areas such as the workplace where the experiences and battles of women have been seen as insignificant. This has been as apparent in the work of social and economic historians on class as in that of those concerned with Jewish immigration

[14] For more information on the ways in which this has affected scholarship on the Jews in Britain see Cesarani's introduction in D. Cesarani (ed.), *Making of Modern Anglo-Jewry*, 1–3.

[15] See e.g. the hospital records of the New York Lying-In Hospital or Chicago Lying-In Hospital (New York Archives, New York City and North-Western Memorial Hospital Archives, Chicago).

[16] Jewish women's experiences of migration to America have been examined in C. Baum, P. Hyman, and S. Michel (eds.), *The Jewish Woman in America* (New York, 1976); S. Stahl Weinberg, *The World of Our Mothers: The Lives of Jewish Immigrant Women* (Durham, NC, 1988); S. Glenn, *Daughters of the Shtetl: Life and Labour in the Immigrant Generation* (Ithaca, NY, 1990). A comparative study of English and American Jewish women appears in Gordon Kuzmack, *Woman's Cause*. Comparative studies of different immigrant groups in America have also tackled gender in their work. See for instance E. Ewen, *Immigrant Women in the Land of Dollars: Life and Culture on the Lower East Side, 1890–1925* (New York, 1985); D. Weatherford, *Foreign and Female, Immigrant Women in America, 1840–1930* (New York, 1986); L. Lamphere, *From Working Daughters to Working Mothers: Immigrant Women in a New England Industrial Community* (Ithaca, NY, 1987); C. Azen Krause, *Grandmothers, Mothers and Daughters: Oral Histories of Three Generations of Ethnic American Women* (Cambridge, Mass., 1991).

and settlement.[17] Some of the neglect of women in British historical scholarship has begun to be addressed by the recent growth in studies of gender.[18] A large literature has emerged on the experience of working-class and middle-class women in British society and the impact of religion on women's lives.[19] This, however, rarely explores the importance of ethnicity.[20]

One obvious obstacle in the path of those who research on ethnicity and gender is related to the difficulties of source material. Immigrant women, like other women, are often obscured in primary documents. Jewish women, however, have suffered the double disadvantage not only because of their gender, but also because of their minority status which has rendered them even more invisible to the recorder's eye.[21] In order to get information on Jewish women new questions have had to be asked of old material and new techniques have had to be deployed, such as oral history. Some historians who have done this have revealed a rich history of Jewish women's lives. Drawing on a fertile collection of oral interviews, Burman, for instance, has explored the importance of gender, class, and ethnicity in the experience of Jewish immigrant women and their children in Manchester in the late nineteenth and early twentieth centuries, focusing particularly on women's role within the family economy and religious sphere.[22] Studies have also begun to examine the role of

[17] For critiques of the way in which social and economic historians have neglected the issue of gender and women's experience see e.g. S. Rowbotham, *Hidden from History: 300 Years of Women's Oppression and the Fight Against It* (London, 1973); and S. Alexander, A. Davin, and E. Hostettler, 'Labouring Women: A Reply to Eric Hobsbawm', *Hist. Workshop J.* (1979), 174–82.

[18] For a useful discussion on the importance of gender in historical research see J. W. Scott, 'Gender: A Useful Category of Historical Analysis', *Am. Hist. Rev.* (1986), 1053–75, and *Gender and the Politics of History* (New York, 1988).

[19] See e.g. J. Lewis, *Women in England 1870–1950* (Brighton, 1984); a collection of essays in J. Lewis (ed.), *Labour and Love* (Oxford, 1986); E. Roberts, *A Woman's Place: An Oral History of Working-Class Women, 1890–1940* (Oxford, 1984) and in G. Malmgreen (ed.), *Religion in the Lives of English Women, 1760–1930* (London, 1986).

[20] For a recent essay on the lack of historical attention to the history of black women in Britain see Z. Alexander, 'Let it Lie Upon The Table: The Status of Black Women's Biography in the UK', *Gender and Hist.* 2/1 (1990), 22–34.

[21] One example of this is the Anglo-Jewish Exhibition in 1887, a major Jewish cultural event. The catalogue to the Anglo-Jewish exhibition primarily lists Jewish religious objects related to male religious practices. While some mention is made of the importance of religion within the domestic sphere, little reference is made to women's preparations for religious rituals within the home. See *Catalogue of the Anglo-Jewish Historical Exhibition* (London, 1888).

[22] R. Burman, 'The Jewish Woman as the Breadwinner', *Oral Hist.* 10/2 (1982), 27–39; 'Growing up in Manchester Jewry: The Story of Clara Weingard', *Oral Hist.* 12/1 (1984), 56–63; ' "She Looketh Well to the Ways of Her Household": The Changing Role of Jewish

Jewish women in social reform and politics within the established Anglo–Jewish community and in the outside world.[23] Such research has shown that the history of Jewish immigration and the social fabric of British society cannot be understood without reference to the importance of ethnicity as well as gender and class.

This book builds on this research by exploring Jewish women's experience of childbirth and infant care in East London in the years 1870 to 1939. As an event which particularly affects women, childbirth is an effective subject for measuring how women fare in society when they are at their most vulnerable. The pain suffered in childbirth can be very hard to deal with, but it can be intensified in situations where communication is difficult and cultural attitudes and prejudices intervene between the patient and her carer. In this context the pain is not only a physical phenomenon but can also be one of mental suffering. For immigrant women childbirth is therefore particularly revealing of the difficulties they encounter as newcomers, coping with language barriers and alien customs.[24]

While childbirth is primarily an event which concerns women, it raises wider questions concerning health overall. With the exception of research by Black on the health of the Jewish poor in East London,[25] issues of health and ethnicity have been ignored by most historians in Britain.[26] Health, however, is critical for understanding not only the social and economic circumstances of an immigrant community, but also the extent to which it integrated into the host society to receive fundamental care at times of life and death, and how it was organized to cope with the inadequacies of

---

Women in Religious Life, *c*.1800–1930', in Malmgreen (ed.), *Religion in the Lives of English Women*; and 'Jewish Women and the Household Economy in Manchester, *c*.1890–1920', in Cesarani (ed.), *Making of Modern Anglo-Jewry*.

[23] Gordon Kuzmack, *Woman's Cause*; E. Black, *The Social Politics of Anglo-Jewry* (Oxford, 1988), ch. 8; R. Cutting, 'The Jewish Contribution to the Suffrage Movement', BA thesis (Anglia Polytechnic, 1988) (copy held at the London Museum of Jewish Life); S. Tananbaum, 'Generations of Change: The Anglicization of Russian Jewish Women in London, 1880–1939', Ph.D. thesis (Brandeis, 1990). Iris Dove is currently writing a Ph.D. at Thames Polytechnic on Jewish girls' clubs in East London.

[24] For an interesting study of the difficulty one Jewish woman faced in encountering anti-Semitism during her childbirth see J. Emanuel, 'The Politics of Maternity in Manchester, 1919–1939: A Study from Within a Continuing Campaign', M.Sc. thesis (Manchester, 1982), ch. 3.

[25] G. Black, 'Health and Medical Care of the Jewish Poor in the East End of London, 1880–1939', Ph.D. thesis (Leicester, 1987).

[26] This is not the case in the USA. See e.g. D. Dwork, 'Health Conditions of Immigrant Jews on the Lower East Side of New York, 1880–1914', *Med. Hist.* 25/1 (1981), 1–40; and G. A. Condran and E. A. Kramarow, 'Child Mortality among Jewish Immigrants to the United States', *J. Interdisc. Hist.*, 22/2 (1991), 223–54.

the host institutions. Indeed, a study of the relationship between ethnicity and health reveals the ways in which a society provides for some of its most disadvantaged members. Central to this book is not only how Jewish women fared in giving birth, but the nature of the medical provision available to them.

The period covered by *Model Mothers*, 1870–1939, saw a marked increase in the provision of medical, nursing, and maternal care. The extent to which this care was provided by institutions with religious affiliations, which often combined an evangelical message with medical attention, is not always appreciated.[27] Clearly, however, the religion of a mother and her family had a profound effect both on the care she would seek and on the attention she could expect to receive. Living in a predominantly Protestant society, Jewish women had specific requirements which were not always catered for by the outside community. For Jewish patients certain difficulties could therefore arise from being attended by those not of their own faith. Unfamiliar with English ways, values, and organizations, Jewish immigrants could find it harder to obtain help and to communicate with health professionals than most non-Jews. This volume examines the ways in which ethnicity and religion affected the provision of health to Jewish mothers and their infants. It not only explores what provision was available to Jewish mothers in the outside world, but also the solutions adopted by the Jews themselves. Many of the problems they faced were not new, but as a religious and ethnic minority they were forced to find new solutions to supplement those provided by host agencies.

In addition to studying the extent to which maternity and infant health services were shaped by ethnic and religious considerations, this book provides the opportunity to understand the complex relationship between ethnicity and the standards of health. Current studies of health care have demonstrated ethnicity to be an important determinant of morbidity and mortality patterns.[28] Arriving penniless and with few possessions in East London, an area already noted for its extreme social and economic

---

[27] A. Summers, 'A Home from Home: Women's Philanthropic Work in the Nineteenth Century' in S. Burman (ed.), *Fit Work for Women* (London, 1979), 33–63. F. K. Prochaska, *Women and Philanthropy in Nineteenth-Century England* (Oxford, 1980); *The Voluntary Impulse: Philanthropy in Modern Britain* (London, 1988); and 'A Mother's Country: Mothers' Meetings and Family Welfare in Britain, 1850–1950', *Hist.* 74 (1989), 379–99.

[28] R. Balarajan and R. Botting, 'Perinatal Mortality in England and Wales: Variations by Mother's Country of Birth, 1982–1985', *Health Trends*, 21 (1989), 79–84; S. E. Curtis and P. E. Ogden, 'Bangladeshis in London: A Challenge to Welfare', *Revue européenne des migrations internationales*, 2/3 (1986), 135–49, 144–7; A. Phoenix, 'Black Women and Maternity Services', in J. Garcia, R. Kilpatrick, and M. Richards (eds.), *The Politics of Maternity Care: Services for Childbearing Women in Twentieth-Century Britain* (Oxford, 1990).

deprivation, it might be expected that the Jewish immigrants experienced very poor health. Yet despite such problems of poverty as well as the disadvantages they faced as an ethnic and religious minority, the Jews did not seem to fare any worse than their neighbours in matters of health and welfare. Indeed, infant mortality—usually considered a reliable measure of social and economic conditions—was strikingly lower among the Jewish poor in East London than that of their neighbours living in comparable social and economic circumstances. Such low rates of infant mortality were manifest among the Jews living not only in East London, but also in other parts of Britain and the world. The book explores this striking phenomenon in East London, showing that it was related to a complex range of factors. These included certain ethnic and religious Jewish customs concerning the importance of hygiene, diet, and breastfeeding as well the types of communal provision available to Jewish mothers and their infants. It would seem, therefore, that ethnicity was as important as social and economic factors in influencing both the patterns of morbidity and mortality as well as the services that were provided.

Jewish infants were not the only group to experience lower rates of mortality. Many Jewish mothers also had low rates of maternal mortality. In this respect, however, Jewish mothers were not dissimilar from other mothers living in East London. Despite living in one of the most impoverished areas of London, mothers in East London were far less likely to die in childbirth than were mothers in many other parts of the metropolis or in the rest of the country. As my research shows, the remarkably low rate of maternal mortality found in East London was linked to the unusually good provision of in-patient and out-patient maternity services in the area. These were available to both native and Jewish mothers. In addition to this, East London appears to have adopted hospital confinements, as opposed to home confinements, much earlier and more rapidly than other parts of London or elsewhere.

Indeed, East London appears to have been exceptional in the scale and variety of health care provision compared not just with other areas of London but with other cities in Britain. This characteristic of the area allows us to examine one of the most interesting questions in the history of maternal and infant care: could an unusually comprehensive provision of maternal and infant care compensate for social and economic deprivation, or was the burden of poverty so great that medical care, however comprehensive and well intentioned, was too feeble to have a measurable effect on the health of mothers and children in terms of rates of maternal and infant morbidity and mortality?

Most existing work on maternal and child welfare services has concentrated on central government policy.[29] Recent local studies of maternal and child welfare, however, have indicated the need for more research on the divergences between local and national maternal and infant welfare provision, and the extent to which this was reflected in different rates of maternal and infant mortality and morbidity.[30] Central to this book are the local forces which shaped the provision of maternity care and infant welfare in East London and how these related to the needs of mothers and their infants in the area, particularly those of immigrants. *Model Mothers* does not cover the full range of services in the area. Instead it focuses on the facilities provided by and for the Jewish immigrants, in order to understand the interaction between immigrants and these services, and the local demands that were made on such provision. The institutions explored here in are voluntary teaching hospitals, Poor Law infirmaries, and domiciliary and district nursing agencies, as well as the communal organizations specifically aimed at the Jewish population in the area.

[29] Davin, 'Imperialism and Motherhood'; D. Dwork, *War is Good for Babies and Other Young Children: A History of the Infant and Child Welfare Movement* (London, 1987); J. Lewis, *Politics of Motherhood* (London, 1980); A. Macfarlane, 'Statistics and Policy Making in the Maternity Services', *Midwifery* (1985), 150–61; R. Campbell and A. Macfarlane, *Where to be Born? The Debate and the Evidence* (Oxford, 1987); Thane, 'Genre et protection sociale'.

[30] E. P. Peretz, 'A Maternity Service for England and Wales: Local Authority Maternity Care in the Interwar Period in Oxfordshire and Tottenham', in Garcia *et al.*, *The Politics of Maternity Care*; 'Regional Variations in Maternal and Child Welfare Between the Wars: Merthyr Tydfil, Oxfordshire and Tottenham', in D. Foster and P. Swan (eds.), *Essays in Regional and Local History* (Hull, 1992); and 'The Costs of Modern Motherhood to Low Income Families in Interwar Britain', in V. Fildes, L. Marks, and H. Marland (eds.), *Women and Children First: International Maternal and Infant Welfare, 1870–1945* (London, 1992); P. A. Waterson, 'The Role of the Environment in the Decline of Infant Mortality: An Analysis of the 1911 Census of England and Wales', *J. Biosoc. Sci.* 18 (1986), 457–70; M. Lodge, 'Aspects of Infant Welfare in Coventry, 1900–1940', in B. Lancaster and T. Mason (eds.), *Life and Labour in a Twentieth-Century City: The Experience of Coventry* (Coventry, 1986); H. Marland, 'A Pioneer in Infant Welfare: The Huddersfield Scheme, 1903–1920', *Soc. Hist. Med.* 6/1 (1993), 25–50.

I

Background: Immigration and Settlement

'IMPOVERISHED' and 'destitute' were the words frequently used by contemporaries to describe the East European Jewish immigrants settling in East London in the late nineteenth century. Migrating from areas facing great upheaval and poverty many of these Jews arrived penniless and without any possessions. Between 1895 and 1902 22 per cent of all the Russian, Romanian, and Galician immigrants arriving at the port of London claimed to be penniless. A further 15 per cent had less than 10*s.* per adult, and the average total was 26*s.* per adult.[1] None the less, despite such poverty, it is a mistake to think of these immigrants as a socially and economically homogeneous group. Each immigrant came with differing levels of skill and economic resources. Some had migrated from towns, others from little villages. Similarly, while some travelled with their family or with friends, others came on their own. Such a variety of backgrounds not only shaped their ordeals on arrival and in subsequent years, but also the future of their children born in East London.

Focusing on the years 1870 to 1939 this chapter examines how the Jews living in East London changed from being a group of immigrants to a well-settled community. This was a lengthy and highly complex process, which not only had implications for the material welfare of the Jewish population but also the strategies they adopted for survival. Furthermore, it affected the ways in which they identified themselves in relation to the wider British society and the way outsiders perceived them. While many of the social and economic insecurities the immigrants faced on arrival faded as they became more settled, and as their children integrated into the wider community, this did not undermine their status as an ethnic and religious minority in British society. Indeed, even the children of the immigrants who were born in East London retained some degree of separate identity. Born in England many of these children did

---

[1] *RC Alien Immigration*, PP 1903 IX pt. I, app., table 62, p. 76. In 1889 Charles Booth estimated that a person needed between 18*s.* and 21*s.* a week so as not to fall into poverty. This is discussed in further detail below. (C. Booth, *Life and Labour of the People in London* (London, 1889), i. 33–61.)

not have the same ties or values their foreign-born parents brought with them from their places of origin. Nevertheless, nor could they always relate to the cultural and social circles of English society.[2] Many of the children of the immigrants were therefore culturally isolated and could sometimes feel as much outsiders as their parents. This was reinforced by the fact that many of the Jewish immigrants and their children in East London resided and worked in places where they were separate from the local population even into the inter-war period.[3]

Yet while the Jewish immigrants and their children living in East London might be considered a closed community with distinct boundaries, this ignores the interaction many of the Jews had with their non-Jewish neighbours in the streets and with their fellow workers in the workplace.[4] Similarly it obscures the enormous changes that occurred in their identity as a result of assimilation. What form this identity took and how it was used differed tremendously and changed over time. The Jewish population shared a sense of common Jewish ancestry and history, as well as religious beliefs and cultural customs, but the weight each Jew placed on these diverse aspects of their identity varied and was subject to continual conflict and negotiation.[5] The identity of the Jewish population therefore cannot be seen as a universal and unified force. Rather it was something which was continually negotiated between the foreign-born and English-born Jews and between different classes within the Jewish community. These conflicts and struggles were bound up with the nature of the East European Jewish migration at the end of the nineteenth century and the ways in which these immigrants and their children were accepted by the better established Jews and wider British society.

[2] R. Livshin, 'Aspects of the Acculturation of the Children of Immigrant Jews in Manchester, 1890–1930', M.Ed. thesis (Manchester, 1982), 256–7, 276–7; T. M. Endelman, *Radical Assimilation in English Jewish History, 1656–1945* (Indianapolis, 1990), 175–9.

[3] E. R. Smith, 'East End Jews in Politics, 1918–1939: A Study in Class and Ethnicity', Ph.D. thesis (Leicester, 1990), 3–5, 22, 32–4. Smith has shown how such segregation within the workplace and in residential patterns placed a serious obstacle to the unity between Jewish and non-Jewish workers. Non-Jewish workers saw even English-born Jews as a foreign and separate category. This perception was also reinforced by the fact that many East End Jews only participated in specifically Jewish organizations, emphasizing their separateness and cultural identity. See also Endelman, *Radical Assimilation*, 181–3.

[4] See e.g. Louis Golding, *Magnolia Street* (London, 1932), 159, which depicts non-Jewish and Jewish children playing together.

[5] For an interesting discussion on the ways in which ethnic identity in America has become a means by which people gain a sense of belonging to a certain community and assert their sense of individuality see M. C. Waters, *Ethnic Options: Choosing Identities in America* (Los Angeles, 1990).

TABLE 1.1. *Total number of Russian, Romanian, and Galician immigrants arriving in Britain and percentage of total aliens, 1895–1902*

Date	Total	% of total aliens
1895	3,494	41.9
1896	6,171	49.9
1897	7,331	54.7
1898	8,283	60.4
1899	9,220	56.5
1900	11,493	60.4
1901	13,940	65.3
1902	11,459	62.0

Source: A Summary of Returns Made to the Board of Trade of Customs, in *RC Alien Immigration*, PP 1903 IX, Report and Minutes of Evidence, app., 76.

Migration

Between 1881 and 1905 approximately a million Jews left Eastern Europe, three-quarters of whom came from Russia. Over 80 per cent went to America, others to Western Europe, South America, and South Africa. Those who migrated to Britain were mostly from Russian Poland, but Galicians and Romanians also arrived between 1890 and 1902.[6] Between 1881–1914 approximately 100,000 to 150,000 East European Jews came to Britain. Table 1.1 reveals that the Russian-Polish, Romanian, and Galician immigrants were the largest group settling in Britain at the end of the nineteenth century, the majority of whom were Jewish. According to the Census of 1901, 95,245 Russians and Poles were living in the United Kingdom, of whom 53,537 were living in the County of London together with 6,189 Austrians and 246 Romanians.[7] In 1903 it was estimated that the total number of foreigners in London was 133,377 with a ratio of 1.4 men to 1 woman.[8]

Tables 1.2 and 1.3 indicate the number, gender, and age of the alien Jews who arrived in Britain and lived in London in the period 1871 to 1911. In the initial years before mass migration, most of the Jewish

[6] For more information on Jewish emigration and its relationship with overall Jewish migratory patterns see M. Wischnitzer, *To Dwell in Safety: The Story of Jewish Migrations since 1800* (Philadelphia, 1948). See also V. D. Lipman, *Social History of the Jews in England, 1850–1950* (London, 1954), ch. 5; L. P. Gartner, *The Jewish Immigrant in England, 1870–1914* (London, 1960), 41–9.

[7] *RC Alien Immigration*, PP 1903 IX I, 22; Lipman, *Social History of the Jews*, 89–90.

[8] *RC Alien Immigration*, PP 1903 IX, census returns given by Mr Reginald Macleod.

TABLE 1.2. *Number and percentage of women among the Russian and Russian-Polish population in London*

Year	Total Russians and Russian Poles in London	Female Russians and Poles in London	Female %
1871	5,294	2,004	37.8
1881	8,709	3,671	42.2
1891	26,742	11,969	44.8
1901	53,537	24,408	45.6
1911	67,733	32,509	48.0

Source: D. M. Feldman, 'Immigrants and Workers, Englishmen and Jews: The Immigrants in the East End of London, 1880–1906', Ph.D. thesis (Cambridge, 1985), 37, table 1.8.

TABLE 1.3. *Number, gender, and age of East European immigrants arriving in Britain, 1895–1902*

Date	Total	Men		Women		Children	
		Number	%	Number	%	Number	%
1895	3,494	1,486	42.5	1,096	31.4	912	26.1
1896	6,171	3,337	54.1	1,686	27.3	1,148	18.6
1897	7,331	4,104	56.0	2,007	27.4	1,220	16.6
1898	8,283	4,850	59.0	2,176	26.0	1,307	16.0
1899	9,220	5,212	56.5	2,398	26.0	1,610	17.5
1900	11,493	6,938	60.4	2,844	24.7	1,711	14.9
1901	13,940	8,208	59.0	3,481	25.0	2,251	16.2
1902	11,459	6,507	56.8	2,937	25.6	2,051	17.9

Source: A Summary of Returns Made to the Board of Trade of Customs, in *RC Alien Immigration*, PP 1903 IX, Report and Minutes of Evidence, app., 76.

immigrants were men, but by 1881 they were being joined by a large number of women and children. The high percentage of women and children among the Jewish migrants during these years, distinguishes them from other migrant groups which were primarily composed of single male wage earners. Such a high profile of families among the Jewish immigrants showed that their migration was generally a permanent move. This contrasted with the pattern of many non-Jewish single male migrants, whose migration was often a transitory search for economic gains before returning to their place of origin. Jewish immigrants not only often travelled together as a family unit, but were also greatly dependent on familial financial support both for their departure from Eastern Europe and for their period of settlement within Britain.[9]

Much of the migration of the East European Jews to Britain was part of a general movement west from Eastern Europe.[10] Such Jewish migration largely stemmed from the hardships the Jews suffered in Eastern Europe, particularly in Tzarist Russia. Tzarist policies had imposed enormous restrictions on the Jewish population, not only in geographical location, but also in employment capability and mobility. The May Laws of 1881 forced Jews out of rural villages into the more urbanized towns and cities of the Pale of Settlement, the area of North West Russia.[11] One of the causes of Jewish migration was the overcrowding in Jewish areas. Between 1820 and 1880 it was estimated that the Jewish population in Russia and Poland rose from 1,600,000 to 4,000,000, an increase of 150 per cent as compared to 87 per cent for non-Jewish residents. By 1897, the Jewish population in the Russian empire had increased to over 5,189,000.[12] The growth was as great in European Russia (without Poland) where the number of Jews rose from 1,023,543 in 1838 to 3,789,448 in 1897. Such growth also occurred in other parts of Eastern Europe.[13]

By the end of the nineteenth century, although mass emigration had reduced the East European Jewish population, it was still extremely congested. The economic structure of Jewish life had failed to expand with the needs imposed by the unprecedented increase in population. Many of

[9] D. M. Feldman, 'Immigrants and Workers, Englishmen and Jews: The Immigrant to the East End of London, 1880–1906', Ph.D. thesis (Cambridge, 1985), 38–40.

[10] Lipman, *Social History of the Jews*, 85.

[11] Z. Gitelman, *A Century of Ambivalence: The Jews of Russia and the Soviet Union, 1881 to the Present* (New York, 1987), 13–14. See also J. D. Klier, 'Russian Jewry on the Eve of the Pogroms', in J. D. Klier and S. Lambroza (eds.), *Pogroms: Anti-Jewish Violence in Modern Russian History* (Cambridge, 1992).

[12] W. J. Fishman, *East End Jewish Radicals 1875–1914* (London, 1975), 22. Given that the Jewish population in these areas had already been reduced by emigration these figures underestimate the true population size by about 1,000,000. See L. P. Gartner, *The Jewish Immigrant in England* (London, 1960, 1973), 21. See also J. Silber, 'Some Demographic Characteristics of the Jewish Population in Russia at the End of the Nineteenth Century', *Jewish Soc. Stud.* 5 (1980), 269–80. For more detail on the demographic growth of the Jewish population in Poland and how this compared with the non-Jews see S. D. Corrsin, *Warsaw Before the First World War: Poles and Jews in the Third City of the Russian Empire, 1880–1914* (New York, 1989), 24–8.

[13] A. Ruppin, *The Jews of Today* (London, 1913), 33; Gartner, *Jewish Immigrant*, 21.

the Jewish petty trades and crafts were increasingly replaced by newer technology and economic developments.[14] Within the Pale of Settlement, Jewish workers also tended to be employed in very small artisan workshops and had very few openings for work in large factories, especially as these were located largely outside the Pale and often refused to employ Jews.[15] In addition Jewish workers often lacked the necessary technical skills. This left Jews no alternative but to pursue artisan occupations, most of which were concentrated in the garment industry. Artisan work meant a menial existence. The small workshops Jews worked in could no longer compete with the large-scale factory production, and skilled Jewish artisans were increasingly displaced by machines. This was an important cause of much of their poverty.[16] In 1900 it was estimated that between 30 and 35 per cent of the Jewish population in the Pale of Settlement depended on relief provided by Jewish welfare agencies.[17] Pogroms in 1881, 1891, and 1905–6, together with continual persecution, further aggravated the situation.[18]

Conditions on Arrival in East London

The East European Jews who migrated to Britain at the end of the nineteenth century joined a Jewish population that had lived in Britain for generations. Originally expelled in 1290, Jews had begun to resettle in Britain in 1656. Many of those who came during the seventeenth century were of German, Dutch, and Sephardi origin, and came as merchants.[19]

---

[14] Gartner, *Jewish Immigrant*, 21.

[15] *RC Alien Immigration*, PP 1903 IX, Q13349, 458.

[16] Klier, 'Russian Jewry', and A. Orbach, 'The Development of the Russian Jewish Community, 1881–1903', in Klier and Lambroza, *Pogroms*, 140–1.

[17] Gitelman, *A Century of Ambivalence*, 78. Gitelman unfortunately does not provide a source for this information. Similarly high statistics are given for the number of Jews existing on charity in the years 1870 and 1890, but again the sources are not revealed (Fishman, *East End Jewish Radicals*, 21–2).

[18] For a detailed examination of the effects of the pogroms see the collection of essays in Klier and Lambroza, *Pogroms*.

[19] Sephardi Jews were descendants of the Spanish and Portuguese Jews who reached England via Holland. For more information on this early settlement see D. S. Katz, *Philo-Semitism and the Readmission of the Jews to England, 1603–1635* (London, 1982), and 'The Jews of England and 1688', in O. P. Grell *et al.* (eds.), *From Persecution to Toleration* (Oxford, 1991), 217–49. See also the collection of essays in V. D. Lipman (ed.), *Three Centuries of Anglo-Jewish History* (Cambridge, 1961); V. D. Lipman, *A History of the Jews in Britain since 1858* (Leicester, 1990), 1–4; T. M. Endelman, *The Jews of Georgian England 1714–1830* (Philadelphia, 1979), and *Radical Assimilation*, chs. 1 and 2.

Some Ashkenazi[20] Jews also arrived from Eastern Europe in the seventeenth century, their immigration growing much larger from the eighteenth century. Their settlement grew greatly in the 1840s with the completion of an efficient and relatively cheap passenger service by rail and sea between Russia and Britain, and in the 1860s when the American Civil War made migration to Britain more favourable than to America. The influx of East European immigrants at the end of the nineteenth century, was therefore not new.[21] The size and nature of their migration, however, was unprecedented, making them numerically the largest group of immigrants Britain had ever received.[22] Having an Ashkenazi background, these East European Jews were most closely identified with those Ashkenazi Jews who had arrived before them, and it was to their institutions they turned in times of need.

Like their predecessors, many of these East European Jews settled in East London. The exact numbers of Jews living in East London is unknown because the censuses never listed the Jews separately. Estimates of the size of the Jewish immigrant population drawn from those residents labelled by country of origin show, however, that in 1871 75 per cent of all Russian and Russian-Polish immigrants were living in the City of London, Whitechapel, St George's-in-the-East, and Mile End Old Town. By 1881 this had risen to 81 per cent. According to the survey carried out by Charles Booth in 1889, East London accounted for 90 per cent of the Jewish population in the capital, the majority of whom resided in Whitechapel and the immediate areas in the borough of Stepney.[23] Stepney

---

[20] Ashkenazi Jews were descendants of the Jews who originally settled in Germany and then migrated to Central and Eastern Europe. They differed from Sephardi Jews in their Hebrew pronunciation, cultural and devotional traditions, and language. Sephardi Jews did not speak Yiddish. Ashkenazi and Sephardi Jews also tended to have separate communal and charitable organizations.

[21] Williams criticizes historians who have seen East European settlement and its impact as a phenomenon which primarily occurred after the 1870s. (B. Williams, ' "East and West": Class and Community in Manchester Jewry, 1850–1914', in D. Cesarani (ed.), *The Making of Modern Anglo-Jewry* (Oxford, 1990), 16–17; See also B. Williams, *The Making of Manchester Jewry 1740–1875* (Manchester, 1976; 1985), 1; Lipman, *Social History of the Jews*, 5–9.)

[22] The largest groups of immigrants who arrived before the Jews, were the Huguenots in the 17th c. and the Irish during the years of the Famine in the late 1840s. Both of these groups also settled in East London. For more information on this see C. Bermant, *Point of Arrival* (London, 1975); R. Gwynn, *The Huguenot Heritage* (London, 1985); J. A. Jackson, *The Irish in Britain* (London, 1963), and 'The Irish in East London', *East London Papers*, 6/2 (1963), 105–19; L. H. Lees, *Exiles of Erin: Irish Migrants in Victorian London* (Manchester, 1979); R. Swift and S. Gilley (eds.), *The Irish in the Victorian City* (London, 1985), and *The Irish in Britain* (London, 1989).

[23] C. Booth, *Life and Labour of the People in London: Religious Influences*, ser. 2 (London, 1902), iv. 9; Feldman, 'Immigrants and Workers', 26–9.

continued to have the highest proportion of foreigners in London through to the turn of the century.[24] In 1911 83 per cent of London's Russian and Russian-Polish population were living in Stepney and Bethnal Green.[25]

Arriving in one of the poorest parts of London, the immigrants found themselves in a place which was already the site of grave concern for many social reformers, and politicians worried about urban degeneracy and the threat of social disorder.[26] Prostitution and crime were considered to be higher because of the presence of a large number of common lodging houses in the district. Many feared such vices would pollute the rest of London.[27] The arrival of immigrants in the East End reinforced such perceptions and attracted more attention to the area. In an effort to counter such detrimental problems, East London became a centre for middle-class philanthropic endeavours in the late nineteenth century, notably through the establishment of the Settlement House Movement and the Charity Organization Society, as well as numerous other voluntary bodies.[28] Each agency had their own objective. Some provided relief while others sought to 'redeem' the poor spiritually and culturally, or through teaching them the ethics of self-help and thrift. Overall, their main priority was to contain the threat of poverty and the social disorder

[24] In 1901 a witness estimated that 44% of the population in Whitechapel were immigrants, while the census enumerated it at 37%. The next highest concentration of immigrants was found in St George's-in-the-East, which a witness estimated to be 31.33%, and the census enumerated at 28%. This was much higher than for the other areas of Stepney which ranged between 3% and 8%. See *RC Alien Immigration*, PP 1903 IX I, 22; table 35 (c) in app., 42. Between 1871 and 1901 the total population in Stepney increased by 24,154, but the number of British-born residents fell by 16,126, representing a decline from 95% to 82% of the borough's total population. (Feldman, 'Immigrants and Workers', 29). Map 2.1 in the next chapter shows in more detail the exact areas of East London where the Jewish population was most concentrated.

[25] Feldman, 'Immigrants and Workers', 26–9.

[26] This is explored in detail by G. Stedman Jones, *Outcast London: A Study in the Relationship Between Classes in Victorian Society* (London, 1971; 1984), 12, 14, 241, 244–5, 283–4. In the 1880s the fear of riots and revolution stemming from poverty was particularly strong as a result of the riots in the centre of the West End. These destroyed the notion that the tranquillity of the middle class could be unaffected by the poverty of areas like the East End. For more discussion of the ways in which the riots and poverty were perceived as threats to the social order see Stedman Jones, ch. 16.

[27] J. White, *Rothschild Buildings: Life in an East End Tenement Block, 1887–1920* (London, 1980), 6–13, 24–30.

[28] Among the most famous Settlements in East London were Toynbee Hall and Oxford House. For a detailed study of the work undertaken by the Settlement House Movement and its relationship with East London see S. Koven, 'Culture and Poverty: The London Settlement House Movement, 1870–1914', Ph.D. thesis (Harvard University, Cambridge, Mass., 1987).

TABLE 1.4. *Population growth in East London, 1871–1911*

Year	Bethnal Green	Whitechapel	St George's-in-the-East	Stepney	Mile End	Poplar
1871	120,104	76,573	48,052	57,690	93,152	116,376
1881	127,006	71,350	47,011	58,500	105,573	156,525
1891	129,134	74,462	45,546	57,599	107,565	166,697
1901	129,680	78,768	49,068	57,937	112,827	168,822
1911	128,282	67,750	47,101	53,798	111,375	162,449

Source: Registrar General, *ARs of Births, Deaths, and Marriages in England and Wales* (1870–1911).

it could cause. Their efforts, however, had little immediate or direct impact on the social and economic deprivation of East London.

Many of the economic and social difficulties of East London were aggravated by the immigrants' arrival, but they were rooted in the social and industrial structure of the area. Demographically, East London had grown tremendously in the late nineteenth century. As Table 1.4 shows, Poplar had witnessed a particularly dramatic growth in the years 1871 to 1881. Although less striking than Poplar, Bethnal Green and Mile End had similarly increased their population size. Whitechapel and St George's-in-the-East also experienced a growth in population, but this was much smaller than in the other districts. In all the areas the population peaked in 1901 and declined thereafter. Much of the growth was the result of the large influx of rural migrants and later immigrants, as well as a high birth rate.[29]

All this increased an already intense competition for resources. Unemployment and underemployment were a serious problem for many living in East London. Much of this was the result of the decline of two of the oldest major industries of East London, silk-weaving and ship-building, from the 1830s.[30] Similarly the availability of work was severely restricted in one of East London's most important industries, the docks, which by the 1880s was shrinking its labour force and sites as a result of fierce

[29] The alien immigrant population of the Metropolitan borough of Stepney increased from 14,030 in 1871 to 54,310 in 1901. The last figure included the British-born children of immigrant parents (*RC Alien Immigration*, PP 1903 IX pt. I, p. 31). For more information on the relationship between the immigrants and the birth rate in East London see Ch. 2.

[30] Stedman Jones, *Outcast London*, 101.

competition.[31] Regular employment was just as difficult to secure in the other important industries based in East London, such as the clothing, footwear, and furniture trades. Often farmed out to specialized work-shops or undertaken as piecework by families within their own homes, these industries were renowned for sweated labour conditions and the amount of work they provided was greatly affected by seasonal fluctuations. Equally seasonal in character was the work offered by jam factories, sweet and chocolate manufacturers, and the cigarette industries which predominantly employed female labour. More permanent work was supplied by a number of breweries and distilleries.[32] The industrial base of East London did not change significantly over the years, and remained relatively untouched by the new industries appearing elsewhere in the city in the inter-war period. Cabinet-making, the clothing trade, transport, warehousing, and distributive trades were some of the areas where there had been an expansion, but these did not provide regular employment.[33]

Casual labour and unemployment were therefore serious problems in East London throughout the years 1870 to 1939. Most of those living in East London at the turn of the century were either surviving or living just below the subsistence level set by Booth at between 18s. and 21s. a week.[34] Llewellyn Smith's survey in 1929 estimated that between 13 and 19 per cent of the East London working class were living below the poverty line calculated at between 38s. and 40s. (at the level set by Charles Booth in 1889), and the remaining number were in a very precarious position. Table 1.5 shows the percentage of population considered to be living in poverty in the years 1889 and 1929. This table reveals that while the level of poverty in East London appeared to diminish in these years, it still ranked as the highest in London and sharply contrasted the rates found in Hampstead, one of the richest districts of the metropolis. In 1929 Poplar was the poorest area of London.[35]

[31] C. Booth, *Life and Labour of the People in London: Industry*, ser. 2 (London, 1902), iv. 419; Evidence given by Ben Tillet to the *House of Lords Select Committee on the Sweating System* (henceforth *Sweating System*), PP 1888 XXI, Qs12620–61. See also Stedman Jones, *Outcast London*, chs. 1 and 5.

[32] Stedman Jones, *Outcast London*, 85; J. A. Gillespie, 'Economic Change in the East End of London during the 1920s', Ph.D. thesis (Cambridge, 1984), 86–7.

[33] Gillespie, 'Economic Change in East London', 22–3, 48.

[34] Booth, *Life and Labour*, i. 33–61.

[35] H. Llewellyn Smith, *The New Survey of London* (London, 1929), iii. 347, 353, 365.

TABLE 1.5. *Percentage of population living in poverty according to the surveys conducted by Booth in 1889 and Llewellyn Smith in 1929*

District	% of poverty Booth's Survey 1889	% of poverty Llewellyn Smith's Street Survey 1929
Bethnal Green	44.6	17.8
Poplar	36.5	24.1
St George's-in-the-East	48.8	*
Whitechapel	39.2	*
Borough of Stepney	35.7	15.5
Hampstead	13.5	1.4
Whole of London (average)	30.7	8.7

* No statistics are available for Whitechapel or St George's-in-the-East in 1929, as these areas were now considered integral parts of the Borough of Stepney.

Source: Booth, *Life and Labour, Poverty*, i. Tables of Sections and Classes, Tables 7, 9–14; Llewellyn Smith, *New Survey of London*, i. *The Eastern Area* (London 1932), 3, 347, 353, 365; and ii. *The Western Area* (London, 1934), 88.

The Process of Settlement

Arriving with their artisan and commercial skills, many Jews were able to utilize the opportunities which were expanding in the East End footwear, tailoring, and furniture trades. Nearly 48 per cent of all 'occupied' Russians and Poles in England and Wales were returned as engaged in tailoring, boot-and shoe-making, or cabinet-making in 1881. Ten years later this percentage had increased to 55 per cent, with cabinet-making accounting for the smallest number.[36] Many of the immigrants employed in these industries worked in appalling conditions in small workshops and for minimal pay. In 1884 the *Lancet* revealed that many Jewish girls and women toiled at their work long after the hours prescribed by the Factory and Workshop Act. 'At all hours of the day and night the [Pelham] street resounds with the rattle and whir of the innumerable sewing machines, the windows shine with the flare of gas, but the street is comparatively

[36] H. Adler, 'Jewish Life and Labour', in Llewellyn Smith, *New Survey* (London, 1934), vi. 283.

deserted.' Police stated that they often heard heavy machinery going on as late as 2 a.m. and beginning again at 7 a.m.[37] These findings were reinforced by the Royal Commission on the sweating trades in 1889. Jewish boot-finishers who worked sixteen or seventeen hours a day, mostly in cellar dwellings, often received a salary of only 12s. a week.[38] The description of one London factory inspector in 1903 sums up the terrible work and living conditions many of the immigrants faced in East London during these years, 'The alien is imprisoned day and night and kept at work in a semi-nude state for a starvation allowance. Family and all sleep in the same room. . . . The effect of this is found in the anaemic and lifeless state of the workers.'[39] While these descriptions sometimes exaggerated the overcrowded and poor working conditions of the Jews on account of an anti-Semitic bias, they none the less reflected the acute poverty a large number of the immigrants suffered in East London.

Yet while poverty and ill-health were very real problems for a large bulk of the East European Jewish immigrants in East London, this was not a uniform experience. One investigation of East End tailoring made in 1886–7 discovered 'an infinite variety of rates of wages'. It showed, for instance, that the earnings of machininists not only differed between different workshops, but even within the same workshop. Remuneration varied also for the assorted tasks within the trade.[40] Such conditions were not static and the social and economic position of the Jewish immigrants changed over time. Concentrated in trades that were clustered around small workshops which demanded only a small outlay of capital, a number of Jewish immigrants found that they could rise from being an employee to the status of a master with their own workshop and workers. By becoming a master, however, an immigrant was not necessarily guaranteed prosperity, as they were just as prone to the vulnerabilities imposed by seasonal fluctuations or economic depressions as their employees. Often an immigrant therefore shuttled between the positions of worker and master.[41] In some cases workers also turned to becoming dealers in order to stave off adversity. During slack seasons it was not uncommon for tailors and furniture-makers to turn to street trading. Yet while the

---

[37] Cited in Fishman, *East End Jewish Radicals*, 51.

[38] *Sweating System*, PP 1888–9, 5th Report: Conclusions and Recommendations, xlii–xliii.

[39] *RC Alien Immigration*, PP 1903, Q11809.

[40] John Burnett, *Report to the Board of Trade on the Sweating System*, 7; cited in Feldman, 'Immigrants and Workers', 108.

[41] Some workers also became costers or travellers during slack seasons. See Feldman, 'Immigrants and Workers', 148–51 n. 59.

immigrants utilized the East End economy to their advantage, only a small number of them succeeded in climbing the social ladder in the late nineteenth and early twentieth century. This changed during the First World War, when the 'demand for shirts, coats, trousers, boots, and other items of apparel, brought prosperity to considerable numbers of small factory owners' including those who were Jewish.[42]

Despite the increasing wealth of some Jewish immigrants and their families during the war and in the years following, many Jews were not so lucky. In 1929 a house sample investigation for the *New Survey of London* showed that in East London 13.7 per cent of Jews were in poverty in the week of investigation, as compared with 12.1 per cent of the whole working-class population. This slightly higher level of poverty was thought to result from the greater percentage of unemployment or part-time or casual labour among the Jews in the area. While 64 per cent of the Jewish workers were employed in the casual labour market only 55 per cent of non-Jewish workers were in a similar position. This partly reflected the greater diversity of occupations among non-Jews who were deployed in the docks, wharfs, warehouses, railway engineering works, breweries, and factories making food and soft drinks.[43] By contrast many of the Jews living in East London in the inter-war years were still employed in the tailoring and furniture-making trades. While conditions in these industries had improved slightly since the nineteenth century they continued to be organized around small workshops and were still subject to seasonal fluctuations and depressions. Some Jews had also entered office work, shop work, and hairdressing, but they remained a small proportion of the total Jewish population living in East London. Conditions in these newer trades were also not much better than in the old trades. Unemployment and underemployment therefore continued to plague the Jewish population living in East London.[44]

The poverty of these Jews was particularly striking in the inter-war years, because of the rapid disappearance of the more prosperous Jews from East London. Indeed, by the end of the First World War, the whole character of the Jewish population living in East London had changed

[42] Endelman, *Radical Assimilation*, 182; H. Pollins, *Economic History of the Jews in England* (London, 1982).

[43] Adler, 'Jewish Life and Labour', 287; Smith, 'East End Jews', 22, 38–42.

[44] Adler, 'Jewish Life and Labour', 271; Lipman, *Social History of the Jews*, 89–90, 168–9; Smith, 'East End Jews', 22–6, 42–3. For more information on structure of work in East London in the nineteenth century and the 1920s see Stedman Jones, *Outcast London*, chs. 2, 3, 4, and 5; and Gillespie, 'Economic Change in East London', 83–4, 88.

from being one that was socially and economically diverse to one that was more homogenously working-class and poor. By 1929 only 60 per cent of the total Jewish population in the metropolis lived in East London, the total number of Jews living in the area having dropped from approximately 125,000 to 85,000 between 1900 and 1929.[45] One immediate cause of the decline was the cessation of immigration during the First World War. This was reinforced by the curbs placed on immigration by the Aliens' Restriction (Amendment) Act of 1919. The shift away from East London was also a reflection of the upward mobility of the Jewish immigrants and their families. The departure of the more prosperous Jews from East London, however, was not a new phenomenon. From the early nineteenth century many of the wealthier and more established Jews had begun to move away to the northern and western parts of London.[46] Part of the dispersal also occurred as a result of policies pursued by the Anglo-Jewish community, who wanted to discourage the concentration of immigrants in one part of London for fear of inciting anti-Semitism. Accordingly, various housing schemes were promoted by leading Anglo-Jewish figures, such as the one developed by the Four Per Cent Dwellings Company which built accommodation in areas such as Camberwell, Dalston, and Stoke Newington after 1892.[47]

Jewish migration from East London to other parts of the metropolis, however, remained relatively small before the First World War. This contrasted with the large exodus that occurred after the war, when many minor professionals and small businessmen, as well as some more economically secure working-class Jews, shifted residence to other parts of London. Many moved northwards to Hackney and beyond.[48] For some Jews the departure from the East End marked the rise in their social and economic status. This, however, was not the case for all those who left. In 1929 a committee of the United Synagogue revealed that many of the Jews who had recently moved to North and North-East London were

[45] Adler, 'Jewish Life and Labour', 271; M. J. Landa in *JC Suppl.* 29, 25 May 1923, p. iv; Smith, 'East End Jews', 28–9. Despite the decline, the Jewish population living in East London was still double that living in Manchester, the second largest Jewish community. In 1920 the Jewish population in Manchester was approximately 32,000. See Williams, 'East and West', 16 n. 4.

[46] For a map detailing the spread of London's Jewish population from East London from the nineteenth century into the twentieth see fig. 7.5 in E. Jones and J. Eyles, *An Introduction to Social Geography* (Oxford, 1977; 1979), 180. See also Lipman, *Social History of the Jews*, 169–70, and Lipman, 'Age of Emancipation', in V. D. Lipman (ed.), *Three Centuries of Anglo-Jewish History* (Cambridge, 1961), 71.

[47] Smith, 'East End Jews', 28.

[48] Endelman, *Radical Assimilation*, 182–3; Smith, 'East End Jews', 21, 28–30.

much poorer than those who had settled there during the nineteenth and first decade of the twentieth century.[49]

The movement of these poorer Jews, was rooted in the changes happening within East London as a whole. Their departure was part of a general movement away from East London during the inter-war period, caused by the clearance of slums, and the conversion of dwellings into offices, shops, and factories. For many the move away from East London was a chance to escape overcrowded housing conditions. According to the 1921 and 1931 censuses, Stepney was the most densely populated borough in London. In 1929 the *New Survey* revealed the most overcrowded part of London to be in the North-West ward of St George's-in-the-East, an area mostly populated by Jews.[50] Many Jews also departed as the result of the relocation to North London (particularly to Hackney and Tottenham) of many of the East End firms such as the tailoring and furniture trades, which traditionally employed Jewish workers.[51]

Most of those who remained in East London tended to be the least economically and mobile of the immigrants and their children. This, however, did not mean that they themselves did not move at all. Within Stepney, which continued to be the dominant place of residence, the Jewish population moved increasingly eastwards from Whitechapel towards Stepney Green and Mile End. Some Jews also began to dwell in neighbouring East End areas. In 1929 a house sample carried out for the *New Survey of London* revealed that '52 per cent of the East London [Jewish] families live in Stepney, 24 per cent in Hackney, 11 per cent in Bethnal Green, and the remaining 13 per cent in Stoke Newington, Shoreditch, and Poplar.'[52]

Social Structures of the Jewish Community

Such geographical mobility within East London and to other parts of the metropolis indicates that the Jews cannot be seen as an unchanging and static group, nor as one community. Although the Jews shared a common heritage and certain religious beliefs and customs, they were as much

---

[49] Smith, 'East End Jews', 29–30.

[50] Llewellyn Smith, *New Survey*, vi. 222, 236, 242, 272; *JC*, 16 Dec. 1932, p. 7, and 9 Mar. 1934, p. 10.

[51] Smith, 'East End Jews', 28–33; Lipman, *Social History of the Jews*, 168–71.

[52] Adler, 'Jewish Life and Labour', 271; Smith, 'East End Jews', 26–7.

divided by class, gender, and generational conflicts as the rest of society.[53] Among the immigrant population there were sharp divisions between those who were able to climb the economic and social ladder, whom Bill Williams has labelled the *nouveaux riches* or 'alrightniks', and those who remained at the bottom. Indeed, many tensions emerged between these *nouveaux riches*, who were the entrepreneurs in the commerce and workshop trades of the East European immigrant community, and the more working-class immigrants. As Williams has shown in the case of Manchester, subtle divisions prevailed among the immigrants. These were 'not simply along the lines of nationality, region of origin or religious preference (although all these existed), but even more in terms of differing degrees of success in the search for economic betterment and social respectability'.[54] In the jostle for improving their status, the clashes not only emerged between the immigrants, but also with the older and more established Anglo-Jews. Bringing their own networks of support and customs, the East European Jews arriving in East London were surrounded by Anglo-Jews who over generations of settlement had also developed their own communal structures and attitudes. Inevitably the relationship between these different groups was not easy.

Much of the tension within the Jewish community was increased by the ever-present threat of anti-Semitism. Although never as virulent as on the European continent, Jews had faced discrimination in Britain for centuries, and had only received full civil rights in 1858.[55] Hostility towards outsiders was prevalent at the turn of the century, most clearly seen in the debate concerning the Aliens Act of 1905 which limited immigration on a permanent basis for the first time.[56] In 1914 the Aliens

---

[53] Much of the earlier literature on the history of the Jews in England tended to deny such tensions. For criticism of this old approach see B. Williams, 'The Beginnings of Jewish Trade-Unionism in Manchester, 1889–1891', in K. Lunn (ed.), *Hosts, Immigrants, and Minorities* (Folkestone, 1980), 263–5; Feldman, 'Immigrants and Workers', 12–13; and 'Introduction', in Cesarani (ed.), *Making of Modern Anglo-Jewry*.

[54] Williams, 'East and West', 18.

[55] For more information on the struggle for civil rights, particularly the fight for entry to Parliament see I. Finestein, 'Jewish Emancipationists in Victorian England: Self-Imposed Limits to Assimilation', in J. Frankel and S. J. Zipperstein (eds.), *Assimilation and Community: The Jews in Nineteenth-Century Europe* (Cambridge, 1992), 43–7.

[56] Lipman, 'The Age of Emancipation', 78; J. A. Garrard, *The English and Immigration: A Comparative Study of the Jewish Influx, 1880–1910* (Oxford, 1971); B. Gainer, *The Alien Invasion: The Origins of the Aliens Act of 1905* (London, 1972). Such antagonism was not confined to the Jewish population. Roman Catholics had also suffered a long history of persecution, and were only granted civil rights in 1829, and certain restrictions had also been attempted to curb the immigration of Irish immigrants in the mid-19th c. See S. Gilley, 'The Roman Catholic Mission to the Irish in London', *Recusant Hist.* 10/3 (1969–70), 123; M. A. G. O'Tuathaigh, 'The Irish in 19th-Century Britain: Problems of Integration', in Swift and Gilley (eds.), *The Irish in the Victorian City*, 27–8.

Restriction Act extended the powers of the 1905 Act, allowing for the control, supervision, detention, and deportation of aliens. More threatening and harsh, however, were the restrictions enacted by the Aliens Act of 1919. This Act provided the police with powers to detain and deport Jews on the slightest pretext, even if they had been settled in Britain for years. Arrests could be made, for instance, if there was any suspicion of causing sedition or industrial unrest. Aliens were also barred from entering the civil service under this act. Anti-Semitism was not only manifested in political agitation, but also in social discrimination, street hooliganism, and other popular expressions of hostility.[57]

While the degree of hostility to Jews changed over the years, being more intense in certain periods than in others, and taking on a different characteristics, it none the less was an issue which constantly underpinned the relationship of Anglo-Jewry with the outside British world. For a number of élite Anglo-Jews, acceptance into wider English society could only be achieved by stressing their bourgeois status. While this identity was rooted primarily in political and economic spheres that largely excluded women's participation, it was none the less greatly influenced by women's activities, particularly in the home. For many of these Jewish leaders, their status was linked to the image of the ideal bourgeois family, for which Jewish women as wives and mothers were held particularly responsible.[58]

For a number of Anglo-Jewish leaders, the appearance of respectability not only rested on bourgeois ideals and attitudes, but also on their ability to be good patriots. In this context it was important for them to make Judaism appear to be solely a set of religious beliefs and practices. Accordingly 'all national aspects of Judaism were relegated to an antique past'.[59] Such a definition of Jewish identity, however, did not always accord with reality, nor was it accepted by all Anglo-Jews or East European Jews. However successfully integrated into British society, Jews

---

[57] Smith, 'East End Jews', 235–6, 240–3; Endelman, *Radical Assimilation*, 191; Finestein, 'Jewish Emancipationists in Victorian England'. For evidence of specific anti-Semitism in Manchester see R. Roberts, *The Classic Slum* (London, 1971; 1977), 171–2, 183; and B. Williams, 'The Anti-Semitism of Tolerance: Middle-Class Manchester and the Jews, 1870–1900', in A. J. Kidd and K. W. Roberts (eds.), *City, Class and Culture: Studies of Social Policy in Victorian Manchester* (Manchester, 1985).

[58] This is also discussed in relation to the role of the Jewish mother in the Introduction. See also M. A. Kaplan, 'Gender and Jewish History in Imperial Germany', in Frankel and Zipperstein (eds.), *Assimilation and Community*, 201–10; and R. Burman, ' "She Looketh Well to the Ways of Her Household": The Changing Role of Jewish Women in Religious Life, *c*.1800–1930', in G. Malmgreen (ed.), *Religion in the Lives of English Women, 1760–1930* (London, 1986).

[59] Feldman, 'Immigrants and Workers', 243.

could also be viewed with disdain, as was illustrated in the case of some very wealthy and highly integrated figures such as Cassel, Rothschild, and Hirsch, whose acceptance into upper-class British society was at times tenuous.[60] The notion of their separateness was also reinforced by the fact that a number of the most assimilated and wealthy Jewish families continued to identify themselves as Jews, marrying only Jewish partners, and dictating the same for their children even when they were indifferent to Judaism.[61]

The acceptance of Jews into the wider community was not only bound up with questions of patriotism and loyalty, but was also linked to the issue of progress as prescribed by theories of liberalism and rational religion. It was therefore important for many élite Anglo-Jews to establish an identity for themselves which showed their religion to have broken with the bonds of traditional Judaism and to have adapted to the demands of a 'civilized' society. This contrasted with the image of the East European Jews, whom some Anglo-Jewish leaders and outside British observers regarded as continuing the practices of an 'irrational' Judaism, and coming from pre-modern states that were still uncivilized and untouched by the effects of liberalism or rational religion.[62] In this way the arrival of the East European immigrants threatened the very position that a number of the Anglo-Jewish élite had so carefully built up for themselves and the principles on which their social institutions were founded.[63]

What was particularly problematic was the overwhelming poverty of the new immigrants, as revealed by the unease of leading members of London Jewry in their discussions with Charles Booth in the 1880s. They saw the poverty and traditions of the newcomers as particularly strange and embarrassing.[64] As one article in the leading Jewish communal newspaper, the *Jewish Chronicle*, expressed it,

If poor Jews will persist in appropriating whole streets to themselves in the same district, if they will conscientiously persevere in the seemingly harmless practice of congregating in a body at prominent points in a great public thoroughfare like the Whitechapel or Commercial Road, drawing to their peculiarities of dress, of language and of manner, the attention which they might otherwise escape, can there be any wonder that the vulgar prejudices of which they are the objects should be kept alive and strengthened? What can the untutored, unthinking denizen of the East End believe in the face of such facts, but that the Jew is an

---

[60] Ibid. 253.   [61] Ibid. 244.
[62] Ibid. 257–8.   [63] B. Williams, 'East and West'.
[64] Charles Booth Collection (BLPES) File B147, pp. 57, 101. B. Williams, *Manchester Jewry*; White, *Rothschild Buildings*. Similar anxieties were present in the Anglo-Catholic community about the Irish poor, who were seen as potentially threatening their newly won rights. See Jackson, 'The Irish in East London', 115–16.

alien in every sense of the word—alien in ideas, in sympathy and in interests from the rest of the population, utterly indifferent to whom he may injure so long as he benefits himself, an Ishmael whose hand is against everyone, and against whom the hand may rightly be.[65]

Such attitudes were not helped by the poor contact between the immigrants and many Anglo-Jews. Communication between these two groups was difficult, because, unlike the new immigrants, most Anglo-Jews did not speak Yiddish. As already indicated, many of the more established Jews were also living in West London and were therefore cut off from daily contact with the immigrants resident in East London.[66]

The conflicts between the Anglo-Jews and the East European Jews were intensified by the antagonism expressed by many members of the host society towards the immigrants. Indeed, East London was already the site of intense anti-Semitism, much of it being fostered by the conditions under which the local population was living. The Jews were seen as the perpetrators rather than the victims of the shortage of housing, the insanitary conditions, and unemployment.[67] Immigrants were also blamed for overcrowding; it was common for Jewish families to take in members of their extended family or friends. Cases of deserted wives and bigamy among Jewish immigrants also provided bait for those who accused the Jews of the breakdown of the social unit, the nuclear family.[68] Gambling,

[65] *JC*, 28 Sept. 1888, 9. See also Fishman, *East End Jewish Radicals*, 67–8.

[66] V. D. Lipman, *A Century of Social Service, 1859–1959: The Jewish Board of Guardians* (London, 1959), 5; Bermant, *Point of Arrival*, 133; E. Black, *The Social Politics of Anglo-Jewry, 1880–1920* (Oxford, 1988), 36–7.

[67] Resentment against the Jews was held not only by the local English population, but also by the Irish immigrants who had settled in East London from the late 1840s. Many of these Irish immigrants and their children were the poorest residents in East London, and as such were living in the worst housing and facing some of the worst economic pressures. For the Irish, the influx of East European Jews was therefore particularly threatening. Much of the hostility the Jews suffered had previously been directed towards Irish immigrants. For more information on the conflicts that emerged between Irish immigrants and the incoming Jews see D. Fitzpatrick, 'A Curious Middle Place: The Irish in Britain, 1871–1921', in Swift and Gilley, *The Irish in Britain*, 45. E. R. Smith has examined the intense political conflicts between the Irish and the Jews in the context of politics in East London in the inter-war years, see 'East End Jews', 229–33.

[68] *RC Alien Immigration*, PP 1903 IX, Q 9418, Q 9780; Gartner, *Jewish Immigrant*, 172; J. Hollingshead, *Ragged London in 1861* (London, 1861; 1986), 25, 45; J. Buckman, *Immigrants and the Class Struggle: The Jewish Immigrant in Leeds* (Manchester, 1983), 159; White, *Rothschild Buildings*, 77; Feldman, 'Immigrants and Workers', 263. An interesting discussion on the way in which perceptions of alien immigration impinged on more national questions concerning social and political questions of physical deterioration, unemployment, high rents, and poverty in Britain appears in D. Feldman, 'The Importance of Being English: Jewish Immigration and the Decay of Liberal England', in D. Feldman and G. Stedman Jones (eds.), *Metropolis London: Histories and Representations Since 1800* (London, 1989).

prostitution, and the selling of illegal alcohol, a lucrative business for some Jewish immigrants, was also seen by a number of Anglo-Jewish leaders to be a blot on the whole Jewish community and potentially inciting anti-Semitism.[69]

Ever conscious of their position and the need to preserve respectability, the Anglo-Jewish élite therefore made stringent efforts to improve the conditions of their members. The characteristic attitude behind these measures was highlighted by one leader comment in the *Jewish Chronicle* in 1881, 'We may not be able to make them rich, but we may hope to render them English in feeling and in conduct. . . . By improving in all directions and educating their children in an English fashion, we can do much to change our foreign poor into brethren who shall not only be Jews, but English Jews.'[70] Indeed, it was felt that the immigrants 'in accepting the hospitality of England . . . owe a reciprocal duty of becoming Englishmen'.[71]

The overwhelming need for respectability and acceptance into wider British society dominated much of the fabric of Anglo-Jewish communal organizations. During the years 1830 to 1870, Anglo-Jewish institutions within London underwent an intensive process of consolidation. This resulted in a remarkable degree of centralization of authority which rested in the hands of a small number of élite families. Their power was drawn from the bonds generated not only through their common religion and wealth, but also from their business connections and marriage ties. This was reinforced by the prestige they wielded in the non-Jewish world. It was these families, such as the Adlers, the Montefiores, the Rothschilds, the Cohens, and the Franklins, who dominated the committees and work of the major Anglo-Jewish institutions.[72] Their authority was not based on any electoral mandate, which limited their powers of coercion. Instead, in order to achieve their goal, they were forced to rely on the tactics of persuasion, moral pressure, or on seeking to meet the needs of the

---

[69] Feldman, 'Immigrants and Workers', 285; Fishman, *East End Jewish Radicals*, 137–8, 285.

[70] *JC*, 12 Aug. 1881. See also Fishman, *East End Jewish Radicals*, 67–8; R. Burman, 'The Jewish Woman as the Breadwinner: The Changing Value of Women's Work in a Manchester Immigrant Community', *Oral Hist.* 10/2 (1982), 27–39, and G. C. Lebzelter, 'Anti-Semitism—a Focal Point for the British Radical Right', in P. Kennedy and A. J. Nicholls (eds.), *Nationalist and Radical Movements in Britain and Germany Before 1914* (London, 1981), 90.

[71] *JC*, 12 Aug. 1881.

[72] Feldman, 'Immigrants and Workers', 17–19; Black, *Social Politics of Anglo-Jewry*, 8–35; C. Bermant, *The Cousinhood: The Anglo-Jewish Gentry* (London, 1971); Finestein, 'Jewish Emancipation', 48–9. Also see n. 76.

immigrants through philanthropic activities, as well as recreational and educational programmes.[73]

Originally established in 1760, the Jewish Board of Deputies was the principal organization by which Jews interacted as an organized body with Parliament and the wider British public. It represented all the synagogues in the country.[74] While the rabbinical court, the *Beth Din*, governed religious matters and arbitrated on civil disputes between Jews, the Board of Deputies, although a lay body, had the statutory authority for registering Jewish marriages as well as the formal custody of certifying new synagogues and burial grounds from 1836. The Board was responsible for negotiating with the state over religious issues which had a secular and political importance, such as sabbath observance and Sunday trading. In this way the Board played a pivotal role not only in representing the rights of Jews to the state as well as in aiding the state to monitor and control the Jewish community. This also meant that among the Jewish population the Board exerted a great deal of power both in determining what constituted correct Jewish practice and in defining the boundaries of Jewish identity.[75]

Equally influential in governing the respectability of Anglo-Jewry was the work of the Jewish Board of Guardians (JBG). Originally established in 1859, the JBG was the most cohesive charitable Ashkenazi institution in the Jewish community.[76] Arising out of an attempt to centralize the relief agencies organized by synagogues and other Jewish associations, the major emphasis in the work carried out by the JBG was on self-help and the prevention of pauperism.[77] Such thinking was in line with policies

---

[73] I am grateful to Bill Williams for this point. See also B. Williams, 'East and West'.

[74] Initially the Board only represented Orthodox synagogues. Only in 1886 were Reform Synagogues permitted entry. They continued to have inferior authority within the Board as late as the 1940s, causing much friction between Orthodox and Reform Jews. See Black, *Social Politics of Anglo-Jewry*, 38.

[75] Feldman, 'Immigrants and Workers', 16–17; Black, *Social Politics of Anglo-Jewry*, 38–43, 262–3; E. R. Smith, 'East End Jews', 7, 38.

[76] The Anglo-Jewish élite families were heavily represented on the committee of the JBG, illustrating the power they held in Anglo-Jewish institutions. For instance between 1859 and 1947, with the exception of 20 years, the presidential office of the JBG was occupied by a member of the Cohen family. The strength of these families on the JBG was not only rooted in the time they devoted to committee work, but also in their financial contributions. See Feldman, 'Immigrants and Workers', 19. A comparable Board of Guardians was set up by the Sephardi Jews in 1879. See Black, *Social Politics of Anglo-Jewry*, 79–80.

[77] Williams, *Manchester Jewry*, 280; Feldman, 'Immigrants and Workers', 197. See also the president's address to the JBG Annual General Meeting, 22 Mar. 1937, 7, 13 (Mocatta Library, box pamphlet BA 28 COH).

of other groups such as the Charity Organization Society. Many of the methods used by the JBG reflected those being used by progressive philanthropists such as Louisa Twining or William Rathbone in the early 1850s.[78] In the 1860s the JBG was among the most progressive philanthropic organizations in England. It undertook a wide range of assistance including the provision of soup, clothes, apprenticeships, and loans for setting up businesses or for further passage to America or South Africa.[79]

None the less, despite its more progressive attitude and abundant forms of aid, the JBG could be just as disciplinary in its treatment of applicants and was as keen to inculcate the ethics of thrift as many parish unions, particularly in times of depression.[80] Full investigations were made of applicants by the JBG to judge their moral integrity and thrift. Newcomers had to prove residence in England of six months and that they were able to support themselves before they were granted help. Those immigrants who appeared unable to maintain themselves were often repatriated by the JBG. Over 24,000 Jewish immigrants were returned by the JBG to Eastern Europe in the years 1881 to 1906. Together with the 7,000 Jews who were also repatriated by the Russo-Jewish Committee between 1882 and 1906, these figures comprised 56 per cent of 'the increase in the total number of Russians and Russian Poles in London between 1881 and 1911.[81] This policy involved harrowing experiences for those it affected.[82] Such harsh measures the JBG saw as important if they were to concentrate their resources on the deserving poor. Not wanting to place the more demoralized cases in the workhouse, repatriation was the only means by which they could eliminate those they saw as the more disreputable poor.[83] Yet this did not prevent them from sometimes using the workhouse as a means of coercion. This was particularly noticeable in the cases of deserted wives, who were seen as a big problem for the Jewish community in the late nineteenth century. Rather than helping a woman and her children, the JBG often insisted that they enter the workhouse. Their attitude to this issue was reflected in an article in the *Jewish Chronicle*: 'To compel these women to enter the workhouse is at the same time the best test of their deserted and destitute condition, the greatest

---

[78] Williams, *Manchester Jewry*, 280.

[79] *Sweating System*, PP 1888 XX, Q1, Q269; *RC Alien Immigration*, Q15233, Q15243; Williams, *Manchester Jewry*, 280, and Feldman, 'Immigrants and Workers', 197; Black, *Social Politics of Anglo-Jewry*, 71–103.

[80] Williams, *Manchester Jewry*, 280; Feldman, 'Immigrants and Workers', 197–8.

[81] Feldman, 'Immigrants and Workers', 203–6.

[82] *RC Alien Immigration*, Qs9774–76, Q15319, Q15629.

[83] Feldman, 'Immigrants and Workers', 203–6.

deterrent to this course of conduct on the part of men, and the most practical way of compelling them to resume their proper responsibility for the support of their families.'[84] Such moral values promulgated by the JBG were also important elements in the foundation of other charitable organizations under its auspices, such as the Sick Room Helps Society which provided help for mothers in childbirth.[85]

Leaders of the JBG saw the Board as providing relief where religious issues were at stake and help was unavailable elsewhere.[86] This was most apparent in its policy on parish relief. Anglo-Jews were particularly concerned about poor Jews accepting aid from the parish since the appearance of Jews on the parish rate could potentially provoke antagonism in the outside world and stigmatize the whole Jewish community. What is more, established Jews feared that their people would be isolated culturally and possibly converted in institutions for the poor.[87] Indoor parish relief, which required residence within the workhouse, limited religious observance. Legally non-Anglican inmates were entitled to attend religious services outside the workhouse on the sabbath and certain festivals, but in reality this was not always adhered to.[88] For this reason many of the efforts of the JBG were directed towards keeping the Jewish poor away from the workhouse. This, however, did not extend to outdoor relief, in particular medical relief, which was much more easily accessible to Jewish claimants because, being provided outside the workhouse, it did not impose the same infringements on religious practice. Seeing medical relief as a lesser need, the JBG no longer provided it after 1873, arguing that no complaints had been heard from the patients themselves or from Poor Law authorities about the treatment of Jewish patients.[89]

---

[84] *JC*, 30 May 1902.

[85] This organization is explored further in Ch. 3.

[86] Lipman, *A Century of Social Service*, 63.

[87] JBG, *AR* 1861, 37; Buckman, *Immigrants and the Class Struggle*, 159; White, *Rothschild Buildings*; and Feldman, 'Immigrants and Workers', 263. For further information on the interaction of the Jews and Poor Law relief see Ch. 5.

[88] M. Steiner, 'Philanthropic Activity and Organisation in the Manchester Jewish Community, 1867–1914', MA thesis (Manchester, 1974), 51–2.

[89] JBG, *AR* (1873), 22; (1879), 18; (1891), 10–11; (1896), 18–19. See also Ch. 3. for more detail on this episode. Contrary to the views held by the JBG, objections to the JBG's policy on medical relief were voiced in 1888. Their withdrawal of relief was thought to have increased the burden on the ratepayers in East London. Jewish patients were thought to be particularly demanding in seeking medical attention from Poor Law authorities (*House of Lords Select Committee on Poor Law Relief*, PP 1888 XV, Revd Billings, Qs2477–8). The withdrawal of medical relief on the part of the JBG was reflected in the type of parish aid the Jews applied for. More Jews appeared amongst those accepting medical and outdoor relief than indoor relief. For more information on this see Ch. 5.

It is impossible to assess the degree to which immigrants accepted such charitable aid and conformed with schemes of Anglicization and assimilation. This ranged not only according to class expectations, but also according to generational differences. As Mr Emmanuel, an Anglo-Jewish character in Louis Golding's novel *Magnolia Street*, published in 1932, observed,

The elder ones did not feel themselves to be in their own land, they looked back to Poland and Russia, they looked forward to America. But he saw the hearts of the younger Jews divided in another way. Not all of them wanted to 'get on'. In these few years of their boyhood and girlhood, they had become more impregnated with English than other foreigners might in two generations. He saw the small boys conforming to the type of small boys opposite. They played football and cricket, and studied the team scores with, if anything more passion. They became, or yearned to be 'sports', and 'decent chaps'. Just as successfully, the little girls were becoming English 'misses'.[90]

Emmanuel's observation not only reflected the generational differences that occurred in the process of Anglicization, but also the gender ones, as shown by the different roles the boys and girls played on the street.

Yet the degree to which Anglicization was achieved in reality is questionable. Much depended on the expectations of the newcomers themselves and their social circumstances. The success of the policies of Anglicization pursued by the Anglo-Jewish élite also rested on their provision of services which met the very real needs of the immigrants. For many of these immigrants, however, the desire to improve their conditions was not merely the result of the Anglicization programme imposed by Anglo-Jewish leaders, but was deeply rooted in their dreams of escaping the drudgery and lack of autonomy they suffered in the sweated workshops they entered on arrival.[91] This was particularly clear in the case of the *nouveaux riches* Jewish immigrants, who, on climbing the social and economic ladder, quickly established their own schemes for Anglicization.

Some of the aspirations of these immigrants can be gauged from the organizations that they set up for themselves apart from those provided by the Anglo-Jews. Approximately 150 Jewish benefit societies existed in East London in 1898. A survey of some streets in Spitalfields in the same year showed that about a half to two-thirds of adult males were members of at least one of these societies. No accurate figures remain on how many

[90] Golding, *Magnolia Street*, 191–2.
[91] D. M. Feldman, 'Historical Review: "There was an Englishman, an Irishman and a Jew . . . ": Immigrants and Minorities in Britain', *Hist. J.* 26/1 (1983), 185–99.

were individual members of these societies. None the less, in 1901 a survey calculated the Jewish friendly societies to have a membership of over 15,500, of which 12,000 probably lived in Stepney. By 1911 42,000 were thought to belong to Jewish friendly societies. Most of these societies were for men only, but in 1907 the Chief Registrar of Friendly Societies listed three Jewish societies which were exclusively for women.[92]

In addition to friendly societies, the immigrants were also involved in a complex range of other organizations such as the *Chevroth*, which were social or voluntary associations often formed out of the congregation of a small synagogue for religious and social welfare purposes. These agencies not only served as a meeting point for similarly minded individuals, but also provided charitable and medical relief.[93] Such associations had their own agendas, some of which matched those of the more established Jews. While many of the organizations established by the immigrants were fragmented along social and class lines, most of them aimed at self-conscious improvement and respectability and stressed their independence from other Jews and wider British society. Many of these societies, while keen to demarcate themselves from both poorer Jews and Anglo-Jewish philanthropists, were none the less the most widely used and long-lasting agencies initiated and maintained by the Jewish immigrants. They were also the chief organizations 'through which the Russian and Polish Jews could create prestige, and express an attempt to legitimize distinctions of social status'.[94]

Less concerned with the ethics of self-help and self-reliance, such as those promoted by the various Jewish benefit societies, and more focused on the goal of collective action and the need for social equality, many Jewish socialist and trade-union activists also pushed for a programme of self-improvement and autonomy within the Jewish East End. Much of the educational aims of Jewish socialist and anarchist groups were aimed at eradicating what they perceived as the ignorance of the Jewish

[92] Feldman, 'Immigrants and Workers', 287; (Black, *Social Politics of Anglo-Jewry*, 196; G. Black, 'Health and Medical Care of the Jewish Poor in the East End of London, 1880–1939', Ph.D. thesis (Leicester, 1987), 92; Williams, 'East and West', 25–6.

[93] Steiner, 'Philanthropic Activity', 22–3. For information on the medical care offered by the various Jewish benefit societies see Black, 'Health and Medical Care of the Jewish Poor', 91–103.

[94] Feldman, 'Immigrants and Workers', 285–98. See also Williams, 'East and West', 17–18, 23–33. Many Jewish activists in the Stepney Labour Party in the inter-war years had gained their political education through their association with friendly societies and other such organizations. It was through these organizations that they had learnt the rules and methods of political procedure. See Smith, 'East End Jews', 78; G. Alderman, *London Jewry and London Politics, 1889–1986* (London, 1989).

immigrants whom they viewed as culturally backward and enslaved to an archaic religion. Accordingly, many articles appearing in the radical Yiddish press urged its readers to learn English. They saw this as a vital step to advancing knowledge in both the political and the scientific world. Socialist and anarchist associations hosted libraries and provided 'lessons in English and arithmetic, and lectures on scientific and literary subjects'. For many participating in these circles, the poverty and discrimination of the Jews could only be solved through Anglicization, trade-unionism, and cultural progress.[95]

Such moves for improvement and Anglicization, whether it be among trade unions or friendly societies, were not totally dissimilar from the values promoted by many of the Anglo-Jewish institutions. Indeed, the extent to which their aims overlapped can be seen from the fact that in the 1920s and 1930s many investigating officers of the JBG (some of whom were themselves the children of immigrants) regarded applicants who were not members of a friendly society as thriftless.[96] Yet, while the importance of self-improvement and self-reliance was shared by the organizations initiated by immigrants and Anglo-Jewish leaders, this did not prevent tension. Indeed, such self-assertion by the immigrant organizations was tolerated only within certain boundaries. Conflicts were particularly strong in the case of the immigrant trade unions and socialist activists (whose efforts for collective action and demands for social equality many Anglo-Jewish leaders saw as a political challenge not only to their own authority and the 'correct' order of the world), but also to the image they had so carefully constructed of the Jewish community in the public domain.[97] Anglo-Jewry was equally worried by the thought that many of the immigrant organizations, such as the *Chevroth*, retained and reinforced many of the ties and customs of the old world which they saw as backward and preventing assimilation.[98]

More importantly, however, many of the relief strategies adopted by these organizations were different from the principles on which the policies of the Anglo-Jewish charitable institutions were founded. Unlike the

---

[95] Feldman, 'Immigrants and Workers', 318–20. See also Fishman, *East End Jewish Radicals*, 97–162.

[96] Interview with Mark Fineman by Gerry Black, Jan. 1986; cited in Black, 'Health and Medical Care of the Jewish Poor', 93.

[97] A number of the *nouveaux riches* immigrant Jews also felt their positions threatened by socialism. See Williams, 'East and West', 30; and Feldman, 'Immigrants and Workers', 315–16.

[98] Steiner, 'Philanthropic Activity', 22–3; Feldman, 'Immigrants and Workers', 287–302; Black, *Social Politics of Anglo-Jewry*, 195–200; Bermant, *Point of Arrival*, 197.

JBG and other such Anglo-Jewish welfare agencies, the associations established by the immigrants carefully aimed to provide relief in a way which would not stigmatize the recipient. One article appearing in 1900 in a Yiddish newspaper primarily aimed at the immigrant readership, which attacked the form of aid given by the JBG, highlighted the differences in approach. It argued,

This is not the form of charity which our learned men have prescribed; the donor should not know to whom he gives, and the recipient should not know from whose hand he takes. . . . The charity of our prominent men is given with noise, alarms and advertisement and is divided with uproar, openly, humiliatingly. No one but a professional beggar can accept it with a light heart, someone who has not sunk so low cannot without it leaving a permanent stain on his conscience.[99]

Such views raised objections from Anglo-Jewish leaders who accused the immigrant associations of indiscriminate almsgiving and causing greater pauperism. The democratic structure of the friendly societies and trade unions also threatened the more paternal approach taken by institutions such as the JBG.[100] In an attempt to undermine the power of the organizations among the immigrants, Anglo-Jewish communal leaders tried to set up their own friendly societies and workmen's clubs and special classes in English, which would instil 'correct' ideas of Anglicization and modes of self-help, but these met with varied success.[101]

The immigrants not only strove for social, economic, and political autonomy, but also for religious independence. This was most noticeable in the struggle for religious education. Some of the most intense conflicts occurred between the religious educational schemes promoted by the immigrants and those instituted by the United Synagogue (the chief representative of Orthodox Jewish synagogues in Britain). Seeing itself

[99] *Der Yidisher Ekspres*, 11 May 1900, 4, cited in Feldman, 'Immigrants and Workers', 301. Such criticism appeared many times in the Yiddish press through the years, particularly in the JBG's response to the large influx of Romanian Jews in the years 1899–1901; see Feldman, 299–302.

[100] For more discussion on this see Feldman, 'Immigrants and Workers', 287–302, and Black, *Social Politics of Anglo-Jewry*, 194–216.

[101] Williams, *Manchester Jewry*, 278–9; Black, *Social Politics of Anglo-Jewry*, 159–60. Another important battle between the immigrant Jews and the more established community was over the establishment of the London Jewish Hospital in East London. Those campaigning for the hospital were accused by the Anglo-Jewish élite, particularly Lord Rothschild, of promoting a scheme which would be seen by the outside world as a move towards exclusivity and separatism. Black has dealt with this episode in 'Health and Medical Care of the Jewish Poor', 251–309. A similar class struggle also occurred in a campaign for the Jewish Hospital in Manchester. See Williams, 'East and West', 2–8.

as the principal representative of Jewish religious life, the United Synagogue asserted a Judaism based on what it perceived to be a modern and rationalized religion that correlated with the demands of British society. Such a vision, however, was not always shared by immigrant religious leaders who abhorred the moves of Anglo-leaders to bring Judaism within the confines of modernity and convenience. This became particularly contentious in a dispute over religious and Hebrew education. Most immigrant children, in addition to going to ordinary schools, were expected to attend *chadorim* (religious schools) in East London. These schools had also existed in Eastern Europe, teaching both Hebrew and the principles of Judaism. Such an education was viewed by many immigrants and their religious leaders as a vital continuation of generations of tradition and learning. This was juxtaposed against what many leaders of the *chadorim* regarded as the ethics of social status and materialism being promoted by the Anglo-Jewish educational programmes. For more Anglo-Jewish leaders, however, the *chadorim* were seen not only as causing children to be overworked, but also, more importantly, as preventing Anglicization, particularly because teaching was done in Yiddish.[102] As one comment in the *Jewish Chronicle* expressed it, the *chadorim* were 'a firmly established evil, ever at variance with our Anglicized ways and doctrines . . .'. Their teachings were thought to be immoral as well as based on superstition.[103]

Many of the struggles over religious issues not only emerged between the immigrants and Anglo-Jewish élite, but also between the Anglo-Jewish leaders. This was most clearly seen in the case of the Federation of Synagogues, established in 1887. Primarily created to represent the immigrant synagogues in East London, the Federation was financially backed by the wealthy Anglo-Jewish figure Samuel Montague. While leaders of the United Synagogue preferred to ignore or oppose the immigrant synagogues, the Federation, largely under the direction of Montague, represented an attempt to reform the immigrant synagogues from within. For Montague the Federation was not only a means of combating socialism as well as promoting Anglicization,[104] but was also a way of reinvigorating Judaism. None the less, while his aims for Anglicization were shared by many leaders within the United Synagogue, they did not necessarily agree with his approach. This was particularly apparent in the

---

[102] Greater detail appears on this struggle in Feldman, 'Immigrants and Workers', 331–9; Black, *Social Politics of Anglo-Jewry*, 217–18.

[103] *JC*, 21 Nov. 1884, and 8 July 1898.

[104] To achieve this Montague forbade the use of Yiddish by the Federation.

struggles over who should have jurisdiction over kosher food and funeral expenses.[105]

Over time such tensions over religious matters and what constituted the 'appropriate' form of Judaism and cultural identity changed considerably. While religious observance was vital to many Jewish immigrants, this was not always the case for their children who regarded religion as an obstacle to assimilation and upward mobility. As one correspondent complained to the *Jewish Chronicle* in 1926, the children of the immigrants regarded the 'things that their parents think are sins' as 'foolish idiosyncrasies'; and thought that their customs were 'but degenerate foibles set by a Rabbinical authority which had to give something concrete to the more prosaic, less imaginative, and sometimes bigoted minds of their parents'.[106] Similarly the children of immigrants resented the use of Yiddish by their parents, and often did not understand it. This resulted in great conflicts between the generations.[107] In this sense it would therefore seem that the Anglo-Jewish programme of assimilation had succeeded. None the less, by the 1920s, many lay and religious Anglo-Jewish leaders were anxious that the process of Anglicization had gone too far, causing many Jews to abandon their religious identity altogether. By this stage, the concern was no longer about raising good British citizens, but rather about bringing children up to be 'true Jews and Jewesses'.[108] It was in this context that a number of Anglo-Jewish leaders launched a series of initiatives in the 1920s to provide more religious education in East London.[109] Much of the focus of their efforts was also aimed at Jewish women, whose educational influence as mothers was seen as the key to the continuation of Jewish ritual and tradition not only within the household but for the whole community.[110]

---

[105] For more detail on the Federation of Synagogues and the battles over funerals and kosher food see G. Alderman, *The Federation of Synagogues, 1887–1987* (London, 1987); See also J. Glasman, 'Assimilation by Design: London Synagogues in the 19th Century', in T. Kushner (ed.), *The Jewish Heritage in British History: Englishness and Jewishness* (London, 1992); Feldman, 'Immigrants and Workers', 302–8, 315–16; Black, *Social Politics of Anglo-Jewry*, 217–18; Livshin, 'Aspects of Acculturation', 149; Smith 'East End Jews', 11.

[106] Letter to 'Auntie', *JC* 12 Nov. 1926. See also Livshin, 'Aspects of Acculturation', 256–9, 276–7, 364.

[107] The loss of Yiddish was a gradual process. While many children of immigrants could not speak Yiddish, they could understand it when spoken to. The degree to which immigrants acquired the ability to speak English also varied. For more detail on the tensions that emerged over Yiddish and the gaps it accentuated between the immigrant generation and their children see Livshin 'Aspects of Acculturation', 229–30.

[108] *JC*, 8 July 1921.   [109] Smith, 'East End Jews', 35–6.

[110] This marked a shift from earlier years when women were seen as peripheral to preserving the fundamental concerns of Jewish religion. For more discussion on this see Burman, 'She Looketh Well'.

Such shifts in the priorities pursued by Anglo-Jewry within the context of religious education, and the increasing secularization of the children of the immigrants indicate the wider changes that had occurred to the Jewish community by the inter-war years. Indeed, by this period, the cessation of immigration and the increasing integration of the Jewish population into English society had transformed the nature of the Jewish East End. Elaine Smith's study of local East End politics among the Jews in the inter-war period, has shown a marked difference in the perceptions and actions of those who were living in the East End in these years from the generation before them. This was not only because many of those living in East London were no longer immigrants themselves, but also because of the social and economic changes that had taken place among the East End Jewish population.[111]

Having been left by the more successfully mobile Jews, East London, by the inter-war years, hosted a Jewish population that was more uniformly poor and working-class. Many of those remaining there also tended to be more radical and politically self-confident than their predecessors. Socialist and anarchist politics had been a feature of the East End from the earliest days of immigration, but by the inter-war years many East End Jews were deeply involved in the newly formed local Labour Party and the Communist Party, and were particularly articulate in the council chamber. Much of their action was galvanized by both the continuing difficulties of poverty and unemployment, which were intensified by the economic depressions of the 1920s and 1930s, and the increasing problem of anti-Semitism and fascism.[112] The involvement of many East End Jews in the local political system did not undermine their ethnic identity. Most of their political work was carried out among fellow Jews within a Jewish environment. Many of these activists also had very clear perceptions about their own ethnicity, which was reinforced by some of the hostility they encountered in the outside world. While their activities concerned the welfare of their fellow Jews, they did not, however, have a distinct Jewish political agenda. Rather, these activists saw their ethnic interests, such as anti-Semitism, as connected to universal issues and not a matter which solely affected the Jews. For these East End Jewish activists there was no contradiction 'between their desire to participate in the local political system as equal members of the general working-class and their desire to retain close ethnic links with fellow Jews'.[113]

---

[111] Smith, 'East End Jews'.
[112] Smith, 'East End Jews'; Alderman, *London Jewry and London Politics*, chs. 3 and 4.
[113] Smith, 'East End Jews', 359–60.

None the less, while the Jewish population in East London appeared to be much more united in their poverty and their radicalism, strong divisions and tensions still remained. This was clearly seen in the struggles between activists involved not only in the Labour Party and the Communist Party circles, but also in Zionist groups.[114] Similarly, great tensions surfaced between the more middle-class Anglo-Jews and the working-class Jews of the East End. As in previous years, at the heart of this struggle were the boundaries of Jewish identity and the right to independence. Many Anglo-Jewish leaders were threatened by the secular and radical perspectives of the East End Jews, which they regarded as undermining the religious and 'respectable' basis of the Jewish community in the outside world. What they especially feared was the assertive political activism of the East End Jews, which they thought would tarnish the whole community as Communist in the outside world, making it seem unpatriotic and even traitorous.[115] Some of the most acute tensions on the political terrain emerged in the conflict over what response should be taken to fascism in the 1930s. While many East End Jews, particularly those involved in the Communist Party, undertook visible protests on the streets against Mosley and his supporters and organized their own defence groups, Anglo-Jewish leaders, particularly those sitting on the Board of Deputies, preferred to adopt action which took a quieter and more private profile.[116]

The intense political strife in the 1920s and 1930s between the more middle-class Jews, who now had a greater concentration in the suburbs, and the East End Jews, reflects the great diversity of expectations and perceptions among the Jews in London in these years. This was not a new phenomenon. Rather, it was rooted in the complex and dynamic processes Jewish immigrants and their children experienced both on arrival and on settling in East London from the late nineteenth century.

Arriving in one of the poorest areas of the metropolis, these immigrants and their children could not escape the economic and social hardships their neighbours suffered. Their history was therefore intricately tied to that of the East End and the conditions they found there. As this chapter has shown, this had a vital impact on the types of occupation they adopted on arrival and affected their degree of social and economic

---

[114] Ibid. 358–61.   [115] Ibid. 356–7.

[116] Divisions also arose between East End Jews over the tactics to adopt in their battle against fascism. Greater detail on the conflicts over the response to fascism appears in D. Rosenberg, *Facing up to Anti-Semitism: How Jews in Britain Countered the Threats of the 1930s* (London, 1985) and Smith, 'East End Jews', 247–90.

mobility. While many of the immigrants and their children benefited from the opportunities offered by East London and then were quick to move away when possible, others were not so fortunate. Such diverse experiences among the Jewish immigrants were reflected in the changing composition of their settlement in East London. By the 1920s the cessation of immigration, together with the shift of the more economically secure Jewish immigrants and their children to other parts of the metropolis, had resulted in a much more homogeneous working-class Jewish population than had existed before the First World War. Such changes had serious implications for the social and economic status of these residents living in the area. While many of these Jews were poor, they were not quite so penniless, nor did they face such bad overcrowding as their predecessors had suffered before 1914. Similarly, many of them had greater access to social and medical services than the generation before them. The following chapters reveal that this not only influenced the material conditions these immigrants and their children experienced between the years 1870 and 1939, but also had repercussions for their health expectations and needs.

Equally as important as the social and economic conditions in East London, was the reception the immigrants received from the Jewish population who were already well settled into British society. Desperate to escape the poverty and persecution in Eastern Europe, many of the immigrants were greeted by a community which had faced its own difficulties and had developed its own strategies for survival. These often differed from and conflicted with the interests of the immigrants and their struggle for self-assertion and integration. Although many of the tensions between the newcomers and the more well-established Anglo-Jews dissipated as many of the immigrants moved up the social and economic ladder, this did not prevent the emergence of new battles. Indeed, subsequent chapters will show that these conflicts were an important force not only in shaping the institutional framework of the community, but also in the kind of welfare and medical relief provided in the Jewish community, particularly for mothers and their infants throughout the years 1870 to 1939. Much of the provision that emerged out of these conflicts had implications for the Jews, as well as for British society as a whole. Furthermore, while many of the philanthropic activities and medical measures undertaken by the Jewish population reflected the strategies adopted in wider British society, many of the measures the Jews took in response to their own specific needs initiated new solutions to old problems in the wider British world.

2

The Health of Jewish Infants and Mothers in East London

If the gentle reader desires to know what kind of blood it is that flows in the Chosen People's veins, he cannot do better than take a gentle stroll through Hatton Garden, Petticoat Lane, or any other London 'nosery'. I do not hesitate to say that in the course of an hour's peregrinations he will see more cases of Lupus, trachoma, favus, eczema, and scurvy than he will come across in a week's wanderings in any quarter of the Metropolis.[1]

SUCH words reveal the fear of many politicians and social campaigners at the turn of the century. They were anxious that the influx of East European Jewish immigrants would bring disease and physically deteriorate the health of the British population.[2] This was a view promoted by ardent anti-Semites, such as the conservative Joseph Banister, as well as by social reformers such as the Fabian Socialists. Arriving at a time of grave anxiety over the future of Britain's economic and military position in the rest of the world, East European immigrants provided a focus for these concerns.[3]

A diminishing birth rate and persistent high infant mortality added to the fears of racial degeneration. During the nineteenth century attempts were made to curb infectious and diarrhoeal diseases among infants, but the issue became a national preoccupation when many recruits failed to pass the fitness tests needed to join the army for the South African War (1899–1902). This was most clearly seen in the Royal Commission on Physical Deterioration in 1904.[4] In a drive to reduce infant mortality, in

---

[1] J. Banister, *England Under the Jews*, 3rd edn. (London, 1907), 61. For similar anti-Semitic remarks see *JC*, 8 Oct. 1897, 18, and 6 Oct. 1901, 18.

[2] Hostility towards the Jewish immigrants was not confined to health. Much of the antagonism towards Jewish immigrants in East London was fostered by local grievances. Jews were blamed for undercutting the wages of the average worker and exploiting the sweated labour system, and for causing a rise in rents. Many of these problems, however, predated the arrival of the immigrants. See Ch. 1.

[3] D. Feldman, 'The Importance of Being English: Jewish Immigration and the Decay of Liberal England', in D. Feldman and G. Stedman Jones (eds.), *Metropolis London: Histories and Representations Since 1800* (London, 1989), 57–8.

[4] A. Davin, 'Imperialism and Motherhood', *Hist. Workshop J.* 5 (1978), 9–66, 49.

1902 legislation was passed, known as the Midwives Act, which regulated the practice of midwives for the first time and was an attempt to raise midwifery standards. Many medical practitioners and policy-makers argued that the solution to infant mortality also lay in the education of mothers through health visiting and schools for mothers, later known as infant welfare centres. Various maternal and infant welfare schemes were also created by voluntary and municipal agencies.[5]

World War I, like the South African War, again prompted anxieties about the reproduction of the nation and led to the Maternity and Child Welfare Act of 1918 which gave more help to local authorities to establish grant-aided child welfare clinics. This legislation also provided money for antenatal care, reflecting a shift in emphasis from the infant to the mother.[6] Concern for maternal mortality appeared in a number of reports from 1875,[7] but it did not achieve national priority in the same way as infant mortality until the early 1920s. While little was done to ease the economic burdens of motherhood, persisting maternal mortality during the 1920s and 1930s caused public outcry over the standards of midwifery care for mothers.[8]

It is against this background that the health of Jewish mothers and their infants is considered. Social and economic conditions of the immigrant living in East London had an enormous impact on the health of immigrant women. Poverty and ill-health were common among the majority of the Jewish population in East London giving credence to the popular image of the immigrants as feeble, unhealthy, and the bringers of disease.[9] Many immigrants suffered poor health before reaching England.

---

[5] School medical inspections were another way to ensure that from childhood to adulthood the nation's population would remain healthy and provide a good workforce and army.

[6] For more information on the development of maternity and child-welfare services see Davin, 'Imperialism and Motherhood'; C. Dyhouse, 'Working-Class Mothers and Infant Mortality in England, 1895–1914', *J. Soc. Hist.* 12 (1979), 248–67; J. Lewis, *The Politics of Motherhood* (London, 1980), and 'The Working-Class Wife and Mother and State Intervention', in J. Lewis (ed.), *Labour and Love: Women's Experience of Home and Family, 1850–1940* (Oxford, 1986); A. S. Wohl, *Endangered Lives* (London, 1983); I. Loudon, 'Deaths in Childbed from the 18th Century to 1935', *Med. Hist.* 30 (1986), 1–41; C. Webster, 'Health, Welfare and Unemployment during the Depression', *P&P* 109 (1985), 204–30.

[7] Loudon, 'Deaths in Childbed', 2.   [8] Lewis, *Politics of Motherhood*, 35–6.

[9] *RC Alien Immigration*, PP 1903 IX, Qs15970–83. See also C. Holmes, *Anti-Semitism in British Society, 1876–1939* (London, 1979), 40; *JC*, 8 Oct. 1897, 18; 6 Oct. 1901, 18. Jewish immigrants were not the only group seen to be spreading disease. A surgeon from Birmingham described the Irish as 'the very pests of society. They generate contagion. More and worse cases of fever, and other infectious diseases of spontaneous origin, occur among them'. The Irish were thought particularly to be the cause of the spread of typhus and smallpox. *RC Condition of the Irish Poor in Great Britain*, PP 1836 XXXIV, p. 480. See also

Some observers believed that the population in the Jewish areas of Poland had physically deteriorated, and this manifested itself in high lunacy rates among the Jewish population.[10]

Determinants of the Health of the Jewish Immigrants

In reality what was the standard of health among the immigrant mothers and their infants? Investigations of contemporary population show ethnicity to be an important factor in determining mortality patterns. It is generally assumed that the health of immigrants is poorer than that of the indigenous population. This has been ascribed to the higher mortality experienced in their countries of origin and the language and cultural barriers to access to health care and social welfare, particularly in the first years of settlement. Migrants, however, tend to be less vulnerable than these assertions would at first suggest.[11] Indeed, many of the Jewish immigrants who arrived at the beginning of the century tended to be those who were more physically and economically mobile. Increasing immigration restrictions, such as the Aliens' Act of 1905, also imposed minimum health requirements, restricting the entry of immigrants who had poorer health. This resulted in a highly select immigrant population, who tended to be healthy young men and women.

Infant Health

An important component in considering the impact of migration and ethnicity on the health of immigrants is the health of the infant. The extreme vulnerability of the infant is often reflected in high rates of mortality in adverse circumstances, still seen in many parts of the world today. An infant's health is not only determined by the conditions under which pregnancy occurs, but also the immediate environment into which he or she is born. The mortality of an infant reflects its health at birth, the health of its mother, the quality of the environment in which it is cared

F. Finnegan, 'The Irish in York', in R. Swift and S. Gilley (eds.), *The Irish in the Victorian City* (London, 1985), 61, and G. Davis, 'Little Irelands', in R. Swift and S. Gilley (eds.) *The Irish in Britain* (London, 1989), 115.

[10] *RC Alien Immigration*, PP 1903 IX, Q11809; *Report of the Interdepartmental Committee on Physical Deterioration* (henceforth *Physical Deterioration*), PP 1904 XXXII, Q1932, Q2199, Q3247, Q3257, Q3457.

[11] For a discussion on the effect of ethnicity and migrancy on current health patterns see A. M. Adelstein and M. G. Marmot, 'The Health of Migrants in England and Wales: Causes of Death', in J. K. Cruickshank and D. G. Beevers (eds.), *Ethnic Factors in Health and Disease* (London, 1989).

for, and the access its family has to health services and effective treatment for life–threatening events.

Mortality statistics for the Jewish immigrants are difficult to separate from the general population in East London in the late nineteenth and early twentieth centuries. None the less, a number of contemporary medical officers of health and other investigators frequently commented on the unexpectedly low rates of infant mortality among the Jewish inhabitants of East London at the turn of the century.[12] This was particularly surprising given that overall infant mortality was slightly higher in East London than in either London as a whole or England and Wales. The high infant mortality in East London was attributable to the terrible social and economic deprivation of the area. This raises a question of interpretation regarding the low infant mortality in areas where there was a high concentration of Jewish immigrants.

In order to test the assertions made by the medical officers about Jewish infant mortality, rates of infant mortality in registration districts of East London taken from the Registrar-General's quarterly returns were calculated for the years between 1881 and 1910 and matched with Map 2.1. This map was reconstructed from two contemporary maps; the first compiled by a house-to-house survey conducted by school inspectors from the London School Board in 1899 to identify areas that were predominantly Jewish,[13] and the second showing the census districts of 1901 which were coterminus with sub-registration districts at the time. One problem in trying to identify the rates of infant mortality in the Jewish areas outlined by the survey is that the boundaries set by the Registrar-General for the collection of the statistics changed in the late 1880s and 1890s. Two Jewish districts, however, whose boundaries appear to have remained the same were Spitalfields and Mile End New Town, where Jews constituted between 75 and 100 per cent of the population in 1899. One other area showing between 75 and 95 per cent of its population as being Jewish was Goodman's Fields. This was also used in the study, but was used with caution as its boundaries changed in 1892 to include Aldgate where the number of Jews was much smaller. Goodman's Fields was included because no separate statistics remain for Mile End New

---

[12] *RC Alien Immigration*, PP 1903 IX pt. II, Dr Shirley Murphy, Q 3960, p. 203; table 17, in S. Rosenbaum, 'A Contribution to the Study of Vital and Other Statistics of the Jews in the UK', *J. Roy. Stat. Soc.* 68 (1905), 528. See also table 1 in L. Marks, ' "Dear Old Mother Levy's": The Jewish Maternity Home and Sick Room Helps Society, 1895–1939', *Soc. Hist. Med.* 3/1 (1990), 61–88, 62.

[13] This map was originally drawn up by George Arkell who used the same method as Charles Booth for his poverty maps of London. The map appeared in C. Russell and H. S. Lewis, *The Jew in London* (London, 1901).

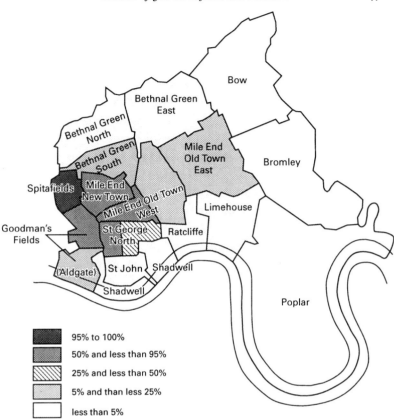

95% to 100%
50% and less than 95%
25% and less than 50%
5% and than less 25%
less than 5%

Note: Proportion of Jewish residents not known for Bow, Bromley, Poplar

MAP 2.1. Proportion of Jewish immigrants to other residents in East London, by census areas, 1899
Source: adapted from map by George Arkell, prepared for C. Russell and H. S. Lewis, *The Jew in London* (London, 1901), and compiled from information gathered by the visitors of the London School Board: boundaries adapted from map of census districts 1901.

Town after 1899, when its boundaries changed, which made it difficult to establish the trend of infant mortality after that date. The districts with a high proportion of Jewish residents were compared with two areas, Limehouse and Bethnal Green East, where Jews constituted less than 5 per cent of the population. Before 1889 Bethnal Green East was part of the area known as the Green, and although the population size changed, this probably did not alter the number of Jewish residents found there.

Figure 2.1 shows a three-year moving average of infant mortality rates

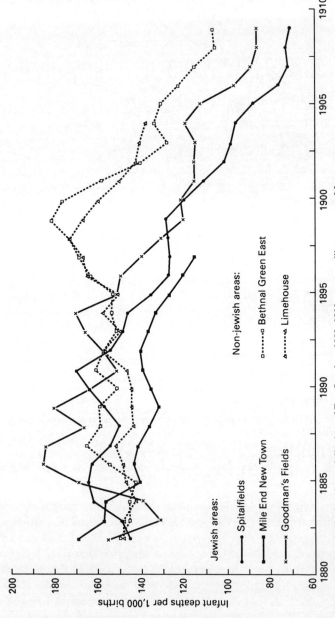

FIG. 2.1. Infant deaths in select subdistricts of East London, 1880–1910, over a rolling average of 3 years
Source: Registrar General, *Quarterly Returns of Births and Deaths for England and Wales* (London, 1880–1910).

for these areas from 1880 to 1910. From 1885 to 1895 rates appear to be higher in Jewish areas than in non-Jewish ones. This, however, appears to be a transient phase occurring at a time of large-scale migration into the area to escape the trauma of pogroms.[14] In 1903 Mr Joseph emphasized this in his evidence to the Royal Commission on Alien Immigration, arguing that infant mortality was especially high among the new immigrants because of the persecution and extreme poverty they had suffered before arriving in Britain and during the initial period of settlement. Many of the infants died on the way.[15] Within a space of ten years, however, the picture changed dramatically, with the infant mortality rate in all Jewish areas below that of other parts of East London by 1895. The decline in infant mortality appeared to start sooner and was more rapid in the significantly Jewish areas (Spitalfields, Goodman's Fields, and Mile End New Town) than those where Jewish immigrants made up less than 5 per cent of the population (Limehouse and Bethnal Green East). The decrease in infant mortality in the Jewish areas Spitalfields and Goodman's Fields in the late 1890s is surprising given that the trend in England and Wales and London was upwards in these years.[16] Figures 2.2 and 2.3 indicate that infant mortality in the Jewish areas was not only below that of other districts in East London, but also below the trend in London as a whole and the rest of England and Wales. By contrast the non-Jewish districts were generally higher or comparable with those of London and the rest of England and Wales. Unfortunately, no separate figures remain for the rates of infant mortality for the separate wards within East London after 1910. This makes it difficult to see whether the infants of the generation of Jews born in Britain had more of an advantage by being born into

[14] *RC Alien Immigration*, PP 1903 IX, Qs15970–83. See also G. A. Condran and E. A. Kramarow, 'Child Mortality among Jewish Immigrants to the United States', *J. Interdisc. Hist.* 22/2 (1991), 223–54, 239. I am grateful to Gretchen Condran and Ellen Kramarow for showing me an earlier draft of this paper and for providing me with a number of references which have been used extensively in this chapter.

[15] Mr N. S. Joseph, *RC Alien Immigration*, PP 1903 IX pt. II, Qs15970–82. High mortality was also found among the infants and young children of those immigrants who travelled to Australia in the nineteenth century. See R. Shlomowitz and J. McDonald, 'Babies at Risk on Immigrant Voyages to Australia in the Nineteenth Century', *Econ. Hist. Rev.* 44/1 (1991), 86–101.

[16] The low rates of infant mortality in Mile End New Town are surprising because of the workhouse in the area, which might be expected to have had an adverse affect on rates of infant mortality. (Illegitimacy rates were certainly much higher as a result of the workhouse, see Ch. 5.) In St John, where there was a workhouse, infant mortality rates were abnormally high, as they were in Whitechapel Church and Shadwell, which might be explained by the existence of London Hospital and the East London Hospital for Children and Women in these two areas. The presence of such institutions in these districts coupled with the abnormally high rates of infant mortality prevented the use of these districts in this study.

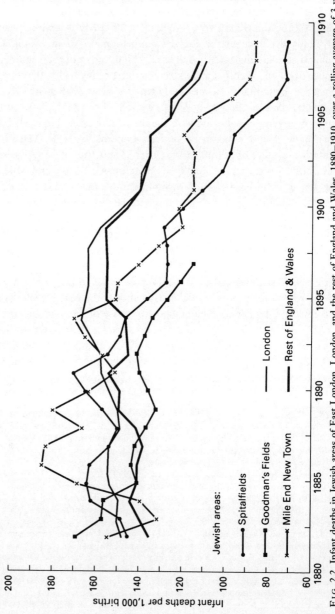

FIG. 2.2. Infant deaths in Jewish areas of East London, London, and the rest of England and Wales, 1880–1910, over a rolling average of 3 years

Source: as for Fig. 2.1.

Jewish areas:
●——● Spitalfields
■——■ Goodman's Fields
×——× Mile End New Town

——— London
——— Rest of England & Wales

Infant deaths per 1,000 births

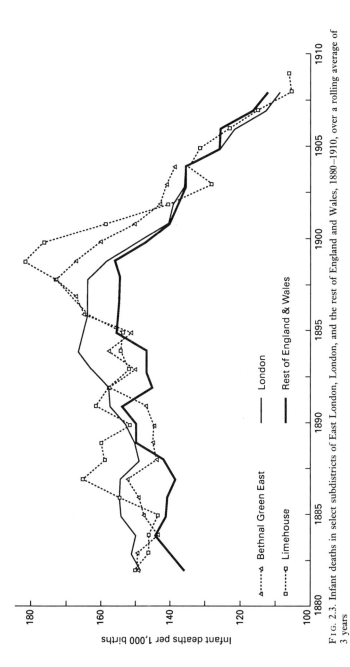

FIG. 2.3. Infant deaths in select subdistricts of East London, London, and the rest of England and Wales, 1880–1910, over a rolling average of 3 years

Source: as for Fig. 2.1.

Legend:
- Bethnal Green East
- Limehouse
- London
- Rest of England & Wales

Y-axis: Infant deaths per 1,000 births (100, 120, 140, 160, 180)

X-axis: 1880, 1885, 1890, 1895, 1900, 1905, 1910

TABLE 2.1. *Infant mortality per 1,000 live births in Manchester,*
1892–1899

Date	Cheetham	Whole of Manchester
1892	124	198
1898	122	196
1899	104	205

Source: S. Rosenbaum, 'A Contribution to the Study of Vital and Other Statistics of the
Jews in the United Kingdom', *J. Roy. Stat. Soc.* 68 (1905), 526–51; Ministry of Health,
42nd AR Infant and Child Mortality (London, 1913), 76, 79.

a more settled and established environment than the infants of the
immigrants.

Lower rates of infant mortality among Jewish immigrants were not
confined to East London alone. In Manchester, infant mortality was
considerably lower in Cheetham, the impoverished area of Manchester
where the Jewish population was most concentrated, than in other parts
of the city (see Table 2.1). Outside Britain similar patterns prevailed.
In 1897 the Russian census showed that the rate of infant mortality in
the (agrarian) Pale of Settlement was 132 for Jewish infants and 259 for
non-Jewish ones.[17] Indeed, the low rate of Jewish infant mortality was
geographically widespread. Jewish infants had a much greater chance of
survival than their non-Jewish counterparts in Asia, Eastern Europe,
Western Europe, and North America.[18] This advantage stretched back to
the mid-nineteenth century and continued well into the twentieth century, reflecting the fact that the Jews had experienced a mortality decline
earlier in the nineteenth century compared to other groups.[19] In the United
States the low rates of Jewish infant and child mortality contrasted with
the higher rates found among other immigrants, such as the Italians and
Poles who arrived during the same period.[20]

[17] R. Salaman, 'Anglo-Jewish Vital Statistics', *JC* Suppl., 29 July 1921, p. v (henceforth
Salaman, *JC*). A. Ruppin, *The Jews of Today* (London, 1913), 79; D. Dwork, 'Health
Conditions of Immigrant Jews on the Lower East Side of New York: 1880–1914', *Med. Hist.*
25/1 (1981), 1–40, 28. See also *RC Alien Immigration*, PP 1903 IX pt. II, Mr J. Prag, Q17877.

[18] For full figures on the rates of Jewish infant mortality and the trend since the mid-19th
c. see U. O. Schmelz, *Infant and Early Childhood Mortality among Jews of the Diaspora*
(Jerusalem, 1971), 15–27, table 2; and Condran and Kramarow, 'Child Mortality', 225–6,
table 1. See also S. D. Corrsin, *Warsaw Before the First World War: Poles and Jews in the
Third City of the Russian Empire 1880–1914* (New York, 1989), 24–8.

[19] Schmelz, *Infant and Early Childhood Mortality*, 13; Condran and Kramarow, 'Childhood Mortality', 224, 227.

[20] Condran and Kramarow, 'Childhood Mortality', 223, 238, table 2.

TABLE 2.2. *Relative age-specific mortality of Jews and non-Jews in selected cities* (per 1,000)

	Jewish	Non-Jewish	Relative risk*
Infant Mortality Rate			
Budapest, 1903–10			
m	103	175	1.7
f	87	149	1.7
Amsterdam, 1961–13			
m	86	113	1.3
f	68	90	1.3
USA, 8 cities, 1911–15	54	108	2
Neonatal Mortality Rate			
Budapest, 1903–10	41.9	56.0	1.3
m			
f	33.9	45.7	1.3
Amsterdam, 1901–13			
m	23.1	30.4	1.3
f	16.5	21.8	1.3
USA, 8 cities, 1911–15	28.1	41.4	1.4
Post-neonatal Mortality Rate			
Budapest, 1903–10	61.1	119	1.9
m			
f	53.1	103.3	1.9
Amsterdam, 1901–13	62.9	82.6	1.3
m			
f	51.5	68.2	1.3
USA, 8 cities, 1911–15	25.9	66.6	2.6

* Reference population for calculation of relative risk is the Jewish population.

Source: U. O. Schmelz, *Infant and Early Childhood Mortality Among Jews of the Diaspora* (Jerusalem, 1971), 38, table 4.

By separating neonatal mortality (deaths within the first 28 days of life) from post-neonatal mortality (deaths after 28 days of life and before 1 year of age), we can begin to see the reasons for the lower rates of Jewish infant mortality. While more detailed statistics do not exist for the rates of neonatal death among Jewish immigrants in East London, it would appear from studies elsewhere in the world that the lower rate of infant mortality amongst the Jews is largely accounted for by the much smaller number of deaths in the post-neonatal period. Table 2.2 shows the neonatal

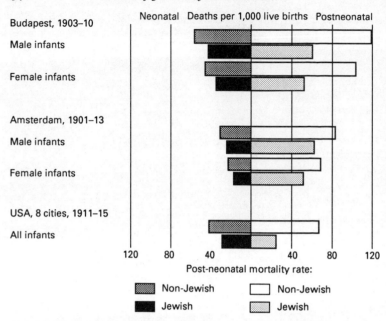

FIG. 2.4. Relative age-specific mortality among Jewish and non-Jewish infants in Budapest, Amsterdam, and the USA, 1901–1915
Source: U. O. Schmelz, *Infant and Early Childhood Mortality among Jews of the Diaspora* (Jerusalem, 1971), 38, table 4.

and post-neonatal mortality rates for Jewish and non-Jewish female and male infants in Budapest (1903–10) and Amsterdam (1901–13), and the overall neonatal and post-neonatal rates for eight cities in the United States (1911–15). Using these statistics Figure 2.4 illustrates this table, with the axis drawn to separate neonatal from post-neonatal deaths. Both the table and the figure show that not only is infant mortality lower overall for Jewish infants, but that there are reductions in both components, though the largest difference is evident in the post-neonatal period.[21] The difference in infant mortality is most apparent in Budapest, where the overall rate of infant mortality was much higher than in Amsterdam. However, the advantage of Jewish infants is even more pronounced in the United States where infant mortality was more like that of Amsterdam. Given that environmental conditions in Budapest were probably much worse than those found in the majority of American cities

---

[21] Stillbirths were also thought to be fewer among the Jewish population, but there are no statistics to confirm this assertion, see Salaman, *JC*, 26 Aug. 1921, p. i.

during these years, these findings suggest that the lower rates in infant mortality among the Jewish population were strongly related to behavioural rather than environmental factors.

The fact that Jewish infant mortality appeared to decline earlier and was considerably lower in the post-neonatal age-group than in the general population indicates that Jewish infants had certain advantages over non-Jewish infants. An infant's chances of survival is dependent on a wide range of factors. Historically, the causes of neonatal mortality are hard to determine, largely due to the absence of recorded material on neonatal mortality before the twentieth century. From the evidence available, it would seem that 'the quality of maternal care probably played a minor, but certainly not a large part' in neonatal mortality, and that there were links with prematurity and congenital deformities as well as environmental conditions, but the relative importance of these factors is hard to determine. Post-neonatal mortality is strongly influenced by breast-feeding customs and environmental and sanitary circumstances and is sensitive to social and environmental deprivation.[22] The lower rates of Jewish post-neonatal mortality therefore appear to indicate that the Jews exerted greater control over some of these conditions than did the non-Jewish population.

When Jewish infant mortality is examined by cause of death this becomes even clearer. Changes in medical diagnosis and knowledge about disease prevents an accurate assessment of the causes of Jewish and non-Jewish infant mortality. None the less, evidence from Europe as well as the United States indicates that Jewish infants were better protected than other infants from diarrhoea (see Table 2.3).[23] Sadly, it is difficult to get statistics directly for East London,[24] but contemporaries thought that diarrhoeal death accounted for a lower proportion of the deaths among Jewish than non-Jewish infants.[25] This is also shown by Figures 2.1 to 2.3 which show a rapid decline of infant deaths in the Jewish areas of East London in the late 1890s, a time when most infant mortality was rising

[22] I. Loudon, 'On Maternal and Infant Mortality, 1900–1960', *Soc. Hist. Med.* 4/1 (April 1991), 29–74, 33, 38–9, 72–3. See also R. I. Woods, P. A. Watterson, and J. H. Woodward, 'The Causes of Rapid Infant Mortality Decline in England and Wales, 1861–1921', pt. II, *Popul. Stud.* 43 (1989), 113–32, 114–15; Schmelz, *Infant and Early Childhood Mortality*, 39; N. Williams, 'Infant and Child Mortality in Urban Areas of Nineteenth-Century England and Wales: A Record Linkage Study', Ph.D. thesis (Liverpool, 1989), 23–5.

[23] See also Ruppin, *Jews of Today*, 77.

[24] One project using death certificates from East London in 1901 is currently being mounted to try and establish both the age and cause of death of Jewish and non-Jewish infants, but it will be some time before any conclusions can be drawn from this study.

[25] *RC Alien Immigration*, PP 1903 IX pt. II, Q 327, Q 3960, Q 5787, Q 5788, Q 21415, Q 21417.

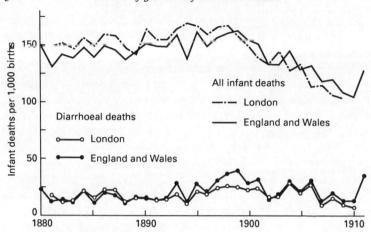

FIG. 2.5. Total infant mortality and rates of infant deaths from diarrhoea in England and Wales and London, 1880–1911
Source: Registrar-General, *74th AR of Births, Deaths and Marriages for England and Wales (for 1911)* (London, 1913), p. xxxiv, table 22.

as a result of diarrhoea caused by the very hot summers in these years.[26] Diarrhoea accounted for nearly a quarter of all the infant deaths in the borough of Stepney in 1901 and was one of the leading causes of death for infants nationally in the nineteenth century.[27] Figure 2.5 shows the rates of infant mortality and infant deaths from diarrhoea in England and Wales. This indicates a rise in the rate of infant mortality from diarrhoea, particularly in England and Wales in the late 1890s, and a corresponding rise in the overall rate of infant mortality.

In Europe and the United States Jewish infants also seem to have had a 'lower mortality from those conditions which were diagnosed in the past as "congenital debility" ' than their non-Jewish counterparts.[28] In addition

[26] Contemporaries noted this in their evidence to the *RC Alien Immigration*, PP 1903 IX pt. II, Q3960, Q3963, Q5787; see also E. W. Hope, 'Autumnal Diarrhoea in Cities', *Publ. Health*, July 1899, 660–5. For more information on the historical trends in infant mortality, and the particular rise in the years 1895–1900, see Woods *et al.*, 'The Causes of Rapid Infant Mortality Decline', pt. I, *Popul. Stud.* 42 (1988), 343–66, 361–2; and pt. II, 120.

[27] Dr D. L. Thomas, *RC Alien Immigration*, PP 1903 IX pt. II, 264. Contemporaries regarded diarrhoea as one of the 'preventable' causes of infant mortality, linking it primarily to bad infant feeding habits. D. Dwork, *War is Good for Babies and Other Young Children: A History of the Infant and Child Welfare Movement* (London, 1987), 49–50; N. Williams, 'Infant and Child Mortality in Urban Areas', 30 and ch. 5.

[28] Schmelz, *Infant and Early Childhood Mortality*, 44–6. See also M. Fishberg, 'Health and Sanitation of the Immigrant Jewish Population of New York', *The Menorah*, 33 (Aug. 1902), 173–4.

TABLE 2.3. *Deaths caused by infantile diarrhoea among Jews and the general population in selected cities, 1901–1915* (per 1,000 new born)

Location	Date	Jews	General Population	Difference %	Cause of death if specified
Berlin	1905	25.7	84.8	−70	—
Hessen	1901–12	m. 18.6	41.1[1]	−55	—
		f. 15.0	36.0[1]	−60	
USA, 8 cities	1911–15	10.5	32.6	−70	Gastric and intestinal diseases
Amsterdam	1901–13	m. 21.7	30.3	−30	
		f. 13.3	23.5	−45	

[1] 1906–10.

Source: Adapted from Schmelz, *Infant and Early Childhood Mortality*, 41–5, table 5.

to this, some contemporary medical experts in England believed that the incidence of contagious diseases such as syphilis which could result in infant deaths was lower among Jewish immigrants, although it was said to rise after the First World War.[29] None the less, these causes were not as influential on the overall rates of infant mortality as other factors. While diarrhoea was one of the chief causes of infant deaths during these years, wasting diseases (particularly of infants under the age of 3 months) and convulsions were also important. Just as Jewish infants seem to have had a smaller propensity to die from diarrhoea than other infants, they were also less liable to die from infectious and respiratory diseases in the same years (see Tables 2.3 to 2.5).

The weight of these causes was very different from those affecting young children which were more likely to be infectious and respiratory diseases.[30] Few statistics are available for young children, but it appears that fewer Jewish children died from infectious and respiratory diseases than non-Jewish ones. As Table 2.6 shows, in Amsterdam (1901–13) young Jewish children under the age of 5 were less likely to die from

[29] Venereal disease was also said to be rare among Jewish women until 1914. See comments by Dr J. Snowman in *JC*, 28 May 1920, cited in G. Black, 'Health and Medical Care of the Jewish Poor in the East End of London, 1880–1939', Ph.D. thesis (Leicester, 1987), 40–2. See also Salaman, *JC* Suppl., 29 July 1921, p. v.

[30] A. Hardy, *Epidemic Streets: Infectious Disease and the Rise of Preventive Medicine, 1856–1900* (Oxford, 1993), ch. 9, table 5.

TABLE 2.4. *Infant deaths caused by infectious diseases (measles, diphtheria, whooping cough, scarlatina) among Jews and the general population in selected cities, 1901–1915* (per 1,000 new born)

Location	Date	Jews		General Population	Difference %	Cause of death if specified
Budapest	1901–5		29.3	36.5 (Cath.)	−20	Excludes whooping-cough
				32.2 (Prot.)	−10	All
Hessen	1901–12	m.	1.5	6.3[1]	−75	All
		f.	3.1	6.4[1]	−50	All
USA, 8 cities	1911–15		4.9	6.4	−25	All
Amsterdam	1901–13	m.	6.3	9.6	−35	Excludes scarlatina
		f.	6.8	9.3	−25	

[1] 1906–10.

Source: Adapted from Schmelz, *Infant and Early Childhood Mortality*, 41–5, table 5.

TABLE 2.5. *Infant deaths caused by respiratory diseases among Jews and general population in selected cities, 1901–1915* (per 1,000 new born)

Location	Date	Jews	General Population	Difference %
Hessen	1901–12	m. 12.1	20.4[1]	−40
		f. 11.1	18.0[1]	−40
Budapest	1901–5	15.6	37.1 (Cath.)	−60
			31.3 (Prot.)	−50
USA, 8 cities	1911–15	8.9	17.9	−50
Amsterdam	1901–13	m. 12.8	21.3	−40
		f. 11.1	17.9	−40

[1] 1906–10.

Source: Adapted from Schmelz, *Infant and Early Childhood Mortality*, 41–5, table 5.

TABLE 2.6. *Child deaths by cause among Jews and general population in selected cities* (per 1,000)

Location	Date	Jews	General Population	Difference %	Cause of death	Population group
Budapest	1886–90	14.4	41.4	−65	Diarrhoea	Below 5 years
	1930–1	3.4	18.5	−80	Diarrhoea	Below 2 years
Warsaw	1931–6	5.2	19.0	−75	Diarrhoea	Below 2 years
Warsaw	1930–2	0.82	1.27	−35	Infectious diseases	Below 5 years
Amsterdam	1910–13	m. 4.1	6.2	−35	Infectious diseases excluding scarlatina	Below 5 years
		f. 3.7	5.9	−35		
New York	1925	3.2	4.0	−20	Pneumonia	Below 5 years

Source: Adapted from Schmelz, *Infant and Early Childhood Mortality*, 41–5, table 5.

infectious diseases, just as young Jewish children in New York (1925) had less chance of dying from pneumonia (see Table 2.6). Deaths from infectious disease were also thought to be much rarer among Jewish children than among their neighbours in England.[31] Tuberculosis, a great killer of adults during this period, fell in the middle range of causes of infants' and children's deaths, being most significant for children aged between 2 and 5.[32] No statistics remain on the incidence or mortality of tuberculosis among Jewish infants and children, but it was a disease known to affect Jewish immigrants working in the cramped and damp conditions of sweated workshops.[33]

[31] E. Hart, 'The Mosaic Code of Sanitation', *Sanitary Rec.* 1 (1877), 183, 198; J. Critchton-Browne, 'The Prevention of Tubercular Disease', *J. Sanitary Institute*, 15 (1894), 455, cited in Hardy, *Epidemic Streets*, ch. 9. See also J. H. Stallard, *London Pauperism Among Jews and Christians: An Inquiry into the Principles and Practice of Outdoor Relief in the Metropolis* (London, 1867), 13. [32] Hardy, *Epidemic Streets*, ch. 9.

[33] Many medical experts showed a rise in the incidence of tuberculosis in East London where the immigrants had settled, but some observers argued that fewer of the immigrants died than the local population. (Dr J. Loane, evidence to *RC Alien Immigration*, PP 1903 IX pt. II, and evidence of Dr D. L. Thomas to the commission; B. A. Whitelegge and G. Newman, *Hygiene and Public Health* (London, 1905), 407; L. P. Gartner, *The Jewish*

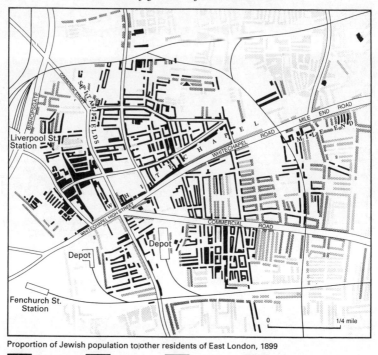

Proportion of Jewish population to|other residents of East London, 1899

| ■ Over 75% | ▨ 50–74% | ▨ 25–49% | □ Less than 24% |

MAP 2.2. Proportion of Jewish population to other residents of East London, by street, 1899
Source: adapted from map by George Arkell, prepared for C. Russell and H. S. Lewis, *The Jew in London* (London, 1901).

   The principal causes of death among infants and young children, be it diarrhoea or respiratory diseases, have a greater chance of spreading where there is poverty, bad sanitation, overcrowding, and poor housing. This raises the question as to whether Jewish immigrants in East London were living in better circumstances than their neighbours. Some comparison of the economic status of the Jewish immigrants and the local population in East London is gauged by matching the poverty map drawn by Charles Booth's investigation for East London in 1889 with the map compiled of the Jewish residents living in East London in 1899. These have been redrawn and are illustrated in Maps 2.2 and 2.3. As the maps show, the level of poverty and the number of Jewish residents varied

Immigrant in England, 1870–1914 (London, 1960; 1973), 160–1; Hardy, *Epidemic Streets*, ch. 9. See also M. Fishberg, 'Health and Sanitation', 174–6, and Dwork, 'Health Conditions', 19–20, for work conditions and tuberculosis among immigrant Jews in New York.)

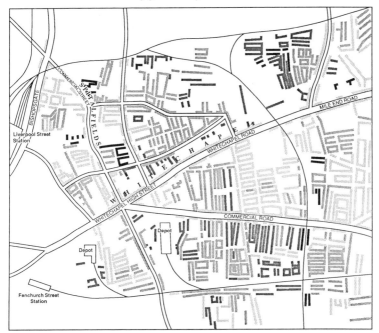

Streets are shaded according to the general condition of the inhabitants:

Lowest class, vicious, semi-criminal

Very poor, chronic want, poor

Mixed, some comfortable, others poor

Fairly comfortable, well-to-do, middle class

MAP 2.3. Degree of poverty in streets with high Jewish population, 1889
Source: C. Booth, *Life and Labour: East London*, 2nd edn. (1889).

tremendously even within individual streets. None the less, it would seem that while some Jews lived in some of the extremely poor areas as well as some more middle-class ones, a large proportion of them were based in districts which Booth classified as mixed, containing some poor and some comfortable residents. This suggests that the Jewish immigrants were therefore neither richer nor poorer than the general population living in these places, and therefore did not have the financial advantages or better housing usually associated with better infant health. No separate figures exist for the specific levels of poverty among the Jewish population, but Booth's investigation of poverty in 1889 revealed that in three heavily Jewish subdistricts in his study the total population living in poverty ranged from 24.1 to 34.6 to 35.7 per cent. When compared with other districts with fewer Jewish residents, it would seem that the level of poverty, although high among the Jewish areas, was in fact lower than in the surrounding non-Jewish ones. While 39.2 per cent of the population living in the predominantly Jewish area of Whitechapel were living in poverty, in Bethnal Green and St George's-in-the-East these were respectively 44.7 and 48.8 per cent.[34]

Recent studies of infant mortality have indicated that while poverty is an important determinant of infant mortality, this can be outweighed by environmental conditions (overcrowding, sanitation, and the disposal of sewerage and refuse). Watterson's study of infant mortality in ninety-seven great towns between the years 1895 to 1910 showed that 'raising private incomes without changing environmental conditions would do little to improve infant mortality levels. Environmental improvement carried out without any change in private incomes would have some effect which would be strengthened in better-off communities'.[35] This is particularly important in the context of Jewish infant mortality. As they were as poor as their neighbours, Jewish immigrants would be expected to have similar housing conditions which were not conducive to robust infants. As one Medical Officer of Health in Stepney, who was puzzled by the lower rates of Jewish infant mortality, commented, 'I was very much interested to learn how it was that people who were living in close courts and crowded alleys under conditions that I was accustomed to find associated with high death rates wherever I had looked in London, had a low death rate.'[36]

Indeed, overcrowding, a factor commonly associated with the spread of infectious and respiratory disease, was significantly high in the areas where Jews were most concentrated. Tables 2.7 and 2.8 show that according to the Census of 1901 the Jewish area of Spitalfields had some of the highest numbers of persons per house and the largest proportion of overcrowding in East London. Contemporaries also claimed that many of the Jewish immigrants resided in crowded situations partly as a result of the practice of taking in lodgers.[37] The situation was slightly better for

---

[34] Feldman, 'Immigrants and Workers', 114–15.

[35] P. A. Watterson, 'Role of the Environment in the Decline of Infant Mortality: An Analysis of the 1911 Census of England and Wales', *J. Biosoc. Sci.* 18 (1986), 457–70. See also Woods *et al.*, 'The Causes of Rapid Infant Mortality Decline', pt. II, 114–15.

[36] Dr Shirley Murphy, *RC Alien Immigration*, PP 1903 IX pt. I, Q3960, p. 203. See also H. J. Ashby, *Infant Mortality* (Cambridge, 1915), 25; *Physical Deterioration*, PP 1904 XXXII, Dr Eicholz, Q475.

[37] *RC Alien Immigration*, PP 1903 IX pt. I, Q3045; *Physical Deterioration*, PP 1904 XXXII, Q1173. Lodging was perceptibly more common among the Jewish immigrants, who often supplied shelter for fellow newcomers, than among the general population. Lodging constituted the provision of shelter as well as the contraction of services such as laundry, mending, tea, and breakfast. The practice of taking in lodgers was relinquished once children entered the workforce.

TABLE 2.7. *Size of population, number of houses and percentage of people per house in selected areas of Stepney, 1901*

Location	Population	Jews %	Houses	Population per house %
Spitalfields	27,969	95–100	1,894	14.76
Mile End New Town	13,259	75–95	1,374	9.65
Whitechapel Church*	33,634	50–75	2,703	12.44
Bethnal Green East	44,694	Under 5	5,253	8.5
Limehouse	32,369	Under 5	4,382	7.39

Note: Houses include those which are listed as inhabited and those which are classified as 'uninhabited' but were occupied.

* Whitechapel Church is not listed separately, but the figures have been compiled from those included in the figures for Goodman's Fields and Mile End New Town under the category 'part of Whitechapel'.

Source: *Census 1901*, table 12, registration county districts and subdistricts with their constitutional civil parishes. Houses and Population 1891 and 1901, pp. 33–4.

TABLE 2.8. *Number and proportion of population overcrowded in selected areas of East London in 1901*

Registration subdistrict	Population overcrowded 1901	% of Population overcrowded to total population	Civil parishes comprised in each rigistration subdistrict
Spitalfields	15,400	55.1	Norton, Folgate, Old Artillery Ground, and Spitalfields
Mile End New Town	12,974	45.2	Mile End New Town and part of Whitechapel
Limehouse	7,322	22.6	Limehouse

Note: Mile End New Town includes Whitechapel Church, which was a more overcrowded area, distorting the figures slightly for Mile End New Town.

Source: Statistical Department of the London County Council, cited in *RC Alien Immigration*, PP 1903 IX, pt. I, p. 32.

Jewish immigrants inhabiting model tenement housing such as Rothschild Buildings, but this was restricted to those who had higher incomes.[38] Most Jews had a limited choice of housing available, made more so by both the general housing shortage as a result of the coming of the railways and the slum clearances in the late nineteenth century, as well as by the discrimination of many non-Jewish landlords against accommodating Jews.[39] Between 1871 and 1901 the number of houses in the whole of Whitechapel diminished from 8,264 to 5,735, increasing the average number of residents per house from 9.14 to 13.74. The overcrowding was at it most extreme in the heart of the Jewish area, where contemporaries argued the average density was 600 per acre as compared with the average in Whitechapel of 286.[40]

Yet despite such overcrowding of the Jewish population, Figures 2.1 to 2.3 suggest that this did not seem to disadvantage Jewish infants. This is even more surprising when we consider the insanitary conditions that many of the Jews were living in. Some of the worst insanitary cases in the borough of Whitechapel and its surrounding area were found where the Jews were most concentrated. This included Old Montague Street, Booth Street, Hanbury Street, and Chicksand Street, based in Spitalfields and Mile End New Town. One investigation by *The Lancet* in 1884 revealed the terrible working and living conditions some immigrants endured:

In Hanbury Street we found 18 workers crowded in a small room measuring 8 yards and a half, and not quite 8 feet high. The first two floors of this house were let out to the lodgers who were also Jews. Their houses were clean but damp as water was coming through the rotting wall. . . . The sink was not trapped, the kitchen range was falling to pieces, while the closet was a permanent source of trouble. A flushing apparatus had been provided but this discharged water outside the pan; the water consequently came out under the seat and flowed across

[38] Rothschild Buildings were constructed in the late 19th c., partly as a result of the concern of more established Anglo-Jews over the poor housing conditions that many of their poorer brethren were facing. Before attaining such accommodation, however, prospective tenants had to prove they had enough income to pay the rent and a certain degree of respectability. For more information on this see J. White, *Rothschild Buildings: Life in an East End Tenement Block, 1887–1920* (London, 1980). See also n. 44 below.

[39] *RC Alien Immigration*, PP 1903 IX pt. I, pp. 31–2, Q1690, Q2480, Q5837, Q15762. See also White, *Rothschild Buildings*, 61. Charles Booth estimated that Spitalfields was the sixth worst place in London for overcrowding in 1889 (C. Booth, *Life and Labour*, final vol., 3–40). Much of the overcrowding was blamed on the Jewish immigrants, and the rise in the practice of 'key' money. For more detail on this see V. D. Lipman, *Social History of the Jews in England, 1850–1950*, 104; D. M. Feldman, 'Immigrants and Workers, Englishmen and Jews: The Immigrant to the East End of London, 1880–1906', Ph.D. thesis (Cambridge, 1985), 77–8; See also *RC Alien Immigration*, PP 1903 IX pt. I, Q2864, Q2878.

[40] Gartner, *The Jewish Immigrant*, 147.

the yard to the wall opposite, which was eaten away at its base . . . the top room
. . . had at times to hold 18 persons, working in the heat of the gas and the stove,
warming the pressing irons, surrounded by mounds of dust and chips from the
cut cloth, breathing an atmosphere full of wooden particles containing more or
less injurious dyes, it is not surprising that so large a proportion of working tailors
break down from diseases of the respiratory organs. . . . In Emily Place . . . we
found 5 persons living in one room, while in another house we came upon a
Jewish potato dealer who kept his wife, 5 children and a huge stock of potatoes all
in one room measuring 5 yards by 6. There was one bed in the room and probably
some of the family slept on the floor.[41]

As this investigation outlined, such conditions were not beneficial
for health. One advantage the Jewish population had, however, was the
visitation and action of a well-organized group of Jewish sanitary inspectors from the Sanitation Committee of the Jewish Board of Guardians
from 1884. This supplemented the work of the local sanitary authorities,
and included visiting individual homes, forwarding complaints to the
local authority and landlords, and distributing educational leaflets among
Jewish inhabitants.[42] The work that they undertook showed a real need
for improvement. In 1884 Jewish sanitary inspectors found that 1,621
of all the Jewish houses inspected were without flushing water in their
indoor or outdoor closets. Similarly, in 1893 Jewish sanitary inspectors
made 5,209 visits to 1,746 dwellings, of which they found 936 (or 54 per
cent) were below the standards laid down by the local public health
authority. This was comparable to the inspections made by the Assistant
Medical Officer of Health for the London County Council, who discovered in 1894, that 58 per cent of the houses he visited in Whitechapel
as a whole had defects.[43] It is impossible to judge the extent to which
the presence of the Jewish sanitary inspectors improved the sanitary

[41] *The Lancet*, 3 May 1884. Similar housing conditions prevailed among the Jewish
immigrants living in New York in the same period. See Dwork, 'Health Conditions of
Immigrant Jews on the Lower East Side of New York: 1880–1914', *Med. Hist.* 25 (1981),
1–40, 5–12.
[42] Between 1898 and 1903 the Sanitary Committee of the JBG annually visited 1,107
dwellings, an annual average of 2,899 visits, to remedy sanitary defects. Gartner, *The Jewish
Immigrant in England*, 150–8. See also E. Black, *The Social Politics of Anglo-Jewry* (Oxford,
1989), 86–90; *RC Alien Immigration*, PP 1903 IX pt. II, Q15400; JBG, President's Address:
AGM, 22 Mar. 1937, 7 (Mocatta Library: box pamphlet BA 28 COH). The work of the
sanitary committee later developed into preventive care of tuberculosis.
[43] The percentage of defects was bigger than those found for nearby Mile End Old
Town, which was 32%, but better than for other parts of London such as Lambeth, St
Pancras, and Kensington, the defects ratios of which were respectively 65%, 70%, and
64%. Dr W. H. Hamer, evidence to *RC Alien Immigration*, PP 1903 IX pt. II.

conditions of the Jewish population, but they may have contributed to the lower rate of Jewish infant deaths.[44]

None the less, while some improvements were made to the sanitary conditions of Jewish homes, this in itself would not have been enough to prevent the spread of infectious diseases which thrived in overcrowded dwellings. Precautions to separate tuberculosis sufferers from their families were undertaken by the Jewish Board of Guardians through the efforts of its sanitary inspectors and health committee from the mid-1890s, and these were among some of the earliest measures undertaken in preventive tuberculosis care.[45] This, however, does not explain the lower rates of respiratory and infectious diseases among the Jewish infants as evidenced in the statistics from Europe and implied by the statements of observers working in East London. Hardy has argued that one reason for the lower rates of infectious disease was that the 'Mosaic Code . . . provided for the isolation of infectious disease cases and for disinfection', but, as she points out, it is impossible to judge the extent to which such precautions were practised in every day life.[46] The isolation of the infected patient away from the rest of the family would have been particularly hard to carry out in the overcrowded and cramped housing of East London.

While it is impossible to measure the degree to which Jewish immigrants followed the religious rulings on the isolation of infectious patients, other religious and cultural traditions were probably greatly influential in reducing infant mortality, particularly from diarrhoea. As Condran and Kramarow have pointed out, much of the behaviour associated with these traditions has been coloured by the attitudes of contemporaries who were quick to cite certain Jewish rituals as a means of prompting the general population to change their lifestyle, rather than because they were based on any true scientific findings.[47] None the less, certain religious requirements and cultural behaviour would have influenced the health of young infants at the turn of the century, particularly the stress laid by Jewish teaching on personal hygiene and cleanliness as well as the intricate preparations around food. This was especially important in the context of

---

[44] Two positive results of the sanitary inspectors' work were that some of the worst problems with the water supply in Whitechapel were addressed, and Lord Rothschild undertook to develop the 4% Industrial Dwellings Co. Ltd, to provide increased and better housing for the Jewish poor (Black, *Social Politics*, 88). See also n. 38 above.

[45] This included the provision of sanatoria, aftercare support and home nursing, and convalescent homes. For more information on this work see Black, *Social Politics of Anglo-Jewry*, 59, 89–90, 101, 165–6.

[46] Hardy, *Epidemic Streets*, ch. 10, See also Hart, 'The Mosaic Code of Sanitation', 183.

[47] Condran and Kramarow, 'Child Mortality', 228–33.

infantile diarrhoea, which is strongly linked to the type of food an infant receives and the conditions under which it is prepared.

Infants who are breast-fed have a far greater chance of survival than those who are given prepared food and drink. Those infants who were hand or bottle-fed at the turn of the century were more susceptible to epidemic diarrhoea, especially in dry and hot summer weather.[48] Breast milk not only provides an infant with the mother's antibodies for fighting infections, but is also much safer than milk which has come into contact with the environment. This was particularly important in the context of working-class homes, where small, overcrowded households lacked their own water supply and water-closets, and had insufficient food storage space. This would have made it impossible to guard milk against the 'bacterial organisms (in particular some strains of Escherichia coli) which, although not harmful to the more developed digestive system of older children and adults, could produce diarrhoea attacks in infants'.[49]

The correlation between the poor environment and the standard of milk was borne out by Newsholme's arguments at the turn of the century. He showed the contradiction that while infants of wealthier parents were more likely to be artificially fed than their working-class counterparts, they were less likely to die. Newsholme concluded that the infants from richer homes were better protected from the hazards involved in artificial feeding because of their parents' income. Wealthy families were not only more likely to be able to afford a better quality of food, but could also prepare it in much safer conditions than in working-class homes.[50] Jewish infants reared in the working-class housing of East London would have suffered the same problems in the preparation and storage of food as their neighbours. None the less, this disadvantage might have been counter-balanced by the Jewish rituals associated with kosher food, which not only weighed heavily against the consumption of infected meat which had undergone inspection before being sold,[51] but also necessitated the separation of milk and meat utensils, and called for a high degree of cleanliness

---

[48] At the turn of the century numerous medical experts showed that infant mortality rose dramatically in the years of hot, dry summers. *RC Alien Immigration*, PP 1903 IX pt. II, Qs21415–17; Q3960. See also V. Fildes, 'Breastfeeding in London, 1905–1919', *J. Biosoc. Sci.* 24 (1992), 53–74, 64.

[49] S. Szreter, 'The Importance of Social Intervention in Britain's Mortality Decline', *Soc. Hist. Med.* 1 (1988), 1–38, 31. See also Hope, 'Observations on Autumnal Diarrhoea in Cities', 662.

[50] See Newsholme, cited in Woods *et al.*, 'Causes of Rapid Infant Mortality Decline', pt. II, 116–17.

[51] For more detail on this see Fishberg, 'Health and Sanitation', 76–7; and Dwork, 'Health Conditions of Immigrant Jews', 29. See also *Physical Deterioration*, PP 1904 XXXII, Q1173.

of implements.[52] Children of Jewish immigrants in London recall that young babies were never given any water or milk without it having been boiled first, thus reducing the likelihood of infection. Jewish religious teaching also demanded hand-washing before and after meals.[53] Adoption of this practice was much slower in the general population, although the use of pasteurized milk gained in strength with the development of milk depots at the turn of the century.[54] Visitors in East London frequently commented that Jewish homes were cleaner than others in the area, which many contemporaries claimed was the result of the dietary and hygienic laws of the Jewish religion.[55] Although it is difficult to establish the degree to which these rituals were followed in Jewish homes in East London, Jewish infants would have benefited where they were adhered to.[56]

Whether Jewish or not, infants of poverty-stricken working-class families living in conditions of bad housing and poor sanitation stood a much fairer chance of survival if they were breast-fed.[57] Contemporaries frequently commented on the high frequency of Jewish mothers breast-feeding their infants, and cited this as one of the reasons for the greater

[52] *RC Alien Immigration*, PP 1903 IX pt. II, Q17900.

[53] Personal hygiene was also said to be high among Jewish immigrants as a result of Jewish religious laws which required both sexes to cut their finger- and toe-nails at least once a week, and for women to attend a ritual bath, the *mikveh*, once a month after menstruating. In addition to the religious rituals, bathing was said to be customary among Jewish immigrants. In New York, as in East London, many more baths appeared with the influx of the East European Jews. For detail on New York see Dwork, 'Health Conditions of Immigrant Jews', 30, and Fishberg, 'Health and Sanitation', 75.

[54] Unpublished letter from Mrs J. J. to L. Marks, 9 Feb. 1992. See also *RC Alien Immigration*, PP 1903 IX pt. II, Q21417; *Physical Deterioration*, PP 1904 XXXII, Q327; and Ashby, *Infant Mortality*, 25–6. For more information on the development of milk depots see Dwork, *War is Good for Babies*, 93–166.

[55] Dr Shirley Murphy, *RC Alien Immigration*, PP 1903 IX, Q3960, p. 203; see also Q17900, Q18311; Salaman, *JC*, 27 May 1921, pp. ii–iii. The degree of cleanliness of the Jewish homes is open to question, as it could largely reflect the attitude of the observer rather than be based in reality. While many contemporaries commented that the Jewish homes were cleaner than most of the general population, others saw them as more slovenly (*RC Alien Immigration*, PP 1903 IX, A. J. Williams p. 9, and Q9418, Q17512; *Physical Deterioration*, PP 1904 XXXII, Q475; *Eastern Post and City Chronicle*, 22 Nov. 1884, cited in Holmes, *Anti-Semitism in British Society*, 17). Such a disparity in views was also present among American observers in this period. See Condran and Kramarow, 'Child Mortality', 231; and Fishberg, 'Health and Sanitation', 75–6.

[56] Over the centuries Jews had continually been noted as a group which escaped the ravages of cholera and typhus epidemics. Such diseases are often spread through contaminated water and raw sewage. The lower rates of these diseases among Jews indicates that they were probably better protected from such insanitary conditions because of the cultural and religious practice of boiling water and thorough cleansing of eating and cooking utensils (see Gartner, *The Jewish Immigrant in England*, 160–1; *RC Alien Immigration*, PP 1903 IX pt. II, Q5105).   [57] Woods *et al.*, 'Causes of Rapid Infant Mortality Decline', 117.

survival of their infants.[58] Widespread breast-feeding, however, was not unique to Jewish mothers. The practice was also said to be common among Irish immigrants, and was very prevalent among the general working-class population in London.[59] It would therefore seem that breast-feeding alone is not the explanation for the lower rate of Jewish infant mortality.[60] Indeed, recent research by Fildes has shown that infant mortality was particularly high in working-class areas of London where breast-feeding was widespread, contrasting with the low rates of infant mortality in the wealthier districts where breast-feeding was less common.[61]

Much depends on the length of time the infants were breast-fed. As Fildes argues, infants who have been breast-fed for 1 or 2 months stand a better chance of survival against infection than those who are bottle-fed from birth, 'whilst children breast-fed for 6 months or longer withstand disease better than both of these groups. Infants for whom breast milk is supplemented with other foods have a better resistance to disease than the wholly artificially-fed, but are more susceptible than children who are exclusively breast-fed.'[62] Medical observers in East London at the turn of the century claimed that Jewish mothers frequently suckled their infants long after they were 9 months old, and that it was difficult to get them to stop even after this period.[63] Prolonged breast-feeding was also widely practised by Jewish immigrant mothers living elsewhere.[64]

The length of term of breast-feeding, however, is not the only determinant in the protection of infant life. Both the quantity and composition

[58] *RC Alien Immigration*, PP 1903 IX pt. II, Q5788, Q18311; *Physical Deterioration*, PP 1904 XXXII, Q636; Ashby, *Infant Mortality*, 25.

[59] Comments relating to Irish breast-feeding appear in *Physical Deterioration*, PP 1904 XXXII, Q475, Qs10985–6, Q11084; Hope, 'Observations on Autumnal Diarrhoea in Cities', 661.

[60] Breast-feeding practices have also been dismissed as an explanation for the long-term decline in national infant mortality. For a summary of this argument see Williams, 'Infant and Child Mortality in Urban Areas', 25–7.

[61] This study was based on the nutritional information for 222,989 infants, which represented 39.2% of all registered births in the 23 boroughs during the years for which figures were available between 1905 and 1919. In the first month of life over 92% of these children received some breast-milk with almost 86% of these having been breast-fed exclusively. Only 7.6% were artificially fed from birth. See Fildes 'Breastfeeding in London', table 1, 56, 59.

[62] Fildes, 'Breastfeeding in London', p. 66. See also R. M. Woodbury, *Causal Factors in Infant Mortality: A Statistical Study Based on Investigations in Eight Cities* (Washington, 1925), 103. See also J. M. Leventhal *et al.*, 'Does Breastfeeding Protect Against Infections in Infants Less than 3 Months of Age?', *Pediatrics*, 78 (5 Nov. 1986), 896–903.

[63] *RC Alien Immigration*, PP 1903 IX pt. II, Q5788.

[64] Woodbury, *Causal Factors in Infant Mortality*, 113–16; Schmelz, *Infant and Early Childhood Mortality*, 50–1.

of breast-milk are vital to sustaining an infant's health. This is partly dependent on the diet and health of the mother. Although still unproven, some research has suggested that while undernourished women can continue to breast-feed, their milk has 'a lower calorific value containing smaller quantities of protein and particularly fat'.[65] Infants of undernourished women who are fed solely on their mother's milk are therefore more likely to be underfed. Fildes claims that many of the infants in early twentieth-century London would have been disadvantaged in this way, as many of their mothers were terribly undernourished and in poor health. Most of these women survived on a staple diet of 'white bread and a scrape of margarine, butter or jam, and weak tea with a dash of milk' with very little fresh milk, vegetables, or meat. This, together with the need to undertake heavy domestic chores and other work immediately after childbirth without an adequate rest, meant that many of the mothers might not have been able to produce a good quality and quantity of breast-milk. Indeed, many health visitors noted, in the poorer areas of London, 'that not only were mothers obviously undernourished but their infants were also small, and . . . by the age of 12 months many [infants], whether breastfed or artificially fed, had still not doubled their birth weight'.[66]

In circumstances where mothers are undernourished, the use of supplementary feeding can help those infants not receiving adequate nourishment from breast-milk. Supplementary feeding and premature weaning were very common in the poorer neighbourhoods of London at the turn of the century. None the less, as already highlighted, conditions under which such food would have been prepared and the inferior nutritional quality of foods used to supplement or replace breast-milk in the early twentieth century probably countered the benefits of supplementary feeding, resulting in higher rates of infant mortality from diarrhoea.[67]

---

[65] Fildes, 'Breastfeeding in London', 67. For more information concerning the controversy over maternal nutrition and infant mortality see J. D. Wray, 'Maternal Nutrition, Breastfeeding and Infant Survival', and A. Lechtig *et al.*, 'Effect of Maternal Nutrition on Infant Mortality', both in W. H. Moseley (ed.), *Nutrition and Human Reproduction* (New York, 1977); R. Morley *et al.*, 'Mother's Choice to Provide Breast Milk and Developmental Outcome', *Archives of Disease in Childhood*, 63 (1988), 1382–5; J. Illingworth *et al.*, 'Diminution in Energy, Expenditure During Lactation', *Br. Med. J.* 292 (15 Feb. 1986), 437–41. See also Great Britain Committee on Medical Aspects of Food Policy, *Present Day Practice in Infant Feeding: Third Report* (London, 1988), especially pp. 8–10 for nutritional value of human milk.

[66] Fildes, 'Breastfeeding in London', 67. For more detail on the staple diet of working-class mothers see M. Pember Reeves, *Round About a Pound a Week* (London, 1913; repr. 1984), ch. 7.

[67] Machine-skimmed condensed milk was a popular supplement in working-class areas. Often this was fed through long-tube feeding bottles which were impossible to clean. See Fildes 'Breastfeeding in London', 67, 68.

The importance of a mother's health and the use of supplementary feeding appears to have been important in the Jewish context. Contemporaries frequently commented on the better care Jewish women received from their husbands and through the social welfare provided by Jewish communal agencies. Jewish women were also praised for ceasing from work early on in their pregnancies.[68] Nevertheless, it is difficult to know whether such favourable conditions for Jewish women improved their health and how far this extended. Indeed, one factory inspector reported that Jewish immigrant women who worked in sweated industries were often found to be 'anaemic' and 'lifeless'.[69] Even Jewish mothers who did not work outside the home appear, like non-Jewish mothers, to have had little rest and to have stinted themselves in order to feed their children first.[70]

While it is impossible to compare the health of Jewish women with that of other women or the effect of that on the quantity and quality of their breast-milk, contemporary observers claimed that Jewish immigrant mothers commonly supplemented their breast-milk with a large variety of extra foods from a very early age. This was not only noted for Russian-Polish Jewish immigrant mothers living in Westminster, but also in American cities, and was said to be a custom they had brought with them on migration.[71] Given the hazards of artificial feeding in these years, such practices might be expected to have caused a higher mortality, but the low rates of infant mortality among the Jewish population contradict this assumption. Russian-Polish Jewish mothers were not the only immigrants to supplement their breast-feeding, Polish mothers also did so, yet in the United States it was shown that their infant mortality rates were much higher and the 'mortality from gastric and intestinal diseases among Polish infants was six times as high as that among Jewish [ones]'.[72] Such a difference in the mortality patterns despite the apparent similarity in feeding practices suggests that the type of food given to Jewish infants and the circumstances under which it was prepared was probably superior in Jewish families.

One indication of the better food on offer in Jewish homes is highlighted by the very low rates of rickets found among Jewish children at the turn of the century. Rickets is a disease commonly associated with

---

[68] *Physical Deterioration*, PP 1904 XXXII, Q327, Q636, Qs1608–9, Q1169, Qs10029–38.

[69] *RC Alien Immigration*, PP 1903 IX pt. II, Q11809.

[70] See the recollections of the children of Jewish immigrants in J. White, *Rothschild Buildings*, 153–6; and B. Aronowitch, *Give It Time* (London, 1974), 23.

[71] Fildes, 'Breastfeeding in London', 65; and Woodbury, *Causal Factors in Infant Mortality*, 114.

[72] Woodbury, *Causal Factors in Infant Mortality*, 114.

deprivation from sunlight and a deficiency in vitamin D. At the turn of the century rickets was widely prevalent among working-class children in Britain and London, causing the Jewish children to stand out as an exception from other poor children.[73] In 1902 50 per cent of children in poor schools in Leeds were found to have rickets. However, in Jewish schools only 7 per cent of the children had rickets, which matched the 8 per cent found in non-Jewish schools classified as 'good'.[74] The high incidence of the disease among the non-Jewish population was attributed to a number of factors. This included air pollution from the dense palls of smoke from industry and domestic heating arrangements, as well as the types of dwellings people lived in which were not designed to let sunlight in. Hardy claims that this, together with 'popular concepts of respectability; and the constraints which kept young children indoors —young mothers lacking in vitality, tenement accommodation, poverty and ignorance' all contributed to a very high incidence of rickets.[75]

Most Jewish children faced the same problems of environmental pollution and lack of sunlight in their homes. One advantage they possessed, however, was that their diet provided a particularly rich source of vitamin D. The vitamin is contained in nearly all fish oils and fish extracts and in most animal fats, eggs, cheese, butter, and milk, all of which were not a regular feature in the staple diet of most working-class homes in the late nineteenth century. Much of the food consumed by these families was 'deficient in the types of fats which prevent rickets, and also calcium and phosphorous, which facilitate the absorption of vitamin D, while they were high in cereals, which prevent its absorption'.[76] This was not the case in Jewish homes. One medical expert in Leeds noted in 1902 that in Jewish homes 'large quantities of oil were used in cooking, even in bread making', and that they generally fried their fish in oil, and that their potatoes, if not fried in oil, were boiled in milk rather than water. Butter and oil were usually added to broth. The normal beverage consumed in Jewish homes was cocoa made with milk which was usually drunk three

[73] *Physical Deterioration*, PP 1904 XXXII, Q327, Q448, Q450, Q475, Q1168; *RC Alien Immigration*, PP 1903 IX pt. II, Q17877.

[74] *Physical Deterioration*, PP 1904 XXXII, Q452.

[75] Hardy, *Epidemic Streets*, ch. 9. See also her 'Rickets and the Rest: Diet, Infectious Disease and the Late Victorian Child', *Soc. Hist. Med.* 5/3 (1992). Air pollution not only blocked out the necessary sunlight, but was probably also an important factor in higher levels of respiratory diseases. Recent research has shown a strong correlation between air pollution and respiratory diseases among young infants and children. See N. Graham, 'The Epidemiology of Acute Respiratory Infections in Children and Adults: A Global Perspective', in *Epidemiol. Rev.* 12 (1990), 149–78, 157.

[76] Hardy, *Epidemic Streets*, ch. 9, and 'Rickets and the Rest'.

times a day, except on days when they ate meat. Eggs, fruit, and vegetables were also abundant in their diet, and Jewish women often combined together in the markets to buy large quantities of the cheaper fish. Herring, a fish rich in oil, figured widely in Jewish diets.[77] Such a diet was therefore probably a strong influence in preventing a high rate of rickets among Jewish children.[78] In addition to this, breast-milk also provides a good source of vitamin D, which, as already stated, was supplied by Jewish mothers for lengthy periods.[79]

The low incidence of rickets might provide one clue for the lower rates of infectious disease among Jewish infants and younger children. While poor nutrition and conditions of overcrowding are the prime determinants of these diseases, Hardy has recently argued that rickets might have had some impact on their incidence, particularly in the case of whooping cough. Rickets commonly struck in late infancy and early childhood, particularly the first two years of life, and had a marked seasonal pattern. Cases of rickets were 'especially numerous in the spring months, and were found to be most severe in children dying at the age of one year who had been born in the previous spring. Infants were at their most vulnerable to rickets when dietary imbalances of the weaning process were compounded by the sunlight deprivation of the winter months'.[80] Hardy has shown that the

seasonality of rickets coincided with that of measles and whooping cough, both of which also achieved maxima during the spring months, and the terrible toll of these diseases, more especially perhaps that of whooping cough, can in part be understood through the prevalence of rickets. Whooping cough is a notably debilitating and exhausting disease. Its acute phase may last up to four weeks, and can involve up to fifty paroxysms of coughing, often followed by vomiting, in twenty-four hours. In very young infants, the immature respiratory system handicaps the response to paroxysms; babies are unable to produce the whoop and resume effective breathing quickly; they become deprived of oxygen and turn blue. Exhaustion is a recognized complication, as is nutritional deprivation. . . . In the nineteenth century, when rickets was so very prevalent among infants, further diminishing their ability to cope with the whoop, and reducing their stamina to resist exhaustion and their defences against secondary infections, whooping cough

---

[77] E. Mellanby, 'Accessory Food Factors (Vitamines) in the Feeding of Infants', *The Lancet*, 17 Apr. 1920, 856–62, 861. See also Ashby, *Infant Mortality*, 26; *RC Alien Immigration*, PP 1903 IX pt. II, Q17900; and Hardy, *Epidemic Streets*, ch. 9.
[78] Low rates of rickets were also found among children on the Hebridean Island of Lewis at the turn of the century, where the diet resembled that of the Jews (Mellanby, 'Accessory Food Factors', 862).   [79] Hardy, *Epidemic Streets*, 19.
[80] Ibid. 11, and 'Rickets and the Rest'.

must have constituted an even more profound threat to their survival. Among older children, too, the physical consequences of rickets impaired the ability to overcome secondary infections.[01]

Contemporaries themselves noted the link between rickets and the survival of young children suffering from measles and whooping cough. The protection Jewish infants and young children had from rickets, therefore, might explain their lower propensity to die from infectious diseases, as shown by the statistics from Europe and the United States.

The Jewish diet was not only rich in vitamin D, but also in vitamin A which was provided through the consumption of fish and fresh vegetables such as carrots. Although not yet conclusive, current research on respiratory disease has begun to show that there might be a link between a deficiency in vitamin A and an increased morbidity from respiratory infection and overall mortality among young children. One hospital-based study in Tanzania also found that vitamin A supplementation helped reduce mortality from measles.[82] Much work still needs to be carried out on vitamin A and its impact on respiratory diseases and measles, but the relationship might help to explain the low number of Jewish infants dying from respiratory diseases as indicated in Tables 2.4 and 2.5.

Jewish infants not only appear to have benefited from the religious and cultural traditions concerning food and its preparation, but also from other social behaviour. Many observers at the turn of the century remarked on the relative absence of alcohol among the Jewish population living in East London.[83] This stood in complete contrast to the local population, where the public house dominated the social scene, especially for men. Contemporaries pointed out that while in many non-Jewish working-class households part of the breadwinner's wages was spent on beer, in Jewish households this was not the case.[84] The overall impression of Jewish immigrants was that they also took very good care of their families. Jewish parents were shown to spend all that they had on their children, and contemporaries commented that it was rare to find a poor Jewish child without shoes, proper clothing, or adequate food. As one Jewish observer, Mr Prag, commented,

---

[81] Hardy, *Epidemic Streets*, 11–12, and 'Rickets and the Rest'.

[82] Graham, 'The Epidemiology of Acute Respiratory Infections', 161–2. See also M. Mamdani and D. Ross, 'Review Article: Vitamin A Supplementation and Child Survival: Magic Bullet or False Hope?', *Health Policy and Planning*, 4/4 (1989), 273–94.

[83] *RC Alien Immigration*, PP 1903 IX pt. II, Q3963, Q21753; *JC*, 19 Aug. 1904; Salaman, *JC* Suppl., 29 July 1921, p. v. See also L. Golding, *Magnolia Street* (London, 1932), 129–30.   [84] Gambling, however, was not an unknown phenomenon in Jewish homes.

You never hear of a Jewish mother taking her child's boots off its feet to pawn them for a drink. On the contrary Jewish parents will make any sacrifices so that their children should be better fitted for the struggle of life. The Jewish alien parent even in his direst poverty will also stint himself so as to pay for extra evening tuition for his children after they have been to the free school for the day.[85]

Jewish mothers, Mr Prag noted, were particularly good in the care they took of their children.[86] Praise lavished on Jewish mothers centred on the meticulous attention they paid to household chores and cooking.[87]

It is difficult to know to what extent Jewish parents were better in the care of their children than other parents. As my Introduction has already pointed out, many of the positive remarks made by contemporaries of Jewish mothers reflected their own middle-class ideals of domesticity and the ideal family unit, which Jewish mothers and their family life appeared to represent. Mothers, as the reproducers of the nation, and infants, as its future citizens, were central to the debates on the physical and industrial deterioration of Britain and her empire.[88] They were the ones on which not only the health of the infant, but also the future of the nation, depended. Much of the blame for the high rates of infant mortality and poor health was placed on the ignorance of mothers, and emphasis was given to the need to teach them the rudiments of cooking and housework. Many contemporary observers also argued that infant mortality was the result of high alcoholism among the working-class, as well as women's work outside the home, which was seen as destroying family life.[89] In this context Jewish mothers therefore symbolized the ideal to which all mothers should strive.

Research on infant mortality in the Third World today has shown wide differentials between a child's survival and a mother's education and her

---

[85] Mr J. Prag, member of St Pancras Health and Insanitary Areas Committee and member of Jewish communal institutions, *RC Alien Immigration* PP 1903 IX pt. II, Q17877. Such comments were also made by non-Jewish observers, see e.g. Ashby, *Infant Mortality*, 25; *Physical Deterioration*, PP 1904 XXXII, Q327, Q21417. This was held true not only for Jews in Britain, but also for those elsewhere in the world. See Ruppin, *Jews of Today*, 77.

[86] Mr J. Prag, member of the St Pancras Health and Insanitary Areas Committee, evidence to *RC Alien Immigration*, PP 1903 IX pt. II, Q17877.

[87] C. Booth, cited in W. J. Fishman, *East End Jewish Radicals, 1875–1914* (London, 1976), 54; *RC Alien Immigration*, PP 1903 IX pt. II, Q18311.; Ashby, *Infant Mortality*, 25–6.

[88] This can be seen in the evidence given to the *House of Lords Select Committee on the Sweating System*, PP 1888 XX, XXI; PP 1889 XIII, XIV; PP 1890 XVI; *House of Commons Select Committee on Alien Immigration*, PP 1888 XI; PP 1889 X; and the *RC Alien Immigration*, PP 1903 IX pts. I and II.

[89] Davin, 'Imperialism and Motherhood'; Dyhouse, 'Working-Class Mothers and Infant Mortality'.

child-rearing knowledge. The level of education and literacy of a mother remains a powerful factor in infant mortality even when socio-economic variables are controlled for. Recent research on infant and child mortality in America in the late nineteenth century, however, has indicated that a mother's literacy skills had far less impact on the level of mortality than socio-economic factors. This is partially explained by the general absence of scientific knowledge about hygiene and the spread of disease in these years, which limited the amount of knowledge that could be passed on to mothers in the care of their infants. This changed once the knowledge became more advanced.[90] No information remains on the education attainment levels of Jewish women, or their literacy skills, but the knowledge they gained in keeping a kosher kitchen and the regulations this placed on food preparation and personal hygiene set them apart from their neighbours.

Jewish women were not only praised for their cooking and household skills, but also for their abstention from working in the outside labour market. The degree to which Jewish married women refrained from working, however, is debatable and cannot necessarily be seen as the cause of the lower rates of infant mortality.[91] Frequent unemployment, illness, or death of the male breadwinner in these families often made the women's contribution to the family income vital. Like non-Jewish women, Jewish immigrant women had to rely on their own resources from early on and frequently had to undertake paid work. A great deal of the work Jewish married women pursued could be carried out within the home while attending to the duties of housework and child care. Those who worked outside the home only did so as a last resort. Jewish women,

---

[90] S. H. Preston and M. R. Haines, *Fatal Years: Child Mortality in Late Nineteenth-Century America* (Princeton, NJ, 1991), 201–2. See also the reviews of this book which appear in 'Forum: Fatal Years' in *Health Transition Review*, 1/2 (1991), 221–44, especially J. C. Caldwell, 'Major New Evidence on Health Transition and its Interpretation', 221–9. The spread of the knowledge about hygiene and food preparation was uneven, and was initially more widespread among the wealthier population, see D. C. Ewbank and S. H. Preston, 'Personal Health Behaviour and the Decline in Infant and Child Mortality: The United States, 1900–1930', in J. Caldwell *et al.*, *What We Know About Health Transition: The Cultural, Social and Behavioural Determinants of Health* (Canberra, 1990), i. 117, 118–19, 120–5.

[91] Contemporaries and historians have continually debated the influence of women's employment and infant mortality. A study of infant mortality in two Swedish parishes showed that the links between women's work and breast-feeding habits and their impact on infant mortality were not straightforward. See A. Brändström, 'The Impact of Female Labour Conditions on Infant Mortality: A Case Study of the Parishes of Nedertorneå and Jokkmokk, 1800–1896', *Soc. Hist. Med.* 1/3 (1988), 329–58. See also Williams, 'Infant and Child Mortality in Urban Areas', 27–9; and Dyhouse, 'Working-Class Mothers and Infant Mortality', 251–4.

however, had an advantage over other women in East London because many of them could find employment within family workshops often situated in their own homes or in close proximity to it. This might have given them more of an appearance of remaining within the home than other working mothers who were more dependent on outside labour which was harder to combine with family needs.[92] The degree to which married women participated in paid employment was dependent on the economic circumstances of their family. While few immigrant women could afford to refrain from work, as Jews became more settled and began to move up the social ladder, so their married women increasingly disappeared from paid labour. This, however, was an uneven process.

Jews were not only praised for their low rates of women working, and for their good family life, but were also thought to be more chaste. Illegitimacy, often linked to very high infant mortality,[93] was said to be rare among the Jewish immigrants.[94] In 1901 William Ward, a vaccination officer for Bethnal Green, showed that while there had been seventy-four illegitimate births among the local population, only two had occurred among the 'foreign Jewish population'. He concluded that Jewish morality was connected to their thrift and domesticity.[95] To what extent these perceptions reflected reality is open to question. The social and economic dislocation families suffered as a result of migration would have increased the likelihood of illegitimacy among the immigrant population.[96] No

[92] A comparison of the type of work married Jewish women undertook in relation to other women in East London and to Irish immigrants appears in L. Marks, 'Irish and Jewish Women's Experience of Childbirth and Infant Care in East London, 1870–1939: The Responses of Host Society and Immigrant Communities to Medical Welfare Needs', D.Phil. thesis (Oxford, 1990), 27–9; and L. Marks, 'Working Wives and Working Mothers: A Comparative Study of Irish and East European Jewish Married Women's Work and Motherhood in East London, 1870–1914', Polytechnic of North London Irish Studies Centre, *Occasional Papers Series*, 2 (London, 1990).

[93] Until the mid-1930s illegitimate infants faced a much greater risk of dying, particularly in the post-neonatal period ('Report of the Infant Committee', *Trans. Obstet. Soc. of London*, 13 (1870), 132–49, 142–3; L. Rose, *The Massacre of the Innocents: Infanticide in Britain*, 1800–1939 (London, 1986), 23).

[94] This was not unique to Jewish immigrants, the Irish were also seen to have low rates of illegitimacy. For more information on the Irish and how they compared with the Jewish population see L. Marks, ' "The Luckless Waifs and Strays of Humanity": Irish and Jewish Immigrant Unwed Mothers in London, 1870–1939', *Twentieth Cent. Br. Hist.* 3/2 (1992).

[95] *RC Alien Immigration*, PP 1903 IX pt. II, Q18311.

[96] Research on single mothers in Paris has shown that migration was a complex dynamic in these women's experiences and their rates of illegitimacy. While many women travelled to the city with the expectation of joining family or friends and some sort of support network, this did not always guarantee economic and social security, let alone sexual protection. See R. G. Fuchs and L. Page Mogh, 'Pregnant, Single and Far From Home: Migrant Women in Nineteenth-Century Paris', *Am. Hist. Rev.* 95/4 (1990), 1007–31, 1009.

figures are available for the rates of illegitimacy of Jews in Eastern Europe, but statistics from select parts of East London show a slight rise in illegitimacy in areas with a high percentage of Jewish immigrants during the late 1870s and 1880s, the years of early settlement (see Figure 2.6). By the late 1880s, however, illegitimacy rates began to fall. Figure 2.7 compares the rates of illegitimacy for selected subward districts identified in Map 2.1 for the 1880s and 1890s, showing the Jewish area of Spitalfields and the non-Jewish area of Limehouse. In both these areas illegitimacy was lower than in London or in England and Wales as a whole. It would therefore seem that although the number of illegitimate births was small among the Jewish population, they did not stand out from the non-Jewish population in this respect in this area of London, making it unlikely to have been a factor in their lower rates of infant mortality relative to non-Jewish components in the East End.[97]

Fertility is another factor which needs to be taken into consideration when examining infant mortality, but this is an area which has been subject to a great deal of historical controversy. One difficulty in isolating the impact of fertility on infant mortality, is that the fall in infant mortality itself might have influenced the decline in fertility. An additional problem in assessing the influence of fertility on infant mortality patterns is their relationship with breast-feeding. Infant mortality and fertility can both be reduced by the widespread use of breast-feeding.[98] While some contemporary medical experts and historians[99] have argued that there was no real correlation between fertility and infant deaths, more recent research has indicated a connection. Woods *et al.* have shown that while fertility declined greatly in the years 1876 to 1899, infant mortality did not fall overall. None the less, they have demonstrated that when 'the diarrhoeal component of infant mortality is ignored because it was critically influenced by short-run meteorological variations, then the underlying long-run trend of infant mortality began to move downward from 1891, if not earlier'. They assert that this means that there could be a positive

---

[97] Although no figures remain on the survival chances of illegitimate Jewish infants in East London, evidence from Budapest for the years 1901–5 suggests that Jewish illegitimate infants suffered similar disadvantages to their non-Jewish counterparts. The gulf between illegitimate and legitimate Jewish infants was comparable to that of non-Jewish infants. In these years the rate of mortality among Jewish infants was 92 per 1,000 births, while among illegitimate infants it was 143. Among Catholics the mortality rate for legitimate and illegitimate infants was 161.9 and 176.8 respectively, and among other creeds it was 136.2 and 148.5 (Ruppin, *Jews of Today*, 78).

[98] Woods *et al.*, 'The Causes of Rapid Infant Mortality Decline', 124.

[99] J. M. Winter, 'Aspects of the Impact of the First World War on Infant Mortality in Britain', *J. Eur. Econ. Hist.* 11 (1982), 713–38, 723.

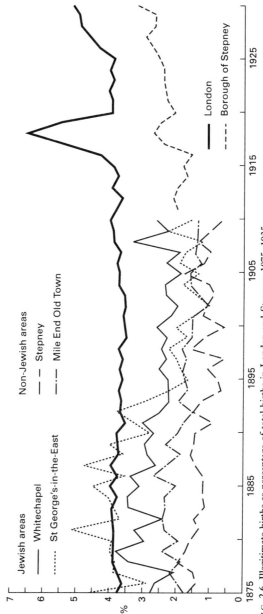

Jewish areas
Whitechapel ————
St George's-in-the-East ··········

Non-Jewish areas
Stepney ————
Mile End Old Town —·—·—

London ————
Borough of Stepney - - - - -

FIG. 2.6. Illegitimate births as percentage of total births in London and Stepney, 1875–1935
Source: Registrar-General, *ARs of Births, Deaths, and Marriages for England and Wales* (London, 1875–1935).

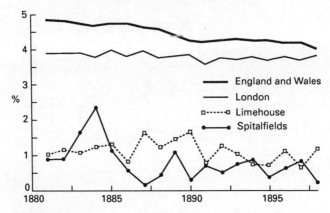

F I G. 2.7. Illegitimate births as percentage of total births in select areas of East London, London, and England and Wales, 1880–1901
Source: Registrar-General, *Quarterly Returns of Births and Deaths for England and Wales* (London, 1880–1910).

link between the decline in fertility and rates of infant mortality and suggest that,

the decline of fertility could have exerted a powerful influence on the subsequent decline of infant mortality not only by relieving the mother of caring for large numbers of offspring, but also because longer birth intervals would tend to improve the chances of an older child receiving adequate care while the mother was nursing a newly born baby (i.e. the high-parity and short birth-interval effects).[100]

The decline in Jewish infant mortality, however, does not appear to have been linked with a reduction in rates of fertility.[101] Many of the Jewish immigrants came from countries which had a higher birth rate than England and Wales (see Fig. 2.8). The Jewish areas of Eastern Europe especially had witnessed a great population explosion in the nineteenth century. Between 1820 and 1897, the Jewish population of the Russian Empire rose from 1.6 to 5.2 million, and in Austria-Hungary from 0.6 to 2.1 million. Such growth is especially noticeable given that it occurred at a time of increased persecution, modernization-secularization, and large-scale emigration which would have had a negative effect on demographic growth. Even in 1897, when the growth of the Jewish population had begun to fade, the Russian Census showed the Jews had a completed

---

[100] Woods *et al.* 'The Causes of Rapid Infant Mortality Decline', 121–6.
[101] For more detail on the patterns of fertility and their impact on infant mortality among Jewish immigrants in America see Condran and Kramarow, 'Child Mortality', 249–51.

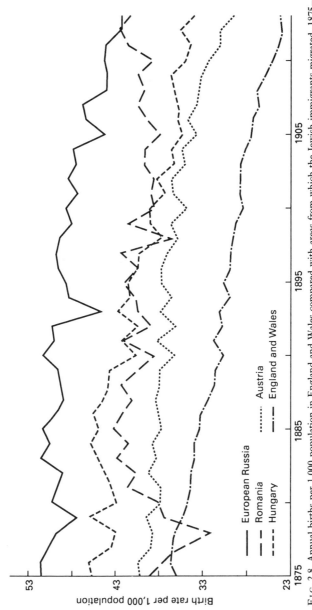

FIG. 2.8. Annual births per 1,000 population in England and Wales compared with areas from which the Jewish immigrants migrated, 1875–1913
Source: B. R. Mitchell, *European Historical Statistics, 1879–1975* (Cambridge, 1980).

fertility rate of 6.2.[102] Such fertility patterns found among the East European Jews differed considerably from those beginning to occur among Anglo-Jewry from the 1850s. Anglo-Jews from the 1850s had already begun to reduce their family size, and this contrasted sharply with the size of East European immigrant families. In the years 1870 to 1885 the completed family size for birth cohorts of ever-married women was estimated to be 3 children among the old Anglo-Jews, while among the East European Jews settling in London it was 7.3.[103] This difference continued into the Edwardian era. In 1903 the crude annual birth rate for the immigrant population in London was 45, while among Anglo-Jews living in the southern counties from 1901 to 1910 it was 33.2.[104] The average completed family size of Jewish immigrants was also higher than the norm of children present among the average British family, or those of manual wage-earners or labourers, which were 3.53, 3.96, and 4.45 respectively in the period 1900–9.[105]

One reason for the high Jewish birth rate was the age structure and marriage patterns of the immigrant community, which contrasted with those found among Anglo-Jews.[106] Jewish immigrants married earlier than many Anglo-Jews. During the 1880s the average age for bridegrooms was 28.2 among the Anglo-Jews in England, while in Russia the average age was 24.5, for brides the respective ages were 21.3 and 24.1.[107] Of the population in England and Wales as a whole, 48 per cent were aged between 15 and 45 in 1901. In the same age group the percentage was 75 per cent among Russian and Russian Polish male immigrants and 71 per cent for female immigrants.[108] The average age for the East European

---

[102] B. A. Kosmin, 'Nuptiality and Fertility Patterns of British Jewry, 1850–1980: An Immigrant Transition?', in D. A. Coleman, *Demography of Immigrants and Minority Groups in the UK: Proceedings of the 18th Annual Symposium of the Eugenics Society* (London, 1981), 247. See also J. Silber, 'Some Demographic Characteristics of the Jewish Population in Russia at the End of the Nineteenth Century', *Jewish Soc. Stud.* 5 (1980), 269–80; and Corrsin, *Warsaw Before the First World War*, 22–9.

[103] Salaman, *JC*, 27 May 1921. See also Kosmin, 'Nuptiality and Fertility Patterns of British Jewry', 253.

[104] See table 6 in Kosmin, 'Nuptiality and Fertility Patterns of British Jewry', 253.

[105] E. A. Wrigley, *Population and History* (London, 1969; repr. 1973), 186–7, table 5.13. See also B. Brookes, 'Women and Reproduction, 1860–1939', in J. Lewis (ed.), *Labour and Love* (Oxford, 1986), 152; *JC*, 10 Apr. 1896, 11. According to the Fertility Census of 1911, in Leeds the number of children born to Russian (Jewish) couples was 3.95, for English couples the number was 2.82 and for Irish ones it was 3.38 (figures from unpublished letter from O. Sandler to L. Marks, 11 July 1989).

[106] Kosmin, 'Nuptiality and Fertility Patterns of British Jewry', 252, see also 255, table 7.

[107] Similar differences also appeared between West European Jews and East European Jews in the 1880s. Kosmin, 'Nuptiality and Fertility Patterns of British Jewry', table 6, and 254–5.   [108] Feldman, 'Immigrants and Workers', 31.

TABLE 2.9. *Marriage rates among Jews and in London per 1,000 aged 15 and over in 1903*

	Jews	London
Men	28.4	27.1
Women	31.7	22.8
Both Sexes	30.1	25.0

Source: Rosenbaum, 'Contribution to the Study of Vital and Other Statistics of the Jews', 549, table 19.

TABLE 2.10. *Proportion of Jewish marriages per 1,000 total population in London 1857–1906*

Date	Jewish marriages per 1,000
1857	9.1
1873	10.0
1884	12.1
1893	21.1
1901	32.2
1906	39.5

Source: *JC*, 31 Jan. 1908.

Jewish brides and bridegrooms in England during the Edwardian period was 22.9 and 25.1 respectively. Among English couples, however, the average marriage age of women was 25.9 while for men it was 26.9.[109] Tables 2.9 and 2.10 show that immigrant Jews not only seemed to marry earlier, but also more frequently than the host community, and marriages became more common as the immigrants became more settled, all of which resulted in a higher birth rate.[110]

Shifting boundaries and population make it difficult to determine the exact birth rates for the specifically Jewish sub-ward districts for which we have rates of infant mortality. None the less, Figures 2.7 and 2.8 and Tables 2.11 and 2.12 show that although the overall birth rate was declining during this period in areas with large numbers of Jews, such as the sub-ward district of Spitalfields or the overall boroughs of Whitechapel

[109] Kosmin, 'Nuptiality and Fertility Patterns of British Jewry', table 6, and 255.
[110] Feldman, 'Immigrants and Workers', 32.

TABLE 2.11. *Birth rate per 1,000 living in Stepney, Southwark, and London, 1886–1900*

Area	1886–90	1891–5	1896–1900	Change 1886–1900
Whitechapel	35.7	40.7	39.2	+3.5
St George's-in-the-East	39.9	41.4	43.3	+3.4
Limehouse	35.3	33.9	33.4	−1.9
Mile End Old Town	37.5	37.6	38.2	+0.7
Whole Borough of Stepney	37	38.3	38.4	+1.4
Borough of Southwark	35.5	35.1	34.3	−1.2
London	32.2	30.9	29.8	−2.4

Source: *RC Alien Immigration*, PP 1903 IX, app., table 74, p. 89.

TABLE 2.12. *Percentage of foreign residents to total population in Stepney, 1891 and 1901*

Area	1891	1901
Limehouse	2.1	3.7
St George's-in-the-East	16.2	28.8
Mile End Old Town	5.3	11.5
Whitechapel	24.1	31.8
Whole Borough of Stepney	11.3	18.2

Source: Stepney MOH, *AR* (1902); *RC Alien Immigration*, PP 1903 IX, table 71, app., Qs 3916–19.

and St George's-in-the-East, the birth rate increased in the late 1890s. In 1908 the Jewish birth rate was still higher than others in East London. The average birth rate for the overall Borough of Stepney was 33.1 per 1,000, whereas in St George's-in-the-East, which had a high concentration of Jews, it was 40.4 per 1,000.[111]

---

[111] Dr Thomas, Stepney MOH, cited in *JC*, 17 July 1908. Family size began to diminish amongst the middle-class from the 1850s, but among the working-class it remained large until the 20th c. Working-class wives married and gave birth earlier than middle-class wives. The Census of 1901 showed distinct class differences in the birth rate whereby the more middle-class area of Hampstead had a rate of 183 births per 1,000 wives aged 15–45, while in working-class Shoreditch the rate was 283. During 1880–1901 the fertility rate declined by 6% in working-class Poplar, whereas in Hampstead it declined by 30%. Only in the inter-war period did family sizes decline in working-class neighbourhoods (E. Ross, 'Labour and Love: Rediscovering London's Working-Class Mothers, 1870–1918', in J. Lewis (ed.), *Labour and Love* (Oxford, 1986) 75–7).

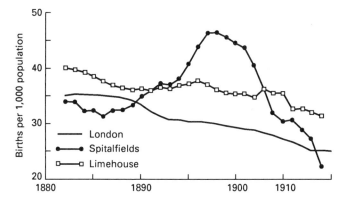

F IG. 2.9. Births per 1,000 population over a 3-year average in select areas of East London and the whole of London, 1882–1910
Source: Registrar-General, *Quarterly Returns of Births and Deaths for England and Wales* (London, 1880–1910).

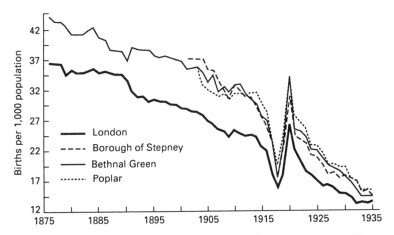

F IG. 2.10. Annual birth rates per 1,000 population in London an selected areas of East London, 1875–1935
Source: Registrar-General, *ARs of Births, Deaths and Marriages for England and Wales* (London, 1875–1935).

By the 1920s, however, when the average rate of marriage was beginning to fall among the Jewish population and the average age of people marrying was rising, the rate of fertility showed a decline.[112] In 1928 the Whitechapel MOH observed

---

[112] Kosmin, 'Nuptiality and Fertility Patterns of British Jewry', 256. The same phenomenon appeared to be happening among the Jewish population in Eastern Europe. (Salaman, *JC*, 27 May 1921, p. ii.)

Whereas up to 1897 the birth rate was rarely less than 40 per 1,000 and remained at 30 to 40 per 1,000 up to 1912, it has now dropped to 13 per 1,000 . . . In Whitechapel the birth rate has been falling for years. You no longer find those big Jewish families which were traditional from patriarchal times. Possibly no part of London shows such a great drop in the birth rate.[113]

Within two generations, therefore, East European immigrants seemed to conform to the English middle-class family size which the established middle-class Anglo-Jewish community adopted from the 1850s.[114] The decline in fertility was not only attributable to the rise in late marriages, but also in the greater use of birth control among the Jewish community. In 1949 a Royal Commission on Population found that 83 per cent of Jewish women married in the 1920s adopted artificial methods of family limitation compared with a national average of 62 per cent.[115]

It would therefore seem that the patterns of marital fertility among the East European immigrant Jews living in East London at the turn of the century were not necessarily beneficial for infant mortality. Indeed the highest period of fertility appears to have occurred in the period when infant mortality dramatically declined. The absence of infant mortality rates for the Jewish population after 1910 makes it impossible to see how the changes in fertility among the immigrants and their children affected infant mortality. One factor which also complicates the picture is birth spacing. Where women were able to space their infants, the chances of survival were much greater. The lengthy periods for which Jewish immigrant women breast-fed, as well as religious restraints concerning sexual intercourse, might have contributed to longer periods between births among Jewish women. According to Jewish law men and women are not supposed to have sexual intercourse during a woman's menstruation, or in the following seven days. During this period a woman is considered impure. Similarly sexual intercourse is forbidden where a woman has given birth and for a period of time afterwards depending on the gender of her offspring. If the woman gives birth to a son, she has to wait forty days before she can regain her purity and have intercourse again. For a

---

[113] *JC*, 6 Jan. 1928.

[114] Kosmin, 'Nuptiality and Fertility Patterns of British Jewry', 252.

[115] E. Lewis-Fanning, 'Family Limitation and its Influence on Human Fertility in the Past Fifty Years', *Paper of the Royal Commission on Population*, 1 (1949), cited in Kosmin, 'Nuptiality and Fertility Patterns of British Jewry', 258. Illegal birth-control was provided to Jewish women on an informal basis by midwives from The London Hospital and the Jewish Maternity Home (this was kindly told to me by a daughter of immigrants who was present when I presented a paper to the Museum of Jewish Life, 7 Apr. 1992).

girl, she has to wait eighty days.[116] The absence of material makes it difficult to see how closely such religious sexual codes were practised and how this affected birth-spacing patterns among Jewish immigrants in East London. Figures from the United States at the turn of the century, however, showed Jewish immigrants had an unusually low proportion of infants born at short intervals after preceding births. None the less, when account is taken of this, the Jewish infant mortality advantage over other groups is not weakened.[117]

Maternal health

Birth spacing is important for the health of the child in relation to the standard of health and amount of energy available to mothers between each individual birth. Not only can childbirth be exhausting, but so is the care subsequently needed for nursing and rearing the infant. Little time and energy was left to many of the mothers who were constantly childbearing at the turn of the century. This would have undermined their ability to care for their infants, and also was an important determinant of their own health and of the risk of dying in childbirth. As already stated it is difficult to know to what extent Jewish mothers had better health than their non-Jewish sisters. Similarly, it is hard to establish whether childbirth was more or less hazardous for Jewish immigrant women than for others. Evidence concerning maternal mortality among the immigrants is less conclusive than that for infant mortality. A much larger number of births is required for an accurate measure of maternal mortality than for infant mortality and this is not available for the sub-ward districts of East London where the Jewish population were most concentrated.

No comparison is possible for the maternal mortality rates of Eastern Europe with England and Wales.[118] Many of the immigrant mothers arriving in Britain at the turn of the century, however, came to a country

---

[116] Lev. 15: 19–33; Lev. 12: 1–8. 'The reason for the lengthy postpartum period of impurity is biological: bleeding often continues for four to six weeks after giving birth. But the reason for the doubling of the impure period after the birth of a girl is unclear.' After the prescribed period of time a woman had to take a ritual bath, a *mikveh*, to be cleansed. For more explanation see R. Biale, *Women and Jewish Law: An Exploration of Women's Issues in Halakhic Sources* (New York, 1984), 151–2.

[117] Woodbury, *Causal Factors in Infant Mortality*. See also Condran and Kramarow, 'Child Mortality', 251.

[118] More is known about the training of midwives, which appears to have been of a high standard. For more information on this see ch. 3 of Marks, 'Irish and Jewish Women's Experience of Childbirth'.

where maternal mortality was still high. After tuberculosis, childbirth was the second most common cause of death among women of childbearing age.[119] Although there were variations over the years, between 1855 and 1934 the maternal death rate in England and Wales averaged around 4.6 per 1,000 live births, totalling some 3,000 to 4,000 maternal deaths a year.[120]

Just why maternal mortality persisted when other forms of mortality diminished has been the subject of much debate among contemporaries and historians. Maternal deaths differ from other kinds of mortality, because they are not necessarily the result of a pathological process, but more usually the result of a normal physiological process going wrong, the occurrence of which should be more readily prevented than disease. It was this viewpoint which, during the inter-war period, formed much of the discussion concerning the persistence of high maternal mortality.[121] Many specialists in the 1930s believed that at least 40 per cent of maternal deaths were preventable through good obstetric care.[122] Yet by the 1930s, when the training and licensing of doctors and midwives had improved, and antiseptic practice had been adopted in most deliveries, the maternal mortality rate remained as high as it had been in the mid-nineteenth century.

By the early 1920s, the obstinacy of maternal mortality caused much concern not only among the medical men, but also among politicians, the general public, and the daily press. Regional studies carried out by

[119] S. Ryan Johansson, 'Sex and Death in Victorian England', in M. Vicinus (ed.), *A Widening Sphere* (Indianapolis, 1977), 163–81; I. Loudon, 'Maternal Mortality: 1880–1950: Some Regional and International Comparisons', *Soc. Hist. Med.* 1/2 (1988), 183–228, 184.

[120] Maternal mortality appears to have declined in England and Wales from 1650 to 1850 before levelling out from about 1850–1934. R. Schofield, 'Did Mothers Really Die? Three Centuries of Maternal Mortality in the "The World We Have Lost" ', in R. Smith, L. Bonfield, and K. Wrightson (eds.), *The World We Have Gained* (Oxford, 1987), 254. 'Even when the rate of maternal mortality was unusually high, at least 96–7% of all deliveries ended successfully. In the context of total deliveries, therefore, maternal deaths were uncommon events.' Childbirth, however, was a common event in society, which made people more aware of the danger of maternal mortality. (Loudon, 'Maternal Mortality', 184.)

[121] In 1924 Sir George Newman wrote: 'Not less than 700,000 mothers in England and Wales give birth to children each year. Of this number approximately 3,000 per annum have died during the last 10 years in the fulfilment of this maternal function. That is a serious and largely avoidable loss of life at the time of its highest capacity and its most fruitful effort. . . . The death rate among women in childbirth has shown but little proportional lessening in the past 20 years.' (Preface to a report by Dr Janet Campbell (Senior Medical Officer to Maternity and Child Welfare Department) to the Department of the Ministry of Health, 1924, cited in *Onward*, 3 (Apr. 1924), 57 (journal issued by City of London Maternity Hospital).)

[122] Loudon, 'Maternal Mortality', 184–5. In 1930 a Ministry of Health Committee investigating 2,000 maternal deaths concluded that 48% of the causes of maternal mortality were preventable (cited in *Onward*, Oct. 1930).

medical practitioners and health officials at the time investigated the impact poverty and social deprivation had on maternal mortality rates, but the importance of these factors was sometimes denied for political reasons.[123] Malnutrition and anaemia certainly weakened many women and made them unable to withstand the effects of haemorrhaging they might otherwise have coped with.[124] Some contemporaries also believed that obstructed labours were caused by deformed pelvises resulting from rickets. The scarcity of rickets among the Jewish population was cited as a reason for the 'considerably less obstructed or abnormal labours' among Jewish mothers than among others.[125] In general pelvis malformation, however, accounted very little for the maternal mortality figures during this period.[126] The conclusion would seem to be inescapable that clinical factors, especially the danger of sepsis, probably had a greater impact on the statistics than factors which could be linked to social and economic causes.[127]

Indeed, contrary to expectations, figures suggest that maternal mortality was surprisingly low in some areas of economic hardship, whereas in more prosperous regions it could be unexpectedly high. In 1931 the maternal mortality rate in middle-class Chelsea was 5.4 per 1,000 births, while in working class Hackney it was 3.2.[128] Middle-class mothers had no more protection against septic infection from doctors who attended them than working-class mothers had from midwives. Indeed, many contemporaries indicated that general practitioners were more likely to medically interfere during a birth than a midwife, increasing the risk of infection. This was especially important given that a middle-class woman was more likely to engage a general practitioner than was her working-class sister. Maternity homes, whose birth attendants were primarily

---

[123] Many in the Ministry of Health, such as Newman, denied that social and economic factors had any bearing on maternal mortality and morbidity so as to avoid the necessity of making wider state welfare provision (C. Webster, 'Healthy or Hungry Thirties?', *Hist. Workshop J*. 13 (1982), 110–29, 122–3).

[124] Loudon, 'Maternal Mortality', 198. Webster suggests that the high rate of anaemia and toxaemia among mothers in depressed areas shows that the vast expansion in maternal and child welfare clinics had little impact on the poor standards of health and nutrition in such areas. More radical solutions were needed in state welfare but ministers were reluctant to undertake them (Webster, 'Healthy or Hungry Thirties', 122–3).

[125] This was also believed to be the reason for the low infant mortality amongst Jews and the low number of still births (Salaman, *JC*, 26 Aug. 1921, p. i). One reason given for the low incidence of rickets in the Jewish community was diet. See above.

[126] Rickets did, however, stunt the growth of children from birth and this was a problem which affected thousands of people. See Wohl, *Endangered Lives*, 56–7.

[127] Infections could be limited by the use of antisepsis, and obstructions through careful obstetric management, but there was no really effective remedy against puerperal sepsis. Recent research suggests that the introduction of sulphonamides in 1936 was one of the most decisive factors in reducing maternal mortality (Loudon, 'Maternal Mortality', 202).

[128] J. Lewis, *Women in England, 1870–1950* (Brighton, 1984), 118.

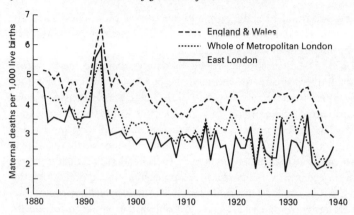

Note: Areas included under the category East London are Bethnal Green, Poplar, and Stepney

F I G. 2.11. Maternal mortality rate in East London compared with England and Wales
and Metropolitan London, 1880–1939
Source: as for Fig. 2.10.

general practitioners, were also favoured by the middle-class women in
the early twentieth century. These homes had some of the worst records
of maternal mortality.

Jewish immigrants settling in East London came to an area which
showed a remarkably low rate of maternal mortality. Figure 2.11 shows
that maternal mortality in East London was much lower than in London
or England and Wales. Given the evidence that the women of the East
End suffered physically from the drudgery of poverty and that they were
often unable to pay for high quality obstetric care, these findings are
surprising. None the less, as the following chapters will show, such low
rates of maternal mortality can be attributed to the access poor women
had to charitable midwifery and skilled medical care in East London
during this period.[129] Although these services could not eliminate the
social deprivation of the area, they seem to have been influential for
maternal mortality.[130]

[129] See contemporary studies done by Lady F. Bell, *At the Works* (London, 1907; repr.
1985); M. Llewelyn Davies (ed.), *Maternity: Letters from Working Women* (London, 1915;
repr. 1984); Pember Reeves: *Round About A Pound A Week*; M. Spring Rice, *Working-Class
Wives* (London, 1939; repr. 1981).

[130] An experiment carried out in the deprived area of Rochdale in the 1930s showed that
maternal mortality could be lowered, despite the prevailing poor social and economic
conditions, through good medical care. By improving the quality of obstetric treatment in
Rochdale the number of maternal deaths was reduced from 90 to fewer than 20 per 10,000,
one of the lowest in the country (Loudon, 'Maternal Mortality', 208).

It would seem, therefore, that while Jewish immigrants arrived in one of the poorest areas of the metropolis, this did not necessarily have adverse affects on their health. This is initially puzzling given that they had left their traditional support networks behind them, and faced a continual struggle of settling in unfamiliar surroundings which were especially deprived. The remarkably low rates of infant mortality among the Jewish immigrants in the late 1890s, however, show that these disadvantages could be overcome by certain practices they inherited from their religious teaching and cultural background. Jewish religious rulings concerning the preparation of food and personal hygiene, together with lengthy periods of breast-feeding, as well as the prevalence of a certain diet, all seemed to guard Jewish infants from an especially harsh environment, giving them an advantage over other infants in the area. The absence of separate statistics for the health of Jewish mothers makes it harder to assess the impact that migration and the period of adjustment had on their morbidity and mortality. None the less, it would seem that by settling in East London where maternity services were especially good and maternal mortality strikingly low, Jewish mothers were well protected against the dangers of childbirth.

Low rates of infant and maternal mortality, however, only tell one part of the story of the health of Jewish infants and mothers in East London. This chapter has concentrated on the effects of ethnicity on particular aspects of health status without exploring the social and cultural implications of ethnicity in gaining access to health-care. Although Jewish immigrants arrived in one of the most impoverished areas of London, the support networks available to them appear to have been wide-ranging and prolific. The existence of these schemes might explain some of the health patterns in this chapter. Subsequent chapters explore the health care systems available to Jewish women in East London and discuss how specifically Jewish medical schemes supplemented those provided by host institutions. In this context ethnicity was not only influential in their experience of host facilities, but also affected the development of their own communal provision.

3

Familial, Neighbourhood, and Communal Resources for Childbirth

IN many societies childbirth is an occasion which relies on the help of the family and the local neighbourhood. The use Jewish women made of these resources was different before and after migration. Unable to call on the kinship and communal ties that had existed in Eastern Europe, Jewish women's experiences of childbirth and infant care in East London were distinct from those of their mothers. Arriving in a new and strange environment, many Jewish women not only faced the difficulties of giving birth separated from their traditional support, but also of being attended by carers who did not always appreciate their customs or speak their language. In this situation childbirth could be a traumatic event, reinforcing the isolation and problems Jewish immigrants experienced when settling in East London.

Yet, despite these disabilities, many Jewish women giving birth in East London in the years 1870–1939 had certain advantages over the local population. Able to draw on Jewish communal resources, Jewish women had access to a variety of services unavailable to non-Jewish mothers. Arising to meet the particular needs Jewish mothers faced as a religious and ethnic minority, such provision was often very different from the types of help provided in the host society. This chapter not only examines the range of facilities provided by Jewish agencies, but also the extent to which they substituted the support many immigrants had previously received from traditional kinship networks in Eastern Europe. The very existence of such communal provision suggests that certain needs were not adequately provided by host institutions.

Some of the schemes developed by the Jewish organizations were advanced for their time, but many of the difficulties they addressed were not new. Indeed, many of the maternal and infant welfare services they established were similar to those being undertaken in society as a whole.[1]

---

[1] For more information on measures being undertaken in maternal and infant welfare services in Britain see Ch. 2.

Jewish women's experience of childbirth and infant care, therefore, cannot be divorced from wider social and medical developments concerning maternity care and infant welfare during this period. This had far-reaching implications not only in terms of the standards of maternity care and infant welfare services, but also as regards the kind of birth attendant available. Central to this chapter are the ways in which the increasing regulation of midwives restricted the use of the traditional birth attendant, the handywoman, and what implications this had for Jewish women who wished to hire attendants whom they knew from Eastern Europe.

Kinship Resources Before and After Migration

In Eastern Europe, the family unit was a significant feature of Jewish life. Whether it be a joyous occasion or a crisis, the family played a critical role, providing not only emotional support but also vital economic and social resources. Indeed, for many young couples, the harsh realities of the first year of marriage could be cushioned by the financial and social aid provided by their respective families. More orthodox Jewish couples also sometimes lived with their parents to enable the husbands to pursue religious study on a full-time basis.[2] Those who did not live with their families often stayed close to them. Privacy might have been rare in these situations, but women could rely on their kin during and after confinement when tasks such as child care and housework were harder to perform.

Although migration often split families, kinship networks continued to perform an important role. Indeed, relatives who either remained behind or had already gone on ahead often paid for the immigrants to make the journey from Eastern Europe to their new abode. In the years 1895 to 1902 between 12 and 24 per cent of the Russian, Romanian, and Galician immigrants who had come via Hamburg, Bremen, and Rotterdam to the Port of London revealed that relatives in Britain had in part or in whole, purchased the tickets for their passage. Those arriving from Libau showed an even higher familial sponsorship in these years, averaging between 25

---

[2] In Eastern Europe a man's prestige was measured by his ability to pursue religious scholarship. For more information on this see C. Baum, P. Hyman, and S. Michel, *The Jewish Woman in America* (New York, 1976), 4; L. Marks, 'Working Wives and Working Mothers: A Comparative Study of Irish and East European Jewish Married Women's Work and Motherhood in East London, 1870–1914', the Polytechnic of North London Irish Studies Centre, *Occasional Papers Series*, 2 (London, 1990), 10.

and 44 per cent.[3] It would therefore seem that while migration loosened many of the traditional kinship ties, it reinforced them in another way. Frequently, the family not only provided essential money for the passage, but also other types of social and emotional sustenance, which continued well into the years of settlement.

Not all of the immigrants arriving in East London, however, came from such a tightly knit family background, nor were all of them greeted by family members on arrival. In the absence of immediate kin many Jewish immigrants were none the less not always totally alone. Indeed, many drew on the support of friends or *landslayt* (those who had migrated from their own towns and villages), or even people they had befriended through chance encounters during their travels or on settling in East London. Newcomers and relatives were frequent visitors in the homes of the immigrants, some of whom stayed for long periods of time. In return for shelter such visitors often shared the burden of running a family and would offer help in crises. Contemporaries commenting on such reciprocity, frequently applauded such strong bonds between Jewish immigrants to which they attributed the good health of the immigrants and their infants.[4] Living in the concentrated Jewish neighbourhood of East London, these immigrants could also call on neighbours who spoke their language and shared their religious beliefs and cultural customs.

Birth Attendants: The Local Handywoman or Untrained Midwife

While family networks often provided crucial help in the event of childbirth and in the days afterwards, one of the most important figures during

---

[3] A very small percentage were assisted by charitable societies abroad. *RC Alien Immigration*, PP 1903 IX pt. II, app., tables 62, 63, 63(a), pp. 76–8. D. M. Feldman has argued that a larger number of those travelling from German ports were probably assisted by families in the USA, which might account for the discrepancy in the figures between those arriving from the German ports and those who came from Libau. 'Immigrants and Workers, Englishmen and Jews: The Immigrant to the East End of London, 1880–1906', Ph.D. thesis (Cambridge, 1985), 40.

[4] Such praise did not come without criticism. Indeed, such hospitality among the immigrants was often cited as the cause of overcrowding and bad sanitation in areas where the immigrants had settled. *Report of the Interdepartmental Committee on Physical Deterioration*, PP 1904 XXXII (henceforth *Physical Deterioration*), Q475, p. 175; Q1172, p. 204. See also Feldman, 'Immigrants and Workers', 40–1. Familial and friendship bonds were not only important among Jewish immigrants, but also among other immigrant groups. Like the Jews, the Irish were accused of causing overcrowding and bad sanitation, but were also noted for their tight familial networks. An interesting account of such ties among Irish immigrants appears in L. H. Lees, *Exiles of Erin: Irish Migrants in Victorian London* (Manchester, 1979), 133–4.

this period was the person who delivered the baby. During the nineteenth century a large proportion of births in Eastern Europe and England were attended by untrained midwives drawn from the family circle or local neighbourhood. Known as *Bobbas* (grannies) in East European Jewish ghettos, or as 'handywomen' in England, these women often had close links with the parturient woman. In some cases they might be a grandmother, mother, or another senior female member of the family. Sometimes they were a local woman who was a familiar face to many in the neighbourhood and was held in special esteem.[5] Most of these midwives were untrained and illiterate, who often undertook midwifery alongside other forms of work including sick nursing and laying out the dead.[6] Many of the midwifery skills they possessed came from watching other handywomen or, in some cases, doctors. In Eastern Europe the Jewish *Bobba* was commonly regarded as 'a medicine woman', whose role was similar to that of 'wisewomen' in other communities.[7]

These women were not only present for the actual birth. In Eastern Europe, a Jewish woman usually engaged the *Bobba* as soon as she knew she was pregnant. A *Bobba* foretold the date of birth by placing her hand on the woman's belly. She would visit the pregnant mother once a week in the early days of the pregnancy, then daily nearer the birth. Her visit was seen as a social occasion when she would talk to the mother and work out the expected birth date.[8] Immediately labour pains began the *Bobba* or handywoman was called in, and she would remain for the whole day, seeing not only to the physical needs of the mother but also attending to housework. It was also customary for her to visit the mother for several days after the confinement.[9]

---

[5] A scarcity of published evidence on these women in Eastern Europe and England makes it difficult to trace their history, and census data on midwives are known to be inaccurate. Most of the evidence available for handywomen in Britain has been drawn from oral interviews. See M. Chamberlain and R. Richardson, 'Life and Death', *Oral Hist.* 10/1 (1983), 31–43. One important source for East European Jewish midwives comes from interviews with Jewish immigrants in New York in the 1940s. See Margaret Mead Papers: Columbia University Research in Contemporary Cultures (henceforth Mead Papers), held in Library of Congress Archives, Washington DC.

[6] Mead Papers (File G48) J302, p. 2; (File G50) J-R33, 1; See also I. Selavan, 'Bobba Hannah, Midwife', *Am. J. Nursing*, 73/4 (1973), 681–3, 681.

[7] Mead Papers (File G50) J-R33, p. 1. In Britain the classic stereotype, 'Jack-of-all-trades' midwives were Sarah Gamp and her partner Betsy, fictional nurses in Dicken's novel *Martin Chuzzlewit*. For more information on this see A. Summers, 'The Mysterious Demise of Sarah Gamp: The Domiciliary Nurse and her Detractors, *c*.1830–1860', *Vict. Stud.* 32/3 (1989), 365–86, 373–4.

[8] Mead Papers (G50) J-R33, p. 1. M. Zborowski and E. Herzog, *Life is with People: The Culture of the Shtetl*, with intro. by M. Mead (New York, 1952), 313.

[9] Mead Papers [G50] J-R33, p. 1. This was not only true for the Jewish Bobba, but also for handywomen in other communities. See e.g. the information on handywomen in Ireland

Few sources remain on the use Jewish immigrants made of these untrained midwives on reaching Britain. More is known about immigrant
midwives in America, where intense struggles between these midwives
and the medical profession has left a rich number of primary sources.[10]
Lacking official qualifications, many of the immigrant midwives aroused
a great deal of derision from American medical professionals. Yet despite
such contempt from the medical profession, immigrant midwives remained vital providers of obstetric care for immigrant mothers in America
through to the 1920s.[11] Immigrants also made extensive use of untrained
immigrant midwives in East London.[12] Advertisements in the local East
End Yiddish press indicate that a number of Jewish midwives practised
in the area from early on. One of these midwives was Mrs Soloman
Rabinovits, an immigrant midwife and sick nurse who lived in Whitechapel
in the 1880s. According to her newspaper announcements she had 'many
recommendations' from doctors and patients for the quality of her services,
and in addition to attending private cases she was willing to care for poor
patients to whom she made no charge for her midwifery skills.[13]

Little evidence remains on the exact number of immigrant midwives
who worked in East London, nor do we know the degree to which their

in L. Ballard, ' "Just Whatever They Had Handy": Aspects of Childbirth and Early Childcare
in Northern Ireland, Prior to 1948', *Ulster Folklife*, 31 (1985), 59–72, 64.

[10] For contemporary accounts of immigrant midwives in America see L. Wald, *The House
on Henry Street* (New York, 1915; repr., 1971), 59–60; F. E. Crowell, 'The Midwives of
New York', repr. in J. Barrett Litoff, *The American Midwife Debate: A Sourcebook on its
Modern Origins* (Westport, Conn., 1986), 36–49; and G. Abbott, 'The Midwife in Chicago',
Am. J. Sociol. 20/5 (1915), 684–99. See also C. G. Borst, 'The Training and Practice of
Midwives: A Wisconsin Study', *Bull. Hist. Med.* 62 (1988), 606–27, and 'Wisconsin's
Midwives as Working Women: Immigrant Midwives and the Limits of a Traditional Occu-
pation, 1870–1920', *J. Am. Ethnic Hist.* (1989), 24–49; E. R. Declercq, 'The Nature and
Style of Practice of Immigrant Midwives in Early Twentieth-Century Massachusetts', *J. Soc.
Hist.* 19 (1985), 113–29; E. Ewen, *Immigrant Women in the Land of Dollars* (New York, 1985),
129–46.

[11] Joseph DeLee, a prominent obstetrician in Chicago, was one of the strongest voices
attacking the practice of midwives, especially immigrant midwives whom he blamed for the
persistently high infant mortality in America. In an attempt to counter the work of immigrant midwives he set up his own midwifery dispensary in the densely crowded immigrant
area of Chicago in the 1890s. See J. W. Leavitt, 'Joseph DeLee and the Practice of Preventive Obstetrics', *Am. J. Publ. Health*, 78/10 (1988), 1353–9; and S. Sessions Rugh, 'Being
Born in Chicago', *Chicago History*, 15/4 (1986–7), 4–21. For more information concerning
change in the use of doctors and midwives in America see J. W. Leavitt, *Brought to Bed, A
History of Childbearing in America, 1750–1950* (Oxford, 1986).

[12] *JC*, 11 Nov. 1904, 9.

[13] *Di Tsukunft* (*The Future*), 24 Dec. 1886. The same advertisement appeared for five
weeks in a row (see 19 Nov. 1886; 26 Nov. 1886; 10 Dec. 1886; and 17 Dec. 1888).

skills and services differed from those of other midwives in the area.[14] In 1896, however, the Royal Maternity Charity, an organization which worked in the East End and was noted for its employment of qualified midwives, found four Jewish midwives whose qualifications matched their regulations. These Jewish midwives could speak Yiddish and were employed specifically for the Jewish mothers for which the Charity catered.[15] In 1904 twenty-eight midwives were estimated to be 'practising among the Jewish poor' in East London. It is not known how many of these midwives were Jewish, but their level of skill was considered to be high. While only eight of these twenty-eight midwives were trained, it was estimated that at least three-quarters of the total could register with the Central Midwives Board (CMB), a new regulating body introduced by the Midwives' Act passed in 1902. This was much better than for most midwives in the whole of the country, only a quarter of whom were eligible for enrolment under the CMB in 1904.[16]

The Rise of the Trained Midwife

The handywoman or untrained midwife continued to practise on a wide scale in Eastern Europe and in Britain well into the twentieth century. By the end of the nineteenth century, however, an increasing number of trained midwives were working, whose emergence was partly linked to

[14] One problem is that midwives are not always listed in census material. For details on the inaccuracy of census data for women's work in general see S. Alexander, 'Women's Work in Nineteenth-Century London', in E. Whitelegg *et al.* (eds.), *The Changing Experience of Women* (Oxford, 1982). In 1881, the Census listed 2,646 midwives in Britain, whereas in 1892 the number of midwives in Britain was estimated to be between 10,000 and 20,000. Of the 800,000 deliveries that took place in Britain in 1892, 450,000, or approximately 50%, were undertaken solely by midwives without the help of medical practitioners. Most of these midwives were thought to be untrained. *Select Committee on Midwives' Registration*, PP 1892 XIV, 144. The number of midwives seems surprisingly low for the number of deliveries during this period. Unfortunately the other forms of assistance given to mothers are unaccounted for. There were also wide variations in the use of midwives between areas. In 1908 50% of all births in England and Wales were attended by midwives. In St Helens, however, it was as high as 93%, while in Newcastle it was 11.2%. In London, where there was a strong tendency for women to engage medical practitioners (74% of all births), certified midwives covered 25% of the total births. *Report from Commissioner, Inspectors and Others on the Midwives Act: Report of the CMB from its Formation to 31st March 1908* (henceforth *Midwives' Act*), PP 1909 XXXIII, Cd. 4822, Q4361, Q4288, Qs4392–3.

[15] *JC*, 7 Feb. 1896, 15. More information on the Royal Maternity Charity appears in Ch. 6.

[16] *JC*, 11 Nov. 1904, 9. See also *Midwives Act*, PP 1909 XXXIII, Cd. 4507, Qs4181–99.

the increasing pressure to regulate the standard and practice of midwives. Legislative attempts to regulate midwives had appeared in most of the European countries where the Jews were based by the late nineteenth century, and midwifery standards were reputed to be high.[17] In Britain many midwifery training programmes had already been established by the late nineteenth century through nursing associations, voluntary hospitals, various charities, and Poor Law institutions, but the first legislation to regulate midwives was only passed in 1902.[18]

As the training process for midwives became more rigorous, a new type of woman began to enter the trade. This transformation started in England in the late 1870s. Gentlewomen and single women began to take up the profession for the first time, some of whom were inspired by religious and philanthropic motives. Married women with family ties were less able to enter the midwifery courses provided by maternity charities and teaching hospitals than single women.[19] These trends were reinforced by the regulation of the midwifery profession. In 1902 the Midwives Bill established a CMB to register certified midwives and to oversee practice.[20] Until 1905, those without a certificate from the CMB had to produce evidence of one year in bona-fide practice as a midwife, but after that date no unqualified midwife could work without a certificate from the CMB.[21] By 1910 any midwife attending a woman in childbirth without a certificate and without the doctor's direction was liable to prosecution. In emergencies the midwife was compelled to call in a doctor.

Such regulations, however, did not transform midwifery standards overnight. In 1908, it was estimated that 73 per cent of midwives in Britain were practising without any form of antisepsis, and 12 per cent were midwives who fitted the drunken stereotype of Sarah Gamp. Until

[17] Different training courses for midwives in Eastern Europe had different admittance procedures and duration. Some courses lasted only 3 months, while others trained applicants for a year. J. S. Baker, 'Schools for Midwives', *Am. J. Obstet. and the Diseases of Women and Children*, 65 (1912) 256–70, repr. in J. B. Litoff, *The American Midwife Debate*, 157–8.

[18] E. W. Hope and J. Campbell, *Physical Welfare of Mothers and Children* (London, 1917), ii. 19; For more information on the training of midwives in England see J. Donnison, *Midwives and Medical Men: A History of the Struggle for the Control of Childbirth* (London, 1977; 1988).

[19] Donnison, *Midwives and Medical Men*, 92, 221. The same claim was made in 1909, see *Midwives Act*, PP 1909 XXXIII, Cd. 4823, Q1383.

[20] For more information on the development of this legislation and the pressures to have it enforced see Donnison, *Midwives and Medical Men*, 80–1, 161, 163.

[21] Hope and Campbell, *Physical Welfare of Mothers*, 23; JC, 11 Nov. 1904, 9.

the late 1920s a large number of midwives were elderly and often unteachable.[22] One of the reasons for the slow decline of the untrained midwife was her popularity among mothers. Often a more familiar face to mothers, the older type of midwife usually undertook domestic work that the newly trained midwives usually did not perform and was cheaper. Some untrained midwives were also thought to be sources of information on abortion and birth-control which increased their appeal for poor mothers, but horrified many medical practitioners.[23]

None the less, despite the reluctance of many mothers to employ the trained midwife, the Bill of 1902 ultimately eliminated the role of the traditional handywoman.[24] In her stead emerged a new professional who often did not share the same class or cultural backgrounds as her patients. This development had a particular impact on the type of midwives serving immigrant Jewish mothers in East London. During the early years of immigration, many of the Jewish midwives would not have had the benefit of the midwifery programmes developing in various parts of Eastern Europe. Restricted to the Pale of Settlement by Tzarist rule, many Jewish women would have found it difficult to attend midwifery courses run in institutions outside the areas in which they were permitted to reside.[25] Even those who migrated in later years who might have had more midwifery training than their earlier counterparts, found their qualifications were often not recognized in England. While many of them found no shortage of clients among their compatriots in Britain, they were forced to retrain in order to ensure against prosecution for illegal practice.[26] Their difficulties were epitomized by many of the cases who sought help

[22] I. Loudon, 'Deaths in Childbed from the Eighteenth Century to 1935', *Med. Hist.* 30/1 (1986), 1–41, 39.

[23] *Midwives Act*, PP 1909 XXXIII, Cd. 4507 and Cd. 4725, 'Report of the CMB from its Formation to 31 March 1908' (henceforth CMB Report), Qs5164–8, 28. See also F. B. Smith, *The People's Health 1830–1910* (London, 1979), 46.

[24] 24. Loudon 'Deaths in Childbed', 39; Hope and Campbell, *Physical Welfare of Mothers*, 22–3.

[25] Russian and Polish universities limited the number of Jewish students they received by a quota system. It is not known whether such restrictions were also imposed on students attending midwifery courses in hospitals. (S. Baron, *Jews Under the Tsars and Soviets* (New York, 1964; 1973), 118; Ewen, *Immigrant Women in the Land of Dollars*, 44; S. Stahl Weinberg, *The World of Our Mothers* (Durham, NC, 1988), 44, 271.)

[26] *JC*, 11 Nov. 1904, 9. Many Jewish communal organizations publicized the risks the immigrants faced should they practise without English qualifications. Notices prepared in Yiddish were placed in the main areas where the immigrants first arrived. Enquiries were also made on behalf of the women to see whether their foreign qualifications were valid. See Sarah Pyke House, General Meeting Minutes, 1907–10, (VI), 25 Mar. 1908, 55; 28 Oct. 1908, 94; 24 Nov. 1909, 177.

from the Union of Jewish Women (UJW).[27] Many of the immigrant midwives who approached the UJW had trained in Russia but lacked the necessary requirements to practise in England.[28] In 1908, for example, one midwife who had learnt her skills from a Russian doctor in Eastern Europe was forced to retrain because her certificates were not recognized in Britain.[29] Language barriers often made retraining for these women difficult, and a great number of those aided by the UJW had to learn English first before they could obtain the CMB qualifications.[30]

Institutionalized Midwifery Training and Jewish Midwives: The Response to Professionalization

Jewish women not only had to overcome the obstacles of language, but also had to cope with the restrictions of training in institutions. According to the Midwives Act of 1902, midwives could no longer train under the supervision of an older midwife or doctor, and were increasingly expected to learn their profession in lying-in hospitals and Poor Law Infirmaries. This gave preference to applicants with some sort of nurse training, which meant that most who entered the course had hospital experience of some kind.[31] For Jewish women this imposed certain difficulties, as many of the institutions that educated nurses and midwives, whether they were voluntary hospitals or Poor Law infirmaries, were affiliated to the Church of England. Several leading hospitals in London, for instance, insisted on their probationer nurses attending Church of England services and allowed no opportunity for non-Anglicans to attend their own worship places. The nature of the work and routine of the hospital also hindered religious observance, and there were fears of

[27] Set up as a result of the first Jewish Women's Conference held in 1901, this organization campaigned for women's rights within the Jewish community and outside. Its main function, however, was to give advice and information to 'necessitous ladies' seeking employment. Part of its work involved providing loans for women training for suitable professions, such as midwifery and nursing.

[28] In the Jewish ghettos the trained midwife usually had a high-school education and a qualification in nurse training. See Mead Papers (G50) J-R36, pp. 3–4.

[29] Sarah Pyke House, General Meeting Minutes, 1907–10, (VI), 25 Mar. 1908, 55; 28 Oct. 1908, 94; 24 Nov. 1909, 177.

[30] UJW, Executive Committee Minutes, 1902–9 (AJ 26/A.1) and Sarah Pyke House, General Meeting Minutes, 1907–10, (VI).

[31] Hope and Campbell, *Physical Welfare of Mothers*, 22. Most midwives in Britain had a nurse training, hence they were often labelled 'nurse midwife', or 'maternity nurse'. By contrast in the USA and on the Continent of Europe midwifery and nursing were usually two separate occupations.

proselytization.[32] Jewish women could also experience anti-Semitism in these institutions.[33]

Although some of these difficulties were overcome through the establishment of specific Jewish hospitals and the creation of Jewish residential nurses homes in the early twentieth century, other problems remained. One major difficulty for Jewish women, as well as for many working-class women, was the educational requirement demanded by the midwifery courses. Despite compulsory education, established in Britain in 1870, few women possessed the reading and writing skills needed for passing the written examinations set by the CMB, which raised many complaints.[34] For instance, one handywoman of Irish descent who helped to deliver many mothers in East London in the 1920s and 1930s, sometimes by necessity on her own, never obtained the necessary midwifery qualifications because she was unable to read or write.[35] Jewish immigrant women also had the disadvantage that English was not their first language.

[32] *JC*, 1 June 1894. Catholic nurses also faced many constraints in the voluntary hospitals and Poor Law institutions (*The Tablet*, 21 Apr. 1894, 621; 20 Oct. 1894, 605). Religious observance was not only difficult within the daily routine, but could also be contravened when they were asked to perform certain medical tasks. A craniotomy operation, for instance, could be particularly problematic for a Catholic attendant. According to Catholic teaching, the life of the unborn child came before that of the mother, a principle not always adhered to by non-Catholic health professionals. Similar problems could also occur over the issue of abortion. For more information on this and the other difficulties Jewish and Catholic nurses and midwives experienced while training in voluntary hospitals and Poor Law institutions see L. Marks, 'Irish and Jewish Women's Experience of Childbirth in East London, 1870–1939: The Responses of Host Society and Immigrant Communities to Medical Welfare Needs', D.Phil. thesis (Oxford, 1990), 85–91.

[33] For more discussion of this, particularly in the context of the anti-Semitism faced by many Jewish medical practitioners in these institutions and within established medical circles as a whole, see K. Collins, *Go and Learn: The International Story of Jews and Medicine in Scotland* (Aberdeen, 1988), chs. 5, 6, and 7; and P. Weindling, 'The Contribution of Central European Jews to Medical Science and Practice in Britain, the 1930s–1950s', in W. E. Mosse *et al.* (eds.), *Second Chance: Two Centuries of German-Speaking Jews in the United Kingdom* (Tübingen, 1991), 243–54.

[34] A report in 1893 showed that 94.6% of the British population could sign the marriage register, but this distorted the real picture. In reality people's reading and writing abilities often did not reach beyond the ability to sign his or her own name. According to Roberts 'about 20% of the poor working-class were illiterate and about as many nearly so' at the turn of the century, see R. Roberts, *The Classic Slum* (London, 1971; 1977), 129–31. For more information on changes in the educational curriculum and the poor literacy rates among the population as a whole in the late 19th c. see D. Vincent, *Literacy and Popular Culture: England, 1750–1914* (Cambridge, 1989), ch. 3. In 1909, CMB refused to lower their examination standards despite the complaints they received. *Midwives Act*, PP 1909 XXXIII, Cd. 4823, Minutes of Evidence, Q1412; Cd. 4725, CMB Report, 15–16; and Cd. 4507, 39.

[35] Mrs M. S., interviewed by Theresa Patton, London, 26 May 1992, transcript, 4–5, 17–19.

Even those who did have the appropriate educational qualifications, were often handicapped by the expenses involved in training. For most immigrant and working-class women, struggling to make ends meet, the fees for training were beyond their reach. In 1908 the cost of a three-month midwifery course in London institutions varied between £14 and £29. The charge for training with a practising midwife was usually £1 per week together with the incidental expenses and fees for lectures.[36] This was not a cost a midwife could easily recoup once qualified, given that most cases only paid her 10s., which on average worked out to £100 for 200 cases in 1908.[37] In addition to the financial obstacles, were the age and marital conditions imposed by midwifery courses. Most programmes preferred single women and would only accept pupils over the age of 21. Those who came to midwifery through nursing had first to encounter the age limit of 23 set by most voluntary hospitals for nurse training.[38] Poor Law institutions required their probationers to be 25 in 1873, which changed to 21 in 1900.[39] A large number of Jewish women were already married by this age, which prevented many of them from entering midwifery courses.[40]

Apart from the above considerations, other factors also weighed against Jewish women taking up the profession. One of the most important determinants was the class and social structure of the Jewish community. From the mid-nineteenth century, many of the women furnishing the higher ranks of midwifery and nursing in Britain were drawn from the wealthier sections of society, who saw the profession as an attractive alternative to marriage and a means of independence. Often these women were the daughters of clergyman or other professionals, who had received an adequate education, part of which had trained them for a spiritual

---

[36] Those who were lucky could get a scholarship from county councils on condition they undertook to work within a specified area for a given period of time once trained. *Midwives Act*, PP 1909 XXXIII, Cd. 4507, CMB Report, Qs365–6, Qs571–2, Qs751–6, Q1816, Q3638, Q4226, Q5011, 31; Hope and Campbell, *Physical Welfare of Mothers*, 29. For more detailed information on the fees charged by the various institutions see L. Marks, 'Irish and Jewish Women's Experience of Childbirth', 96, table 3.1.

[37] *Midwives Act*, PP 1909 XXXIII, Cd. 4507, CMB Report, Q4194–5.

[38] In a study of four provincial hospitals in Manchester, Leeds, Southampton, and Portsmouth, Maggs found that the average age for recruits in the later 19th c. was between 25 and 35. The age range varied on the demand for nurses in each area, but overall older women were preferred. The same was true in London. See C. Maggs, 'Nurse Recruitment to Four Provincial Hospitals 1881–1921', in C. Davies (ed.), *Rewriting Nursing History* (London, 1980).

[39] M. A. Crowther, *The Workhouse System, 1834–1929* (London, 1981), 177.

[40] *JC*, 3 Feb. 1911, 26. See Ch. 2 for more information on the age of marriage among Jewish immigrants.

vocation suited to nursing and midwifery.[41] No comparable women, however, existed among the Jewish population.[42] Similarly Jewish women were not drawn to the lower ranks of nursing (often a route into midwifery), which many associated with domestic work, an activity despised by most Jewish women.[43]

Given all these constraints on the Jewish women's entry into midwifery and nursing, it is not surprising that few joined these professions. In an attempt to solve this problem, Jewish organizations such as the UJW and Sick Room Helps Society (SRHS) provided loans for Jewish midwives and nurses to train in English institutions.[44] None the less the shortage of Jewish nurses and midwives continued to be a problem.[45] In 1911 the UJW revealed that thirty vacant posts in Jewish institutions for Jewish nursing staff were not being filled.[46] Similarly, only two candidates replied to an advertisement to become a probationer for maternity or midwifery training at the recently opened Jewish Maternity Home in 1911. Both were found inappropriate for the job.[47] One possible reason for the scarcity was that many of those who were helped by the UJW and SRHS emigrated or married after completing their studies and therefore did not practise in East London.[48]

---

[41] M. Vicinus, *Independent Women: Work and Community for Single Women, 1850–1920* (London, 1985), ch. 3. [42] *JC*, 3 Feb. 1911, 26.

[43] This attitude is confirmed by interviews with 300 Jewish immigrants conducted in Manchester. Only one woman of those interviewed worked as a charwoman. (R. Burman, 'Jewish Women and the Household Economy in Manchester, *c*.1890–1920', in D. Cesarani (ed.), *The Making of Modern Anglo-Jewry* (Oxford, 1990), 59.) Many women preferred nursing to domestic service but Jewish women did not go into either occupation, preferring instead to take family work-shop employment which did not isolate them from their families. As Ch. 2 has shown, such work might also have enabled Jewish women to breast-feed their infants better than other mothers. Such work patterns among Jewish women contrasted with Irish immigrant women who entered domestic service and nursing in large numbers, seeing it as a means of climbing the social ladder. See Marks, 'Working Wives and Working Mothers', 16–7, and 'Irish and Jewish Women's Experience of Childbirth', 28–9, 92–4. In contrast to their East European sisters before them, German-Jewish women refugees coming to Britain in the 1930s entered domestic service in large numbers. Domestic employment was often their only means of securing entry into the country. See T. Kushner, 'An Alien Occupation: Jewish Refugees and Domestic Service in Britain, 1933–1948', in Mosse *et al.* (eds.), *Second Chance*, 555–78.

[44] Between 1903 and 1909, the UJW advised and placed 35 Jewish women in hospitals and infirmaries as nurses, 3 of whom became probationers at the London Hospital and 25 of whom were registered as midwives (*JC*, 1 Feb. 1907, 30; 1 Jan. 1909).

[45] The scarcity of Jewish nurses was one of the issues at the Jewish Women's Conference in London in 1902. See UJW, *AR* (1902), 13 and *AR* (1912), 15–16.

[46] *JC*, 8 Sept. 1911. [47] *JC*, 9 Feb. 1912, 42.

[48] The CMB reported similar problems. Many pupil midwives did not practise midwifery once qualified. Only 16.7% of the successful midwifery candidates at the City of London Maternity Home and London Hospital intended to practise in 1913 (*Midwives' Act*, PP 1913

Medical Care during Times of Sickness and Confinement

The shortage of Jewish midwives and nurses in East London had serious repercussions for Jewish mothers giving birth in the years 1870–1939. Without recourse to midwives from their own community, they were forced to turn elsewhere for help. Much of their experience with these services was affected by the nature of medical and maternity provision during these years. In the late nineteenth century, most maternity care, other than that offered by the parish, was purchased privately by those able to pay, or supplied by local charities. Some women also had access to care through friendly societies. Membership of these societies, however, was restricted to those whose husbands were in regular employment, and the medical provision such societies offered did not necessarily extend to wives or include maternity care.[49]

The financial expense of attendance in childbirth therefore rested primarily on the mother and her family, causing great hardship to countless mothers. In 1870, the average fee charged by an English midwife was 7s. After the Midwives Act of 1902 a registered midwife could cost between 2s. 6d. and 21s. while an unregistered midwife usually charged 5s. By 1910 the average fee for a midwife was 10s.[50] This was a large sum for most working-class families. Before the First World War a woman was lucky if her husband gave her 25s. regularly every week. Out of this she was expected to pay for rent, food, and clothing for the whole family.[51] Nothing remained for the additional outlay expected for maternity. On top of payment for the midwife there might be the additional expenses of hiring a nurse or someone to do the housework during the first few days after the birth, and the provision of necessities for the baby. The frequent loss of wages on the part of the mother during her confinement also made these costs harder to bear. In all, decent maternity care before the First World War could amount to as much as £5.[52]

The financial anxieties of mothers were not eased by the introduction

---

XXXIV, CMB Report, Cd. 6755, app.; see also *Midwives' Act*, PP 1909 XXXIII, CMB Report, Cd. 4822, Q4189 and Q4361).

[49] M. W. Flinn, 'Medical Services under the New Poor Law', in D. Fraser, *The New Poor Law in the Nineteenth Century* (London, 1976).

[50] Chamberlain and Richardson, 'Life and Death', 33. E. Ross, 'Labour and Love: Rediscovering London's Working-Class Mothers, 1870–1918', in J. Lewis (ed.), *Labour and Love: Women's Experience of Home and Family, 1850–1940* (Oxford, 1986), 78.

[51] M. Llewelyn Davies (ed.), *Maternity: Letters from Working Women* (London, 1915; repr. 1984), 5. See also M. Pember Reeves, *Round About a Pound a Week* (London, 1913; repr. 1984), 75–93. [52] Ross, 'Labour and Love', 78; Llewelyn Davies, *Maternity*, 5.

of National Health Insurance in 1911 which made no special provision for childbirth. By this Act, husbands who were in full employment could receive 30*s.* on behalf of their wives, but women did not receive this directly.[53] The creation of Maternity Benefit in 1913 met, for the first time, some of the costs women were expected to pay for their confinements. This was limited, however, to those whose husbands had regular work. Given the prevalence of casual labour and unemployment in East London, many women could not hope to claim the benefit. In 1913 one East London maternity hospital reported that many of their mothers, whose husbands were involved in dock work and casual labour, could not 'even get work to keep their Insurance cards up to date (or for 26 stamps)' and were 'therefore ineligible even for Maternity Benefit'. Even those who could claim maternity benefit found it insufficient.[54] Until 1918 the maternity benefit, like other social benefits, was also restricted to those who had been a member of a friendly society before the passing of the National Insurance Act, and to those who had been British citizens for over five years. This had severe implications for Jewish immigrants, many of whom remained 'aliens' because they could not afford the £10 charged for naturalization.[55] Many Jewish women therefore found that they were unable to draw maternity benefit because of their immigrant status, and even when it was possible they usually did not receive the full amount.[56]

Few mothers in East London could therefore rely on the maternity benefit, but they had the advantage of living in an area which hosted a large range of charitable maternity care. East London not only had a high number of teaching hospitals, but also numerous district nursing associations, dispensaries, and medical missions which offered free district and in-patient midwifery care.[57] Although free, such services made certain

[53] E. Ross, 'Women's Neighbourhood Sharing in London before World War One', *Hist. Workshop J.* 15 (1983), 4–27.

[54] East End Maternity Home, *AR* (1913), 19–20.

[55] Together with the expenses involved in becoming a British citizen, many Jewish immigrants were put off by the lengthy process involved in attaining citizenship which was often full of delays imposed by the Home Office. Not surprisingly the number of immigrants who were naturalized was very low. See E. R. Smith, 'East End Jews in Politics, 1918–1939: A Study in Class and Ethnicity', Ph.D. thesis (Leicester, 1990), 26.

[56] For more information on the disadvantages Jewish immigrants faced in claiming National Insurance and other social benefits see S. Cohen, 'Anti-Semitism, Immigration Controls and the Welfare State', *Critical Social Policy*, 13 (1985), 73–92. Jewish immigrants also suffered discrimination from the regulation imposed by the laws governing Unemployment Insurance. This was a problem which continued into the inter-war years. See Smith, 'East End Jews', 240–1.

[57] The amenities provided by these organizations are explored further in Chs. 4 and 6.

demands of their patients. As in the case of Jewish women training to be midwives and nurses, what was especially problematic for Jewish patients was the religious orientation of many of the agencies providing such care. Much of the nursing in the nineteenth century was undertaken by Anglican religious bodies, who attached a spiritual message to their medical care.[58] This was not only true of medical missions, who had a powerful evangelical purpose behind their medical care, but also of district nursing associations which had been strongly influenced by the new religious zeal of the mid-nineteenth century.[59] Voluntary hospitals were less concerned about converting souls, but were frequently patronized by organizations from the Church of England and had an Anglican chaplain attached to the hospital staff. No distinction was made as to the religion of patients, but most hospitals and district nursing associations had prayers in the ward or at the bedside in the home. This could make non-Anglicans feel awkward. It was bad enough for the patients to feel an object of charity, let alone to feel that their beliefs and customs did not comply with those caring for them.[60]

Although by the late nineteenth century a number of hospitals had secured some arrangements for their non-Anglican patients to be visited by those of their faith, undermining some of the discomfort experienced by non-Anglican patients, certain difficulties none the less remained. For Jews a fundamental problem in having non-Jews administer medical care was when death occurred—particularly during childbirth. According to Jewish law the life of the mother is more important than that of the unborn child, which could occasionally present anxieties when non-Jews attended a difficult childbirth.[61] Complications could also arise over the need for certain Jewish sacraments to be administered before death. Jewish law indicates that a Jewish dead body should be watched and prepared

---

[58] For more information on the way in which religion shaped medical and nursing care in late Victorian Britain see F. K. Prochaska, 'Body and Soul: Bible Nurses and the Poor in Victorian London', *Hist. Research*, 60/143 (1987), 336–48.

[59] During a discussion over whether the Jewish community should provide a Jewish dispensary in East London, great concern was expressed over the enticement of the Jewish poor by the Yiddish-speaking staff working in the dispensaries provided by the medical missions (*JC*, 6 Nov. 1896, 16; 20 Nov. 1896). [60] See Chs. 4 to 6.

[61] According to Jakobovits, Jewish law insists that in any 'mortal conflict between mother and child', a mother's life 'enjoys priority, if necessary at the expense of the child, provided its head or the greater part of its body had not yet emerged from the birth-canal (which is the legal definition of birth). Judaism, therefore . . . would regard it as a grave offence against the sanctity of life to allow a mother to perish in order to save her unborn child' (Chief Rabbi, Dr I. Jakobovits, 'Jewish Medical Ethics', St Paul's Lecture (publication), 23 Nov. 1976, 2). This ruling was totally the reverse of Catholic teaching. See n. 32 above.

solely by Jews and buried within 24 hours, a custom not usual in English society. An additional ritual which could be problematic was the circumcision, or *bris*, of baby boys on the eighth day after birth. Jewish dietary laws also made institutional care and district nursing of Jewish patients complicated. By the late nineteenth century most voluntary hospitals in East London provided kosher food, but difficulties remained, particularly for those caring for the Jewish patients on the district. Most non-Jewish nurses were not trained in the requirements of kosher kitchens and kosher cooking, an important concern in most East End Jewish homes no matter how small and poverty-stricken they might be.

Further complexities for Jewish patients could also arise as a result of their linguistic difficulties. Many of the first generation of East European Jewish immigrants only spoke Yiddish, making communication with health professionals hard. This was especially difficult in cases of confinement, as the Chairman of the Royal Maternity Charity stressed in 1896. His compassion was great for the 'poor foreign Jewess' who 'could seldom speak the language' and was 'in the midst of strangers . . . in the hour of her trial and distress'.[62] One midwife who worked for London Hospital stated that many of her patients 'could only speak Yiddish', and she often 'found communication with them difficult'.[63] On hospital premises some patients spoke Yiddish which could ease some of the communication barriers. Similarly, sometimes neighbours were on hand to translate for health professionals working on the district level.

For Jewish mothers, childbirth was therefore not only an event which caused financial and medical anxieties, but also one which raised apprehensions over religious and cultural matters which extended beyond the birth itself to questions of maintaining the family and the household while she was incapacitated. For those Jewish women unable to call on their family or friends, or to engage someone who understood their religious and cultural background, childbirth could be a very stressful occasion. Evidence presented by a non-Jewish midwife, Mrs Ayers, to the Royal Commission on Alien Immigration, revealed the great hostility shown by some carers who lacked sympathy for the culture of those they attended. Protesting against what she saw as the improper behaviour of her Jewish patients, Mrs Ayers was particularly offended by their offer of a glass of brandy rather than the customary cup of tea. Similarly, she protested that it was difficult to get rid of the children and husbands from

[62] *JC*, 7 Feb. 1896, 15.
[63] Cited in A. E. Clark Kennedy, *The London: A Study in the Voluntary Hospital System* (London, 1963), ii. 191.

the birth chamber in Jewish homes.[64] Her statements are somewhat surprising given the taboos concerning childbirth within the Jewish religion, but they indicate the clashes that could occur between Jewish mothers and those who attended them. Another non-Jewish midwife attending a Jewish woman in Whitechapel in 1913 made similar remarks, complaining that the patient continually recited Hebrew prayers, and was so noisy that she was unable to open the windows or the door of a very hot birthchamber for fear of attracting outside attention. This situation, she argued, was made worse by the fact that other women in the house joined in the wailing. Much of the tension on this occasion was also increased by the fear of the patient that her baby was going to be born dead. Lacking a common language and not appreciating the cultural values of the patient she attended, the midwife was unable to allay such anxieties.[65] Such difficulties as shown by this midwife and Mrs Ayers highlight the very real tensions that could emerge between Jewish mothers and non-Jewish carers.

Jewish Communal Institutions Providing Aid During Confinement

Recognizing the difficulties many Jewish women experienced in giving birth in the host society, a number of Jewish organizations had set up their own kinds of aid from early on. Many of the resources they offered to women in childbirth were shaped by the nature of medical relief as a whole. Prior to 1861 most of the help supplied to parturient Jewish women rested with a number of synagogues. This changed in 1861 when medical relief and maternity care became the responsibility of the JBG, funded by grants from the conjoint synagogues. As part of this development the JBG provided its own dispensary and medical officer, and supplied expensive medicines such as quinine and cod-liver oil, as well as other things such as wine, gin, brandy, blankets, bath tickets, coal and food. A subscription was also taken out with the Royal Maternity Charity which secured the attendance of a midwife and other help for poor lying-in women.[66]

[64] *RC Alien Immigration*, PP 1903 IX Q 9425; *JC*, 22 Aug. 1902, 14.
[65] Case reported in Midwifery School Register, 1911–19, British Hospital for Mothers and Babies, Woolwich (GLRO file H14/BMB/C1/1/1).
[66] JBG, *AR* (1862), 18, 40.

By the early 1870s the JBG discovered that its medical relief was surpassing general relief and seemed to have expanded beyond what was deemed to be necessary. In 1870 it was estimated that the number of attendances at the surgery had increased by 380 per cent in the past 8 years, while the number of general applicants had increased by only 25 per cent.[67] Disturbed by this trend, the JBG decided to discontinue its outdoor medical relief in 1873, believing that adequate medical provision for the poor was made available under the Poor Law. Similarly, the JBG claimed 'many of those who sought the medical officer of the Board were, in reality, *poor*, but not *ill*, and that they so sought him as a means of obtaining food, or its equivalent'.[68] For similar reasons the JBG also discontinued its dispensary in 1879, refusing to reopen it in response to a plea from the Federation of Synagogues in 1891.[69]

Nevertheless the JBG did not entirely abandon the provision of medical relief. It promised to continue its maternity subscription and to supply medical extras not provided by the Parish. In addition to this, it gave some financial relief to women in childbirth. Indeed, as Tables 3.1 to 3.3 show, the general annual expenditure on overall relief and medical relief increased greatly in the years following 1873, rising most sharply in the late 1890s and early twentieth century. After the National Insurance Act of 1911 the total expenditure by the JBG on medical relief did not diminish and continued to be a large proportion of the total expenditure on relief, indicating the difficulties Jewish immigrants had in claiming the benefits under the National Insurance scheme. By the 1920s the sum spent on medical relief was still high, but no longer constituted such a large percentage of the total relief, indicating the cessation of immigration and the stabilization of the Jewish population in these years.

Table 3.1 demonstrates that, although constituting only a small percentage of the total sums spent on medical relief, the money allotted to maternity and midwifery cases was also increasing in these years, particularly in the 1890s and early twentieth century. However, with the exception of 1917, 1921, and 1923, expenses on maternity cases began to diminish after 1913. While this might have been the result of the Maternity Benefit Act of 1913, this is unlikely given the disadvantages Jewish women suffered in obtaining such benefits. Such a decline more probably reflected the diminishing immigration after 1914, as well as the increasing

---

[67] Ibid. (1870).   [68] Ibid. (1873), 23. Emphasis in the original.
[69] Ibid. (1891), 10–11.

TABLE 3.1. *Maternity grants as percentage of total money relief from the JBG, 1872–1893*

Year	Total money relief	Maternity cases	Maternity cases as % of total
1872	£1,891	£52 15s	2.80
1873	£2,091	£72 10s	3.39
1874	£2,010	£60	2.98
1875	£2,065	£60 5s	2.90
1876	£2,343	£48 5s	2.05
1877	£2,791	£56 10s	2.04
1878	£3,397	£62	1.82
1879	£3,451	£87 10s	2.55
1880	£4,069	£77 15s	1.89
1881	£4,283	£69 15s	1.61
1882	£4,381	£115	2.62
1883	£4,268	£99 10s	2.34
1884	£4,395	£79	1.80
1885	£4,566	£99	2.17
1886	£6,103	£130 10s	2.13
1887	£5,324	£119 10s	2.24
1888	£5,472	£132	2.41
1889	£5,147	£114 10s	2.23
1890	£5,884	£122	2.07
1891	£8,352	£167	2.0
1892	£9,049	£243	2.68
1893	£10,822	£343	3.17

Source: JBG *ARs* (1872–93), expenditure tables.

maternity care offered by voluntary hospitals and other charitable agencies during and after the First World War.

Supplementing the medical work of the JBG was the provision made by the Visitation Committee of the United Synagogue set up in 1881, and by the Ladies Conjoint Visiting Committee of the JBG founded in 1882. Both organizations visited the sick Jewish poor in their own homes, in hospitals, workhouses, and other such institutions. In 1884 the Ladies Committee began to supply nourishment and clothing in times of illness, and engaged a Jewish nurse in 1885 to care for the sick poor. Trained at The London Hospital, this nurse was maintained at the expense of Lady

TABLE 3.2. *Subscription to maternity charity and relief for midwifery cases as percentage of total medical relief from the JBG, 1872–1893*

Year	Total medical relief balance	Subscription to maternity charity	Subscription as % of medical relief	Special midwifery cases	Midwifery cases as % of medical relief
1872	£380 11s 5d	£6 5s	1.57	£27 15s	7.35
1873	£357 6s 6d	£4 3s	1.12	£14 17s 6d	4.20
1874	£384 8s 9d	£16 15s	4.43	£11 12s	3.12
1875	£400 8s 8d	£15 15s	4.66	£35	10.20
1876	£343 4s 8d	£29 8s	7.25	£38 5s	9.5
1877	£381	£26 5s	6.82	£27	7.08
1878	£378 16s 5d	£23 6s	6.08	£25 14s 6d	6.86
1879	£399 15s 3d	£22 5s	5.5	£12 15s	3.25
1880	£301 6s 2d	£26 9s	8.64		
1881	£324 2s 8d	£24 7s	7.40		
1882	£310 15s 6d	£26 9s	8.40		
1883	£319 10s 8d	£26 5s	8.15		
1884	£264 5s 3d	£26 5s	9.85		
1885	£316 12s 8d	£15 15s	4.56		
1886	£351 1s 11d	£15 15s	4.55		
1887	£280 15s 11d	£15 15s	5.70		
1888	£268 15s 1d	£15 15s	5.95		
1889	£236 0s 4d	£15 15s	6.78		
1890	£255 10s 6d	£15 15s	6.25		
1891	£275 0s 9d	£15 15s	5.82		
1892	£365 16s 1d	£15 15s	4.37		
1893	£325 16s	£15 15s	4.91		

Source: JBG *ARs* (1872–93), expenditure tables.

Rothschild and Mrs Lionel Lucas.[70] The Committee also established a nourishment fund for the sick in 1886.

By the early 1890s, however, the JBG realized that despite these measures certain medical needs remained. An investigation carried out by a JBG committee in 1895 revealed that poor Jews had a much greater number of their infants dying than wealthier Jews. While infant mortality

[70] JBG, *AR* (1886).

TABLE 3.3. *Breakdown of funds at free disposal of the JBG with special reference to medical relief and maternity cases, 1893–1930*

Year	Total relief given	Medical relief	Medical relief as % of total relief	Expenses on maternity cases	Maternity cases as % of total relief
1893–5	£51,644	£1,225	2.4	£944	1.8
1896–1900	£84,800	£2,184	2.6	£1,214	1.4
1901–5	£81,973	£3,697	4.5	£1,545	1.8
1906–10	£115,988	£8,408	7.2	£1,599	1.4
1911–15	£80,785	£12,792	15.8	£557	0.7
1916–20	£128,782	£12,494	9.7	£351*	0.3
1921–5	£145,731	£11,147	7.6	£547*	0.4
1926–30	£134,401	£9,878	7.3	£182	0.13

* Although the amount of money given to maternity cases was decreasing overall, the sum increased for no accountable reasons in 1917 and 1921.

Source: JBG *ARs* (1893–1930), expenditure tables.

formed 20 per cent of the total deaths among Jews, and 36 per cent among middle-class Jews, among pauper Jews infant mortality constituted 81 per cent of the total figure.[71] These findings were substantiated by a group of workers who visited and relieved the Jewish poor. The committee concluded that many of the infant deaths were attributable to the living and working conditions of East London and inadequate nursing among the Jewish poor. Seeing many of these deaths as preventable, the JBG recommended increasing the number of skilled nurses for the Jewish poor.[72] One Jewish philanthropist, Mrs Lionel Lucas, had already begun to address the problem in 1891 when out of her own money she paid for two Jewish nurses to care for the Jewish poor, one of whom attended confinements.[73] These nurses, however, could not cover the desperate needs for nursing among the Jewish poor.

[71] These figures do not give an accurate account of infant mortality because they do not measure the number of infant deaths per 1,000 live births. For more accurate statistics on Jewish infant mortality see Ch. 2. More prosperous Jews began to limit their family size from the 1850s which could explain their lower rate of infant mortality compared with poorer Jews. (I am grateful to Richard Smith for making this point.)
[72] JBG Committee on Infant Mortality, *Report*, 4 June 1895, 3, 6, 7 (Charles Booth Collection, LSE file: B197). JC, 10 Apr. 1896, 11.
[73] These nurses worked under the direction of the Ladies Conjoint Visiting Committee. *JC*, 31 Mar. 1905.

The Sick Room Helps Society and its Home Helps Scheme

With the creation of the SRHS in 1895, a new service appeared.[74] Established under the auspices of the JBG and the guidance of Mrs Alice Model, the SRHS nursed the sick poor and maternity cases in their own homes.[75] Partly inspired by a similar Jewish foundation in Frankfurt am Main, the 'Hauspflege Verein', the object of the society was to 'provide women help in all cases where Jewish mothers are unable, owing to poverty, to provide for themselves proper nursing and have no relatives to look after the home during their illness'.[76] Based in Underwood Street, the heart of Whitechapel and the East End, its services were available to a wide number of Jews living in the area. All cases needing help were to be referred to the SRHS by the Ladies' Conjoint Committee of the JBG or by sick nurses funded by Mrs Lionel Lucas.[77]

The SRHS undertook to supply nurses to its sick poor, and midwives to parturient women, but its chief provision was in the supply of home helps.[78] These home helps were to fill in the gaps between the visits of the nurse, as many district nurses were over-worked and had inadequate time to care sufficiently for the patient. In addition home helps attended to the work usually performed by mothers, such as housework, shopping, and cooking as well as child care. The work of the home helps gave the mother the much-needed mental and physical break from chores which otherwise hindered any real convalescence.[79] Poor mothers who had formerly 'grudged themselves even a few days of enforced idleness', the SRHS claimed, no longer feared loss of time during confinements because of the home-helps scheme. Difficulties which had frequently occurred as a result of premature activity were now, the SRHS stated, eliminated.[80]

One of the guiding principles of the SRHS was the 'maintenance of the

---

[74] See also L. Marks ' "Dear Old Mother Levy's", The Jewish Maternity Home and Sick Room Helps Society 1895–1970', *Soc. Hist. Med.* 3/1, (1990) 61–88. For a discussion resulting from this article see E. Fox, 'The Jewish Maternity Home and Sick Room Helps Society, 1895–1939: A Reply to Lara Marks', and my response 'Ethnicity, Religion and Healthcare', both in *Soc. Hist. Med.* 4/1 (1991), 117–28.

[75] Mrs Alice Model, later labelled the 'Florence Nightingale of the Jewish Community' was the leading figure in the SRHS for over 40 years (*JC*, 29 Sept. 1911).

[76] *JC*, 15 Nov. 1901, 21.

[77] *JC*, 3 Jan. 1896. The JBG agreed that it would refer its cases of pregnant women to the SRHS at the cost of 10s. per case (JBG, *AR* (1900), 21).

[78] From 1912 many of the nurses supplied came from the Queen's Jubilee nursing organization.   [79] *JC*, 3 Jan. 1896, 9.

[80] *JC*, 9 Dec. 1904, 28.

integrity of the home when the mother is laid up through sickness or during the lying-in period'.[81] A mother's infirmity often placed a heavy burden on the husband, who was forced to forgo his daily earnings in order to care for his wife and the children, ultimately entailing destitution for all concerned. It was in this context that organizers of the SRHS defended themselves against the idea that their work pauperized those it was caring for. As they claimed, 'All that tends to improve the conditions of health, must increase the prospects of self-dependence among those who are not only immersed in the depths of poverty, but whose children likewise have . . . succeeded to an inevitable heritage of sickness and suffering.'[82]

Jewish home helps were essential in a situation where Jewish nurses were scarce. Whilst nurses of whatever religion could undertake the general nursing care, the need for someone with a knowledge of Jewish dietary habits remained. Such requirements had made the SRHS adopt a policy which was ahead of its time. Many other nursing and midwifery associations, keen to distinguish their medical expertise from domestic work did not embrace the idea of home helps as fully as the SRHS. The Royal Maternity Charity, for instance, which cared for a substantial number of Jewish patients in East London, provided assistance at the time of delivery but no post-natal care.[83] Similarly district nurses, such as those employed by the East London Nursing Association, usually did not undertake the preparation of food or any housework.[84] Some district nurses, such as Mrs Ranyard's Bible nurses or those from Catholic nursing associations which nursed among the Irish poor in East London, undertook some housework alongside their nursing care, but this was not given the same priority as the care provided by the home helps supplied by the SRHS.[85] What was unusual about the SRHS was therefore not that it provided help within the home, but rather the balance it achieved in the division of

---

[81] *Charity Organization Review*, Apr. 1914, 187.   [82] *JC*, 30 Oct. 1896.

[83] E. Black, *The Social Politics of Anglo-Jewry, 1880–1920* (Oxford, 1988), 162.

[84] M. E. Baly, *A History of the Queen's Nursing Institute, 1887–1987* (London, 1987).

[85] *Catholic Directory* (1890), 439–40; E. W. Whitehead, *A Form of Catholic Action: The Little Sisters of the Assumption* (London, 1947), 58–62; *Magazine of the Sacred Heart* (Parish Magazines of St Mary and St Michael Catholic Church, Commercial Road—kept at THL), Aug. 1927, p. iii; Notes on the background of the Little Sisters of the Assumption (NSP archive). For more detail about Mrs Ranyard's nurses see Prochaska, 'Body and Soul', 336–48 and F. Ducrocq, 'The London Biblewomen and Nurses Mission 1857–1880: Class Relations/Women's Relations', in B. J. Harris and J. K. McNamara (eds.), *Women and the Structure of Society* (Durham, NC, 1984). More information on the comparison between the SRHS and the Catholic nursing associations appears in Marks, 'Irish and Jewish Women's Experience of Childbirth', ch. 4.

domestic labour and professional nursing. It was careful to stress that while the home help was a 'valuable adjutant' to the midwife and nurse, providing hot water and helping with the patient generally, on no account was she to 'interfere with professional duties'.[86]

One Catholic nursing association working in East London, the Nursing Sisters of the Poor (also known as Little Sisters of the Assumption), were assisted by Lady Servants or Lady Helpers, whose task was to provide clothes, medicine, and food for the patients, and undertake the menial housework tasks. The background of these Lady Helpers and the motives behind their employment were somewhat different from those of the home helps engaged by the SRHS. While the Lady Helpers came from a wealthy background and their purpose was seen as breaking down the antagonisms between the classes, thus unifying the Catholic Church, many of the home helps of the SRHS came from the same poor background as their patients.[87] Many of them were Jewish widows or deserted wives struggling on the poverty line, which made them more able to understand the cultural and financial difficulties of the poor women they served. Indeed, many home helps used their work to stave off destitution.[88] As a letter to Mrs Model pointed out,

with very few exceptions, the 'Helps' are taken from that class of helpless widows who formerly had to receive weekly dole from our Boards of Guardians for the maintenance of their families. Surely, it is no small matter to have introduced a useful and helpful class of work, and thus to have given these poor women the opportunity of earning their own bread.[89]

One Jewish woman interviewed remembered the financial desperation which pushed a home help to aid her mother during her confinement in 1921, in spite of her own illness.

She was a middle-aged widow who was very very ailing. In the bedroom there was my mother in her bed and across the way there was an old-fashioned sofa and this poor woman used to lie on the sofa and she would ask me to run down to the shops to get her headache powder. And if she went shopping I had to go with her

---

[86] *Charity Organization Review*, Apr. 1914, 187.
[87] Whitehead, *A Form of Catholic Action*, 64. By contrast the nuns, whose life was meant to be one of moderation and frugality, were closer to the living conditions of those they served.
[88] *JC*, 9 Dec. 1904, 28. A similar practice existed in rural Poor Law institutions from the 18th c. Many of the elderly and sick who were dependent on the parish were cared for by women who were long-term recipients of relief themselves (M. E. Fissell, 'The "Sick and Drooping Poor" in Eighteenth-Century Bristol and its Region', *Soc. Hist. Med.* 2/1 (1989), 35–58, 43).   [89] *JC*, 9 Dec. 1904, 28.

because she couldn't carry the shopping bag. I was only about six and a half years old then. She begged my mother to give her a good report when the 'lady' from the [Jewish Maternity] home called to inspect, because she needed the money.[90]

Arguing that the home helps provided a valuable service for the community, the SRHS strongly advocated that they should be properly remunerated. Viewing their home helps as 'scientific charwomen', the SRHS felt their home helps did 'arduous' work and did not want to appear to be doing anything which savoured of 'sweating' their employees.[91] Home helps often worked from 8 in the morning till 8 at night. They were paid according to the number of days they worked. By 1913 their payment ranged from 5s. a week for part-time work to 11s. a week for full-time employment.[92]

Remuneration and Funding

Eager not only to promote independence and self-help among those it employed, the SRHS also fostered the same spirit among its patients through its Provident Fund set up in 1897. Based on a model established by the Jewish organization in Frankfurt am Main and other nursing associations, the SRHS Provident Fund was a scheme to which mothers contributed on a weekly basis. Thus the scheme not only made provision for the mother and her family when she was ill, but managed to 'educate' her 'in habits of thrift' and prevented the 'stigma of pauperization'.[93]

Contributions to the Provident Fund were built up slowly. In 1897 Jewish mothers contributed £31 in pennies. This was a considerable sum for them, but could only cover 6 per cent of the Society's costs. By 1904, however, their contributions amounted to £630, or 29 per cent of the total expenditure (£2,200).[94] While 1,543 cases were attended by the Society in 1904, 2,450 poor women were contributing weekly payments of a penny to insure cover during periods of confinement.[95] Such weekly

---

[90] Miss T.G., interviewed by L. Marks, London, 22 Jan. 1988, transcript p. 4.

[91] *JC*, 11 July 1913, 22.

[92] *Charity Organization Review*, Apr. 1914, 188. This again contrasted the work of the Catholic Lady Helpers and the nursing nuns who worked for free. Whitehead, *A Form of Catholic Action*, 64.

[93] *JC*, 24 Nov. 1899, 23; 15 Nov. 1901. Unlike the SRHS Catholic nursing organizations in East London provided free nursing care. Nursing nuns were not even allowed to accept a cup of tea for fear that patients would feel inadequate. To survive, the Catholic nursing associations relied on donations, subscriptions, and door-to-door collections. *Catholic Directory* (1890), 439–40; Publicity leaflet calling for donations (NSP archive).

[94] Black, *The Social Politics of Anglo-Jewry*, 162.

[95] In this year 80–90 women a week were being helped by home helps (*JC*, 9 Dec. 1904, 28).

instalments, although small in amount, were significant in saving the society from collapsing in 1908. Although not enough to cover the full costs of the expenditure, the weekly payments from the mothers covered a third of the society's expenditure in 1909. This proved that the society was no longer merely dependent on philanthropy, but was founded on the core of the people it intended to serve.[96] By 1911 almost 5,000 provident members contributed £1,300, equalling 36 per cent of the Society's total budget. The number of provident members assisted now also outweighed the charitable cases sent by the JBG.[97]

Preventive Work

Much of the work of the SRHS constituted preventive health care which was already a concern in the world outside and within the wider Jewish community. From the mid-nineteenth century, mothers' meetings set up by various Protestant and Catholic groups had become an important part of the social scene. Although initially spiritual in aim, these meetings were a crucial contact for mothers. By the turn of the century mothers' meetings were increasingly focusing their attention on infant care.[98] Lessons on infant and domestic management and sewing, all of which were seen as being the essence of 'good motherhood', were provided by various Jewish mothers' meetings.

In 1895 an association called the East End Jewish Mothers' Meetings was established by Mrs E. Jacobs and Miss Bella Lowy under the auspices of the JBG. This organization helped organize mothers' meetings for Jewish women in East London. By 1898 about fifty women attended the meetings held twice a week. During these meetings needlework was

---

[96] *JC*, 5 Feb. 1909. Another institution which was built up on pennies contributed by the Jewish poor was the London Jewish Hospital. At the end of the 19th c. many poor Jewish immigrants were campaigning for the establishment of a separate Jewish Hospital, arguing that non-Jewish hospitals such as the London were not meeting their needs. Unlike the Sick Room Helps Society which was supported by the established community, the campaign for the London Jewish Hospital initially met with strong resistance from wealthier members of the community. Finally in 1919 the London Jewish Hospital was established. For more details on the history of the London Jewish Hospital and the tensions between the established community and the immigrants on the issue see G. Black, 'Health and Medical Care of the Jewish Poor in the East End of London, 1880–1939', Ph.D. thesis (Leicester, 1987), Ch. 7.

[97] *JC*, 24 Feb. 1911, 23. The rise in provident members and the decline in cases sent by the JBG might have been linked to the introduction of National Insurance in that year, although, as already incidated above, Jewish immigrants were handicapped in claiming such benefits. See Black, *Social History of Anglo-Jewry*, 163.

[98] See F. K. Prochaska, 'A Mother's Country: Mothers' Meetings and Family Welfare in Britain 1850–1950', *Hist.* (1989), 379–99, 391.

taught and readings were given alongside health talks. Mothers could also buy clothes at the cost of the material only. Reported as 'glad to attend these meetings', the mothers saw them as an escape from their 'cheerless surroundings'. Such meetings provided an important source of support, offering not only a social occasion, but also an opportunity for mothers to gain advice, and, in later years, to have the health of their infants checked by a doctor.[99]

In addition to such meetings, mothers were visited in their own homes by a district nurse lent by the JBG, as well as by Jewish ladies from the Association and West London Synagogue. During these visits advice was given, and women were taught how to economize their household budgets.[100] This supplemented the work of sanitary inspectors and health visitors originally appointed by the JBG in the late nineteenth century, whose aim was to educate the Jewish poor in East London in habits of cleanliness.[101] By the turn of the century health visitors were increasingly focusing their attention on proper infant care, and were circulating leaflets in Yiddish and English on proper infant management.[102] Jewish girls were also drilled in the disciplines of proper domestic management and infant care through various girls' clubs and the Domestic Training Home established in 1893.[103] Alongside these activities, staff from the SRHS provided lessons in sewing, infant feeding, and house management.[104] Special attention was directed towards expectant mothers. Following the trend set by the parliamentary debate concerning midwifery standards in 1902, visitors for the Provident Fund of the SRHS took the 'opportunity to advise the mothers as to the importance of securing properly qualified medical men and midwives to attend them in confinement'.[105]

According to one writer to the *Jewish Chronicle* such preventive work was vital. While admitting that the Jewish poor did not waste money on beer and alcohol, the correspondent still admonished Jewish mothers for

[99] For more information on the meetings see *East End Inquiry Commission*, June 1898, 14–15, pamphlet in United Synagogue Council Minutes, vol. 2, 1891–1902 (CRO archive); *Caroline Franklin, 1863–1935: An Appreciation* (book written and printed by friends for private circulation, 1936—copy held at British Library, (10861 cc.15)), 43–4; *JC*, 9 May 1902.

[100] *East End Inquiry Commission*, June 1898, 14; *Caroline Franklin*, 43–4.

[101] *JC*, 14 July 1901.

[102] C. Davies, 'The Health Visitor as Mother's Friend: A Woman's Place in Public Health, 1900–1914' *Soc. Hist. Med.* 1/1, (1988), 39–59, 52.

[103] Jewish Association for the Protection of Girls and Women, *AR* (1896–8), 18; *JC*, 9 Aug. 1895, 5, and 3 Mar. 1899, 12.   [104] *JC*, 9 July 1909.

[105] *JC*, 28 Nov. 1902.

their incapacity for thrift and called for their better domestic education.[106] Similarly the SRHS argued that the teaching on hygiene could not be left to neighbours and friends, who 'having no sense of cleanliness or order in their own dwellings', could not 'bring these desirable factors into the homes of others'.[107] Ideally the SRHS saw the home helps as eliminating this problem by combining the teaching of cleanliness with their other tasks, but even home helps were thought to be 'totally ignorant and backward'.[108]

Maternity Care and Hospital Provision

Initially providing help for ordinary cases of illness and for families where the mother was in hospital or convalescing, financial difficulties in 1899 obliged the society to concentrate its efforts on maternity nursing and home care.[109] Between 1898 and 1908 the number of maternity cases rose from 378 to 2,693, an increase of 2,315.[110] In 1911 the SRHS extended this maternity work with the provision of a Maternity Home. Known as the Jewish Maternity Home (JMH), or more affectionately as Mother Levy's, the home was based at 24–6 Underwood Street, Whitechapel.[111] Together with provision of a nurses' home and headquarters for the SRHS, the Home included two maternity wards accommodating a total of twelve patients, an isolation ward, an operating theatre, a waiting room for applicants, and a midwifery training school. In-patients of the maternity wards included those who had paid the weekly penny to the Provident Fund as well as poverty-stricken mothers who could not pay anything.[112]

Two years after opening, the Jewish Maternity Home was already getting too small, and this became a severe problem in subsequent years. Much of the pressure on the in-patient facilities of the JMH was part of a wider trend towards hospital maternity care within East London. Indeed, the area was unusual in its early resort to hospital confinements as

---

[106] *JC*, 14 July 1901, 8.   [107] *JC*, 3 Jan. 1896, 9.   [108] *JC*, 24 Nov. 1899, 23.
[109] SRHS, *6th AR, 1899* (London, 1900); *7th AR, 1900* (London, 1901); *8th AR, 1901* (London, 1902); cited in Black, *Social Politics of Anglo-Jewry*, 162–3.
[110] *JC*, 30 Oct. 1896; 24 Nov. 1899, 23; 19 June 1910.
[111] The money came from the Lewis-Hill Bequest, which had been left directly for the purposes of establishing a maternity home. This was supplemented by a donation from Sir Marcus Samuel (later Lord Bearsted). The establishment of the Jewish Maternity Home contrasts the difficulties incurred in setting up the London Jewish Hospital which was continually unable to raise funds from the wealthier members of the Jewish community. *JC*, 24 Dec. 1911, 23; 'Report on the Jewish Maternity Home', in the King's Fund Papers (GLRO file: A/KE/526 [7]).   [112] *JC*, 29 Sept. 1911, 10.

opposed to domiciliary midwifery.[113] The high rate of hospital births was especially noticeable in Stepney where the JMH was based. A significant reason for the high proportion of hospital births in East London was that many of the hospitals were teaching hospitals, which by the 1920s preferred to accept in-patients rather than district cases for greater ease in instructing pupil midwives and medical students. While some women saw hospital confinements as expensive and inconvenient because of their needs to care for children and the home, others regarded hospitals as attractive alternatives to giving birth in the cramped and insanitary housing they lived in. One woman, who had her babies in the early 1920s chose the JMH, as opposed to remaining at home, because she lived in a cramped flat at the top of the house, with no lavatory or bathroom, except in the back garden which seemed a long way to go when she was feeling weak.[114]

Heavy demands on the in-patient facilities at the JMH made it necessary to impose severe restrictions on the number of admissions. In 1920 the number of applications for entry into the wards of the JMH outnumbered the number accepted for admissions by about three to one. A certain number of those registered for admission in 1921 were cared for by the district midwives attached to the home, but as administrators of the hospital reported there were 'many women far more suitable for in-patient treatment, frequently on account of destitute or overcrowded conditions, apart from medical considerations'.[115] The tight squeeze on beds became worse in 1925 when the London County Council instructed the home to allow only nine of the beds to be booked. The remainder were to be kept for emergencies.[116] A large number of patients therefore had to be turned away to other hospitals in the area.[117] Many women said that they had to book a long time in advance in order to get into the home; otherwise there was no guarantee of admission. One woman, forced to book a hospital bed at a late stage in her pregnancy when complications arose, was immediately excluded from the JMH because it required early booking to secure a bed. This caused her some disappointment, preferring to go to Mother Levy's 'because they had chicken soup there every day and they were fed very well'.[118]

---

[113] The reasons behind this were multifarious and are discussed in greater detail in the next chapter.

[114] *JC*, 15 May 1925. Letter from Mrs I.T. to L. Marks, London, 31 Oct. 1987; 26 Nov. 1987, typed excerpts, p. 5.

[115] 'Report on the JMH'.   [116] *JC*, 3 May 1925, 7.   [117] 'Report on the JMH'.

[118] Miss T.G., interview transcript, p. 5.

Plans to develop the home were finally realized in 1927. The extension included four new wards accommodating twenty-three more beds, two operating theatres, an observation nursery, and more accommodation for the nursing staff and administration.[119] Despite such extensions the demand for hospital births pushed the JMH to plan further expansion in 1937. By the late 1930s, however, it was no longer viable to retain the same location because the majority of the Jewish community had moved northwards and the hospital staff were complaining that consequently many of their probationer midwives were unable to get sufficient district midwifery cases.[120] It was proposed to build the new hospital in Stoke Newington, but building was halted with the onset of war.[121]

Despite increasing problems of space within the home and the problems imposed by the shift of the Jewish population, the presence of the JMH in East London distinguished the Jewish population from other minorities in the area. Indeed the Irish poor, another significant ethnic group in the district, who had access to their own Catholic Nursing Associations, had no maternity home of their own.[122] This reflects the different orientation and needs of the Irish from those of the Jews. Funds were not quite so scarce among the established Jewish community as they were for the Irish, whose welfare resources came primarily from the Catholic Church. Most of funds at the disposal of the Catholic community were directed towards building churches and providing Catholic schools, which left little to build a hospital. However, the need for a maternity hospital was perhaps more urgent among Jews. Catholic patients faced similar discomforts to Jewish patients when not attended by those of their own denomination in a hospital environment, but their needs were easier to satisfy than those of Jewish patients. The disadvantages Catholic patients suffered could be eased by the attachment of a Catholic priest to hospital premises and by the Catholic visitors.[123] Jewish patients, however, needed more than this. Ritual requirements concerning diet and circumcision as well as the handicap of language barriers made the need for a specifically Jewish maternity hospital more important.

---

[119] *JC*, 1 Nov. 1927, 18.   [120] JMH, *AR* (1936), 11; 'Report on the JMH'.
[121] During World War II the hospital was evacuated to Hampton Court where 30 beds were provided in 1940. Work recommenced on the new hospital in Oct. 1945 and eventually the hospital was opened in 1947 as the Bearsted Memorial Hospital.
[122] Indeed, there were no Catholic hospitals at all in East London. However there were some in other parts of the country, such as the Hospital of St John and St Elizabeth in Great Ormond Street in London.   [123] *Catholic Directory* (1895), 483.

Preparation for Motherhood and Infant Care

As the numbers of SRHS maternity patients increased so did the range of work the Society undertook. From 1912 it provided an Infant Welfare Centre. Like many other centres, that of the JMH gave lessons on hygiene and thrift, and taught women how to make clothes for their babies and nightdresses for their confinements.[124] Seeing themselves as crucial agents of social work and cleanliness, a staff of health visitors based in the Infant Welfare Centre promoted educational schemes.[125] The *Jewish Chronicle* highlighted the methods they devised for getting their message across. One technique was the use of simple drawings:

> One deals with the evils of a deadly fly, and depicts, in vivid fashion, the disease-carrying *musca domestica* and the havoc it brings. Here, too, is an enlarged picture of a baby's comforter that has fallen in the street and collected a few thousand stray germs. The picture of the 'dummy', with its coloured representation of clinging disease disseminators, is enough to make a mother think. Literature is all very well, but one cannot always get the mothers to read it. They have no time. It is the picture that tells the story, and a lurid, necessary story it is.[126]

Realizing the importance of adequate nutrition for nursing mothers, the SRHS, through the Infant Welfare Centre, provided milk supplements and vitamins for those mothers who had difficulties in breast-feeding. Unlike the other services such as the home helps system (which was partially means tested), the milk supplements and other such items were free.[127] Some Jewish nursing mothers could also obtain meals at the cost of 1½d. through a Mothers' Dinner Fund run by the Jewish Day Nursery.[128] For the many nursing mothers who arrived at the nursery in the middle of the day exhausted, 'over-heated', and incapable of breast-feeding, these meals were vital.

[124] Letter from Mrs R.G. to L. Marks, London, 10 Feb. 1988, typed excerpts from letters, p. 2; Mothers attending such classes were also given lectures on hygiene and infant welfare (*ELO*, 4 May 1929).

[125] 'Sick Room Helps Society', paper presented to the Jewish East End Museum research group, author and date unknown, p. 2. Paper kept at the Museum of Jewish Life, London.

[126] *JC*, 12 Apr. 1912, 26.

[127] JMH, *AR* (1936), 23; Miss T.G., interview transcript, p. 8.

[128] Set up by Mrs Model in the late 1890s, the nursery primarily catered for the children of those who were forced to undertake waged work outside the home, such as widows and deserted wives. While in 1914 728 such meals were given to mothers by the nursery, by 1915 the number had risen to 1,157. These meals seemed to have increased during the war years, but declined by 1916–17 when only 480 meals were served (Jewish Day Nursery, *ARs*, 1914–17). The initial increase might have been a way of remedying the problems created from the growing unemployment and poverty amongst women in the initial years of the war.

Other Jewish organizations provided similar centres, most notably the Jewish Mothers' Welcome and Infant Welfare Centre established by the Jewish Mothers' Meetings association in 1908.[129] Following the methods of St Pancras Mothers' School, created in 1907, the Jewish Mothers' Welcome supplied salaried health visitors who visited the homes of Jewish mothers before and after the birth of all the babies, and held frequent infant consultations under the direction of an approved medical officer. Most of those babies who came to the centre before the First World War were sent by The London Hospital, which provided the centre fortnightly with a list of all the new Jewish babies. The centre concentrated its efforts on those mothers who only had one or two children, feeling that they could 'do more good with the young mother, who had not already buried half a dozen'. They not only saw young mothers as 'more open to teaching', but also that they were more likely to continue to put into practice with their future children what they had learnt.[130] Attached to the centre was also a Mothers' Committee, established in 1922 so that 'mothers could express their own views'.[131] By 1926 the staff at this centre included a medical practitioner and two trained health visitors. Mothers could come with their babies for medical consultations three days a week, or come for the treatment of minor ailments any day. Access to a crèche was also provided for mothers attending the special health lectures at the centre. A dispensary was housed on the premises which supplied dried milk and simple drugs. In later years the work of the centre was subsidized by the Local Government Board.[132]

One of the recommendations of the Maternity and Child Welfare Act of 1918 was an increase in antenatal care.[133] From 1918 the JMH was

---

[129] Initially the centre was based in the premises of Lady Magnus' Working Girls' Club in Leman Street, but when it grew too big it moved to Toynbee Hall in 1916 and then to Great Alie Street the following year. From 1915 the centre was based in Camperdown House in Half Moon Street, and had another branch in Betts Street. In 1930s this centre was moved to Bernard Baron Settlement. See *Caroline Franklin*, 44–5; Stepney, 'Public Health Survey', 1932, app. D (b), p. xiii (PRO: MH 66/392).

[130] C. Franklin, 'Address to Members of the Jewish Mothers' Welcome and Infant Welfare Centre', in *Caroline Franklin*, 81–2. [131] *Caroline Franklin*, 45.

[132] Stepney, 'Public Health Survey', 1932, app. D (b), p. xiii (PRO: MH 66/392); Jewish Mothers Welcome and Infant Welfare Centre *ARs* (1932–3, 1934–5, and 1938–9; The origins of the centre are described in *Caroline Franklin*, 44–5, 82–5. Caroline Franklin used the centre to launch a Standing Joint Committee of Jewish Infant Welfare centres in Stepney in 1928, which became the Federation of Jewish Infant Welfare Centres the following year.

[133] J. Lewis, *The Politics of Motherhood: Child and Maternal Welfare in England, 1900–1939* (London, 1980), 151. The Maternity and Child Welfare Act called on local authorities to provide maternity services with the aid of government funding. This was not mandatory

running its own antenatal care sessions, one of the earliest hospitals to do so. In 1926 the Jewish Mothers' Welcome and Infant Welfare Centre also hosted an antenatal clinic. The JMH undertook continuous contact with mothers before their confinements and until the child reached school-age.[134] By 1929 over 1,970 mothers had attended antenatal clinics held at the JMH twice a week. These were attended by medical practitioners, one of whom was Jewish.[135]

Circumcision

Through its association with the Initiation Society, the SRHS guaranteed its patients (whether nursed in the JMH or on the district) financial help with circumcisions. Established thirty-five years prior to the SRHS, the Initiation Society financially assisted those who otherwise could not afford the circumcision of their child. Their work was seen as important in preventing Jewish infants from being taken away from the Jewish faith. By 1908, the Society was an official educational body, training *mohalim* (religious men who performed the circumcision) and insisting that all its members undertake antiseptic precautions whilst performing the operation.[136] Although provision for circumcision was made in other local East London Hospitals and other maternity schemes, the SRHS ensured circumcision as a standard part of their services.[137]

Patients' Response

One difficulty in tracing the response of the patients to the Jewish communal resources is that much of the material preserved was written by those who financed and controlled the services provided. Newspaper reports and the few remaining annual reports, although biased, imply that many cherished the care they received. This did not mean that differences did not emerge. One criticism came from a Jewish mother who observed 'We are not like the *goyim* (Gentiles), we do not want to be talked to or taught, we do not drink, and we know how to bring up our children religiously and soberly.'[138] In 1930 some hostility was also

and local authorities undertook such provision in varying degrees around the country. For more information on how this affected East London see Ch. 6.

[134] 'Jewish Charities', *ELO*, 1 May 1926, 2.
[135] *ELO*, 11 May 1929, 6; Dr Muriel Landau acted as the Medical Officer of Health for the JMH from 1922 (JMH, *AR* (1936), 12).
[136] *Jewish World*, 7 Apr. 1911, 10.   [137] See Ch. 4.
[138] Recorded in Lady Constance Battersea, *Reminiscences* (London, 1922), 417.

expressed to the idea that the JMH now had a midwifery school and was allowing its patients to be used as guinea-pigs for probationers.[139] None the less, while conflicts arose, the JMH was remembered with particular affection by those interviewed, and received much praise in reports that appeared in the *Jewish Chronicle* and the *East London Observer*. The support which came from the Jewish mothers to prevent the collapse of the SRHS in 1908 also reflected the affinity these mothers felt with the organization.

Although the SRHS was initiated and run by the more middle-class Jewish community, this did not seem to alienate the poorer patients. The JMH had a reputation for being a homely place. Mother Levy, the superintendent of the SRHS for twenty-five years, was a much-cherished figure in the community. It was through her care and that of her nursing staff that many Jewish women found the JMH 'a much cosier place than the enormous London hospital'.[140] As one woman stated

People weren't asked as many questions at Mother Levy's. It was a very homely sort of place—they made provision for older children so they could come when their mothers were there. Very often women had children close in age so they could bring the other children with them and take them to a little play area with toys.[141]

Many mothers chose the SRHS and its maternity home because it was Jewish and less alienating than the other schemes provided by host institutions. It was more comfortable to be surrounded by a nursing staff who were sympathetic to Jewish rituals and culture. In addition, although many of the nursing staff employed in the Maternity Home were not Jewish and did not necessarily understand Yiddish, the mothers were surrounded by familiar Jewish faces from their neighbourhood who on occasion could translate for them.

Communal organizations and the wider community

Many contemporary observers expressed admiration for the facilities provided by the Jewish community for their poor, particularly in the case of the JBG.[142] One institution, however, which gained overwhelming praise

---

[139] Letter from Barnett Hyman, *ELO*, 10 May 1930, 6.
[140] Letter from I.T. to L. Marks, London, 31 Oct. 1987; 13 Nov. 1987, typed letter excerpts, p. 5.   [141] Miss T.G., interview transcript, p. 8.
[142] See e.g. evidence contained in the following parliamentary reports, *House of Commons Select Committee Alien Immigration*, PP 1889 X, Q1361, Qs 1378–9; *House of Lords Select Committee on Poor Law Relief*, PP 1888 XV, Q4939; *RC Poor Law Relief*, PP 1909 XL, Q17387, Q17490, Q19062.

was the SRHS, which the outside community regarded as innovative and pioneering.[143] This was partly the result of its own active publicity. In 1910 recommendations made by Alice Model for home helps were seriously considered by a Charity Organization Society during their enquiries into provident nursing.[144] Similarly, in 1920 Alice Model's expertise was called upon by the Stepney Maternal and Child Welfare Committee during an investigation into the provision of home helps for the area.[145] Many of Alice Model's suggestions were not adopted, but her ideas and the scheme established by the SRHS were influential during these discussions.

One of the most enthusiastic followers of the SRHS was the Central Committee on Women's Employment (CCWE), which created its own home-helps training scheme in November 1914. The CCWE used many of the ideas already voiced by the SRHS in the 1890s. Margaret Bondfield, an ardent advocate of the scheme, stated in 1915 that the home help worked in conjunction with the nurse, undertaking the housework, cooking, and childcare, chores which so often hindered the speedy recovery of mothers.[146] Using the model set up by the SRHS, the CCWE drew its home helps from women who struggling to secure work, such as middle-aged women and those who had been thrown out of work by the war. Thus, it was argued, these women could become self-sufficient and at the same time help others. Initially employed in the workrooms of the Queen's Work for Women Fund, these women were then, if deemed suitable, selected to train as home helps. Those chosen were scrutinized for their personal character and ability to maintain their own homes. They were sent to classes (some provided by settlements and others by the London County Council) in cookery, laundry, housewifery, hygiene, and infant care. Like the SRHS the CCWE was adamant that its home helps should be paid well for their work. During their training the home helps were paid 11s. 6d. per week, but the Committee recommended that once qualified they should be paid 5d. per hour, or 12s. 6d. per week, with food. Some home helps were able to find work for 14s. per week.

By 1915 the CCWE had two large centres for recruiting home helps, one in the West End and one in the East End, and had trained 100 women in eight months. The areas covered by the office in East London

[143] *ELO*, 1 May 1915, 5.

[144] Charity Organization Society, Proceedings of Council, 12 May 1910, 304 (GLRO file: A/FWA/C/A3/45/1).

[145] Stepney Maternal and Child Welfare Committee Minutes, 11 May 1920, 149 (THL file: 1083).   [146] *ELO*, 19 June 1915, 6.

included Stepney, Bethnal Green, Hackney, Poplar, and Shoreditch. Like the SRHS, Margaret Bondfield stressed that the scheme should be self-supporting through the collection of weekly instalments. According to her vision, home helps were the solution for those women who could not afford servants. She saw the scheme as opening up 'boundless opportunities' and urged the municipal authorities to adopt it.[147] As Chapter 6 shows, however, municipal authorities were slow to take up Miss Bondfield's suggestion and their responses varied.

Given that Jewish mothers were living in a predominantly Anglican society, it was important that they be served by those familiar with their religious and cultural needs. Those who were lucky were able to rely on the support of relatives and friends who had migrated with them from Eastern Europe, but many Jewish women left behind them those who understood them most. Added to these problems was the increasing disappearance of the traditional birth attendant, the handywoman, as a result of the tightening regulations on midwifery training and practice. The demise of the local handywoman had repercussions for all mothers giving birth in East London, but her disappearance was harder for Jewish immigrant women. Indeed, as the legislation tightened the regulations for midwifery, so it became harder for Jewish women to continue to practise and train as midwives. Midwifery skills could no longer be transmitted between generations because of migration. Those who wanted to train and practise midwifery now had to obey state regulations which involved learning in institutions unsympathetic to their cultural and religious needs. All this contributed to a scarcity of Jewish midwives in East London.

In the absence of family support, local handywomen, and midwives of their own persuasion, Jewish mothers were increasingly forced to rely on other forms of help for childbirth such as that provided by Jewish communal organizations. Although Jewish communal facilities could not cover all Jewish mothers living in East London, those who were assured of their care received a vital source of support. To what extent these agencies compensated for the adverse economic and social circumstances facing East European Jewish expectant mothers is hard to estimate given the dearth of statistics concerning the health of these mothers and the small numbers involved. What is apparent, however, is that certain needs which could not be met easily in host institutions made the Jewish organizations search for schemes which provided a new answer to old problems. Religious and cultural factors, quite as much as clinical considerations,

[147] Ibid.

provided the spur to innovation in domiciliary practice. Such help was invaluable to mothers striving to bring healthy infants into the world, and it provided a model for other less specialized agencies to follow. The SRHS was most engineering in this respect. By 1915 the SRHS proudly claimed to be the pioneer of the home-helps scheme. Good care during confinements involved not only skilled medical attention but also reliable domestic aid and child care. Home helps or maternity nurses were expensive and beyond the pocket of many women in East London, but the SRHS proved that home helps could be made available to even the poorest.

Apart from supplying home helps the SRHS provided a host of services with the help of the JBG. Jews living in East London not only had access to home helps, but also a maternity hospital, maternal and infant welfare clinics, health visitors, and a Jewish Day Nursery. An important indication of the quality of the services provided by Jewish agencies such as the SRHS was also their incorporation into maternity and infant welfare schemes after the Maternity and Child Welfare Act of 1918. Indeed, as Chapter 6 shows, the Jewish agencies retained a strong hold on the services in East London up to 1939.

Such services did not exclude the possibility of Jewish mothers seeking help from other organizations. Instead these facilities were seen as supplementary to those already provided in East London, which gave the Jewish population an advantage over other residents. This also contrasted with the experience of the Irish Catholic poor, another immigrant population in the area, who faced similar discomforts to the Jews when nursed by those not of their faith. Although served by a number of Catholic nursing associations, they did not have access to the highly centralized medical and maternity relief schemes as provided by the JBG and SRHS among the Jews, nor could they call on a Catholic maternity hospital. The Jewish community therefore stood out from their neighbours not only in its prolific provision, but also in the innovative types of care it provided.

4

Local Voluntary Hospitals and Maternity Care

IN addition to the alternative schemes set up by Jewish communal organizations, Jewish mothers had particularly good access to maternity care from host institutions. Despite, or possibly because of, its poor social and economic situation, East London was characterized by a large number of charitable maternity services from early on. Such provision was vital to mothers facing the continual strain of bearing infants on a low income. Although the abundant maternity facilities in the area could do little to prevent the economic and social hardships many mothers suffered, they none the less appear to have had an important influence on the rate of maternal mortality. As has been shown, maternal mortality was much lower in East London than the rest of London or England and Wales (see Fig. 2.11).

Chapters 5 and 6 examine what was provided by Poor Law institutions, as well as charitable agencies such as district nursing associations and later municipal centres. The focus of this chapter is on hospital provision which was especially good because of the numerous voluntary teaching hospitals in East London. From the 1880s these hospitals played an increasingly important role in delivering mothers on an in-patient and out-patient basis, and were the leading exemplars of maternity care in the area. Indeed, East London, by comparison with the rest of London and England and Wales, was distinguished for its early resort to hospital births. Like the Jewish communal schemes examined above many of the measures these hospitals adopted reflected the broader concern of infant and maternal mortality, and were influenced by the developments occurring to maternity and infant welfare services as a whole.

The hospitals were unusual in both the types of help they provided and their attitude towards their patients. Based in the heart of East London, these hospitals had to deal with not only the severe problems of social and economic deprivation, but also a large immigrant population, which made special demands on their services. This chapter concentrates on the ways in which the special conditions of East London fostered a sense of communal responsibility within the hospitals and shaped the services they provided. Among the themes explored are the responses of the hospital administrators and staff to the specific cultural and religious needs of the Jewish patients. In studying the access Jewish patients had to these hospitals, I hope to examine the degree to which their experience differed from that of other patients. In this chapter I not only compare the hospitals' facilities with those available through Jewish communal organizations as well as other agencies in the area, but also look at how they were perceived by the patients they served. Evidence on Jewish mothers is difficult to assess because Jewish mothers are not listed separately within the primary sources. Relevant information has therefore been teased from evidence on the hospitals and their patients in general.[1]

Voluntary Hospital Maternity Services in East London

Those voluntary hospitals which provided maternity care on a charitable basis in East London included The London Hospital, often known as 'The London',[2] the City of London Maternity Hospital (CLMH), the East End Maternity Home (EEMH) and the Salvation Army Mothers' Home (SAMH). All these hospitals had training programmes for teaching midwives, and some also trained monthly or maternity nurses as well as medical students. Tables 4.1 and 4.2 show the average number trained in each institution per year, and the average number of in-patients and out-patients treated by each hospital per year in the period 1885–1940.

Established in 1750, the CLMH was initially a lying-in institution which, from 1872, also provided a domiciliary or 'district' midwifery service. Based in Aldersgate Street, the hospital served a very large district, predominantly the more central areas of the city like Islington, Clerkenwell,

---

[1] By contrast records in the USA tend to list the nationality of each patient and sometimes that of their husbands. Some examples of this are the registers from New York Lying-In Hospital or Chicago Lying-in Hospital. (New York Hospital Archives, New York City, and North-Western Memorial Hospital Archives, Chicago). For more information on these hospitals see also N. S. Dye, 'Modern Obstetrics and Working-Class Women: The New York Midwife Dispensary, 1890–1920', *J. Soc. Hist.* 20 (1987), 549–64; V. A. M. Quiroga, *Poor Mothers and Babies: A Social History of Childbirth and Child Care Hospitals in Nineteenth-Century New York City* (New York, 1989); and S. Sessions Rugh, 'Being Born in Chicago', *Chicago History*, 15/4 (1986–7), 4–21.

[2] More detailed information on the maternity services provided by The London Hospital can be found in L. Marks, 'Mothers, Babies and Hospitals: "The London" and the Provision of Maternity Care in East London, 1870–1939', in V. Fildes, L. Marks, and H. Marland (eds.), *Women and Children First: International Maternal and Infant Welfare, 1870–1945* (London, 1992).

TABLE 4.1. *Average number of midwives, maternity and monthly nurses, and medical students trained per year at East London hospitals, 1885–1940*

Year	CLMH			EEMH		LH	SAMH
	Midwives trained	Monthly nurses trained	Medical students trained	Midwives trained	Maternity nurses trained	Midwives trained*	Midwives trained
1885–90	25	127	—	—	—	—	—
1891–5	32	132	—	11	9	—	—
1896–1900	46	154	—	17	17	—	—
1901–5	49	133	—	23	24	—	—
1906–10	55	101	—	46	16	—	—
1911–15	69	60	23	59	19	40	27
1916–20	79	8	47	49	8	—	41
1921–5	67	8	55	58	5	41	92
1926–30	46	3	36	39	13	—	53
1931–5	47	—	34	46	12	23	31
1936–40	51	—	37	50	—	—	39

Note: Figures are not available for all years. The averages are based on the total number of years available and divided accordingly.

* Figures in this column represent total numbers trained in one year, not averages.

Source: CLMH, EEMH, London Hospital (LH), and SAMH, *ARs* (1885–1940).

TABLE 4.2. *Average number of total in-patients and out-patients per year in East London hospitals, 1870–1939*

Year	CLMH Hospital	CLMH District	EEMH Hospital	EEMH District	LH Hospital	LH District	SAMH Hospital	SAMH District
1870–5	487	407	—	—	—	880	—	—
1876–80	371	927	—	—	—	954	—	—
1881–5	274	1,235	—	—	—	2,135	—	—
1886–90	379	1,342	150*	—	—	2,304	—	—
1891–5	471	1,628	202	258	—	2,140	—	—
1896–1900	553	1,658	271	563	—	2,131	—	—
1901–5	599	2,345	323	416	—	3,576	—	—
1906–10	764	2,779	498	720	—	4,896	—	—
1911–15	977	1,478	540	1,017	—	4,118	456	1 648
1916–20	1,383	430	774	1,066	—	2,788	902	1,259
1921–5	1,691	356	1,031	1,227	314	2,645	1,136	1,375
1926–30	1,581	240	1,300	745	586	2,201	1,533	1,013
1931–5	1,585	253	1,494	415	1,373*	609	1,557	783
1936–8	1,626	268	1,519	283	2,191	442	1,614	917

Note: Figures are not available for all years. The averages are based on the total number of years available and divided accordingly.

* This figure represents the total patients in one year and is not an average.

Source: *AR*s from CLMH, EEMH, LH, and SAMH (1885–1940).

and St Lukes, but it also received a large number of patients from further East, such as Bethnal Green and Shoreditch, as well as a few from Spitalfields and Whitechapel.[3] Initially the hospital's outdoor midwifery service only covered the area within a mile of the hospital, but it grew quickly and by 1880 the district midwives were attending over 1,000 patients a year, three times more than the total number of in-patients (see Table 4.2). Until the late 1880s the CLMH's out-patients department was one of the largest in London. In 1913, however, the hospital deliberately reduced its outdoor department when maternity benefit was introduced, because, it argued, many women would no longer need its charitable midwifery services.[4]

By contrast with the other hospitals in studied here, The London was not specifically set up to be a maternity hospital. Founded originally as a general voluntary and teaching hospital in the mid-eighteenth century, The London began to accept maternity patients in order to train their medical students in 1853. Known as the 'Green Charity', this was a district midwifery service run by medical students who delivered patients in their own homes. Such provision for maternity patients was unusual for general hospitals during this period.[5] In 1885 a 'White Charity' was also introduced which provided maternity care through the hospital's midwifery students. As Table 4.2 indicates, the maternity department of The London was one of the largest outdoor departments in the area by the late 1880s. Initially the hospital only accepted patients within a one-mile radius of Whitechapel Road, where the hospital was based, but later patients were taken from further afield. Although the service was predominantly domiciliary, by the early twentieth century maternity wards, such as the Marie Celeste ward, catered for in-patients. Table 4.3 shows that in the years 1906 to 1938 the number of cases delivered by midwives, as opposed to maternity assistants (probably medical students), varied between 39 and 64 per cent, with the highest proportion of midwife cases occurring during the years of the First World War, when many medical men departed the civilian services for the war effort.

Much smaller than The London was the East End Maternity Home.

---

[3] A detailed breakdown of the geographical location of patients appears in L. Marks, 'Irish and Jewish Women's Experience of Childbirth and Infant Care in East London, 1870–1939: The Response of Host Society and Immigrant Communities to Medical Welfare Needs', D.Phil. thesis (Oxford, 1990), 184, table 6.3.

[4] CLMH, *AR* (1913).

[5] F. B. Smith, *The People's Health, 1810–1930* (London, 1979), 29–30; J. H. Woodward, *To Do the Sick No Harm: A Study of the British Voluntary Hospital System to 1875* (London, 1974), 45.

TABLE 4.3. *Number of out-patients attended by maternity assistants and midwives at The London, 1906–1938*

Year	Total cases	Maternity assistant cases	Maternity assistant cases as % of total	Midwife cases	Midwife cases as % of total
1906–10	24,478	15,567	64	8,911	36
1911–14	17,340	9,423	54	7,917	46
1915–17	8,796	3,392	39	5,404	61
1919	2,817	1,263	45	1,554	55
1921–5	13,226	6,325	48	6,901	52
1926–8	6,826	3,731	55	3,095	45
1930–5	5,023	3,041	61	1,982	39
1936–8	1,327	646	49	681	51

Note: Maternity assistants probably referred to cases undertaken by medical students. The midwife cases refer to those cases undertaken by trained midwives or pupil midwife under the supervision of trained midwives.

Source: London Hospital, *ARs* (1906–38).

Established in 1884, the EEMH initially aimed to provide charitable institutional care for an average of six patients at a time, but extended to provide district midwifery care in 1891.[6] Its outdoor service was soon much larger than its in-patient one (see Table 4.2). The hospital was not only a place of treatment, but also provided midwifery training. Located further east and south than The London, it served an area closer to the docks.

Unlike the three other hospitals, the Salvation Army Mothers' Hospital grew out of an institution which primarily catered for unmarried mothers. The Salvation Army's rescue work, begun in the 1880s, had revealed a desperate need for a maternity home for single mothers. Its first home, founded in Chelsea in 1886, was one of the few alternatives to the workhouse for unmarried mothers at that time.[7] Five years later a nurses' training school was launched by the Army at Ivy House, Hackney,

[6] M. S. Sumner, 'Hospital Visits', in A. A. Leith (ed.), *Every Girl's Annual, Extra Supplement* (1887); *ELO*, 30 May 1908. The Hospital was formerly known as the Mothers' Lying-in Hospital until 1912 when it changed its name to the East End Maternity Hospital.

[7] Founded in 1752, Queen Charlotte's Hospital was the first lying-in institution to assist not only poor married women but also 'deserving' single women. In 1865 more provision was made for unmarried mothers through the establishment of the General Lying-in Hospital. These hospitals helped about 550 cases a year. (A. R. Higginbotham, 'The Unmarried Mother and Her Child in Victorian London, 1834–1914', Ph.D. thesis (Indianapolis, 1985), 92.)

which in 1894 became a maternity home for single women. In the late 1890s its maternity services extended into a district midwifery service for married mothers, and in 1913 the Mothers' Hospital appeared.[8] Based in Clapton, the hospital initially restricted its patients to women from that area and Bethnal Green, but as its district outposts opened so its catchment spread further east.

Located in different parts of East London, these hospitals provided an extensive network of maternity care for a range of patients. Records from the CLMH and the EEMH are particularly interesting because they show the occupation of each woman's husband. Based on the outskirts of the East End and nearer to the city, the CLMH had relatively more prosperous patients. The majority of husbands were involved in artisanal or semi-skilled labour, although there were also some whose occupation was more casual and subject to the fluctuations of the seasons.[9] Casual jobs, however, were more common among husbands of the women confined in the EEMH, who were primarily employed as dock labourers near the hospital. The London had more varied patients than those of the EEMH, including those whose background was rooted in dock work, textiles, and furniture-making. Established in Clapton, the SAMH had a slightly wealthier constituency. Such variations, however, were small, and as the hospitals aimed at providing care for poor women, most of their patients came from comparable backgrounds of poverty.

The hospitals showed some perceptible differences in the kind of immigrants they accommodated. Registers from the different hospitals do not list the patients separately by their religious or immigrant status, which makes it difficult to get an accurate picture of the number and type of immigrants using the hospitals. The only sources available are the surnames of the patients registered, although it is difficult to know whether these names are those of immigrants or whether they are of people already well settled in East London. Of all four hospitals, the EEMH registered far more women with surnames common in Ireland. This was partly because the hospital was so near to the docks, where many of the Irish immigrants had settled.[10] Some Jewish patients used the EEMH in

[8] J. Fairbanks, *Booth's Boots: Social Service Beginnings in the Salvation Army* (London, 1983); 'The Mothers' Hospital', *The City and Hackney Health Authority Newsletter*, 12 (May 1986), 1.
[9] CLMH Out-patients Register and District Case Books and EEMH Out-patients and In-patients Registers, 1875, 1885, 1895, 1905, 1915, 1925, 1935.
[10] One nun working in East London emphasized the popularity of the hospital among Irish immigrants and their families. Sister P., Sister of Mercy, interviewed by L. Marks, London, 9 Dec. 1987, transcript, p. 3.

later years, but they appeared more regularly in the registers of the other hospitals which were further north-west from the docks, indicating the predominantly Jewish areas that these hospitals were based in.

Hospital Regulations and Procedures

Of the four hospitals, the SAMH was most religious in its outlook and evangelical in its aim. The mission of the hospital was not only to provide medical services, but also to spiritually heal their patients. They saw the work of their midwives as dealing 'with souls as well as bodies'.[11] Their aim was not merely spiritual consolation during illness, but also the more long-term goal of conversion.[12] According to the Salvation Army their missionary efforts had its rewards, claiming that many mothers who previously would not have prayed were converted by their efforts.[13] Even Jewish patients were reported to be affected by the spiritual ministrations of the Salvation Army.[14] It was customary for the SAMH nurses to hold prayers at the bedside of the patients in their homes as well as in the hospital wards. Mrs E.C., who worked in the hospital and was delivered in her own home by a midwife from the SAMH, recalled prayers during breakfast and 'plenty of singing' in the Home.[15]

Religious practice was not confined to the Salvation Army.[16] In the 1880s the CLMH invited women to attend the churching and thanksgiving ceremony as well as to baptize their infants in the hospital's Anglican chapel. Fees from the collections at these baptisms went towards the running of the hospital. This undoubtedly would have caused some problems for Jews, who do not believe in baptism, and for Catholic women, who might have preferred the ceremony performed by a Catholic priest. Once they left the hospital women were entreated to continue the private prayers they had said whilst in the institution and also to attend public worship.[17] Reports from The London and the EEMH did not specify their religious orientations. Although not compulsory, the stress laid upon religious ceremonies in the SAMH and CLMH implies that those who did not attend these occasions, such as Jewish mothers, would have felt themselves to be outsiders.

[11] *The Deliverer*, Feb. 1899, 114 (newspaper issued by the Salvation Army).
[12] SAMH, *AR* (1933), 4.   [13] Ibid. 16, and (1934), 9.
[14] Ibid. (1934), 10.
[15] Mrs E.C., interviewed by L. Marks, London, 13 Jan. 1988, transcript, pp. 7–8.
[16] See 'Inquiry as to Charges to Proselytize: Jewish Patients in the German Hospital', 22 Feb. 1894, 3–4, in United Synagogue Visitation Committee Minutes, 1 (1871–1902) (CRO).
[17] CLMH, *AR* (1871), 9.

In addition to experiencing religious alienation, some Jewish mothers might, in common with other mothers, have been discomforted by the paternalistic attitudes of the hospital authorities. The explicit intention of these hospitals was to provide a charitable service for the benefit of all poor women. As charitable objects, however, the patients had to satisfy certain requirements before they were permitted entry.[18] Keen to show prospective donors the respectability of the hospitals, they all stressed that only married women with good moral characters were admitted. To gain treatment women had to produce letters of recommendation from a Governor or subscriber of the hospital, and certificates of marriage.[19] The EEMH made it explicit that such letters were to confirm that those they treated were worthy of help and in real need.[20] Frequently women had to walk for miles, as well as spend much time waiting, before they could obtain such references, making them think twice before applying for help.[21]

Increasing concern for the plight of the unmarried mother and her child at the end of the nineteenth century led to many voluntary hospitals admitting single mothers for the first time in the 1880s.[22] However, only those who could prove it was their first confinement, or were considered exceptional cases, were admitted.[23] Illegitimacy continued to be taboo in the years up to 1939, but the policies of the hospitals towards unmarried mothers softened over time.[24] In 1905, when The London opened the Marie Celeste ward, women no longer had to prove their marital status, and by 1922 hospital staff thought nothing of helping a woman who was clearly cohabiting.[25] Some unmarried mothers were picked up through

[18] Smith, *People's Health*, 28–30.
[19] This was a common policy for voluntary hospitals throughout the 19th c. (Smith, *People's Health*, 29–30; A. E. Clark Kennedy, *The London: A Study in the Voluntary Hospital System* (London, 1963), ii. 33). In 1870 the CLMH, anxious to curb false certificates, told their Governors to check the character and respectability of women before they gave out letters of recommendation (CLMH, *AR* (1870), 18).
[20] 'Report on EEMH', *c*.1908, King's Fund Papers (GLRO file: A/KE/248/1).
[21] Smith, *People's Health*, 28–30; Clark Kennedy, *The London*, 33.
[22] See A. Higginbotham, 'Respectable Sinners: Salvation Army Rescue Work with Unmarried Mothers, 1884–1914', in G. Malmgreen (ed.), *Religion in the Lives of English Women, 1760–1930* (London, 1986).
[23] CLMH, *AR* (1908), 15; *Onward*, 8 (1925) 178 (journal issued by CLMH); *The Deliverer*, Apr. 1902, 127.
[24] For further information on unmarried mothers see Higginbotham, 'Respectable Sinners', and L. Marks, ' "The Luckless Waifs and Strays of Humanity": Irish and Jewish Immigrant Unwed Mothers in London, 1870–1939', *Twentieth Cent. Br. Hist.* 3/2 (1992), 113–37.
[25] Minutes of a subcommittee appointed to consider the working of the new Marie Celeste ward, n.d. but presumed 1905 (London Hospital Archive, Blue File LM/5/22).

the venereal disease department at London Hospital. Many single mothers applied to The London for assistance from all over London and other parts of the country. No girl was 'sent away without every effort having been made to help her in her trouble'. A few of the single mothers were confined in the hospital, but many were referred to other agencies specially organized to deal with the plight of the single mother, such as the Salvation Army.[26] The policy of the hospital was to keep in touch with the girls 'as far as possible'.[27] When compared with the overall numbers of mothers cared for by The London, the percentage of single mothers, however, remained relatively small. The highest percentage of single mothers treated by the hospital was 2 per cent of the total admissions in 1921 (42 cases), but in most years little more than 1 per cent were admitted. Similarly other hospitals, such as the EEMH, also showed very few unmarried mothers on their registers. This probably reflected the small number of unmarried mothers in East London in general as well as hospital restrictions.[28]

The hospitals also placed certain constraints on married women. In an area like East London, where maternity teaching hospitals flourished after the 1880s, access to hospital facilities might have been easier because of the need to provide teaching cases for medical and midwifery students. But the numbers treated were determined by the number of staff and the number of beds. Outdoor and indoor patients had to produce references to secure admission even in the 1930s, and mothers had to book early if they wanted to be sure of care.[29] Hard decisions had to be taken as to who should be taken into hospital rather than attended in their own homes in the district. Those ordered by doctors to go into hospital were taken without question, but others had to be judged according to their housing conditions and how cramped these would be for a home confinement.

Although hospital staff were not perturbed by cohabitation, in 1922 one woman who was helped and the man living with her clearly felt the necessity of proving their respectability to the Hospital, so that no one would feel anything had been done 'behindhand'. E. W. Morris (House Governor), 'Report of a Visit to the District Maternity Charity with Miss Nicholls, District Midwife', 19 Dec. 1922. The same story was repeated in an article in *London Hospital Illustrated* (1933), 10–11.

[26] For more information on agencies helping the unmarried mother and her child, see Higginbotham, 'Respectable Sinners', and Marks, ' "Luckless Waifs and Strays of Humanity" '.

[27] The London Hospital, *ARs* (1921), 187; (1926), 203.

[28] See Ch. 2 for rates of illegitimacy in East London. See Marks, 'Irish and Jewish Women's Experience of Childbirth', 192, table 6.5, for detailed numbers and percentage of single mothers cared for by The London in 1922–9.

[29] Mrs E.C., interviewed by L. Marks, London, 13 Jan. 1988, transcript, p. 3.

Given the general state of housing in the East End this would have been a hard decision for anyone.

Hospital provision was usually made for those with first confinements or those who had more than five previous pregnancies. Table 4.4 and Figures 4.1 to 4.3 show how those accepted as in-patients at the CLMH tended to have had fewer pregnancies before their confinement than those treated as out-patients. Figure 4.1 indicates a steady rise in the number of in-patients with no children from the early 1900s, continuing through to the inter-war years. As Figure 4.3 shows, by 1913 over 80 per cent of all first-time mothers cared for by the CLMH were treated as in-patients. This was much higher than those women who had given birth before. This trend continued into the inter-war period. By the 1930s over half the in-patients were first-time mothers. This was most striking when compared to those patients who had been pregnant before, particularly those with over five previous pregnancies. Figure 4.2 also shows that among the total out-patients, the percentage of first-time mothers was low. The high proportion of first-time mothers among the in-patients was not unique to the CLMH. In 1925 the majority of cases admitted to the EEMH had no previous pregnancies.[30]

The large number of hospital cases among first-time mothers found for the CLMH and the EEMH can be explained by a number of factors. One of the most important reasons was the introduction of effective antenatal care in the 1920s, as well as the increasing emphasis hospitals placed on hospital care for first-time mothers as well as for abnormal cases. Indeed a substantial proportion of the in-patients accepted by the EEMH were not only first-time mothers, but also those who developed complications during pregnancy or during labour.[31] In addition to this was the heightened awareness among women of the dangers of maternal mortality and their increasing demand for more hospital care. The increasing emphasis on abnormal or first-time cases had serious implications for the overall outcome of hospital care, as those now being admitted were those who faced the highest risk of dying. The pressures that this put on the hospitals were not eased by the fact that they were also the places where most emergencies were sent.

None the less, while increasing attention was paid to first-time mothers and abnormal cases, a large proportion of the women cared for in the hospital were those who had two to four pregnancies before. Indeed, Figure 4.1 shows that the percentage of these women as a total of the

---

[30] EEMH, *Clinical Report* (1925), 3.   [31] Ibid.

TABLE 4.4. *Deliveries, maternal deaths, and number of previous births of CLMH patients at 5-yearly intervals, 1870–1939*

	Year	Total deliveries	Maternal deaths	Number of previous births		
				0	2–4	Over 5
In-patients	1880	383	12	82	171	130
	1885	259	5	61	117	81
	1890	423	1	87	193	143
	1895	490	1	86	235	169
	1900	599	1	142	266	191
	1905	611	1	147	302	162
	1910	842	4	259	371	212
	1915	1,011	16	432	413	166
	1920	1,847	11	943	659	245
	1925	1,657	11	738	729	190
	1930	1,552	7	734	637	181
	1935	1,587	6	930	484	173
	1939	1,531	6	839	629	63
Out-patients	1880	1,050	4	48	413	589
	1885	1,118	1	51	427	640
	1890	1,333	3	82	439	812
	1895	1,585	4	126	596	863
	1900	1,753	2	170	663	920
	1905	2,575*	3	252	995	1,328
	1910	2,742	1	180	1,038	1,524
	1915	658	0	25	263	370
	1920	543	0	6	202	335
	1925	270	0	15	137	118
	1930	275	0	27	132	116
	1935	283	0	45	144	94
	1939	256	0	47	155	97

Note: After 1913 the number of out-patients declined as a result of a decision made by the hospital to limit its out-patient department because of the introduction of maternity benefit.

* This figure does not correspond with Table 4.2. 30 cases are unaccounted for.

Source: CLMH, *ARs* (1870–1939).

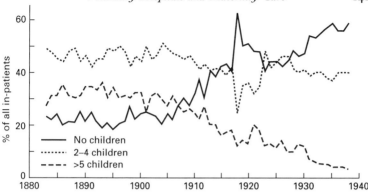

FIG. 4.1. Percentage of in-patients according to the number of previous births before confinement at the CLMH, 1883–1939
Source: CLMH, *ARs* (1883–1939), table 3.

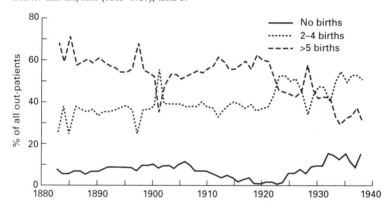

FIG. 4.2. Percentage of out-patients according to the number of previous births before confinement at the CLMH, 1883–1939
Source: as for Fig. 4.1.

in-patients at the CLMH, except during the years of World War I, remained relatively stable from 1880 to 1930. In contrast was the reduction in the number of in-patients with more than five previous pregnancies. The decline in the number of such women among the indoor patients might be attributed to the general decline in fertility and family size during this period. However, women with more than five previous pregnancies continued to be the majority of those who were out-patients. After 1913 the gap in the number of outdoor patients with and without previous pregnancies closed substantially, which might be explained by the limitations the hospital imposed on out-patients in 1913. Even with

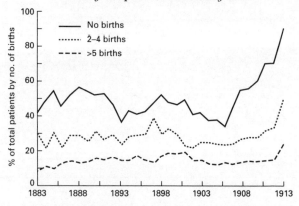

FIG. 4.3. In-patients as percentage of total CLMH in-patients and out-patients by
number of previous births, 1883–1912
Source: as for Fig. 4.1.

this development, however, the overall percentage of women who had
already had a large number of pregnancies continued to be very high
among those treated as out-patients. This trend reflected the general
attitude of the medical profession in these years. While today women who
have had more than five pregnancies are seen as having as great a risk as
first-time mothers and to be in need of special attention, this was not the
case before the Second World War. Indeed, before the war most obstetricians saw those who had a large number of births as safe and not in need
of hospital care. It is therefore not surprising to see that the percentage
of women with more than five previous pregnancies was relatively small
among those treated as in-patients.[32]

Quality of Care Available from the Hospitals

Changing priorities over which women should be cared for within the
hospitals reflected the medical advances that occurred to hospital maternity care over the years. The safety of all births was greatly dependent on
the training and skill of the medical attendants. While the risk of infection

[32] I am grateful to Irvine Loudon for this point. The trend shown in the CLMH cannot
be taken as a general pattern, as the women coming in reflected the demography of the area
in which the hospital was based. In some years the number of women with no previous
pregnancies was high and then dropped and was overtaken by those with more than one
baby a year or so later. This pattern might be a reflection of many of the same first-time
mothers later entering motherhood for a second or third time a few years later.

in hospitals diminished greatly in the 1880s with the introduction of antisepsis and the improvement in medical training, the incidence of puerperal sepsis continued to be far higher in hospitals than in the home through to the twentieth century. Although home births themselves were not without danger, those who could secure district midwifery care from voluntary hospitals were probably assured of better treatment, especially from the 1880s with the growing emphasis on antisepsis and better medical training.

None the less a high standard of treatment was not always guaranteed. One medical student in 1905 remembered the exhaustion he suffered when, with very little previous clinical experience, he was expected to deliver fifty-four mothers in a fortnight. 'I lost all sense of time, I did not know whether it was yesterday, today or tomorrow. It sounds absurd but it is true. The month we spent on maternity was itself enough to undermine the stoutest constitution.'[33] The gruelling hours students worked could undermine the work of even the best-trained students and must have had some impact on the type of care they could give.

By 1919 the situation had changed very little in The London Hospital. Both medical students and midwifery pupils were expected to undertake district deliveries with very little previous training and minimal supervision. Medical students had sole responsibility for conducting the labours and the after-care of the mother and infant for the following ten days. Such students were in their fourth year and had taken a course of lectures on midwifery, but their clinical experience was minimal. During their first three labours on the district they were supervised by the junior resident accoucheur, but after that were left to their own devices. Assisted by the junior resident accoucheur, medical students also conducted their first two labours each week in the Marie Celeste lying-in ward. Any abnormalities of labour were reported to the junior resident accoucheur. In 1919 the authors of an official hospital report were amazed that there had been no public outcry against the negligent midwifery training and standards of midwifery care offered by The London. Indeed, they claimed that it was 'a wonder that the public have tolerated it for so long'. Calling for a reform of these conditions, they argued that medical students and pupil midwives could only gain adequate practical teaching of the clinical conduct of labour in the environment of an in-patient maternity department.[34]

---

[33] R. N. Salaman, 'The Helmsman Takes Charge' (unpublished memoirs, n.d.), 27–8.
[34] Dr E. Holland, 'Report on the External Maternity District and on the Urgent Need of Reforming the Work of Students thereon', Apr. 1919, 5 (London Hospital Archive file: LH/A/17/35).

The London Hospital subsequently increased its in-patient intake in the 1920s.

No investigations over the quality of care remain for the other hospitals. In the wider world, however, the EEMH was often praised as exemplary in its maternity care. In 1930 it was commended for its success in lowering maternal mortality despite the high number of abnormal cases it received. Of the 37,171 mothers delivered as in-patients by the EEMH 1884 to 1938 there were 73 deaths, which was a rate of 1.96 per 1,000 births. The maternal mortality rate for out-patients was much lower; out of a total 31,233 deliveries there were 22 fatalities, or a rate of 0.70 per 1,000 births.[35] Unfortunately, these figures cannot be compared with London Hospital or the SAMH, but figures from the CLMH suggest that the EEMH had a remarkably low rate. In the years 1870–1939 out of a total of 62,143 in-patients there were 374 deaths at the CLMH, or a rate of 6.01 per 1,000. Its record for out-patients was 123 deaths out of 74,049 deliveries, the equivalent of 1.66 per 1,000 births. Table 4.5 shows the number of maternal deaths during five-year periods in the CLMH and EEMH for the years 1870–1939.

One reason for the low maternal mortality rate at the EEMH was its clinical practice. One medical officer commented, 'The essence of the East End Hospital practice is not wait and see, but see and wait. That that is the basis of sound midwifery, results abundantly testify.'[36] The hospital had a reputation for very little instrumental interference in its births. Although the rate at which it used forceps for its deliveries varied over the years (see Table 4.6), its overall rate of forceps delivery was 2.9 per cent of all births. It also had a low induction rate which was 1.21 per cent. For every 1,000 births only 0.1 per cent Caesarian sections were performed. All these rates compared very favourably with the rates considered reasonable during this period.[37] Table 4.7 shows the rates for the CLMH, where the forceps rate was not as low as at the EEMH. How the treatment given at the CLMH and the EEMH was reflected in the infants' survival can be seen in Tables 4.8 and 4.9. These tables indicate that the rate of stillbirths and neonatal deaths was lower among the out-patients of the two hospitals than that found among in-patients. In earlier

---

[35] The low rate of maternal mortality at the EEMH was discussed in the *Br. Med. J.* 15 Feb. 1930, 294–5, 294; *ELO*, 17 May 1930, 5; 23 May 1931, 6; and *Med. Offr.*, 25 Aug. 1928, 79–81; 31 Jan. 1931, 45.

[36] 'The East End Maternity Hospital', *Med. Offr.*, 31 Jan 1931, 45.

[37] The standard rate considered reasonable for forceps was 7% of all deliveries ('The East End Maternity Hospital', *Med. Offr.*, 31 Jan. 1931, 45).

TABLE 4.5. *Number of in-patient and out-patient deliveries and maternal deaths at CLMH and EEMH, 1870–1939*

	In-patients				Out-patients			
	CLMH		EEMH		CLMH		EEMH	
Year	Total cases	Total deaths	Total cases	Total deaths	Total cases	Total deaths	Total cases	Total deaths
1870–5	2,436	39	—	—	1,629	7	—	—
1876–80	1,484	31	—	—	4,734	8	—	—
1881–5	1,369	37	—	—	6,239	11	—	—
1886–90	1,894	8	—	—	6,708	14	—	—
1891–5	2,354	6	1,009	7	8,139	19	1,033	3
1896–1900	2,763	6	1,237	6	8,284	24	1,349	4
1901–5	2,994	11	1,614	2	11,725	20	2,081	2
1906–10	3,882	16	2,492	5	13,896	10	3,600	0
1911–15	4,883	44	2,696	7	7,392	7	5,084	3
1916–20	6,915	47	3,868	8	2,151	3	5,332	5
1921–5	8,456	44	5,154	7	1,724	0	6,134	2
1926–30	7,904	33	6,496	8	1,199	0	3,727	1
1931–5	7,925	35	7,470	10	1,534	0	2,080	2
1936–9	6,505	17	4,558	8	1,072	0	849	0

Note: CLMH: 1870–1939 total in-patients 62,143 with 374 deaths = 6.01 per 1,000 births; 1872–1939 total out-patients 74,049 with 123 deaths = 1.66 per 1,000 births. EEMH: 1884–1938 total in-patients 37,171 with 73 deaths = 1.96 per 1,000 births; 1891–1938 total out-patients 31,233 with 22 deaths = 0.70 per 1,000 births.

Source: ARs from the CLMH and EEMH (1870–1939).

years the CLMH had a higher rate of stillbirths and neonatal mortality among its in-patients than those of the EEMH. By the 1930, however, the two hospitals had comparable rates. Table 4.10 shows that the overall neonatal death rates per 1,000 births was much lower for the EEMH and CLMH than for England and Wales nationally. This suggests that these two hospitals provided for safe deliveries. Table 4.11 also demonstrates that the stillbirth rate was also much lower for these hospitals than for the whole country. This might have been the result of the scrupulous attention the hospitals paid to the mothers during their pregnancies.

TABLE 4.6. *Percentage of in-patient and
out-patient deliveries at the EEMH in which forceps were used*

Year	Forceps rates %
1925	2.5
1926	2.5
1929	4.1
1930	3.6
1931	4.8
1932	3.2
1934	4.1
1935	4.4
1936	4.2
1938	5
1939	5

Source: 'Clinical Report' in EEMH, *ARs* (1925–39).

TABLE 4.7. *Number and rate of instrumental deliveries at the CLMH*

Year	Forceps	%	Caesarians	%	Induction	%
1912	115	11.7	10	1	7	0.7
1913	50	5.9	10	1	23	2.7
1914	105	9.9	11	1	19	1.8
1919	155	11	4	0.4	26	1.8
1922	150	8.8	8	0.5	47	2.7
1923	125	7.4	13	0.8	58	3.4

Source: CLMH, *ARs* (1912–23).

In-patient Confinements

The preference for hospital confinements in The London's report for 1919 should be considered against the background of a more general public debate concerning the dangers of childbirth. Until the 1920s childbirth was predominantly an event which occurred at home and not in hospital. As early as 1920, however, the Ministry of Health was arguing for an increase in the number of maternity hospitals and homes to

TABLE 4.8. *Number and rate of stillbirths and neonatal deaths at the EEMH, 1911–1939*

Year	Total births	Stillbirths	Stillbirth rate	Neonatal deaths	Neonatal death rate
Out-patients					
1911–14	3,961	85	21.5	—	—
1925–6	1,989	38	19.1	29	14.5
1929–30	1,237	26	21.0	10	8.0
1931–5	2,072	30	14.5	15	7.2
1936–9	860	15	17.4	9	10.5
In-patients					
1911–14	2,131	49	22.9	27	12.6
1925–6	2,337	72	30.8	30	12.8
1929–30	2,781	78	28.0	43	15.5
1931–5	7,521	190	25.2	124	16.5
1936–9	4,316	123	28.4	59	13.6

Note: Neonatal and stillbirth rates = deaths per 1,000 births.
Source: EEMH, *ARs* (1911–39).

compensate for bad housing conditions.[38] Similar attitudes were voiced by many East London hospitals including The London. Deploring the terrible state of housing, the London Hospital by 1930 was arguing for the extension of in-patient care. It called for the creation of 'sufficient lying-in accommodation for every woman who requires it', which it claimed would be for 'the good of the community'.[39] This view, which became orthodox after the Second World War, was extreme in 1930. The College (later Royal College) of Obstetricians and Gynaecologists, founded in 1929, with its emphasis on building the speciality of obstetrics and gynaecology, endorsed the government policy for a national maternity service in the 1930s which was based on home deliveries by midwives and general practitioners as the backbone of the service, with hospital deliveries reserved only for 'social' admissions, high risk cases, and emergencies.[40]

[38] Ministry of Health Memorandum,'Maternity Hospitals and Homes' (1920), 1.
[39] London Hospital, *AR* (1930), 210.
[40] E. Peretz, 'A Maternity Service for England and Wales: Local Authority Maternity Care in the Inter-war Period in Oxfordshire and Tottenham', in J. Garcia, R. Kilpatrick, and M. Richards (eds.), *The Politics of Maternity Care: Services for Childbearing Women in Twentieth-Century Britain* (Oxford, 1990), 31–2; O. Moscucci, *The Science of Woman: Gynaecology and Gender in England, 1800–1929* (Cambridge, 1990), 185–7.

TABLE 4.9. *Number and rate of stillbirths and neonatal deaths at the CLMH, 1870–1939*

Year	Total births	Stillbirths	Stillbirth rate	Neonatal deaths	Neonatal death rate
Out-patients					
1872–5	1,650	58	35.1	11	6.6
1876–80	4,698	185	39.4	73	15.5
1881–5	6,262	243	38.8	64	10.2
1886–90	6,733	308	45.7	81	12.0
1891–5	8,250	325	39.4	154	18.6
1896–1900	8,401	379	45.1	139	16.5
1901–5	11,874	426	35.8	205	17.2
1906–10	14,096	450	31.9	200	14.2
1911–15	7,478	170	22.7	89	11.9
1916–20	2,187	31	14.2	41	18.7
1921–5	1,793	27	15.1	22	12.2
1926–30	1,210	19	15.7	9	7.4
1931–5	1,283	29	22.6	12	9.3
1936–7	532	10	18.7	6	11.3
In-patients					
1872–5	1,667	—	—	28	16.7
1876–80[1]	1,500	—	—	43	28.6
1881–5	1,381	—	—	60	43.4
1886–90	1,941	59	30.4	46	24.0
1891–5	2,176	80	36.8	73	33.5
1896–1900	2,806	107	38.1	98	34.9
1901–5	3,033	116	38.2	95	31.3
1906–10	3,867	148	38.3	200	51.7
1911–15[2]	3,954	203	51.3	181	45.7
1916–20	7,117	311	43.7	205	28.8
1921–5	8,569	300	35.0	245	28.5
1926–30	8,032	—	—	129	16.0
1931–5	8,027	—	—	141	17.6
1936–7	3,352	—	—	65	19.4

[1] Hospital closed in 1878, no figures for this year.
[2] No figures for 1912.

Source: CLMH, *ARs* (1870–39).

TABLE 4.10. *Number of births, neonatal deaths, and neonatal mortality rate for England and Wales, EEMH and CLMH, 1929–1939*

Year	England and Wales Neonatal mortality rate	EEMH Total births	EEMH Neonatal deaths	EEMH Neonatal mortality rate	CLMH Total births	CLMH Neonatal deaths	CLMH Neonatal mortality rate
1906–10	34.3	—	—	—	17,963	400	11.1
1911–15	35.6	—	—	—	11,432	270	23.6
1916–20	41.2	—	—	—	9,304	246	26.4
1921–5	43.9	—	—	—	10,362	267	25.7
1926–30	46.8	6,152[1]	93	15.1	9,242	138	14.9
1931–5	50.5	9,593	139	14.4	9,310	153	16.4
1936–40	52.8	5,176[2]	68	13.1	3,884[3]	71	18.3

Note: Neonatal mortality rate = deaths per 1,000 births.

[1] Years 1927 and 1928 not included.
[2] Years 1937 and 1940 not included.
[3] Year 1940 not included.

Source: ARs for EEMH and CLMH (1929–39), and A. MacFarlane and M. Mugford, *Birth Counts: Statistics of Pregnancy and Childbirth, Tables* (London, 1984), table A3.4, 10–11.

TABLE 4.11. *Number of births and stillbirths and stillbirth rate for England and Wales, EEMH and CLMH, 1929–1939*

Year	England and Wales stillbirth rate	EEMH			CLMH		
		Total births	Stillbirths	Stillbirth rate	Total births	Stillbirths	Stillbirth rate
1929	40	1,937	49	25	—	—	—
1930	41	2,081	46	22	—	—	—
1931	41	1,974	52	26	—	—	—
1932	41	1,941	44	22	—	—	—
1933	41	1,784	36	20	—	—	—
1934	40	1,979	45	23	1,809	44	24
1935	41	1,915	43	22	1,891	40	21
1936	40	—	—	—	1,898	63	33
1937	39	—	—	—	1,986	63	32
1938	38	1,766	45	25	—	—	—
1939	38	1,589	46	29	—	—	—

Note: Stillbirth rate = stillbirths per 1,000 births.

Source: *ARs* for EEMH and CLMH (1929–1939), and MacFarlane and Mugford, *Birth Counts*.

An interesting aspect of the hospital maternity services in East London is the rapidity with which they increased their number of beds and hence their number of hospital confinements in the 1920s. Some of this stemmed partly from the increased birth rate in the years immediately following the First World War (see Fig. 2.8). Even when the number of births began to decline in the late 1920s, however, the hospitals were still accepting a very large number of in-patients. Figure 4.4 shows that despite the drop in the birth rate the total number of women accepted as in-patients in all four hospitals rose or remained high in the late 1920s. While this might have been due to the drop in out-patients, the smaller number of total births in the outside population and the steady inflow of in-patients, seems to indicate that the hospital in-patient services were reaching more women than they had in previous years.

By comparison with other areas, East London was unusual in the high level of in-patient hospital facilities. As Table 4.12 reveals, from the 1920s, East London had a much higher rate of hospital births than home

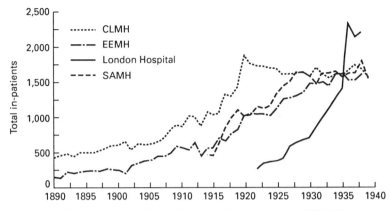

FIG. 4.4. Total number of in-patient births in East London hospitals, 1890–1939
Source: CLMH, EEMH, London Hospital, and SAMH, *ARs* (1890–1940).

ones compared with the rate for other major cities such as Liverpool and Birmingham or than nationally. Figures from other parts of London, such as St Pancras, Woolwich, and Hampstead indicate that London generally had a much higher rate of hospital births than other cities. Within London, however, East London showed an even higher rate of hospital confinements than most other parts of the metropolis. Stepney (where London Hospital and the EEMH were located) showed an extremely quick transformation to hospital confinement. In 1927 nearly 81 per cent of all the births occurred at home; by 1936 this had been reduced to just under 27 per cent. Similar trends were seen in Poplar and to some extent in Bethnal Green. In contrast to other London hospitals such as Queen Charlotte's Hospital in Marylebone and the General Lying-in Hospital in Lambeth, hospitals in East London were accepting a much greater proportion of in-patients from the 1920s (see Table 4.13 and Fig. 4.6 and 4.9).

The presence of numerous teaching hospitals in East London partly accounts for its high proportion of in-patients.[41] Throughout the period home confinements had better records on maternal mortality, but medical staff faced many difficulties when delivering cases at home. Students also had certain advantages in treating women in hospital rather than at home, where help during an emergency was not quite as forthcoming. By the

---

[41] St Pancras had a high rate of hospital births which was accounted for by the high number of teaching hospitals and lying-in institutions in the area (J. Lewis, *The Politics of Motherhood* (London, 1980), 120–1).

TABLE 4.12. *The percentage of home and institutional confinements in East London and other areas, 1915–1946*

Place	Year	% home confinements	% hospital confinements
East London			
Bethnal Green[1]	1931	56.3	43.7
	1932	53.39	46.6
	1933	54.2	45.8
	1935	41.2	58.8
	1936	43	55.3
	1937	44.6	55.4
Poplar[2]	1915	88.7	12.3
	1920	87.8	10.2
	1925	75	23
	1930	62	38
	1932	50.1	49.9
	1935	38.72	58
Stepney[2]	1920	79	21
	1927	56	44
	1935[3]	26.6	73.4
Elsewhere in London			
Hampstead	1926	60	40
	1932	41	59
	1938	33	67
Kensington	1924	72	28
	1930	68	32
	1934	67	33
Woolwich	1925	67	33
	1930	53	47
	1933	41	59
	1936	33	67
St Pancras	1915	87.5	12.5
	1935	44	56
Birmingham	1915	>97	<3
	1935	67	33
Hull	1915	>97	<3
	1935	88	22
Liverpool	1915	>97	<3
	1935	59	41

TABLE 4.12. (*Cont.*)

Place	Year	% home confinements	% hospital confinements
National	1927	85	15
	1933	76	24
	1937	75	25
	1946	46	54

Note: Hampstead figures are worked out on the basis of the number of births occurring at home. Kensington figures are based on the numbers of mothers reported to be giving birth in various institutions—this might be an underestimate because it does not include all the institutional births.

[1] The figures are taken from hospital sources only which might account for the stress on hospital care. The figures cited are for home and hospital deliveries undertaken by the major hospitals in Bethnal Green.

[2] These percentages are calculated from births notified by doctors, midwives, and parents as home confinements and births notified by hospitals. Some births are unaccounted for and therefore the percentages are approximates and do not add up to 100%.

[3] The figures for this year are calculated according to an investigation undertaken by the Stepney MOH in 1935 on the level of skilled midwifery in the area and are therefore more accurate than most statistics for the time.

Sources: Poplar MOH, *ARs* (1915–35); Bethnal Green MOH, *ARs* (1930–9); Stepney MOH, *ARs* (1920, 1927, 1935); Hampstead MOH, *ARs* (1926–36); Kensington MOH, *ARs* (1924–34); Woolwich MOH, *ARs* (1925–38); national figures and data for other areas taken from J. Lewis, *The Politics of Motherhood* (London, 1980), 120.

late 1920s hospitals could deal more effectively with emergencies and abnormal cases from the antenatal clinics.

However, one of the most important causes for the high rate of hospital confinements in East London was undoubtedly the housing conditions in the area. Reflecting on his midwifery training at London Hospital in 1905 Salaman recalled undertaking district deliveries in homes which were

the poorest imaginable and often totally unprepared for the event. Once I attended a woman in a naked garret, reached by a ladder. There was a broken down bed and a single bed with a single blanket, a chair without a back, a tin basin without a towel, and the poor mother herself was practically naked. Of food and drink there was none.[42]

Cramped housing also meant there was no escape from noise and the arguments of families in the background. Salaman remembered on one

[42] Salaman,'The Helmsman', 27–8.

TABLE 4.13. *Total number of in-patients and out-patients of five hospitals in East London compared with four non-East London hospitals, 1922–1938*

	In-patients				Out-patients			
Year	Total for 5 East London hospitals[1]	%	Total for 4 non-East London hospitals[2]	%	Total for 5 East London hospitals	%	Total for 4 non-East London hospitals	%
1922	4,415	44	3,900	20	5,589	56	15,555	80
1923	4,435	46	4,163	21	5,212	54	15,897	79
1924	4,401	48	4,102	23	4,716	52	13,756	77
1925	4,668	50	4,203	22	4,630	50	15,325	78
1926	4,860	54	4,177	23	4,142	46	14,292	77
1927	5,214	60	4,540	23	3,544	40	15,003	77
1929	5,917	67	4,784	28	2,908	33	12,012	72
1930	6,047	69	5,088	29	2,770	31	12,670	71
1931	6,072	71	4,519c	27	2,510	29	12,184[3]	73
1932	6,042	72	3,958c	25	2,378	28	11,695[3]	72
1933	—	—	4,561c	28	—	—	11,628[3]	72
1934	—	—	5,023c	27	—	—	13,866[3]	73
1935	6,354	78	5,023c	28	1,811	22	12,906[3]	72
1936	—	—	5,017c	29	—	—	12,828[3]	71

Note: This table does not show the overall trend of hospital confinements. It is limited to showing the pattern for voluntary hospitals and does not take into account what was occurring in Poor Law institutions or among district midwifery agencies.

[1] Five East London hospitals include the City of London Maternity Home, East End Maternity Home, Jewish Maternity Home, London Hospital, and Salvation Army Mothers' Hospital.

[2] Non-East London hospitals include the British Mothers' Lying-in Hospital (Woolwich), Clapham Maternity Hospital, General Lambeth Hospital, and Queen Charlotte's Hospital (Marylebone), 1922–31.

[3] After 1930 there are no figures for Clapham Hospital.

Sources: CLMH, EEMH, JMH, LH, and SAMH, *ARs* (1922–36); London County Council, 'Statistics of Hospitals in Greater London not under Public Management', in *London Statistics* (1922–36).

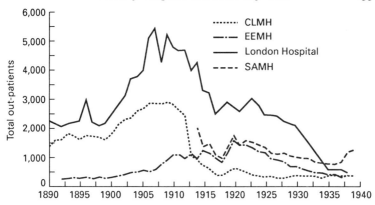

F I G. 4.5. Total number of out-patient births in East London hospitals, 1890–1939
Source: as for Fig. 4.4.

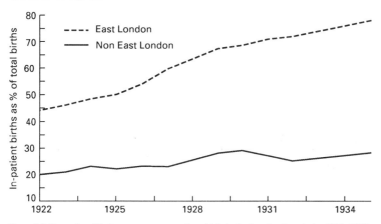

F I G. 4.6. In-patient births as percentage of total births in London hospitals, 1932–1936
Source: CLMH, EEMH, JMH, London Hospital, *ARs* (1922–36); LCC, 'Statistics of Hospitals in Greater London not under Public Management in *London Statistics* (1922–36).

occasion using the excuse of needing some boiled water to get some respite from a fight between a father and daughter in the next room.[43] Similar descriptions appeared in reports from other hospitals. In 1913 the EEMH declared that 'Without doubt, the best place for a poor woman to be confined is not her own home.'[44] The picture drawn by Salaman in 1905 was also described by the House Governor of London Hospital in 1922.[45]

---

[43] Salaman,'The Helmsman', 30.   [44] EEMH, *AR* (1913), 12.
[45] Morris, 'Report of a Visit to the District Maternity Charity', 3–4.

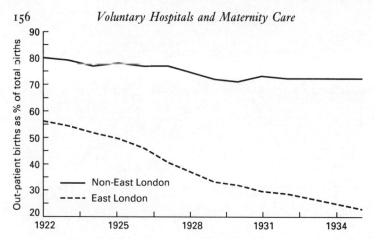

FIG. 4.7. Out-patient births as percentage of total births in London hospitals, 1922–1936
Source: as for Fig. 4.7.

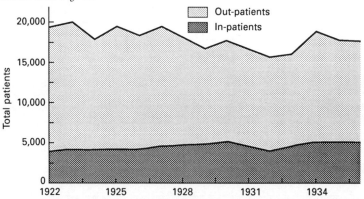

FIG. 4.8. Annual out-patients and in-patients of non-East London hospitals, 1922–1936
Source: as for Fig. 4.6.

By the 1920s new blocks of flats, with bathrooms and electric light, were appearing in East London but the rent charged for such accommodation was 'quite prohibitive' to most living in the area. Many were therefore forced to continue living in overcrowded, insanitary, tenement houses.[46] Bugs were also a problem. In the house where Miss B. carried out her first delivery the walls had just been whitewashed. She waited most of the night for the baby

[46] The London Hospital, *ARs* (1925), 197; (1921), 187; and (1924), 187; Miss M.B., interviewed by L. Marks, London, 7 July 1987, transcript, 4.

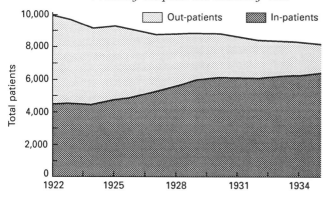

FIG. 4.9. Annual out-patients and in-patients in five East London hospitals, 1922–1936
Source: as for Fig. 4.6.

and once the gas was lit the bugs crawled through the new whitewash and came out through the walls, and before I'd got the baby I'd used up all the swabs killing bugs so I had to send father across to hospital to get another packet of swabs. Of course I'd used them all up. . . . And I was told that I shouldn't . . . have used them . . . of course, you weren't dirty because you'd bugs, the bugs were in the walls, they didn't belong to the person . . . I can remember bathing another baby, and you know I'd dressed it up and there it was lovely and clean and I picked it up to kiss it and there was a bug crawling up its gown. . . .[47]

In early years hospitals appeared to appreciate that many women found it impractical to be confined in hospital as it would entail leaving their house and their 'little children to the care of a kind but casual neighbour'.[48] By 1925, however, the EEMH was arguing that housing conditions, many of which lacked the 'common necessities of life' placed normal cases of birth at serious risk.[49] This emphasis grew stronger each year, and by the 1930s the EEMH was stressing the comforts that hospitals could afford the mothers and the nurses. It reported that twice in one year a ceiling had fallen down while an infant was being born at home, leaving the mother less perturbed than the nurses. Given such housing circumstances it was not surprising that the SAMH saw the 'convenience of the wards' as 'a boon'.[50]

According to the medical reports women themselves were demanding hospital rather than home confinements.[51] Why then was the new

[47] Miss M.B., interview transcript, 6.   [48] EEMH, *AR* (1913), 12.
[49] Ibid. (1925), 13.   [50] Ibid. (1931); SAMH, *AR* (1933), 3.
[51] Ministry of Health Memorandum, 'Maternity Hospitals and Homes' (London, 1920), 1.

generation of women calling for hospital confinements when their mothers, whose living conditions were often comparable or worse, had stayed at home?[52] The CLMH took the view that the change had come about during World War I which had brought thousands of soldiers and civilians into contact with hospitals, making the prospect of confinement in hospital less daunting.[53] Similarly the EEMH argued that women's growing choice to be confined in hospital stemmed from an increase in the number of women educated 'in the matters of health and sanitation'.[54] With the improvements in obstetric care and the expansion in the number of beds, hospital confinement became an alternative closed to women a few decades before.

Some women preferred to go into hospital because it got them away from the claustrophobic atmosphere of home. In 1927 The London claimed that there was 'an even greater desire for in-patient treatment than in former years, owing no doubt to the abominable home conditions which prevail in many quarters'.[55] Some mothers saw the time they spent in hospital as a holiday, as testified by one patient interviewed by the SAMH:

This is my fourth, and all my babies were born here. I came to the Mothers' Hospital to be properly looked after and to have a holiday. It is the only real rest I have, and I make the most of it. My husband is in steady work, but we have only two rooms, and there is a great deal of racket and noise in the house. I think I should have gone crazy if I had had my baby at home; and I know that I should have been dreadfully irritable with my husband and children.[56]

Both the EEMH and the SAMH were prepared to take women in a few days before their actual confinement so that the mothers could catch up on some rest. This, the SAMH argued, spared many mothers the extra exhaustion they would have normally suffered had they remained at home, and also built up the women's constitution before they returned home.[57] The length of time mothers spent in hospital and how many beds were available for them at the CLMH and EEMH can be seen from Table 4.14. While the beds increased in number over the years, the length of stay remained at about a fortnight. Between 1905 and 1915 the

---

[52] In 1924 the SAMH reported, 'In these days of acute housing problems, surely everyone should realise that history repeats itself over and over again, and there is actually "no room" in the impossibly small spaces in which some families live for the little, expected new-comer to arrive. The Mothers' Hospital has been a boon to many such' (*AR* (1924), 7).

[53] *Onward*, 3 (1925), 58.   [54] EEMH, *AR* (1927), 6.

[55] The London Hospital, *AR* (1927), 201.

[56] SAMH, *AR* (1926), 7–8; see also EEMH, *AR* (1934).

[57] SAMH, *ARs* (1916) and (1926).

TABLE 4.14. *Number of patients and beds and average length of stay at the CLMH and EEMH, 1887–1939*

Year	City of London Maternity Home			East End Maternity Home	
	In-patients admitted	Average no. of beds daily occupied	Average stay in days occupied	In-patients admitted	Total no. of beds
1887–90	1,188	17.9	16	—	7
1892–5	1,899	21.3	16	866	13
1896–1901	2,814	24.5	16	1,187	18
1902–5	1,820[1]	23.9[1]	15[1]	1,416	26
1906–10	3,822	30.1	15	2,492	33
1911–15	4,883	41.8	15	2,696	33
1918–20	4,518	61.0	13	2,546	33
1921–5	8,456	67.7	14	5,154	38
1926–30	7,904	64.9	15	6,496	56
1931–5	7,925	67.9	15	7,470	56
1936–9	6,505	71.7	15	4,558	59

Note: The average length of stay is not given for the EEMH.

[1] For years 1903–5.

Source: ARs for CLMH and EEMH (1887–1939).

average number of beds occupied by in-patients at the CLMH almost doubled from 24 to 46, a trend which was reinforced in the inter-war years. The number of beds also doubled at the EEMH in the twenty years between 1902 and 1920. Such a rise in the number of beds indicates the shortage of beds the hospitals in East London experienced in the inter-war years. During the 1920s The London continually lamented that it had to turn women away because it could not give them the in-patient care they were seeking. Table 4.15 shows that as many as 250 women (44 per cent of the total applications for in-patient care) seeking in-patient care at The London were referred elsewhere in 1923, and even when the hospital expanded its number of beds in 1926 a large number of women continued to be turned away in the following years.[58]

How much the choice of the women to be confined in hospital stemmed

[58] See The London Hospital, *ARs* (1921–6).

TABLE 4.15. *Number and percentage of patients wanting in-patient treatment but turned away compared with those accepted at London Hospital, 1921–1930*

Year	Total in-patients treated	Patients wanting in-patient care and referred elsewhere	% patients referred elsewhere
1921	—	142	—
1922	252	167	40
1923	314	250	44
1924	344	191	36
1925	347	214	38
1926	387	204	35
1927	569	159	22
1928	605	251	29
1929	692	276	29
1930	677	310	31

Note: The London acquired more beds in 1926 which explains the increase in the number of in-patients after that date.

Source: London Hospital, *ARs* (1921–30).

from the pressure from the medical staff is hard to judge. Certainly the housing standards required by hospitals to carry out a district delivery were high as revealed in instructions to mothers who were to receive district midwives from the CLMH in 1936.

The room should be the best available in the house with as much sun and air as possible, and near the bathroom is advisable as it saves endless steps for the nurse. Do not have more furniture in it than is really needed. Good lighting should be considered. The carpet should be rolled up, or if this is not possible, it should be well protected with sheets. A single bed is preferable and with a foot end. Plenty of bed linen and some old sheets, also a small one, are needed.[59]

The descriptions of housing in East London, as noted above, imply that such conditions could not be achieved in many East London homes.

During his midwifery training at London Hospital at the beginning of the twentieth century, Salaman observed that Jewish homes tended to provide better conditions for confinements than others. In his experience Jewish homes were 'immeasurably better' because 'however poor the

[59] *Onward*, 49 (Jan. 1936), 36.

home, there would be clean linen, hot water and several women neigh-bours to comfort the mother and assist the doctor'.[60] Years later Miss M.B., who worked as a nurse and midwife for The London in the 1920s and 1930s, confirmed Salaman's judgement.[61] By contrast medical profes-sionals stressed that the homes of Irish patients were much poorer and were less well equipped for childbirth and other medical treatment than those of other local residents. Irish families also seemed to be noticeably larger than other families.[62]

Although many women were clamouring to be delivered in hospital by the late 1920s, this was not the whole picture. A number of women told by their doctor to go into hospital refused to do so because they 'didn't trust their husbands, and wouldn't leave them'.[63] Many women could not rely on their family or neighbours to look after the children in their absence. Financial restraints also limited the possibility of employing someone to undertake such work. Aside from the help that could be gained from the Sick Room Helps Society and later the council, home helps or maternity nurses were expensive and beyond the pocket of many women in East London.[64] Before World War I most handywomen were paid 10s. for ten days with food, which increased to a minimum of 15s. per week after the war. This was a large sum compared with the average working-class wage of 25s.[65]

Although not in half as bad a condition as many of the houses in East London, the EEMH itself had many disadvantages for confinements. In 1932 the Stepney Public Health Survey reported: 'The building consists of an old house and a chapel converted into a hospital . . . It presents all the disadvantages of an adapted building—numberless narrow corridors on varying levels and awkward narrow stairways.' The equipment of the hospital was also 'simple in quality and minimum in quantity'. In addi-tion the hospital's practices were unorthodox: only antenatal cases selected by the senior tutor were medically examined by doctors; babies

---

[60] Salaman, 'The Helmsman', 27–8.   [61] Miss M.B., interview transcript, 4.

[62] Salaman, 'The Helmsman', 27–8; Recollections of a private nurse from 1899. One of the cases the nurse treated was from an Irish Family, see 'Two Private Cases', *League of London Hospital Nurses Review*, 8 (1939), 44.

[63] Miss M.B., interview transcript, 6.

[64] Ministry of Health, *Report*, 8 May 1920, (PRO file: MH 52/202). For more informa-tion on home helps see Chs. 3 and 6 and L. Marks, '"Dear Old Mother Levy's": the Jewish Maternity Home and Sick Room Helps Society, 1895–1939', *Soc. Hist. Med.* 3/1 (1990), 61–88, 76–8.

[65] The London Hospital, *AR* (1921), 186; M. Llewelyn Davies (ed.), *Maternity: Letters from Working-Class Wives* (London, 1915; repr., 1984), 5. See Chs. 3 and 6 for the fees charged by midwives.

slept together with their mothers in the wards; septic cases were retained as long as possible; and no masks or gloves were used for confinements. Yet, the report continued, 'the hospital is an outstanding example of how good workmen can obtain excellent results with bad tools. The medical and nursing staff are devoting all their energies to the care of patients.' It concluded that 'in spite of everything the statistics in the past years have left nothing to be desired'.[66]

While the number of hospital deliveries was obviously increasing, the number of home confinements remained quite high. Home confinements were cheaper for the hospital than hospital births. In 1914 the total cost of each in-patient per week at the EEMH amounted to 17s. 7d., whereas the average cost of each out-patient cost 6s. 10d., less than half of the sum to keep an in-patient in for a week.[67] Hospital staff tried to make the best of the situation they found in patients' homes.[68] Indeed, it would seem they were largely successful, as despite the lack of facilities in the homes, the majority of the deliveries ended with a healthy mother and baby.[69] This result was reflected in a report by the EEMH in 1932, which regretted the recent flow of expectant mothers to hospitals because district work had 'shown through many years, that normal cases can be treated in poor and sometimes dirty homes with no fatalities'.[70]

Other Services

Follow-Up Care

All the hospitals had some kind of follow-up care for their district cases whereby the midwives or medical students visited the mothers several times. In some cases maternity nurses could also be brought in for the following weeks to help not only with medical care but with some housework as well. While their help was not as extensive as that of home helps provided by philanthropic organizations and municipal schemes, maternity nurses did go some way to helping mothers burdened with housework and child care during confinement.

From 1922 The London Hospital (in collaboration with Bethnal Green Council from 1925) was supplying maternity nurses and labour nurses to

---

[66] Stepney, 'Public Health Survey', 1932, pp. xvi–xvii (PRO file: MH 66/391).

[67] EEMH, *AR* (1914); London Hospital *AR* (1929), 209.

[68] EEMH, *AR* (1930), 13; London Hospital, *AR* (1929), 209.

[69] In its annual report for 1932 the EEMH stated that of the 8,200 cases attended by the EEMH on the district for the years 1922–32 there were no maternal deaths.

[70] EEMH, *AR* (1932), 8.

accompany their district medical students and pupil midwives.[71] Labour nurses assisted the students during the deliveries, and maternity nurses took care of the patient for the following ten days.[72] Often maternity nurses also provided extra nourishment, groceries, and baby garments for their patients. These nurses were reported to be in high demand by the patients.[73] In 1922 12 per cent of the maternity out-patients received maternity nurses. By 1934 this had risen to 58 per cent, but this increase was due to the significant drop in the number of out-patients in the early 1930s rather than because of an increase in the number of maternity nurses supplied.[74]

Preventive Work

Apart from the immediate task of nursing women during their confinements, all the hospitals undertook preventive health care. These services had roots in activities which had operated since the nineteenth century such as health visiting, the establishment of schools for mothers, and Babies' Welcome Clubs. Patients cared for by the EEMH in its earliest years, for instance, received lessons on the necessity of cleanliness and 'how to wash and dress and feed a baby' alongside the medical care they received.[75] This educational policy continued into the twentieth century and was also pursued by the other hospitals. Lessons on hygiene and infant management were provided at sessions when the women booked into the hospitals and at a later date through antenatal and postnatal clinics. Guidance was given on breast-feeding and extra nutriments were supplied for pregnant nursing mothers along with milk for their infants.[76]

[71] The London Hospital, *AR* (1926), 202.

[72] Ibid. (1927), p. 201. The London Hospital separated the nursing work undertaken during the delivery and the lying-in period between labour and maternity nurses. Much of the work undertaken by these two types of nurse was probably rooted in the traditional work of a 'monthly nurse'. A monthly nurse had less midwifery training than a midwife, and could not practise as an independent midwife. Her main task was to carry out the menial tasks alongside a medical practitioner during a delivery and to nurse the mother during the lying-in period. Many upper-class women during the 19th c. preferred to employ independent midwives with full midwifery training to act as their monthly nurses when delivered by a medical practitioner. For more information see J. Donnison, *Midwives and Medical Men: A History of the Struggle for the Control of Childbirth* (London, 1977; repr., 1988), 62.

[73] The London Hospital, *AR* (1928), 215.

[74] For exact number of maternity nurses and the number of patients these covered see Marks, 'Irish and Jewish Women's Experience of Childbirth', 216, table 6.16.

[75] EEMH, *AR* (1932), 8.

[76] Bethnal Green MOH, *AR* (1910–11), 36; Stepney MOH, *AR* (1910), 22; (1914), 55–7. The MOH of Stepney reported that education concerning breast-feeding was especially needed if the following could be taken as a common problem: 'Quite recently when one of the Health Visitors called at a certain house, she found the mother and her first baby, aged

By the 1920s antenatal care became a regular part of the services offered by East London hospitals. The persistence of high maternal mortality during the 1920s increased public awareness on the need to institute proper antenatal services.[77] Antenatal care had an extremely high profile in the 1920s because it was seen as the only way to reduce maternal mortality. In 1932 the Departmental Committee on Maternal Mortality estimated that the lack or failure of antenatal care accounted for 15 per cent of the primary avoidable factors in maternal deaths in the years 1930 to 1932.[78] The persistence of high maternal mortality during the inter-war years increased public awareness of the need to institute proper antenatal services which became a regular part of the maternity services in these years.[79] Effective antenatal care relied on the co-operation between midwives, general practitioners, and hospital consultants, which was rare in the inter-war period. Often antenatal services were split between many different institutions, clinics, and general practitioners' surgeries with minimal communication between all parties. In addition antenatal practice during this period only consisted of testing urine and measuring blood pressure. This was useful for identifying toxaemia cases, for which treatment was limited.[80]

Antenatal care as practised in East London hospitals, however, probably came closer to the attainable ideal than elsewhere. Their policy of deliberately identifying high-risk mothers and their provision of special attention before, during, and after labour was perhaps the greatest service antenatal care could provide during this period.[81] As at other hospitals, most women who wanted maternity care from The London and EEMH could only book by attending the antenatal sessions.[82] Young women who were expecting their first confinement were expected to attend the antenatal clinics more often than those who had already had children. The department at The London kept 'strict watch' on 'possible defaulters'.[83] According to The London Hospital's reports very few women failed to return to these clinics and most took full advantage of the facilities.[84]

---

3 weeks, at breakfast. The mother was having bacon and eggs and the baby, bacon fat and the yolk of egg!' (Stepney MOH, *AR* (1914), 57).

[77] London Hospital, *AR* (1927), 201.

[78] Ministry of Health, *Final Report of the Departmental Committee on Maternal Mortality and Morbidity* (London, 1932), 23.   [79] London Hospital, *AR* (1927), 201.

[80] See I. Loudon, 'Some Historical Aspects of Toxaemia Pregnancy: A Review', *Br. J. Obstet. &. Gynaecol.* 98 (1991), 853–8.

[81] For a detailed description of the antenatal care practice of the EEMH see W. H. F. Oxley, 'Prophylaxis in Midwifery', *Med. Offr.*, 25 Aug. 1928, 79–81.

[82] Ibid. 81.   [83] The London Hospital, *AR* (1925), 197.

[84] Ibid. (1927), 201.

Medical staff working in the antenatal clinics saw their role as educational. The CLMH stressed that an expectant mother should live

a normal healthy life, not overworking, or doing heavy lifting, avoiding sudden exertion, and trying, as far as possible, to be normal. She should rest every afternoon on her bed for an hour with her clothes off, and really relax. This will help her not to become very tired, and will also help her child. She should have regular outdoor exercise for at least one hour per day, walking or gardening.[85]

Unfortunately such advice was not necessarily practical for many mothers of East London whose lives were dominated by incessant housework and child care.

By the late 1920s maternity services extended into postnatal care carried out by the Infant Welfare Centres, including those established by the hospitals. Considerable emphasis was placed by the infant welfare department at The London on the vaccination of infants. Much of the postnatal work only constituted 'an examination of the new-born infant and the giving of advice to the mother, rather than a physical examination of the latter'.[86] Most of the advice given was on breast-feeding, which was a continuation of old policy. How effective such education was is debatable. Despite decades of warning against artificial feeding, according to one medical officer, ignorance remained.

What is most annoying is the mother who comes once, with a breast-fed baby satisfactory in every way and then never again [until] about 18 months or two years later, when she brings a miserable, pasty, undersized child with bow legs. When reproached she *invariably* says that, as to the bow legs, the lady next door, or her mother, or her grandfather (and sometimes the doctor) says 'He will grow out of it as he gets older.'[87]

Hospital reports were slightly more sympathetic to the reasons behind the continuance of artificial feeding, which they saw as the result of 'the strenuous lives' that the mothers lived. The EEMH felt that much of this could be corrected by educating mothers to apply for extra food from the Borough.[88] In 1929 The London Hospital claimed that since it had opened its antenatal department, its mothers had become 'more solicitous, not only for advice for their infants but for themselves in matters of health during pregnancy'.[89] Tables 4.16 to 4.18 reveal the numbers of mothers who attended the various clinics at the CLMH and SAMH. Reflecting

[85] Matron, 'Mother's Circle', *Onward*, 48 (Oct. 1935), 409. Similar advice was given by the EEMH, see its *AR* (1927), 12.
[86] Stepney, 'Public Health Survey', 1932, pp. xx, 44 (PRO file: MH 66/391).
[87] Bethnal Green MOH, *AR* (1924), 14.   [88] EEMH, *AR* (1928), 13.
[89] The London Hospital, *AR* (1929), 201.

TABLE 4.16. *Number of cases and attendances at the child welfare centre and antenatal clinics of the CLMH, 1921–1939*

Year	Child Welfare Centre		Antenatal clinic		
	No. first-time attenders	Total attendance of all cases	Total cases	Total attendance	Average no. visits to the clinic per mother
1921	530	6,322	—	—	—
1922	738	5,690	2,242	3,363	1.5
1923	701	5,836	2,145	3,453	1.6
1924	422	5,234	2,137	3,453	1.6
1925	500	4,876	—	3,726	—
1926	—	4,717	—	5,832	—
1927	389	4,839	2,277	6,001	2.6
1928	354	4,854	2,227	6,730	3.0
1929	431	4,639	2,070	7,555	3.6
1930	345	4,674	2,083	7,856	3.8
1931	358	4,114	2,161	8,305	3.8
1932	389	4,134	2,225	8,189	3.7
1933	344	3,996	2,098	10,035	4.8
1934	334	4,191	2,181	10,278	4.7
1935	304	4,076	2,749	10,282	3.7
1936	280	3,302	3,369	9,990	2.9
1937	277	3,444	3,003	10,248	3.4
1938	241	3,145	2,908	9,972	3.4
1939	280	2,580	2,832	9,646	3.4

Source: CLMH, *ARs* (1921–39).

the increasing drive for antenatal care, Table 4.16 indicates that the average number of times a mother visited the antenatal clinic at the CLMH increased between 1921 and 1934, thereafter stabilizing in the following years. It is difficult, however, to know whether the increase in attendance was the result of a decision on the part of the mothers or pressure from the medical professionals.

Hospital Social Welfare Schemes

A recurrent theme in the hospitals' reports was of the unemployment and poverty faced by the overwhelming majority of its patients. Such

TABLE 4.17. *Number of cases and attendances at the antenatal and child welfare clinics for district cases at SAMH, 1921–1940*

Year	District births	Child Welfare Clinic		Antenatal Clinic	
		Sessions	Attendances	Sessions	Attendances
1921	1,340	94	2,050	92	296
1922	1,493	1,878	2,922	138	1,844
1923	1,424	58	2,146	148	1,878
1924	1,346	103	3,652	155	2,922
1925	1,270	101	1,528	153	1,923
1926	1,050	100	1,933	160	1,579
1927	1,024	97	1,707	248	2,121
1928	1,074	110	1,792	275	3,276
1929	988	141	1,558	245	3,142
1930	927	130	1,185	223	3,000
1931	881	104	776	202	2,701
1932	887	54	636	204	2,896
1935	676	—	158	—	3,092
1936	685	—	143	—	3,167
1937	750	—	—	—	3,437
1938	1,099	—	—	—	6,802
1939	1,134	—	—	—	9,515
1940	1,133	—	—	—	9,146

Source: SAMH, *ARs* and *The Deliverer*, 1921–39.

deprivation meant that many of its mothers could not 'provide themselves adequately with what they need for their infants'.[90] One way in which the hospitals tried to ease this problem was through their social welfare schemes. From early on the SAMH offered some welfare relief such as garments and food through its mothers' meetings (established in 1895). Such meetings not only aimed to provide religious knowledge, but also to give mothers a cup of tea and a respite from the daily drudgery of housework, and an opportunity for women 'to open their hearts' to sympathetic nurses.[91]

District midwives also advised mothers on what was wrong and where to get the required care.[92] Coming into contact with the women in their

---

[90] Ibid. (1925), 198.
[91] For further information on mothers' meetings see Chs. 3 and 6, and F. K. Prochaska, 'A Mother's Country: Mothers' Meetings and Family Welfare in Britain, 1850–1950', *Hist.* 74 (1989), 379–99. [92] *The Deliverer*, Feb. 1899, 114.

TABLE 4.18. *Number of cases and attendances at various clinics held at the SAMH for in-patients and out-patients, 1920–1939*

Year	Hospital: Number of births in hospital	Antenatal clinic		Child welfare clinic		Postnatal clinic		Dental clinic	
		Sessions	Attendance	Sessions	Attendance	Sessions	Attendance	Sessions	Attendance
1920	1,002	156	3,959*	104*	3,575*	—	—	—	—
1921	1,011	139	4,534	139	3,668	—	—	—	—
1922	1,129	142	6,987	142	3,407	—	—	—	—
1923	1,104	185	6,407	185	2,833	—	—	—	—
1924	1,138	221	6,598	221	3,646	—	—	—	—
1925	1,300	338	14,463	338	6,198	—	—	—	—
1926	1,420	355	11,987	355	6,948	—	—	—	—
1927	1,483	342	14,942	148	7,594	42	210	29	372
1928	1,605	345	16,475	151	7,548	53	219	30	454
1929	1,607	397	18,359	148	6,663	—	—	—	—
1930	1,549	403	19,380	145	5,658	96	—	25	501
1931	1,447	397	17,728	153	6,031	101	—	25	557
1932	1,583	408	19,392	154	6,560	89	—	25	593
1935	1,534	—	20,154	—	7,130	—	2,311	—	511
1936	1,596	—	20,978	—	7,782	—	2,093	—	468
1937	1,595	—	21,290	—	7,561	—	2,544	—	444
1938	1,756	—	22,316	—	9,017	—	2,851	—	395

* It is not clear whether the session and attendance belonged to the hospital or district clinics.

own surroundings, midwives from all the hospitals gained a good knowledge of the conditions these women were facing. Their work often supplemented that of the health visitor, as was revealed in one report from
the EEMH: 'In our visiting we cannot restrict ourselves to maternity
only, but incidentally send children to Hospital, consumptive men to
Dispensaries and Infirmaries, and in fact, if the mother is in any kind of
trouble, from being knocked about by her husband to the death of her
child, she comes at once to tell "Matron".'[93] The midwives also provided
certain necessities from the samaritan funds attached to each hospital.
Such funds were an acknowledgement that medical care alone would not
suffice in an area of great deprivation. The samaritan fund of each hospital operated in different ways, providing baby clothes and nightgowns for
confinement, and food. At Christmas time there were extra activities
provided by the hospitals, such as a special tea and gifts of coal, as well
as food and additional garments.

The EEMH appears to have been particularly sensitive to the needs
of its patients. During the dockers' strike of 1911 women were allowed to
come into hospital ahead of their confinement (in some cases three months
before delivery), because of the stark prospects many faced should they
remain at home where money was scarce and food not forthcoming.
Many women admitted to the hospital were found to be starving.[94] In 1912
the EEMH reported,

Never have our visits revealed such unparalleled poverty as during the past year.
The coal strike was terrible, but when it was followed by the long dock strike it
was indeed disastrous. To face a succession of crises as our people have been
through is almost beyond the limit of their endurance. To insufficient food the
patients are inured, but to no nourishment and to work hard and to nurse a baby
has been the too common lot of our women.[95]

Like the EEMH the Salvation Army was aware of the burden of poverty
and its influence on malnutrition and ill-health, and would take in women
in advance of their confinements.[96] Other hospitals acknowledged the social
deprivation facing many of their patients, but did not show quite as much
concern as the EEMH or the SAMH.

An important part of the assistance given through the Samaritan Fund
was the financial aid given to those who needed to go to a convalescent
home. Such help was vital if a mother was to regain her strength before
embarking for the first time or yet again on the burdens of motherhood.[97]

[93] EEMH, *AR* (1911), 15.   [94] Ibid. 14–15.   [95] Ibid. (1912), 14.
[96] SAMH, *AR* (1933), 6–7.   [97] EEMH, *AR* (1910), 15.

The London recognized that 'though confinement is not necessarily an illness, a fortnight's rest and change from the continual routine of home life is a great boon to the mothers of large families and indeed if they are to maintain a good standard of health, it is almost imperative that they should have this short rest after the confinement'. Most of the women from The London were sent to the St Mary's Convalescent Home in Birchington on Sea. Such help was not unique to The London. Other maternity hospitals in East London ran similar schemes. Yet while these services were important they were not enough to eliminate the greater part of the deprivation in the area, and difficulties arose over child care for the remaining children in the mother's absence. They could only help in a limited way. No more than 2 per cent of all the maternity cases at The London Hospital were given aid to go on convalescence.[98] Most of the hospitals, including the most sympathetic hospital, the EEMH, also reserved such help only for 'deserving' cases.

Fees Charged

Although these hospitals were established with the explicit aim of providing medical care on a charitable basis, it is a mistake to presume such services were entirely free.[99] Viewing themselves as agents of social reform, they aimed to make their patients self-supporting citizens. It was clear from the earlier reports of the CLMH that although a charitable institution it was not to be 'considered as a Poor House'. No woman was to take advantage of institutional care without due cause. According to the rules of 1870 a woman was only allowed to remain in hospital free of charge for 48 hours before her confinement. Should she remain beyond that time previous to her confinement she would be expected to pay at the rate of 18*d*. per day.[100]

This policy became less stringent over time, but women were still expected to contribute towards the costs of their care, because, it was argued, the service could not be entirely self-supporting.[101] By 1892 the Salvation Army was running a scheme whereby women could subscribe

---

[98] The London Hospital, *ARs* (1922–34).

[99] The Salvation Army made it clear that 'To the maternity home any woman is admitted upon payment of a subscription of 1*s*. per week for 10 weeks, the object being rather to train nurses in midwifery than to afford charitable relief' (SAMH, *Report of the Committee of Inquiry upon the Darkest England Scheme* (1892), cited in Fairbanks, *Booth's Boots*, 36).

[100] CLMH, *AR* (1870), 10–11.

[101] This was stressed by a plea for money by the Salvation Army in *The Deliverer*, Feb. 1899.

to the maternity home 1*s*. per week for 10 weeks to ensure treatment. In 1897 the standard fee charged by a Salvation Army district nurse for nine days' attendance was 7*s*. 6*d*., but this was not required of patients who were too poor to pay.[102] Three years later the institution was charging between 7*s*. 6*d*. and 10*s*. 6*d*. according to the circumstances and the husband's wages, for 'ten days thorough nursing and keeping the home tidy'.[103] Patients could pay the sum in small amounts every month. In 1908 the EEMH charged 3*s*. 6*d*. for women being attended in their own homes. Women were given back 1*s*. of the fee if they kept certain 'simple rules' set by the hospital. What the rules were is unclear.[104] In the 1930s London Hospital charged 14*s*. for an in-patient delivery.[105]

Like many voluntary hospitals by the beginning of the twentieth century, The London Hospital had its own Lady Almoner.[106] It was the task of the Lady Almoner to see that rigid economies were observed, and that the services of the hospital were not 'abused' by those who could afford private care. She was to assess the degree to which patients could be expected to pay for the services offered by the hospital. Inevitably, she was not a popular figure. Any tendency on the part of the patient towards thriftlessness and dependence was frowned upon in the almoner's reports.[107] In line with this tradition, rather than offering material support, the Lady Almoner put families in touch with other charitable agencies already organizing for this purpose. This even included various apprenticeship and skilled employment associations, so as to help the children of their patients to gain suitable trades.[108]

Such attitudes underlay the questioning mothers had to undergo in order to gain the benefits of the maternity care offered by the hospital. Although women were always expected to pay some contribution towards the care they received, with the introduction of the maternity benefit in 1913 many women who previously were unable to pay were now expected

---

[102] *All the World*, May 1897, 216 (newspaper issued by the Salvation Army); *The Deliverer*, Jan. 1897.

[103] *The Deliverer*, July 1900, 11. By the early 1930s the Salvation Army was charging '£1 and 2*s*. the first, a £1 for each of the others. If you had a woman come in to help you, you would pay 10*s*. or 10 bob.' Mrs E.C., interview transcript, p. 4.

[104] *ELO*, 30 May 1908, 3.

[105] Mrs D.G., interviewed by L. Marks, London, 28 Sept. 1987, transcript, p. 13.

[106] For more information on the introduction of payment into voluntary hospitals and the establishment of Lady Almoners see G. Rivett, *The Development of the London Hospital System* (London, 1986), 49–50, 119, 144.

[107] *First Report of the Lady Almoner*, 1 Feb. 1910–31 Jan. 1911, cited in G. Black, 'Health and Medical Care of the Jewish Poor in the East End of London, 1880–1939', Ph.D. thesis (Leicester, 1987), 217–18.   [108] Black, 'Health and Medical Care', 219.

to cover some of the expense of their confinement. The amount was dependent on their husband's income. One Jewish woman remembered how humiliated her mother felt by the personal questions she was always asked by the Lady Almoner, often after a long wait. As a Jewish patient she felt even more resentful of the ignorance shown by the staff in spelling her name.[109]

Jewish Patients' Attitudes and the Jewish Community's Response to the Hospitals

Aside from the embarrassment some women felt when asked judgemental questions by the Lady Almoner, what were the perceptions of patients to these hospitals in general? The experience of patients treated by these hospitals altered over time and was partly tied to the changes affecting hospital policies as a whole. Rules governing the CLMH, for instance, seemed paternalistic in their approach to patients during the 1870s. Those admitted were expected to behave with the appropriate decorum. They were to arrive with clean apparel and linen, and were expressly forbidden to take any kind of spirituous liquors as they were 'highly injurious' to both the mother and the infant. After confinement women were required by the rules of the hospital to show their gratitude by waiting on the Governor or Governess who had 'kindly recommended' them and to present them with a letter of thanks and to acknowledge the help they had received from the hospital.[110] Other hospitals in East London were not explicit in such procedures, but the policy pursued by the CLMH was common for many voluntary hospitals during the nineteenth century. In practice such rules were probably moderated over time.

Despite the patronizing attitudes of the hospitals, there was an element of warmth and sympathy for the poverty-stricken patients they were serving. Although the Lady Almoner was not necessarily the most popular person, the midwives and maternity nurses of these hospitals were looked upon as friends or 'angels' of the poor, or even 'angels of mercy'.[111] By the 1930s all the hospitals were serving a third generation of women, having previously helped their mothers and grandmothers. As administrators at the SAMH reported,

---

[109] Miss T.G., interviewed by L. Marks, London, 22 Jan. 1988, transcript, p. 8.
[110] CLMH, *AR* (1871), 9.
[111] *The Deliverer*, Jan. 1897, 301; Oct. 1906, 157; *London Hospital Illustrated*, c.1936, 5; SAMH, *AR* (1913–14), 7.

In the East End there are now whole families of children who have been attended into the world by Salvation Army nurses; sometimes young wives, booking the services of the older nurses, will say, 'Do you remember? When I was four I used to hold the soap for you and roll up the binders! Mother always had you and so must I!'[112]

This suggests that the patients must have had some kind of satisfaction if daughters were being persuaded by their mothers to go to the same hospital.

Despite the barriers of language and cultural differences and moments of tension it seems that these hospitals were by and large sympathetic to their Jewish patients' needs. In his years at London hospital as a medical student, Salaman recalled that he had hardly been affected by any anti-Semitism, nor seen any real mistreatment of Jewish patients. He claimed that 'The record of the "London" in those days of the Aliens Bill agitation was indeed a proud one.' Similarly he stated that Catholic patients were treated at The London Hospital in the same way as other patients, and were not made subject to any 'hostility or ribaldry' from the staff or other patients.[113]

Part of the reason behind the good treatment of the Jewish patients was that key Anglo-Jewish leaders took a keen interest in financing and running these hospitals. In all of the hospitals Jewish benefactors were active in funding-raising schemes, and often sat on the hospitals' various committees; Jewish women being conspicuously active in the ladies' associations and Needlework Guild.[114] Through their donations the established Jewish patrons were able to gain positions of authority which enabled them to safeguard the rights of their co-religionists in hospital institutions. To gain the financial sponsorship of wealthy Jewish patrons, many of these hospitals went out of their way to make special provision for Jewish patients. Where hospitals did not concede to their demands Jewish subscribers changed their allegiances. This was most clearly seen in the case of the German Hospital in London which was accused in 1894 of allowing its Jewish and Catholic patients to be proselytized and forced to listen to Protestant prayers. These allegations proved groundless, but many Jewish subscribers protested by redirecting their sponsorship to

---

[112] SAMH, *AR* (1932), 5.   [113] Salaman, 'The Helmsman', 23, 37.

[114] Catholic benefactors also appeared on subscription lists in the EEMH, *AR* (1910). Mrs Lionel Rothschild was president of the Needlework Guild for the EEMH (EEMH *AR* (1937)). Lord Rothschild was one of the most famous Jewish benefactors and fund-raisers for the London Hospital. For more details on the relationship between the Jewish community and hospitals see Black, 'Health and Medical Care', ch. 6.

other hospitals and the established Jewish community transferred its allegiance to the Metropolitan Hospital instead, which guaranteed that Jewish rituals would be more easily observed.[115]

All the East London hospitals providing maternity services allowed their non-Anglican inmates to be visited by those of their respective faiths. At the EEMH and The London, Catholic nuns and priests were able to visit Catholic and non-Catholic patients freely.[116] Salaman remembered one Catholic priest in particular who was always welcomed by patients at The London. This contrasted with the official Anglican clergy, who seemed to be 'colourless, impersonal officials'. Their 'influence' was 'negligible', and their visits often 'aroused derision amongst the nursing staff as well as the patients'. Jewish patients had similar arrangements and they were often attended by a rabbi or lay Jewish visitor from a nearby synagogue or from the United Synagogue Visitation Committee.[117]

The religious needs of Jewish patients were much more elaborate and complex than those of Catholic patients, making them a more conspicuous group in hospital records than other minorities. One of the most pressing needs for Jewish patients was the provision of kosher food. From its early days London Hospital had a kosher kitchen attached to its special Jewish wards. In 1928 the CLMH established a special kosher kitchen with the financial support of the Jewish community.[118] Other hospitals did not possess kosher kitchens, but they managed to bring in kosher food from outside for their Jewish patients.

Another concern for the Jewish patients was provision for the circumcision of baby boys on the eighth day after birth. In 1906 The London Hospital received correspondence from the Jewish Initiation Society, which dealt with circumcision, calling for the notification of the birth of a male Jewish child so that a qualified Jewish *mohel* could perform the rite. The letter expressed fear that several Jewish women who were confined in the Marie Celeste ward 'through ignorance' had not had 'their children circumcised according to Jewish law on the 8th day'.[119] Arrangements were

[115] More information relating to this episode can be found in 'Inquiry as to the Charges to Proselytise: Jewish Patients in the German Hospital', United Synagogue Visitation Committee, Minutes, 1 (1871–1902) (CRO); *JC*, 9 Mar. 1894, 11; and Black 'Health and Medical Care', 229–34, 322.

[116] Sister P., Sister of Charity, interviewed by L. Marks, London, 14 Dec. 1987, notes, p. 3.

[117] According to Salaman, 'In one large ward, "Sister" used to suspend a doll in clerical garb from the chandelier with the avowed object of scoring off the visiting chaplain' (Salaman, 'The Helmsman', 35).   [118] *JC*, 9 Jan. 1925; 14 Sept. 1928.

[119] The London Hospital Archive: Blue File LM/5/27. Letter from the Society for Relieving the Poor on the Initiation of their Children into the Holy Covenant of Abraham to the Secretary of the London Hospital, E. W. Morris.

TABLE 4.19. *Number of Jewish in-patients treated at The London Hospital, at five-yearly intervals, 1871–1938*

Year	Total patients	Jews %
1871	4,781	5
1875	6,338	3.9
1880	6,312	5.9
1885	8,565	6.8
1890	9,105	7.7
1895	10,559	8.4
1900	12,746	9.1
1905	13,552	12.2
1910	16,884	12.4
1915	17,637	14.2
1921	18,770	10.4
1925	18,077	11.1
1931	14,304	14.7
1935	15,409	14.7
1938	15,902	13.7

Source: The London Hospital, *ARs* (1885–1938).

made by the hospital for the wishes of the society to be adhered to, and other hospitals had a similar practice.[120] Staff at The London looked forward to the celebration because relatives would bring a huge feast which they were invited to join.[121]

The extent to which these hospitals provided for the needs of minority patients can be most clearly seen in the records for The London which had a large proportion of Jewish patients among its general in-patients and out-patients. Table 4.19 shows how the number of Jewish patients accepted by The London Hospital increased over the years 1871 to 1938. No statistics remain for how many Jewish patients used the out-patient service. However, in 1907 it was calculated that between 20 and 30 per cent of the total out-patients were Jewish. Accurate figures do not remain for the number of Jewish mothers using the maternity services. In 1907 it was estimated that approximately half the home births attended by the hospital's midwives were Jewish.[122] In 1925 it was thought that, of a total 1,800 in- and out-patients treated at the CLMH, 450, or 25 per cent,

[120] SAMH, *AR* (1933), 9.   [121] Miss M.B., interview transcript, pp. 1–2.
[122] *JC*, 8 Mar. 1907.

were Jewish.[123] Unfortunately no statistics remain for the Jewish patients who used the other hospitals.

Various people I interviewed implied that Jewish patients cherished the care they received at the hospitals. Although Jewish patients were seen by the health professionals to be slightly strange in their habits and their language, they were considered more grateful than many for the treatment they received. Miss M.B., who worked at The London, argued that 'the attitude of the Jewish patients was excellent', and the relatives helping during confinements were very co-operative. She also claimed that 'they were always trying to show their gratitude by giving presents to the medical staff'.[124]

One Jewish woman who gave birth at The London Hospital in 1936 had fond memories of the place and said that many held it in great esteem.[125] Others, however, also commented on how large and impersonal the hospital was.[126] The EEMH was smaller than The London, and had a mixed response from its patients. One Catholic nun who frequently visited the place had the impression that the EEMH was a 'very happy place, but the accommodation was very limited and it wasn't laid out very well', a verdict borne out by the 'Public Health Survey' for Stepney.[127] Despite this, she argued, many women chose to have their babies there and 'loved it'.[128]

Less happy memories came from the daughter of a Jewish mother who gave birth in the EEMH in the 1920s:

Mother was very ill during the pregnancy and she felt that she had to go into hospital as she could not risk a home delivery. I went to visit once—the food was atrocious. Absolutely appalling. Mother couldn't eat any of the food there. They used to give them boiled pudding, and peas with worms crawling out of it. Mother couldn't eat anything. She was there a fortnight, and when she came home she was very weak because she hadn't eaten anything. The baby was all right to start off with. The EEMH was very poverty stricken.[129]

---

[123] *JC*, 9 Jan. 1925. As Ch. 5 shows, Jewish mothers only entered a Poor Law institution as a last resort, preferring to have their care either at home, or from another agency. Unfortunately, no evidence remains on whether there was any differentiation in the use made by Jewish mothers of the in-patient and out-patient hospital services. Hospital staff saw Jewish homes as better than others which might have resulted in more mothers giving birth at home. However, Jewish patients were also known to want the best possible medical care they could get, which in this period often meant a hospital birth.

[124] Miss M.B., interview transcript, pp. 2–3.

[125] Mrs D.G., interview transcript, p. 20.

[126] Miss T.G., interview transcript, p. 8.

[127] Stepney, 'Public Health Survey', 1932, pp. xx, 44 (PRO file: MH 66/391).

[128] Sister P., Sister of Mercy, interviewed London, 9 Dec. 1987, transcript, p. 3.

[129] Miss T.G., interview transcript, p. 4.

Another non-Jewish woman, Mrs E.C., booked to have her baby at the EEMH in the early 1930s. Her initial experience of the home changed her mind. She resented having to get a reference before she was admitted, and when she was admitted before she was due she found conditions so unbearable she decided when her proper time came she was not going to give birth in the hospital. 'I didn't like it one bit seeing all these people screaming and hollering, because I wasn't. So I decided I wasn't going to have the baby there.'[130]

This woman decided instead to engage a Salvation Army midwife in her own home, whom she described as 'really nice to me and gentle'. Mrs E.C. said that 'they talked a lot about religion and all that', but she was not bothered by this and felt that it gave the place a more 'homely' atmosphere than the EEMH.[131] Jewish women who gave birth in the home stated they also had not been unduly affected by the prayers in the hospital.[132]

Whatever the attitudes of the patients, these hospitals seemed to offer a service which reflected the social and economic requirements of the patients they served. Based in an area of great poverty, the hospitals to some extent understood the need for facilities which stretched beyond medical care to a large number of social services. To what extent such provision compensated for the living conditions facing most mothers in the area is hard to estimate, but it would seem that these services could account for the remarkably low maternal mortality in East London in the years 1870–1939. Indeed, the medical and social care offered by these hospitals provided a vital network of communal aid in an area where the burdens of motherhood were worsened by terrible poverty. For the standards of the time these hospitals did remarkably well in terms of maternity care and were leading forces in providing facilities which poor mothers could not otherwise have purchased for themselves. While many patients might initially have felt unwelcomed by the scrutiny of the Lady Almoner, many cherished the services provided by the hospitals. Like all voluntary hospitals, those based in East London, catering for poor mothers, suffered increasingly from lack of funds as the twentieth century progressed, resulting in the need for rigid economies.[133]

---

[130] Mrs E.C., interview transcript, p. 3.

[131] Mrs E.C., interview transcript, pp. 4, 7.

[132] Interview with Jewish Women's League by L. Marks, London, 9 Apr. 1990, tape.

[133] In 1920 desperate shortages of finances pushed The London to charge patients a guinea a week for their maintenance (*ELO*, 14 Aug. 1920, 4). In 1930 the EEMH had a deficit of £26,000 because it built new buildings (*ELO*, 17 May 1930, 5). For more discussion on the financial difficulties many voluntary hospitals faced in London during the 1920s see Rivett, *Development of London System*, 185–91.

Based in an area of high immigration these services had an extra challenge. While there might have been tensions between immigrants and the hospital professionals and authorities, overall immigrants were not distinguished from other sections of the local community in terms of treatment. That their cultural and religious needs were considered is most clearly seen in the context of the Jewish patients. This is not to say that these immigrants never felt isolated in the hospitals. Indeed, as outsiders the Jews felt the need to establish their own organizations for helping mothers during confinement, which often complemented the other maternity services in East London. It could be argued that the Jewish women were more fortunate than the local population because they had supplementary provision.

5

Poor Law Institutions and Maternity Care

Visitors to the infirmaries, especially in the East End, will agree that the conditions in these places are altogether unsuited for Jews. The feeling between the Jew and non-Jew patients is somewhat strained, and the staff generally would rather prefer to dispense with the Jewish element. Here again the language difficulty is the main trouble. The very name 'Infirmary' seems to terrify the East End Jew.[1]

S U C H words used by Revd Wolf in 1909, vividly portray the discomfort many Jews experienced in Poor Law institutions. In these institutions Jews not only suffered the stigma of parish relief like everyone else, but also were disadvantaged by their immigrant status and non-Anglican background. This chapter explores what implications this had for Jewish mothers who, unable to seek care from their traditional or communal networks of support or to gain help from other host agencies, were forced to rely on the parish for their maternity care.

Parish relief always allowed for some form of medical assistance during illness or childbirth for the very poor, but its character altered significantly over the centuries and was linked to the nature of Poor Law provision as a whole. This not only affected the types of maternity care offered but also the access patients had to its facilities. Much of the care offered by the parish for mothers was bound up with the changes in the Poor Law medical provision as a whole. In 1834 parish relief was transformed by the Poor Law Amendment Act, which drastically restricted outdoor relief. Those who wanted assistance now had to enter an institution, the workhouse, and faced the loss of voting rights.[2] Before 1834 many destitute sick were given minimal outdoor relief and were left in their own homes to be cared for by family and neighbours or by charitable dispensaries and voluntary hospitals.[3] Some parish authorities set aside

---

[1] *JC*, 5 Feb. 1909, cited in G. Black, 'Health and Medical Care of the Jewish Poor in the East End of London, 1880–1939', Ph.D. thesis (Leicester, 1987), 183.

[2] In 1834 most of the men seeking parish relief would have been disqualified from voting because of their lack of property, as would all the women, because of their sex.

[3] Much of the charitable care offered by dispensaries and voluntary hospitals was targeted to the 'deserving poor'. For an interesting discussion on this and the role of the

rooms for the sick poor, while others provided separate infirmaries. The legislation of 1834 made no provision for the sick within the workhouse, but by the 1840s an increasing number of workhouses were evicting the able-bodied poor because of the overwhelming need to admit the sick.[4] Medical provision for the poor was better in some parishes than others.[5]

Only in 1867 were the sick formally separated from the able-bodied poor by the Metropolitan Poor Law Amendment Act. Under this Act, London Poor Law unions could combine to build large district asylums which were to be managed by the Metropolitan Asylums Board. This made the classification and institutional treatment of the sick, infirm, and insane poor easier.[6] Many of the developments after 1867 were rooted in the 1834 Poor Law Amendment Act which enlarged the local unit of Poor Law administration and resulted in the construction of larger institutions. These allowed for the more effective segregation of the various classes of paupers.[7] None the less, recipients of Poor Law infirmary care were as stigmatized as those confined in the workhouse. Only in 1885, under the Medical Relief (Disqualification Removal) Act, were those who accepted medical relief from the parish able to retain their right to vote.[8] Despite this legislation the stigma attached to such services took time to be eroded.

Much of the assistance given by Poor Law Guardians to mothers during childbirth was shaped by these changes in parish and medical relief. Under the new Poor Law legislation of 1834 women continued to be regarded as the appendages of their husbands, and, apart from single women, were not entitled to relief on their own behalf. Only in the 1840s did legislation begin to tackle the problem of able-bodied women and mothers. None the less, the degree to which provision changed depended on local Boards of Guardians, many of whom pursued policies well into

dispensary in providing medical services for the poor in Huddersfield see H. Marland, *Medicine and Society in Wakefield and Huddersfield* (Cambridge, 1987), ch. 3.

[4] R. G. Hodgkinson, *The Origins of the National Health Service* (London, 1966), 451.

[5] Some enlightened provision for the sick poor was made by parishes in Norfolk well before 1834. See A. Digby, *Pauper Palaces* (London, 1978), 161–79.

[6] P. Ryan, 'Politics and Relief: East London Unions in the Late Nineteenth and Early Twentieth Centuries', in M. E. Rose (ed.), *The Poor and the City: The English Poor Law in its Urban Context, 1834–1914* (Leicester, 1985), 140–1; G. Stedman Jones, *Outcast London: A Study in the Relationship Between Classes in Victorian Society* (London, 1971; repr. 1984), 253–5.

[7] For more information on this see F. Driver, 'The Historical Geography of the Work-house System in England and Wales, 1834–1883', *J. Hist. Geog.* 15/3 (1989), 272, 282, 283.

[8] M. W. Flinn, 'Medical Services Under the New Poor Law', in D. Fraser (ed.), *The New Poor Law in the Nineteenth Century* (London, 1976), 64–5.

the twentieth century which neglected the needs of women in child care and paid no attention to their economic status as deserted wives or widows.[9]

As recipients of parish relief, mothers could not specify whether they wished to give birth at home or within a Poor Law institution. Until the early twentieth century the Poor Law relieving officer decided whether a woman was to be confined in her own home or in the workhouse. Unlike some unions which refused to help pregnant mothers outside the workhouse, unions such as St George's-in-the-East and Whitechapel in East London (both of which were renowned for highly restrictive outdoor relief policies) did provide some outdoor midwifery care, albeit on a very limited scale.[10] This usually entailed the provision of midwifery care by the district medical officer, or a local midwife. With the cuts in outdoor relief as a whole, however, maternity care in East London was increasingly dispensed within the Poor Law institution rather than in the patient's home.

Given the demeaning experience suffered by many when applying for parish or union relief, it is not surprising that women turned to the parish for help during their confinement only as a last resort. Until the late 1880s, when voluntary hospitals began to accept single mothers for the first time, unmarried mothers formed the largest group of women seeking maternity care from the Guardians. Three-quarters of those mothers delivered in 634 workhouses in England and Wales in the period 1871–80, and half of those helped by the Bethnal Green workhouse in the years 1871–1911, were unmarried.[11] By the early twentieth century, however, much of the stigma attached to parish maternity services was diminishing. Concern for infant and maternal morbidity and mortality, together with developments in maternity care as a whole in the early twentieth century, such as the regulation of midwives and the increasing adoption of antisepsis and antenatal care in voluntary teaching hospitals, spurred many parishes to improve provision for expectant mothers. Coinciding with these measures was the growing use of the service by mothers, who,

[9] For more information on the male-centred focus of Poor Law policies see P. Thane, 'Women and the Poor Law in Victorian and Edwardian England', *Hist. Workshop J.* 6 (1978), 29–51; M. A. Crowther, *The Workhouse System, 1834–1929* (London, 1981), 102.

[10] The cut in outdoor relief by unions in East London is examined in more detail in Ryan, 'Politics and Relief', 136, 142–51; Stedman Jones, *Outcast London*, 250, 274–6.

[11] F. J. Mouat, 'Notes on Statistics of Childbirth in Lying-In Wards of Workhouse Infirmaries of England and Wales for Ten Years, 1871–1880', *Trans. Internat. Med. Cong.* 4 (1881), 393; Bethnal Green Guardians, *Reports* (1871–1911) (GLRO file: Be BG 261/3). See also E. M. Ross, 'Women and Poor Law Administration, 1857–1909', MA thesis (London, 1956), 158.

in a poverty-stricken area like East London where casual labour was prevalent and wages irregular, were greatly dependent on Poor Law midwifery care.

This chapter focuses on the unions of Bethnal Green, Poplar, Whitechapel, and St George's-in-the-East.[12] Based in an area of acute poverty and deprivation, these unions illustrate the difficulties Poor Law authorities faced in providing medical care as a result of rapid urban transformation and upheaval. Additional problems arose from the influx of various groups of migrants (including the Jews) who, cut off from their family and friends, could find themselves isolated at times of sickness or confinement. Here, I consider how Poor Law maternity provision in East London was affected by the national policies on maternal and infant health as well as the local economic and social conditions of the area. A central theme is the impact this had on the tensions between the aims of local guardians and national policy-makers, as well as the demands of the mothers who used the services. As I will show, in the context of the experience of Jewish mothers, parish provision was more responsive to local needs and perhaps less punitive than has traditionally been believed.

East London and its Unions

Located in one of the poorest parts of the metropolis, the unions in East London faced heavier burdens than most in London. Although the overall levels of poverty and the strain faced by these unions was higher than elsewhere in the metropolis, each union varied in the demands made of it, reflecting its different location (see Map 5.1). In his study of poverty, Booth argued that St George's-in-the-East was the poorest area of London, because of its lack of major industry and high number of casual labourers. Bethnal Green where the occupational base was dependent on the furniture trade and the casual labour market ranked second.[13] Comparable levels of poverty were also found in Whitechapel where the population was overwhelmingly employed in small trades such as clothing and cigar-making. Of all the unions, Whitechapel had the largest group of Irish and Jewish immigrants to deal with and the highest number of lodging houses. Poplar, with one of the largest unions in the area, had more factories and

---

[12] Most of the material relating to these institutions is held by the GLRO. Henceforth footnotes will only give the place of the union, the date, and file number for reference to Board of Guardians' minutes etc.

[13] C. Booth, *Life and Labour of the People in London*, ser. 1. (1889), i. 37. See also Table 1.5 above.

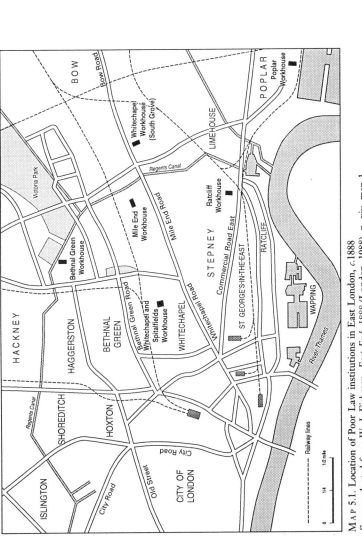

MAP 5.1. Location of Poor Law institutions in East London, c.1888
Source: adapted from W. J. Fishman, *East End, 1888* (London, 1988), p. xiv, map 1.

large employers than the other places, which meant that it had a more varied occupational base of unskilled and semi-skilled workers.[14] By 1929, however, Llewellyn Smith listed Poplar as the most poverty-stricken part of London, its industries having been hit particularly badly by the post-war slump and economic depression of the late 1920s.[15]

Despite being situated in a poverty-stricken area, East London unions, because they were part of London, could rely on the support of the Metropolitan Common Poor Fund after 1867. This enabled them to be more centralized administratively and financially than provincial unions. None the less, East London unions still faced difficulties in raising their funds because of the absence of middle-class ratepayers and the lack of rates equalization. In 1889 the percentage of middle-class residents was respectively 2.5 per cent in St George's-in-the-East, 4.2 per cent in Bethnal Green, 4.8 per cent in Poplar, and 6.2 per cent in Whitechapel.[16] A comparison of the rateable values of Bethnal Green and Kensington in 1874 shows the great disparity of rates within London. Both had similar populations, and yet the rateable value of Bethnal Green was £289,940, while in Kensington it was more than three times this amount at £1,117,030. Similarly, in 1904, the average value assessed per head of population in Poplar was half that of London as a whole, and was lower still in Bethnal Green and St George's-in-the-East. The East London unions were therefore caught, as Ryan has argued, in a 'trap familiar to modern local authorities; a high demand for local social service provision from their poverty-stricken inhabitants, the provision of which was found to increase the burden of rates, on both rich and poor ratepayers'.[17]

All these factors hindered the amount of relief the East London unions could offer. Some of the unions were more radical in their spending than others. The largest union in this study, Poplar, was renowned for its generous outdoor relief. This was partly influenced by the cohesive Labour Party in Poplar, which drew its strength from the trade unions of the dock industries and large factories in the area.[18] Other parishes, where

[14] Booth, *Life and Labour*, 63–9, 71.

[15] H. Llewellyn Smith, *The New Survey of London*, i. *Eastern Area* (1930) 347, 353, 365; See also G. Rose, 'Locality, Politics and Culture: Poplar in the 1920s', Ph.D. thesis (London, 1988), introduction.

[16] Booth, *Life and Labour: Poverty*, Tables of Sections and Classes, 7, 9, 14. See also Ryan, 'Politics and Relief', 137.

[17] Ryan, 'Politics and Relief', 137. See also Bethnal Green Board of Guardians, *Report* (1900), 16 (Be Bg 261/2).

[18] For more information on the percentage of outdoor and indoor paupers to the population as a whole in different parts of East London see Chance Bart, 'London Pauperism, 1891 and 1901', extract of a paper read before the Royal Statistical Society, in Bethnal

workers were less organized and the Labour Party was weak, were more restrictive in their relief policies.[19]

It is difficult to determine the impact the politics of the different unions had in relation to maternity services. The sheer volume of material for each parish in East London makes the task of uncovering the history of Poor Law maternity care in the area complicated. The documents examined for this study include minutes, registers, and reports from the Boards of Guardians and their infirmaries, and reports from government commissions. Many of these sources contain only indirect evidence concerning maternity care. Indoor maternity provision is better documented in this material than outdoor services, which makes it hard to judge the extent of Poor Law maternity care in East London and its impact on the health of mothers and infants in the area. Furthermore, formal records of patients were not officially required of Poor Law medical staff until 1913, resulting in a lack of information on the types of mothers using indoor and outdoor parish maternity services.

Poor Law provision and the Jewish population

Very little is known about the Jews who applied for help from Poor Law institutions. Contemporaries argued that the lower rates of application for poor relief in East London were a reflection of the large numbers of immigrants in the area who relied on relief from elsewhere, but, with the exception of a few comments from Ryan, few historians have explored this connection further.[20] Even less is known about the Jewish mothers who used the Poor Law maternity services. Part of the problem in understanding their experiences in these institutions is that, overall, Jews were reluctant to use infirmary facilities and therefore do not show up readily

Green Board of Guardians, *Report* (1903) (Be BG 261/3). See also Bethnal Green Board of Guardians, *Report* (1909) (Be BG 261/5), which shows Poplar as having not only a much larger amount of poverty overall, but also a higher number of recipients of outdoor relief than other unions and parishes in London in 1908. While outdoor paupers in Whitechapel numbered 0.5 per 1,000, in Bethnal Green it was 3.3, and in Poplar 30.9.

[19] Ryan, 'Politics and Relief', 139, 165–6. The radical politics of Poplar and the forces behind this during the 1920s are examined in Rose, 'Locality, Politics and Culture', and J. A. Gillespie, 'Poplarism and Proletarianism: Unemployment and Labour Politics in London, 1918–1934', in D. Feldman and G. Stedman Jones (eds.), *Metropolis London: Histories and Representation Since 1800* (London, 1989).

[20] *RC Poor Law Relief of Distress*, PP 1909 XXXVII, evidence of Henry Lockwood, inspector for the Metropolis, Qs12855–73, Q13819; Ryan 'Politics of Relief', 148.

in the records.[21] The experience Jewish women had in these institutions can partly be judged by the religious provision Poor Law Guardians made for non-Anglican inmates and their attitudes towards them.

Much of the access Jewish mothers had to the maternity services provided by the Poor Law authorities was dependent on the position of Jewish women under the Poor Law. As in the case of any migrant, Jewish newcomers' claims to parish support were tenuous without the proper residential qualifications. After 1846 those who applied for parish relief had to prove they had lived continuously in an English district for five years. Such restraints were primarily directed at the large number of Irish immigrants arriving in Britain as a result of the Famine in these years.[22] In 1865, the Union Chargeability Act (28 & 29 Vic. cap. 79) revised the laws of settlement and removal to require just one year's residence.[23] Despite the frequent protests over the expense involved in enforcing orders of removal, the laws remained unchanged well into the twentieth century.[24] Jewish East European immigrants arriving in the 1870s faced the same dangers of removal as many Irish immigrants had experienced before them.

Whatever the changes in the residential requirements, their existence highlighted the continual anxiety of parish relief officers that they would be inundated with an influx of newcomers.[25] In the 1840s such anxieties were focused on the Irish immigrants, but by the late nineteenth century attention had turned to the East European Jews. Many investigations

---

[21] G. Black also discusses this difficulty, see 'Health and Medical Care', 189. Irish immigrants are even harder to locate in Poor Law sources. Although a large percentage of the Catholics applying to Poor Law authorities were Irish, the material does not always specify their place of origin. The only clues available to the researcher are the surnames generally common to Ireland, but, as in the Jewish case, these do not show whether they belong to immigrants or their children. One means to get at this material would be to look at census schedules, but this material demands time-consuming scrutiny to get any meaningful data and they are only available for the years 1871, 1881, and 1891, which leaves out the majority of the years examined in this book.

[22] Before 1846 Irish residents in English parishes had no rights of settlement, and those found to be a burden on the rates were frequently shipped back to Ireland. In the early 19th c. thousands of Irish migrants were removed from English parishes in this way. Many avoided applying for relief for fear of removal (Crowther, *Workhouse System, 1834–1929*, 225).

[23] M. Rose, 'Settlement, Removal and the New Poor Law', in Fraser (ed.), *New Poor Law*, 31, 38–9.

[24] In 1875 Whitechapel Board of Guardians signed a petition with the Guardians of St Pancras, City of London, Hackney, St Marylebone, the Strand, St George's, and Paddington in protest against the Irish Removal Bill in Parliament that year (Whitechapel, 25 May 1875; 1 June 1875 (St BG/Wh/57)). In 1880 Whitechapel Guardians petitioned the government against the proposed Irish Removal Bill (Whitechapel, 27 July 1880 (St BG/Wh/62)).   [25] Rose, 'Settlement and Removal', 39.

were undertaken to estimate to what extent East European immigrants had taken away the work and livelihoods of the local population and what impact this had had on the level of pauperism within London.[26] Most of these surveys concluded that pauperism had not increased as a result of the immigration and that the East European Jews were not a large number of those claiming parish relief.[27] The fact of these continual investigations, however, gave cause for concern for many well-established Anglo-Jews, who feared that the appearance of their fellow poor on the parish rates would result in anti-Semitism.

The tenuous position of Jews was highlighted in the Royal Commission on Alien Immigration in 1903 and the Aliens Act that followed it in 1905.[28] Under this Act the Home Secretary could deport any alien who had committed a criminal offence or had, within twelve months of arrival, 'been in receipt of any parochial relief as disqualifies a person for the parliamentary franchise or been found wandering without ostensible means of subsistence. . . .' Within four years of the passage of the Act, 1,378 people had been deported.[29] Pregnant women were particularly vulnerable under this Act. In 1906 the Whitechapel Board of Guardians approached the Home Office over the question of destitute alien women arriving alone in Britain 'in a condition of advanced pregnancy, and who must of necessity become a charge to the ratepayers'. It was said that such cases were on the increase. The Home Office assured the Guardians that the Aliens Act not only intended to prevent alien, pregnant, pauper women gaining entry into the country, but that the Home Office would relieve the Guardians of any such women.[30] Such restrictions were later reinforced by the Aliens Restriction (Amendment) Act of 1919 which extended the powers of medical officers based at ports to reject aliens on arrival. It was within their jurisdiction to grant only conditional landing to parturient women.[31]

---

[26] In particular see Whitechapel Board of Guardians, *Report on Immigration of the Foreign Poor*, 1–2 (Whitechapel, 1 Nov. 1887, 257 (St BG/Wh/70)) (henceforth *Report on Immigration*). See also, for references to ongoing questions from LGB to Guardians about the number of aliens receiving relief in individual parishes: Bethnal Green, *Triennial Report* (1897), 7 (Be BG/261/1); Bethnal Green Hospital, Committee Minutes, 1903 (Be BG/161/3); Poplar, 6 July 1892, 193 (Po BG/34); 17 Feb. 1909, 742 (Po BG/55). See also Stedman Jones, *Outcast London*, 244.   [27] *Report on Immigration*, 5.

[28] *RC Alien Immigration*, PP 1903 IX, 24–5.

[29] *JC*, 24 June 1910, cited in S. Cohen, 'Anti-Semitism, Immigration Controls and the Welfare State', *Critical Social Policy*, 13 (1985), 73–92, 81.

[30] *ELO*, 8 Dec. 1906, 8.

[31] Edmund Leigh White, 'The Work of an Aliens Medical Officer', *Med. Offr.*, 1 Oct. 1921, 147.

Many applying to the parish for relief found the process repugnant. As outsiders, however, Jewish claimants could experience the additional problem of anti-Semitism from Poor Law officers. On a number of occasions Whitechapel recorded abuse to Jewish patients by the District Medical Officer, Mr Braye. In 1879 Mr Braye recorded the following in the register:

People in good condition. Ratepayers, shopkeepers, better clothes than I can afford. Would never have had pauper visiting order if they had not been Jews. Have been paying Doctor Swyer for private-attendance. A pauper's order is invariably given to these Jews who are sent on from the Jewish Relief Officer without compelling the head of the family to come for order—in many cases their servants.

When attending a Jewish mother he noted: 'Nothing amiss except pregnancy. No order would have been given if they had been Asians instead of Jews.' In another instance Mr Braye called a Jewish woman a 'dirty Jewish bitch'.[32] The Guardians put him on probation, but his behaviour did not improve. Only in 1881, however, did the Guardians force him to resign.[33]

Jewish newcomers who entered workhouse infirmaries also faced the prospect of being culturally and religiously isolated. As Anglican institutions, Poor Law workhouses and infirmaries made very little provision for their non-Anglican inmates. This could be especially problematic for religious observance. Jewish inmates had to apply specially for permission to abstain from work on the traditional Jewish sabbath in the workhouse of St George's-in-the-East Union.[34] In addition to this it was difficult for non-Anglicans to worship and practise their religion in the workhouses and infirmaries.[35] Many Jews, as well as Catholics, were also anxious that correct spiritual consolation was unavailable for those dying in workhouse institutions and infirmaries.[36] Death among Jewish inmates was compli-

[32] Whitechapel, 25 Nov. 1879, 51–2 (St BG/Wh/106/1). The reference to 'Asians' indicates that Jews were not the only ones subjected to hostility from parish relieving officers.
[33] Complaints continued against Mr Braye. See Whitechapel, 2 Dec. 1879 (St BG/Wh/62); 2 Feb. 1880 (St BG/Wh/63). For the discussion concerning his resignation see 18 Jan. 1881, 8 Feb. 1881, and 1 Mar. 1881 (St BG/Wh/63).
[34] United Synagogue, Visitation Committee, Minutes, 7 Mar. 1904 (CRO).
[35] Problems were not confined solely to Jewish inmates. Frequent complaints were also made about the Catholic poor in workhouses, who had no access to Catholic prayer books, rosaries, tale-books, or newspapers, and were often forced to worship in uncomfortable surroundings. See B. Bulbeck, 'Catholic Poor in Workhouses', *The Tablet*, 12 Apr. 1873, 470; 'The Cries from our Poor in the Workhouses', *The Tablet*, 4 Feb. 1893, 177.
[36] *The Tablet*, 18 July 1880, 361.

cated by the stipulation that only a Jewish person could lay out the dead person, and that the body had to be buried within twenty-four hours.[37] Over the years the East London Boards of Guardians became more willing to make religious provision for their non-Anglican inmates and by 1906 most of the unions in East London had done so.[38] They also helped finance special Catholic and Jewish chaplains and instructors, and supplied Bibles and ritual objects.[39] In later years the Guardians of St George's-in-the-East made sure that a Yiddish newspaper and some Yiddish books were supplied to the infirmary.[40]

Anglo-Jews were particularly concerned about the supply of kosher food for their compatriots in both the workhouse and the infirmary. While Guardians ensured the provision of fish for Catholics on Fridays,[41] the dietary requirements for Jews were more complex. A prolonged debate by the Whitechapel Guardians during the 1870s about the provision of kosher food illustrated the difficulties Jews faced in such institutions. The Board finally decided to buy kosher meat but not to allow 'special rations'.[42] Remarkably, precautions were also taken to separate milk from meat utensils and to cook Jewish food away from non-kosher food in the infirmary.[43] Years later a clerk from the St George's-in-the-East Board of Guardians opposed a proposal to provide kosher food for Jewish inmates of the infirmary, regarding Jewish patients who refused to eat non-kosher food as 'bigoted'.[44] The discussion that ensued revealed the vulnerability of Jewish inmates. Yet despite such hostility, Guardians increasingly

---

[37] Outside the Jewish community similar importance was attached to preserving the identity and integrity of the dead body. After the Anatomy Act of 1832 the unclaimed corpse of anyone who died on the parish could be used for dissection purposes. Many feared that their spirit would be unable to rest or be resurrected without proper burial. The possibility of being used for dissection therefore caused great fear of dying in the workhouse. It therefore became very important for the working-class that they should be able to provide a decent funeral and burial for themselves. Even those who had meagre incomes set aside money for the burial society. For further information on this see R. Richardson, *Death, Dissection and the Destitute* (London, 1988, 1989), 272–81.

[38] *Returns with Reference to Religious Services at Metropolitan Unions and Parishes* (1906), in Bethnal Green Infirmary, Minutes, 26 Apr. 1906 (Be BG/150).

[39] Whitechapel, 3 May 1870, 342 (St BG/Wh/50); Poplar, 1 June 1888, 211 (Po BG/34); 23 July 1924, 87 (Po BG/71).

[40] Whitechapel, 20 Sept. 1907, 241 (St BG/SG/45).

[41] Alice Mackie, 'Memories of the Poplar Workhouse, 1932–1939', in Settlement of the Holy Child, *AR* (1962/3), 25.

[42] It is not clear what was meant by 'special rations' but it might have been the provision of food which was kosher for Passover (Whitechapel, 25 Oct. 1870, 240–3 (St BG/Wh/51); 28 Mar. 1876 (St BG/Wh/57)).

[43] Whitechapel, 10 Feb. 1880, 74 (St BG/Wh/106/1).

[44] *ELO*, 29 Feb. 1908, 2.

understood the importance of providing kosher food for their Jewish inmates. In 1910 the Board of Guardians in Mile End noted that 'the recovery of such patients may be retarded owing to the food supplied to them being prepared in a way contrary to their principles' and followed the example of other East London Guardians in supplying kosher food.[45]

Much of the increase in the religious provision for non-Anglicans in these institutions stemmed in part from the pressure of Anglo-Jewish and Catholic communal leaders. Fearing that their poor would be culturally isolated or converted in workhouse institutions, many of the wealthier members of the Catholic and Jewish communities attempted to safeguard the religious and cultural interests of their poor by securing positions on the Boards of Guardians and by making other representations. In the Jewish community the United Synagogue's Visitation Committee and the Jewish Board of Guardians (JBG) was in constant contact with Poor Law authorities on the question of religious provision for Jewish inmates.[46] Often the Visitation Committee arranged that the initial supply of kosher food would be financed by Jewish agencies.[47] The extent of visiting work undertaken by the Visitation Committee to Jewish inmates in Poor Law institutions can be seen in Table 5.1.[48] Similar action was taken by the Catholic community to win religious concessions for their poor.[49] The Catholics established their own Catholic Guardians Association with the explicit purpose of getting Catholic Guardians appointed.

[45] *ELO*, 2 Apr. 1910, 2.

[46] Formed in 1871, this Committee's purpose was to visit Jewish inmates in Poor Law institutions, voluntary hospitals, and prisons. This was the main organization undertaking such work, but it was joined by other groups and individuals within the Jewish community, such as the Ladies' Conjoint Committee, the Ladies' Loan Society, the Jewish Ladies' West End Society, and the Minister of the East End Visiting Committee. (United Synagogue, Council Minutes, pamphlet on the East End Scheme, p. 12; United Synagogue, Visitation Committee, Minutes 1871–1902 (CRO)). See also Whitechapel, 24 May 1892, 461–2 (St BG/Wh/74).)

[47] United Synagogue, Visitation Committee, Minutes, 1871–1902, 11 Nov. 1909 and 12 Apr. 1910.

[48] Members of the Committee were allotted specific places to visit. Many of the lady visitors on the Committee were drawn from the West London Synagogue (United Synagogue, Visitation Committee, Minutes, 17 Nov. 1913, 297).

[49] One of the most burning issues in the Catholic community was the placing of Catholic children in Poor Law schools. This issue was continually raised by the Catholic priests to the Boards of Guardians in Whitechapel and St George's-in-the-East. Many of the children mentioned had surnames common to Ireland. (Whitechapel, 3 Nov. 1878, (St BG/Wh/60); 5 Oct. 1880, 16 Nov. 1880, 4 Jan. 1881 (St BG/Wh/62); 19 Dec. 1881 (St BG/Wh/106/1); St George's-in-the-East, 31 Mar. 1871 (St BG/SG/13); *ELO*, 8 Mar. 1873.) *The Tablet* also reported extensively on difficulties faced by Catholic children in the workhouse and the need for Catholic schools (*The Tablet*, 12 Apr. 1873, 470; 20 Apr. 1878, 787; 20 Aug. 1881; 27 Aug. 1881, 337–8; 3 Nov. 1881, 377; 26 Nov. 1881, 359; 12 Sept. 1885, 429).

TABLE 5.1. *Average number of visits to Jewish inmates in various Poor Law institutions made by the United Synagogue Visitation Committee per year, 1873–1912*

Institution	Year	Average no. visits	Average no. inmates visited	Average no. admitted in last year	Average no. visitors
Whitechapel Union					
W & I	1873–9	8	6	—	—
	1880–4	12	17	17	—
	1890–1	52	19	—	—
	1896–7	60	19	—	—
	1901	101	23	179	—
	1905	134	42	158	5
	1910–12	141	62	137	7
St George's-in-the-East					
W	1873	1	0	—	—
	1875–9	2	—	—	—
	1880–4	4	2	2	—
	1890–1	21	7	7	—
	1896–7	24	5	24	—
W & I	1901	50	16	89	—
	1905	126	22	156	5
	1910–12	72	26	240	5
Poplar and Stepney	1901	2	1	1	—
Sick Asylum	1905	24	3	3	2
	1910	31	3	10	2
	1912	25	4	11	3
City of London					
W	1873	2	0	—	—
W & I	1874	12	8	—	—
W	1875–9	4	4	—	—
	1880–4	5	6	8	—
	1890–1	17	5	10	—
	1896–7	7	5	2	—
	1901	52	7	12	1
	1905	12	1	0	1
	1910–12	46	4	14	2
Bethnal Green					
W	1874	1	0	—	—
	1884	1	1	1	—

TABLE 5.1. (*Cont.*)

Institution	Year	Average no. visits	Average no. inmates visited	Average no. admitted in last year	Average no. visitors
	1890–1	16	6	4	—
	1896–7	13	—	—	—
	1901	18	—	—	—
W & I	1905	56	13	15	4
	1910–12	90	25	105	—
Mile End	1882	1	2	2	—
W	1890–1	20	4	6	—
	1896–7	9	7	10	—
	1901	40	15	53	—
W & I	1905	50	38	137	4
	1910–12	70	46	355	6
Shoreditch	1890–1	14	1	2	—
	1896–7	9	—	—	—
	1901	18	4	13	—
	1905	22	4	29	1
	1910–11	22	4	15	2

Note: It is unclear whether certain institutions are infirmaries or workhouses; where possible I have indicated when numbers refer to the workhouse or the infirmary: W = workhouse only; W & I = workhouse and infirmary.

Source: United Synagogue, Visitation Committee, minutes, 1902–14 (CRO).

Despite this, difficulties remained. Commenting on Jewish patients, Reverend A. Green remarked

much care is bestowed at the infirmary and great desire exists to do all that is possible for the welfare of the patients. But a workhouse infirmary is a workhouse infirmary when all is said and done, and there is a difference indeed between that and such a place as the Jewish wards of the London Hospital. In the Union Infirmary the status of the average patient is naturally not of the highest. The Jew who comes in *qua* Jew is regarded more or less as an alien, and when he can speak only Yiddish this is accentuated . . . it often happens that a Jew who wants to put on his hat when he takes his meals, and who wants to put on tephilin[50] and say his

[50] *Tephilin* (phylacteries) are small black boxes with small parchments of extracts from the five books of Moses bound by leather thongs to the forehead and left arm, and worn by Jewish men during weekday morning prayers.

prayers in the morning, is assailed with all manner of comment, ribald and blasphemous, which renders his stay a perfect purgatory.[51]

Jewish patients, as in dealing with other agencies, also had linguistic problems in workhouse infirmaries. Not surprisingly most Jewish mothers therefore tried their utmost to avoid Poor Law authorities. A number of them, however, had no choice but to receive help from the parish during their confinement. The experience Jewish mothers had with these services was bound up with general developments in parish maternity care as a whole.

The Structure and Quality of Poor Law Maternity Care in East London

Such shifting attitudes towards non-Anglican inmates reflected a wider change occurring to parish relief as a whole. This was particularly clear in the case of medical care, the provision of which altered substantially following the Metropolitan Poor Law Amendment Act of 1867 and the establishment of the Metropolitan Asylums Board. Under this legislation a new form of hospital was initiated with the increasing separation of Poor Law infirmaries from the workhouse. Paid nurses began to supplement able-bodied pauper women as the carers in Poor Law infirmaries, and consultants and resident medical staff were appointed. Buildings and equipment also changed to meet the advancing standards of medical knowledge. Much of this was financed by the LGB and was no longer reliant on the budgets of Guardians.[52] By taking some of the administration and finances out of the hands of the Guardians, the Act finally secured the possibility for progress in indoor medical care, albeit slow and uneven.

Of all the Poor Law medical services, maternity wards were the slowest to improve, and were greatly dependent on the policy of individual unions.[53] Most indoor maternity care continued to be provided in workhouses rather than in infirmaries. In 1903 more than two-thirds of the metropolitan unions and parishes accommodated their maternity wards in the workhouse. Only a third of maternity wards were in infirmaries, and most of these were in the same location as the workhouse.[54] In East

---

[51] Revd A. A. Green, originally born in East London, was minister of Hampstead Synagogue between 1892 and 1930. He wrote under the pseudonym 'Tatler' in *JC*, 1 Jan. 1909.

[52] Flinn, 'Medical Services', 64–5.

[53] Thane, 'Women and the Poor Law', 39; S. and B. Webb (eds.), *The Break-Up of the Poor Law: Being Part One of the Minority Report of the Poor Law Commission* (London, 1909), 84–5.

[54] Bethnal Green Board of Guardians, *Report* (1903), 14 (Be BG/261/2).

London, St George's-in-the-East and Whitechapel were the earliest in providing separate maternity wards within their infirmaries, in 1873 and 1877 respectively.[55] Maternity wards began to appear in the Poplar and Bethnal Green institutions in 1894 and remained part of the workhouse until the early 1920s.[56]

It is commonly assumed that the conditions under which mothers gave birth were worse in Poor Law institutions than in voluntary hospitals or patients' homes. Indeed, before the development of separate maternity wards the conditions under which mothers had to give birth were often appalling, as Louisa Twining recalled in the case of one workhouse:

> The lying-in ward . . . which was only a general ward without even screens, had an old inmate in it who we discovered to have an ulcerated leg and cancer of the breast; yet she did nearly everything for the women and babies, and often delivered them too. The women's hair was not combed, it was 'not lucky' to do so, and washing was at a discount. The doctor and myself could not imagine at first why the temperatures went up, and the babies nearly always got bad eyes and did badly.[57]

Such an environment was not conducive to ensuring healthy mothers and infants, and many believed the risk of dying in childbirth or infancy was greater in a Poor Law institution than elsewhere.

Unfortunately, the absence of official records on deaths in childbirth within workhouse institutions and the absence of reliable statistics on maternal mortality makes these assumptions difficult to assess. None the less, one study carried out by Gathorne Hardy, the president of the Poor Law Board, in 1865, suggested that the rates of maternal mortality in metropolitan workhouses compared favourably with those of larger lying-in hospitals. Table 5.2 shows that of the 2,728 confinements in thirty-nine London workhouses there were sixteen deaths, all of which occurred in nine workhouses. Overall, the maternal mortality rate in the workhouses was 6 per 1,000 births, which was slightly lower than the British Lying-In Hospital based in London, where the rate was 7 per 1,000 births. Queen Charlotte's Hospital, however, which was also located in London and primarily catered to unmarried mothers, had a much higher maternal mortality rate of 40 per 1,000 births. The admission of unmarried mothers may have played a part in the wide difference between

---

[55] St George's-in-the-East, 11 July 1873, 115–16 (St BG/SG/16); Whitechapel, 14 Oct. 1873 (St BG/Wh/54); 23 Oct. 1877 (St BG/Wh/60).

[56] Poplar, 13 June 1894, 102 (Po BG/41); 20 July 1921, 72 (Po BG/75); Bethnal Green, 29 Nov. 1900, 82 (Be BG/147); 4 Sept. 1924, 139–40; 18 Sept. 1924, 154 (Be BG/161).

[57] L. Twining, *Workhouses and Pauperism* (London, 1898), 201.

TABLE 5.2. *Number of confinements and maternal deaths in London workhouses and selected lying-in hospitals*

Institution	Number of deliveries	Maternal deaths	Death rate per 1,000 cases
Queen Charlotte's Hospital 1857–63	2,268	90	40
Rotunda Hospital, Dublin			
1857–61	6,521	169	26
British Lying-In Hospital 1849–61	1,581	11	7
39 London Workhouses 1865	2,728	16	6
Outdoor midwifery department,			
St George's Hospital 1856–63	2,800	10	3.5

Source: 'Workhouse Death-Rate in Childbirth', *J. Stat. Soc.* 30 (1867), 171–3, 172.

this hospital and the workhouses. A more significant reason, however, was that from 1850 hospitals such as Queen Charlotte's Hospital tended to admit a high proportion of selected abnormal cases and referred emergencies who often arrived with complications or in a moribund state. By contrast, workhouses accepted all women without any prior clinical selection which meant that they had to deal with fewer abnormal deliveries which probably resulted in a lower rate of maternal mortality.[58] Overall, however, district midwifery care was shown to be the safest form of confinement.[59]

Another study carried out for the years 1871 to 1880 of 87,726 deliveries in 634 workhouses confirmed these findings. The overall rate of maternal mortality in these institutions was 8.7, which compared unfavourably with the rate of 4.7 registered by the Registrar-General for the same years.[60] Table 5.3, however, shows that a large number of the deaths in the workhouses were not connected with childbirth. Listed as 'other causes' in the table, most of these women died from pneumonia, phthisis, smallpox, scarlet fever, or heart disease. Some of these causes, such as phthisis, were linked to the social and economic deprivation these women had faced before entering the workhouse.

The investigation revealed that most of those women who died in

[58] I. Loudon, 'Deaths in Childbed from the Eighteenth Century to 1935', *Med. Hist.* 30 (1986), 1–41, 21.

[59] G. Hardy, 'Workhouse Death-Rate in Childbirth', *J. Stat. Soc.* 30 (1867), 171–3, 172.

[60] Registrar-General, *Decennial Supplement of Births, Deaths and Marriages for England and Wales* (1871–80).

TABLE 5.3. *Causes of maternal deaths in workhouse infirmaries, 1871–1880*

Cause of death	Provinces			Metropolis			Combined		
	Births	No. of maternal deaths	MMR*	Births	No. of maternal deaths	MMR	Births	No. of maternal deaths	MMR
Post-partum haemorrhage		48	0.74		22	0.95		70	0.79
Puerperal convulsions		79	1.22		13	0.56		92	1.04
Puerperal fever: metria and peritonitis		217	3.36		73	3.16		290	3.30
All other causes		215	3.32		93	4.02		308	3.51
Unaccounted		2	0.03		3	0.13		5	0.56
TOTAL	64,609	561	8.7	23,117	204	8.8	87,726	765	8.7

Note: Puerperal fever was the cause of the largest group of deaths in the workhouse institutions during this period, owing to the very high rates found in the general population in the 1870s; the highest rates ever recorded occurred in 1874–5. Death rates from puerperal fever in the 1860s and 1880s would probably have been considerably lower.

* MMR = maternal mortality rate.

Source: Adapted from 'Statistics of Childbirth in Workhouse Infirmaries', in LGB, *11th AR* (1882), in *Reports of Commissioners*, PP 1882, XXVIII, Cd. 3337, p. xlvii.

connection with causes from childbirth in the metropolitan and provincial workhouses died from puerperal fever. Puerperal fever was the greatest killer of women in childbirth until the 1930s and was particularly high in the 1870s. The overall rate of puerperal fever found in workhouses was 3.3 per 1,000 births in the years 1871 to 1880. This was higher than the rate of 2.08 given by the Registrar-General for England and Wales for the same years.[61] None the less, the difference in the rate of puerperal fever between the workhouse and the general population was probably less than these figures suggest. Many doctors tended to classify puerperal fever under other causes of death which meant that the rates of puerperal fever listed by the Registrar-General were probably underestimates.[62] When compared with other lying-in institutions the rate of puerperal fever in the workhouses was even more striking. In the years 1870 to 1874 the estimated rate of puerperal fever in Queen Charlotte's Hospital was 17.6 per 1,000 deliveries, while at the Glasgow Maternity Hospital the estimated rate was 20 per 1,000 in 1873.[63] Those conducting the study of workhouses concluded that, in the context of puerperal fever, a pauper woman confined in the workhouse had 'as fair a chance of life . . . as a poor woman confined in her own home'.[64]

These studies indicate that parish maternity care was much better than traditionally assumed and outweighed the social and economic disadvantages experienced by many of the pauper mothers. Loudon has shown that the standard of care provided by birth attendants is a vital determinant in maternal mortality. The quality of care is dependent both on the birth attendant's knowledge of basic obstetric procedures (judged by the standards of the time), and on the amount of unwarranted interference. As Loudon has argued, these factors are more important than 'social and economic determinants except in so far as these determined the type and quality of birth attendant. High maternal risk could be associated with cheap untrained midwives or expensive over-zealous and unskilled

[61] Hardy, 'Workhouse Death-Rate in Childbirth', 172; Registrar-General, *Decennial Supplement* (1871–80).

[62] For more information on this see I. Loudon, *Deaths in Childbirth: An International Study of Maternal Care and Maternal Mortality, 1800–1950* (Oxford, 1992), apps.

[63] W. Williams, *Deaths in Childbed* (London, 1904); F. Nightingale, *Introductory Notes on Lying-In Hospitals* (London, 1876).

[64] LGB, 'Statistics of Childbirth in Workhouse Infirmaries', in LGB, *11th AR* (1882), in *Reports of Commissioners*, PP 1882 XXVIII, Cd. 3337, p. xlix. Among the lowest rates of puerperal fever in the 19th c. was that recorded by the Royal Maternity Charity, which was 1.2 per 1,000 in the years 1831–43. All births attended by the Royal Maternity Charity took place within the patient's home (F. H. Ramsbotham, 'The Eastern District of the Royal Maternity Charity', *Lond. Med. Gaz.* NS 2 (1843–4), 619–25).

doctors. Sound obstetric practice by well-trained midwives could produce low levels of maternal mortality even in populations which were
socially and economically deprived.'[65]

One possible reason for the low maternal death rate was that more of
the births in Poor Law institutions were attended by midwives than by
medical practitioners. Low payments offered by the parish to midwives
would not have attracted the most skilled attendants, but the midwives
employed were less likely than medical practitioners to interfere during
birth, thereby reducing the risk of infection. Women confined in workhouses were also probably protected from infection, since the majority of
maternity wards were not accommodated in the infirmaries. This was
confirmed by a study in 1901 which showed that mothers who gave birth
in infirmaries were much more likely to contract erysipelas and puerperal
fever than those confined in workhouses.[66]

The level of care infants received in Poor Law institutions is more
complicated to assess than that offered to mothers, partly because an
infant's survival is determined by a wider range of issues. As Chapter 2
has shown, the causes of infant mortality vary for infants at different ages.
Post-neonatal mortality (deaths after 28 days of life and before 1 year of
age) is commonly associated with bad sanitation or poor breast-feeding as
well as social and economic deprivation. The historical causes of neonatal
mortality (deaths within 28 days of birth) are harder to discern, but are
linked to prematurity and congenital deformities as well as environmental
conditions and the quality of maternity care.

A substantial number of the infants cared for within the Poor Law
institutions were illegitimate, a group which was particularly vulnerable
in wider society. Until the mid-1930s illegitimate infants faced a much
greater risk of dying, especially in the post-neonatal period.[67] Many of these
deaths were caused by the absence of social and medical resources for
unmarried mothers and their infants. Yet an investigation into workhouse
conditions in 1907 showed that the protection and food illegitimate infants enjoyed in such places during the post-neonatal period 'removed
the presumption against the survival of illegitimate infants'.[68] This was
highly dependent on the conditions of individual unions.

---

[65] I. Loudon, 'On Maternal and Infant Mortality, 1900–1960', *Soc. Hist. Med.* 3 (1990),
61–81, 72.

[66] Bethnal Green Board of Guardians, *Report* (1903), 15 (Be BG/261/2).

[67] 'Report of the Infant Committee', *Trans. Obstet. Soc. of London*, 13 (1870), 142–3; L.
Rose, *The Massacre of the Innocents: Infanticide in Britain, 1800–1939* (London, 1986), 23.

[68] Webbs, *Break-Up of the Poor Law*, 102.

None the less, while illegitimate infants may have benefited in some Poor Law institutions, the inquiry of 1907 indicated that most infants fared worse than those cared for in outside workhouses. The social and economic conditions that had driven the mothers to seek parish support often counted against their infants. Overall infant mortality was two to three times greater in Poor Law institutions than among the general population in 1907. In the case of neonatal mortality, it was shown that out of every 1,000 babies born in the population at large, twenty-five died within a week, while the number dying in the same period in Poor-Law institutions was between forty and forty-five.[69]

The higher rates of neonatal mortality in workhouse infirmaries are difficult to explain. The three main causes of neonatal mortality are generally assumed to be prematurity, birth injury, and congenital malformations. Loudon has shown that where there were numerous doctor deliveries and a tendency by doctors towards a high rate of interference, the result could be high rates of neonatal mortality due to birth injury. Evidence from the United States supports this.[70] However, this explanation is unlikely since there were few deliveries by doctors in the workhouse infirmaries. As already indicated above, low rates of maternal mortality in the workhouses also suggest that an absence of medical men delivering women resulted in less medical intervention in childbirth which contributed to a lower incidence of infection. It is also doubtful that the workhouse population showed higher rates of prematurity or congenital malformation than the general population.

A more probable explanation was that the causes of neonatal and post-neonatal deaths are not always separate from each other and sometimes overlap. 'Endogenous' (or inherent) causes of infant death could operate after the end of the first month, and some deaths in the first week were due to 'exogenous' (or environmental) causes such as infection. Neonates could, and still occasionally do, succumb to infections, such as gastro-intestinal and especially respiratory infections, and this can happen even in the first week. Erysipelas was also a not uncommon cause of early neonatal death, usually when the mother had puerperal fever; and this nearly always occurred in the first few days of life. But erysipelas alone is unlikely to have been the only factor.

Thus the high rate of neonatal mortality in crowded workhouses may have been due to an excess of deaths from infections, such as infantile pneumonia, diarrhoea, or erysipelas, or a combination of all three. The

[69] Ibid.   [70] Loudon, 'On Maternal and Infant Mortality', 41, table 4.

environment of the workhouse might well have made this likely. But this is speculation, and it would be easier to make a case for this explanation if we were discussing late neonatal mortality (end of first week to end of third) rather than early neonatal mortality. The truth is that we still lack detailed data on neonatal mortality by cause in the late nineteenth and early twentieth centuries, and especially on the incidence of prematurity which may have been markedly different in this period from the incidence seen in the mid- to late twentieth century.[71]

The most striking feature of the investigation in 1907 was the high rate of post-neonatal mortality in the workhouses. In the general population 132 infants per 1,000 births were likely to die within the first year of life, while in workhouses the rate was between 286 and 392. The investigation attributed the high rate of post-neonatal mortality to the unsanitary condition of many workhouse nurseries and the ease with which infection could spread among the children.[72] Although Poor Law infirmaries were endeavouring to copy the sanitary standards set in voluntary hospitals, this was not always achieved. In 1899 a visitor revealed a particularly low level of cleanliness in the children's ward of Whitechapel Infirmary. Infants often remained unwashed and one flannel was used to clean all of them. In addition the system of 'cleansing the babies' bottles' was 'very unsatisfactory'. She concluded that the unhygienic conditions were largely due to defective management and overworked nurses.[73] Given the inferiority of the services offered to infants in workhouses, it is not surprising that a large number of the infants cared for in this environment died before reaching their first birthday.

The Quality of Midwifery Staff in Poor Law Institutions

The standard of maternity care offered within the workhouse was subject to the quality of its nursing staff and medical officers. Until the late nineteenth century many infirmaries in East London expected their nurses to combine midwifery care with general nursing duties. In earlier years many of these nurses lacked not only midwifery training but also basic nursing skills. By 1865 the Poor Law Board was encouraging Guardians to employ salaried nurses, but many continued to use paupers for nursing work until it was officially forbidden by the Poor Law Board in 1897.[74] As large institutions with more resources, the infirmaries in East London

[71] I am grateful to Irvine Loudon for this explanation.
[72] Webbs, *Break-Up of the Poor Law*, 102–3.
[73] Whitechapel, 31 Oct. 1899, 384–5, St BG/Wh/81.
[74] Crowther, *Workhouse System*, 177.

T ABLE 5.4. *Proportion of student nurses to total staff employed in East London infirmaries, 1902*

	Total no. of nursing staff	Total no. of probationer nurses	% probationer nurses
Bethnal Green	85	30	35
Hackney	68	35	52
Poplar and Stepney Sick Asylum	84	67	80
City of London	50	23	46
Shoredtich	50	18	36
St George's-in-the-East	30	24*	80
Whitechapel	39	10	26

* This figure includes both probationers and staff nurses.

Source: Adapted from *Returns of Nursing Staff Employed at Infirmary*, Bethnal Green, 30 Oct. 1902 (Be BG/148).

appear to have been more capable than others of funding salaried staff to care for their patients. Bethnal Green employed salaried nurses for its workhouse infirmary from the unusually early date of 1853, while similar policies were undertaken in Poplar, Mile End, St George's-in-the-East, and Whitechapel from the 1870s.[75] Throughout the years Guardians reported difficulties in securing nursing staff because of inadequate wages and bad accommodation.[76]

In an attempt to eliminate the acute shortage of trained nurses in workhouse infirmaries, Poor Law authorities began to train their own nurses.[77] By the turn of the century most of the workhouse infirmaries in East London were providing facilities for probationer nurses, as can be seen in Table 5.4. Returns taken in 1902 showed Poplar and Stepney Sick Asylum had the largest number of probationer nurses, and Whitechapel the smallest.[78] Probationer nurses constituted a vital component of the nursing staff, Poplar having one of the highest percentages. The level of

[75] Bethnal Green, 13 June 1853 (Be BG/17).
[76] Whitechapel reported in 1885 and 1892 that their nurses kept on retiring because their salaries were too low (6 Oct. 1885, 64 (St BG Wh/106/2); 8 Nov. 1892, 195 (St BG/Wh/75)). In 1905 Bethnal Green Infirmary called on the LGB to support a rise in the wages for its sisters, because they were being paid far less than elsewhere. The salary was raised from £30 to £35 (9 Nov. 1905 (Be BG/150)).
[77] For further detail on nurse training see Crowther, *Workhouse System*, 176–8.
[78] *Returns of Nursing Staff Employed at Infirmary*, in Bethnal Green, 30 Oct. 1902 (Be BG/148).

training nurses received in workhouse infirmaries was highly variable until a national syllabus was set by the Nurses Registration Act in 1919.

The standard of nurse training was especially important given that they undertook much of the midwifery care in workhouse infirmaries. In 1894 Poplar Guardians complained that their midwifery care was carried out by the general nursing staff because they did not have a separate nurse to staff their maternity ward.[79] They finally obtained an additional nurse with special midwifery qualifications to look after the maternity ward in 1895. The employment of trained midwives to work on the maternity wards, however, was slow, as can be seen in Table 5.5, which shows only one resident midwife at the Hackney institution in 1906.

Where midwifery duties were carried out in conjunction with more general nursing care the risk of infection was great, as the local government inspectors commented when visiting the Whitechapel Infirmary during the 1890s. Only after 1903 was a certified midwife appointed to attend the maternity ward in the Whitechapel Infirmary, duties which had previously been carried out by a sister of the Infirmary.[80] Similar moves were made by Bethnal Green. On opening its hospital in 1900 Bethnal Green immediately appointed a sister who had undertaken a midwifery course at Queen Charlotte's Hospital to take charge of its maternity ward, with the help of assistant nurses. The duties expected of the midwife were to ensure all the wards were clean and that the records were kept accurately. Midwives were directly under the authority of the matron and medical officer.[81]

Until the early twentieth century midwifery training was offered in only a handful of Poor Law infirmaries.[82] In 1907 Whitechapel Infirmary became one of the first Poor Law training schools for midwives in England. The LGB and other public authorities regarded its training to be of the highest standard.[83] Pupil midwives from both Whitechapel and Bethnal Green attended midwifery lectures by a doctor authorized by the Central Midwives Board (CMB) and funded by the LGB.[84] St

[79] Poplar, 13 June 1894, 102; 20 Nov. 1895, 337 (Po BG/41).
[80] Whitechapel, 3 Mar. 1903, 45 (St BG/Wh/82).
[81] Bethnal Green, Waterloo House Minutes, 9 Feb. 1905 (Be BG/234).
[82] J. Donnison, *Midwives and Medical Men: A History of the Struggle for the Control of Childbirth* (London, 1977; repr. 1988), 119. Bethnal Green, 29 Nov. 1900, 82 (Be BG 147); 24 Nov. 1904, 181 (Be BG/149).
[83] Dr H. Larder, Medical Superintendent at Whitechapel Infirmary, letter to *ELO*, 9 Oct. 1909, 5.
[84] Whitechapel, 13 Mar. 1906, 453 (St BG/Wh/87); Bethnal Green Infirmary, 15 May 1910, 238 (Be BG/152).

TABLE 5.5. *Number of patients and type of nursing staff employed at infirmaries in East London, 1902*

	Bethnal Green	Hackney	Poplar and Stepney Sick Asylum	City of London	Shoreditch	St George's-in-the-East	Whitechapel
No. of beds	669	606	770	511	515	396	590
No. of patients	483	443	754	376	462	266	556
Patients per bed	5.6	6.5	8.9	7.5	9.2	8.8	14.2
Matron	1	1	1	1	1	1	1
Assistant matron	1	1	2	1	1	1	1
Superintendent nurses	2	1	2	2	1	1	1
Home sisters	1	—	—	1	1	—	—
Midwife	—	1	—	—	—	—	—
Maternity pupils	—	1	—	—	—	—	—
Ward sisters or head nurses	15	9	10	9	8	6	4
Staff nurses	40	24	7	18	24	24*	25
Probationers	30	35	67	23	18	10	10
Total nursing staff	85	68	84	50	50	30	39

* Includes probationers

Source: *Returns of Nursing Staff Employed at Infirmary*, in Bethnal Green, 30 Oct. 1902 (Be BG/148).

George's-in-the-East sent each of its nurses to the East End Maternity Home to receive midwifery training. Each nurse was to receive four months' training at the voluntary hospital for a fee of £19 10s.[85]

By the early twentieth century, the standard of midwifery training among those caring for mothers within Poor Law institutions had advanced greatly since Twining's days. In 1909 the CMB considered Poor Law institutions good models in their midwifery training for other schools, especially as they had a wider range of patients than the ordinary lying-in institutions.[86] Comparing it to the training given by maternity charities and lying-in hospitals, the Carnegie Trust argued in 1917 that the Poor Law institutions offered more satisfactory training because it embraced 'the general training of the nurse'.[87]

District Maternity Care Provided by Poor Law Institutions

District midwifery, usually classified together with other forms of outdoor medical relief, did not progress as fast as the maternity wards of Poor Law institutions. The 1867 Metropolitan Poor Law Amendment Act did not alter the arrangements made for outdoor medical relief by the Medical Order Act in 1842. Each union was divided into districts which could easily be covered by a district medical officer.[88] In larger districts more than one medical officer was employed. Most district medical officers' salaries were low and the duties expected of them often overwhelming.[89] Midwifery formed a minor part of their work. Frequently their work in this area was supplemented by local midwives, who could call in a medical practitioner or the district medical officer when an emergency arose.

---

[85]   St George's-in-the-East, 16 Dec. 1915 (St BG/SG/79/1).

[86]   Many Poor Law infirmaries had a high percentage of women who were suffering from chronic alcoholism, destitution, and infectious diseases, and who were not allowed into general lying-in hospitals (*Report from Commissioner, Inspectors and Others on the Midwives Act*, PP 1909 XXXIII, Cd. 4823, Q3682; see also Q3625, Q3642, Qs3648–89).

[87]   E. W. Hope and J. Campbell, *Report on the Physical Welfare of Mothers and Children: England and Wales* (London, 1917), i. 22. In areas such as Merthyr Tydfil in Wales, where voluntary hospitals did not provide midwifery, Poor Law institutions constituted the main providers of midwifery services and training right through to the late 1920s (E. Peretz, 'Local Authority Maternal and Child Welfare Services in England and Wales, 1919–1939: A Comparative Study of Three Local Areas', Ph.D. thesis (Middlesex University, 1992)).

[88]   Flinn, 'Medical Services', 49.

[89]   The difficulties faced by medical officers working within Poor Law institutions and in the district, and the lack of incentives they had for improving services, is examined in detail in M. A. Crowther, 'Paupers or Patients? Obstacles to Professionalization in the Poor Law Medical Service Before 1914', *J. Hist. Med.* 39 (1984), 33–54.

For much of the nineteenth century Guardians were more interested in cutting their outdoor medical relief budgets than in offering appropriate financial incentives to secure good midwifery care, and this constituted a very small part of outdoor medical relief.[90] Midwifery orders only formed 5 per cent of the total medical orders provided by the parish of St George's-in-the-East in the months of 1870. The same was true for Bethnal Green in the years 1898 to 1911; of the total medical orders, those for midwifery cases varied between 0.27 per cent in 1900 and 1 per cent in 1908. This was a slightly smaller proportion of total medical orders than those for London as a whole, where midwifery orders never rose above 1.37 per cent of the total medical orders in the years 1883 to 1913. In Bethnal Green, in the years 1898 to 1911, a greater proportion of the cost of medical relief was devoted to the cost of the general nursing of patients in their own homes or the treatment of patients at the dispensary attached to the infirmary.[91]

Limits on the provision of midwifery orders did not necessarily reflect the desire of mothers. Indeed, Jewish mothers, like many other mothers, would probably have preferred to be confined at home on the parish than in the more restrictive environment of a Poor Law institution. This was especially important for Jewish mothers given the constraints on their religious observance in such institutions. The freedom of Jewish mothers to give birth at home would, however, have been limited by the restraints operating in the outdoor parish midwifery services. Paupers needing outdoor medical relief could only be cared for once referred by the union's relieving officer, whose job was to assess entitlement to relief. A woman had to secure a midwifery order from a relieving officer before she could secure help during her confinement. This entitled her to engage a midwife or, in an emergency, a medical practitioner, employed by the parish. As stated above, on occasion officers could make it difficult for Jewish patients to obtain such orders.

Although the relieving officer could be bypassed in some urgent

---

[90] F. B. Smith, *The People's Health, 1810–1930* (London, 1979), 53; Crowther, *Workhouse System*, 163–5. Even in the early 20th c. outdoor medical care was seen as more costly and ineffective than indoor medical care. An example of Guardians' complaints in this regard can be seen in Bethnal Green Board of Guardians, *Report* (1909), 118 (Be BG 261/6).

[91] St George's-in-the-East, 9 Dec. 1870, 310 (St BG/SG/13); Bethnal Green Board of Guardians, *Reports* (1898–1911) (Be BG/261/2); LGB, *ARs*, contained in *Reports from Commissioners* (PP 1883–1914). For fuller figures see in L. Marks, 'Irish and Jewish Women's Experience of Childbirth and Infant Care in East London, 1870–1939: The Responses of Host Society and Immigrant Communities to Medical Welfare Needs', D.Phil. thesis (Oxford, 1990), 269–70, tables 7.9–11.

situations, the requirement for a midwifery order could lead to problems. A common complaint among medical officers was that relieving officers were not medical experts and therefore could not know the needs of their patients, including maternity cases.[92] The Minority Report complained in 1909 that some unions refused to provide outdoor midwifery orders, or restricted them to an extent which prevented most mothers from obtaining them. Some unions refused orders to mothers with three or four children, at the same time as granting the request of unmarried mothers or those who were being confined for the first time.[93]

In East London unions these restrictions were not extensively applied and a range of women were given midwifery orders. Securing midwifery orders, however, could sometimes be obstructive to good care, especially in times of emergency when speed was vital. In 1894 Whitechapel Infirmary held an inquest on a woman who had died because of negligent medical care during childbirth. The medical practitioner who responded to the call refused to attend the case without a larger fee, for which extra permission had to be secured.[94] Because the first relieving officer was absent, and no subsequent call was made on another officer, no extra order was secured. The woman only received skilled attention three days later, by which time it was too late. She died in the infirmary a fortnight later.[95] Summing up the case, the coroner concluded that the medical officer had been legally correct in refusing to attend the patient without an order from the relieving officer, but added that 'for years past, he had advocated a system whereby the necessitous poor would be allowed to call in the nearest doctor in cases of urgent sickness'. He argued that funds for paying the doctor for his first visit should be taken out of the rates. Poplar Guardians had already adopted the system, and he advised that Whitechapel Guardians should do the same.[96] The following year Whitechapel Guardians sent a letter to medical practitioners in the area, informing them that, if a district medical officer was not available, the Guardians would be prepared to pay all the fees entailed by the medical practitioner for the first visit and for any medicine. Any doctor making such a visit between the hours of 10 p.m. and 8 a.m. was to be paid 7s. 6d., and 3s. 6d. between 8 a.m. and 10 p.m.[97]

---

[92] Flinn, 'Medical Services', 49–50.

[93] Webbs, *Break-Up of the Poor Law*, 89–90.

[94] Without proof of a midwifery order, neither medical men nor parish midwives were assured of payment for their work.

[95] Whitechapel, 18 Dec. 1894, 195 (St BG/Wh/77).   [96] Ibid. 196.

[97] Ibid. 2 July 1895, 427–8.

In 1898 the situation was slightly eased with the passing of Section (2) in the Poor Law Amendment Act. This empowered Guardians to pay medical men called in to undertake urgent medical care and midwifery work. Individual unions were to set the scale of payment.[98] Medical practitioners in the parish of St George's-in-the-East were unwilling to attend any urgent midwifery cases without the guarantee that they would be paid a minimum fee of £1 1s.[99] On occasions Guardians forgot or delayed payment for the midwifery care carried out by local doctors, which could lead to resentment. In 1908 a doctor in St George's-in-the-East refused to attend a case on the grounds that he had not been paid for two former attendances.[100] Only in 1918 was the dispute over who should pay the medical men for emergency work settled with the passing of the Midwives Act. Under this legislation local authorities were required to pay the fee whenever the patient's family was unable to do so. The fee could be recovered at a later stage, but in many cases it never materialized.[101]

Except in emergencies, much of the midwifery work undertaken by the parish was done by local midwives.[102] Until the regulation of midwives in 1902 there was no guarantee that the midwives hired by the parish were qualified. Indeed, given the low wages offered by the parish for such work, it might be assumed that women hired were not among the best qualified.[103] Nevertheless, by the 1870s Guardians were hiring professional midwives, as they were doing with their nursing staff in the infirmaries. From the 1870s onwards Whitechapel Guardians took a particular interest in securing qualified midwives. In 1872, prompted by allegations that they were employing an unqualified woman, the Whitechapel Guardians thoroughly investigated her training with the Royal Charity of Midwives. Satisfied with her skills they continued to employ her.[104] She was under strict instructions that in cases of emergency she was to send

---

[98] St George's-in-the-East, 23 Aug. 1907, 209 (St BG/SG/45).

[99] Ibid. 15 Nov. 1907, 328; Whitechapel Guardians were paying similar fees to the doctors they were hiring for such cases (Whitechapel, 31 Dec. 1907, 277 (St BG/Wh/89)).

[100] Poplar, 10 Jan. 1908, 408 (Po BG/SG/45).

[101] Donnison, *Midwives and Medical Men*, 185.

[102] The fees Guardians paid for such services were 6s. for each district midwifery case in Whitechapel in 1884. By 1904 the fees had been raised to 7s. 6d. for each case, which compared favourably with private cases. Of the 420 midwives who were reported to be working in London in 1909, only 32 were working entirely within either Poor Law institutions or lying-in hospitals. Many more midwives were reported to be working from their own homes for charitable or Poor Law institutions, or taking private patients. (Whitechapel, 1 Jan. 1884 (St BG/Wh/66); 8 Nov. 1904, 322 (St BG/Wh/86); 'The Supervision of Midwives in the County of London', *Med. Offr.*, 21 Jan. 1911, 29.)

[103] Smith, *People's Health*, 48.

[104] Whitechapel, 17 Sept. 1872, 121, 195; 15 Oct. 1872, 156–7 (St BG/Wh/54).

for a medical officer, and to make sure she sent for him from the correct district. The midwife was provided with a map for the purpose.[105]

Standards among the midwives employed by the parish Guardians almost certainly improved with the implementation of the Midwives Act in 1902 and the creation of midwifery schools within workhouse institutions and in unions, such as Whitechapel, where efforts were made to pay midwives fees which compared favourably with those of private cases.[106] Yet although incentives were increasing for midwives to work for the parish, their numbers remained low. This was partly because most midwives preferred to be independent. Of the 420 midwives who were reported to be working in London in 1909, only thirty-two were working entirely within Poor Law institutions or lying-in hospitals.[107]

Attitudes Towards Mothers Confined in Poor Law Institutions

As already highlighted, much of the Poor Law policy was not sympathetic to the needs of women, and pregnant women had a particularly ambiguous position until the turn of the century.[108] Expectant mothers were not viewed as 'impotent' like the infirm or the elderly, and were often classified together with the 'able-bodied' poor.[109] Most women had to prove themselves destitute before they could get any parish support for their confinement. As late as 1909 some unions insisted on providing maternity care only within the workhouse.[110] This approach stemmed largely from the fact that the great proportion of pregnant mothers supported by the parish midwifery services were unmarried.[111] Like the 'undeserving' poor,

[105] Ibid. 12 Nov. 1872, 205. In 1890 the Whitechapel Guardians again ensured that they hired a certified midwife of the Royal Maternity Charity (Whitechapel, 15 Apr. 1890, 456–7 (St BG/Wh/72)).

[106] Whitechapel, 1 Jan. 1884 (St BG/Wh/66); 8 Nov. 1904, 322 (St BG/Wh/86).

[107] 'The Supervision of Midwives in the County of London', *Med. Offr.*, 21 Jan. 1911, 29.

[108] Thane, 'Women and the Poor Law', 29–35; Ross, 'Women and Poor Law Administration', 161.

[109] Smith, *People's Health*, 47; M. Chamberlain and R. Richardson, 'Life and Death', *Oral Hist. J.* 10/1 (1983), 31–43, 33; Thane, 'Women and the Poor Law', 39.

[110] Webbs, *Break-Up of the Poor Law*, 87. See also *RC Poor Law Relief*, PP 1909 XXXVII, 246.

[111] The Poor Law Amendment Act of 1834 cut outdoor relief for unmarried mothers and decreased the assistance available from the father of the illegitimate child. After 1834 unmarried mothers were therefore increasingly forced to seek relief within the confines of the workhouse. For more information concerning the attitudes towards unmarried mothers and the provision of services see A. R. Higginbotham, 'The Unmarried Mother and Her

the moral conduct of unmarried mothers was regarded as questionable. Even the workhouse social reformer, Louise Twining, argued that the lying-in wards should be 'in the workhouse rather than the infirmary' so 'as to induce a proper sense of shame in the mothers'.[112]

By the 1890s some of these attitudes had altered slightly to arguing that the girls should be detained in the workhouse 'in the interests of the women themselves'. For the sake of the health of the women and infants, the Poplar Guardians in 1898 urged the LGB 'to promote legislation to enable Boards of Guardians to detain unmarried inmates of Lying-in Wards for three weeks after the birth of their children'.[113] Such views were common for the period. In 1900 Bethnal Green refused permission for visitors to attend mothers confined in its lying-in wards and mothers were unable to leave the wards on the usual visiting days.[114] By contrast, the Whitechapel Board of Guardians was more lenient and reluctant to adopt the policy proposed by Poplar.[115]

Vestiges of the old attitudes none the less remained. In 1903 Dr Downes opposed the transferral of the maternity wards from the Bethnal Green workhouse to the infirmary, because they would be abused in the same way as the infirmary. Many patients were inefficiently occupying space in infirmaries when, he argued, they should be accommodated in the workhouse. Should the maternity wards be placed in the infirmary they too would be used too freely.[116] Some Poor Law officers also continued to feel that parish maternity services invited immorality. In 1909 one lady

Child in Victorian London, 1834–1914', Ph.D. thesis (Indianopolis, 1985), 2, and ' "Sin of the Age": Infanticide and Illegitimacy in Victorian London', *Vict. Stud.* 32/3 (1989), 319–38, 321. See also Crowther, *Workhouse System*, 100–1.

[112] Some women Guardians were more sympathetic to the plight of the unmarried mother and were not only active in mounting rescue work among unmarried mothers, but also searched for employment for women once they had left the workhouse, and found foster-mothers for illegitimate children. None the less, while in later years a number of women Guardians promoted strong feminist views in their work and helped to soften workhouse discipline for defenceless inmates, most of the women Guardians elected took a conventional view of women's duties and emphasized the moral codes of conduct women were supposed to follow in the workhouse. For more information on this and the election of women Guardians see Crowther, *Workhouse System*, 69, 77–9, and Ross, 'Women and Poor Law Administration', 162–6.   [113] Poplar, 12 Jan. 1898, 15 (Po BG/45).

[114] Bethnal Green, Waterloo House, Minutes, 9 May 1900 (Be BG/234). No reason was given for this decision.   [115] Whitechapel, 1 Apr. 1890, 444–5 (St BG/Wh/72).

[116] Bethnal Green, 1903, 15 (Be BG/261/3). Dr Downes also expressed this view in 1909 (see *RC Poor Law Relief*, PP 1909 XL, Q23155, and app. XV (D), 437). As late as 1920 many workhouses were still refusing to provide outdoor relief to unmarried mothers on the pretext that to do so would invite immorality. Returns from Jan. 1920 demonstrated that 79% of unmarried mothers relieved were provided with indoor relief (Crowther, *Workhouse System*, 100).

inspector complained that women who were confined within the work-house were not separated into specific categories. She claimed,

Nowhere is classification more needed than in the maternity wards. The unavoidable and close intercourse between the young girl, who often enters upon mother-hood comparatively innocent and the older woman who is lost to all sense of shame and who returns again and again to the maternity wards for the birth of her illegitimate children, constitutes a grave danger. Too often the older woman invites the friendless girl to share her home on leaving.[117]

Guardians remained uneasy about providing maternity care even on an outdoor level. In 1910 Poplar Guardians protested against a clause in the Midwives Bill which proposed to compel Guardians 'to pay the fee of the doctor whom a midwife is required to send for in cases of emergency' whether it was for a destitute case or not. They argued that it would not only put a new burden on the rates, it also went against the principles of Poor Law institutions. In effect, they claimed, the proposal would 'bring families to whom it applied into contact with the Poor Law without their consent and without any application on their part'.[118] Yet such restrictive views and policies were not universal and some unions had a more lenient approach. Whitechapel Union, for instance, was reluctant to detain its unmarried mothers and in 1904 was one of the first unions to adopt the policy of the Registrar-General that births occurring in workhouses should not be registered as such.[119] On a national level, evidence suggests that the embarrassment of giving birth with the help of the parish was also changing. In 1909 the Royal Commission on Poor Law Relief commented that many more women were entering workhouse institutions for their confinements than previously assumed. The Minority Report of the Commission calculated that the annual number of births in the Poor Law institutions of the United Kingdom probably exceeded 15,000. Nearly 2,000 births occurred annually in the thirty-four lying-in wards of the Poor Law institutions of the Metropolis.[120]

Frequently women were using the workhouse solely as a maternity hospital. They normally stayed ten days in total and rarely took any other form of relief afterwards. According to the Minority Report of 1909,

---

[117] Webbs, *Break-Up of the Poor Law*, 95. See also Miss Stansfeld, *RC Poor Law Relief*, PP 1909 XXXVII, pt. VIII, ch. 4, pp. 563–4.

[118] Poplar, 28 Sept. 1910, 328 (Po BG/56); See also *East End News*, 30 Oct. 1930.

[119] Whitechapel, 1 Apr. 1890, 444–5 (St BG/Wh/72); 8 Nov. 1904, 322–3 (St BG/Wh/86); *RC Poor Law Relief*, PP 1909 XXXVII, 246.

[120] *RC Poor Law Relief*, PP 1909 XXXVII, pt. V, ch. 1, p. 245; Webbs, *Break-Up of the Poor Law*, 93.

many of these mothers were not in the 'ordinary sense of the term, destitute persons.' Indeed editors of the report argued: 'it is generally assumed that the women admitted to the Workhouse for lying-in are either feeble-minded girls, persistently immoral women, or wives deserted by their husbands. Whatever may have been the case in past years, this is no longer a correct description of the patients in what have become, in effect, Maternity Hospitals.' In England and Wales during 1907, 30 per cent of the women who gave birth within Poor Law institutions were married women. Married women constituted between 40 and 50 per cent of those confined in London Poor Law institutions.[121] None the less, while the stigma attached to parish maternity services appeared to be lessening on a national level, it was not totally eroded. In East London some women still showed a resistance to parish maternity care, perhaps reflecting the less sympathetic approach of certain unions such as Poplar and Bethnal Green. During the dock strike of 1911, the East End Maternity Home reported that some of its patients had been forced through economic circumstances to be confined in the workhouse rather than the hospital. Many of these mothers had used the workhouse only as a last resort.[122] During World War I, however, attitudes towards parish maternity care changed greatly, when the numbers of patients entering Poor Law infirmaries increased substantially. This not only made Poor Law infirmaries a more familiar communal institution for many of those who had no previous experience of their care, but also forced Poor Law authorities to show more flexibility in their provision. In 1917, for example, the LGB funded Whitechapel Infirmary to establish a new ward to receive non-pauper women for their confinements during air-raids.[123]

Such developments not only showed a change in public attitudes towards Poor Law infirmaries, but also perhaps a shift in the sensitivity of Guardians to the needs of the community. Although the original aim of Poor Law maternity services was to provide for those who could not afford maternity care in any other way, a wider public increasingly utilized the facilities. In 1920 Poplar Guardians considered whether they should allow 'ordinary' maternity patients to use their lying-in wards, subject to approval from the Ministry of Health. West Ham Union had already

---

[121] Webbs, *Break-Up of the Poor Law*, 95–6. One observer to the commission was reported as saying that in some large cities the advantages of the maternity departments were 'so much appreciated that various underhand expedients' were 'adopted to secure admission to the wards'. Married women were reported as pretending they were single or deserted in order to gain admission (*RC Poor Law Relief*, PP 1909 XXXVII, pt. V, ch. 1, p. 245).

[122] East End Maternity Home, *AR* (1911), 14–15.

[123] Whitechapel, 4 Dec. 1917, 432 (St BG/Wh/97).

instituted such a policy.[124] Similarly in 1922 the Whitechapel Infirmary committee recommended that the Infirmary should accept paying patients, subject to the consent of the Ministry of Health, at a fee of 1 guinea per week. Preference was to be given to those who were living within the Whitechapel Poor Law area.[125] Some of the maternity beds offered in Poor Law infirmaries were also funded by the local borough council.[126] In 1927 Poplar Guardians allotted eight of their beds to the borough council.[127]

Many of the improvements made by Poor Law authorities to their maternity services stemmed from increasing public demand for the high rate of maternal mortality to be curbed. Their policies and views were similar to those of voluntary hospitals. In 1921 the Poplar Guardians argued that 'in view of the overcrowded conditions of many of the homes in the district, and of the fact that trained certified staff are engaged at the maternity wards', they thought 'that endeavours should be made to induce expectant mothers to come into the wards during the period of confinement'.[128]

By the early 1920s the focus of maternity care by East London Poor Law authorities was on in-patients, and its rate of hospital confinements, as in the case of the voluntary hospitals examined in the previous chapter, was high compared to the rest of London or the country as a whole. While Poor Law infirmaries, taken over by the Local Government Board in 1929, showed an increase in the number of in-patients in Stepney by the late 1920s, this was slightly slower than in voluntary hospitals whose number of in-patients increased dramatically in the years after 1915 (see Figs. 5.1 and 5.2). Table 5.6 shows the number of maternity patients in Poor Law infirmaries from 1890 onwards.

No accurate figures can be found for the proportion of mothers who were being confined within the maternity wards of Poor Law institutions as opposed to being confined on the district. It is clear, however, that the number of maternity beds provided by the Poor Law authorities was increasing. Initially the Poplar maternity wards only accommodated twenty-eight mothers with their babies. The number confined in the hospital rapidly increased, as Table 5.7 demonstrates. By 1926 the demand for entry was so great that there was pressure to develop a municipal maternity hospital, which was finally realized in 1929 with the establishment of a

[124] Poplar, 21 July 1920, 74 (Po BG/67).
[125] Whitechapel, 28 Nov. 1922, 232–3 (St BG/Wh/102).
[126] For more information on this and other services provided by the council see Ch. 6.
[127] Poplar, 27 July 1927, 112 (Po BG/74).
[128] Poplar, 20 July 1921, 72 (Po BG/75).

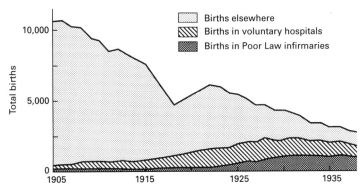

Note: No figures available for 1914, 1916, and 1919–21.

F I G. 5.1. Annual births of Stepney residents in voluntary hospitals, Poor Law infirmaries, and elsewhere, 1905–1938
Source: Stepney MOH, *ARs* (1905–38).

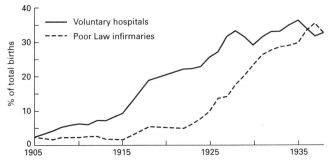

Note: No figures available for 1914, 1916, and 1919–21.

F I G. 5.2. Percentage of births of Stepney residents in voluntary hospitals and Poor-Law infirmaries, 1905–1938
Source: as for Fig. 5.1.

maternity ward at St Andrew's Hospital (one of the first Poor Law hospitals established after the 1867 Metropolitan Poor Law Act). This ward provided twelve beds and twelve cots.[129]

Social Services Provided for Mothers by Poor Law Institutions

From their earliest days Poor Law institutions had provided relief other than medical care for destitute mothers. This ranged from general relief,

[129] *ELO*, 10 Aug. 1929, 3.

T ABLE 5.6. *Total number and percentage of in-patient births of Stepney
and Poplar residents in Poor Law infirmaries and voluntary hospitals*

Borough	Year	Total births in the borough	Infirmary births		Voluntary hospital births	
			No.	%	No.	%
St George's-	1890–4	7,840	381	5	—	—
in-the-East	1895–9	8,756	283	3	—	—
Whitechapel	1890	2,730	105	4	—	—
	1894–9	18,759	716	4	—	—
Stepney	1905–9	51,116	981	2	1,993	4
	1910–13	34,375	692	2	2,166	6
	1922–5	22,744	1,464	6	5,142	23
	1926–30	22,542	3,828	17	6,728	30
	1931–5	17,383	4,768	27	5,759	33
	1936–8	8,445	2,820	33	2,740	32
Poplar	1905–9	26,642	441	2	918	3
	1910–14	25,317	341	1	1,212	5
	1915–20	20,082	467	2	1,414	7
	1920–2	13,564	—	—	1,033	8

Notes: St George's-in-the-East and Whitechapel became part of the Borough of Stepney
in 1900. Poor Law infirmaries came under municipal control after 1929. By the early
1920s many of the infirmaries had dropped the title 'infirmary' and instead used
'hospital', e.g. Whitechapel Infirmary was listed as St Peter's Hospital and the infirmary
in St George's-in-the-East was called St George's Hospital in 1923.

Source: St George's-in-the-East and Whitechapel MOH, *ARs* (1890–9); Stepney and
Poplar MOH, *ARs* (1905–38).

such as food and clothes, to shelter within the workhouse. Securing such
services from Poor Law authorities frequently entailed demanding investigations into families' circumstances, a process which was not unfamiliar
to those who asked for comparable services from the Lady Almoner in a
voluntary hospital. Lying-in wards improved partly as a result of the
general advances being made in nursing care in workhouse infirmaries
and the outcry against infant and maternal mortality, but elsewhere the
provision of food and other forms of support to mothers and their babies
was closely tied to outdoor relief which Guardians were increasingly
trying to reduce in these years, and this hindered any progress on that
front.

TABLE 5.7. *Number of births in All Saints' Maternity Hospital,*
1921–1928

Year	No. of births
1921	30
1922	67
1923	112
1924	212
1925	314
1926	512
1927	581
1928	561

Source: *ELO*, 10 Aug. 1929, 3.

The hardship this imposed was illustrated by one midwife, working in Poplar, who in 1906 complained about the difficulties mothers faced with Poor Law officials when seeking parish support. She had sent the unemployed husband of one of her patients to the relieving officer to ask for food for his wife, but he had been refused. Instead he was offered an order for the whole family to go into the workhouse. At this point the midwife tried to intervene and approached the relieving officer, but with no success. If it had not been for the help of the midwife and the neighbours the woman 'might have starved'. In another instance where a mother did not have enough breast milk to feed her baby the inability to secure help from the parish proved fatal for the infant.[130]

Alongside these two cases, the midwife claimed that she had seen many other cases where relief had been refused to the husband applying on behalf of the wife, causing them great shame. One man whom the midwife told to approach the relieving officer had said that 'he would rather lie in the gutter than go again'. Desperate for advice about what to do in these circumstances, the midwife asked Sir Shirley Murphy what she should do to get help for such cases. She pleaded,

We, as district midwives, are told we are responsible for the health of the mothers and babies under our care, and how can we care for them if mothers have no food? I often, out of my own pocket, pay for milk and food because there seems no other

[130] Poplar, 12 Dec. 1906, 434–5; 6 Feb. 1907, 536, (Po BG/75). The first case was of a woman with a surname common in Ireland.

way to help them. I am only a woman earning my own living and cannot keep doing this.[131]

Sadly the evidence given by this midwife was common, reflecting the restrictions imposed on outdoor relief as a whole. In 1909 the Minority Report criticized the Poor Law authorities for inadequate and variable social services for mothers and their infants. 'An expectant mother, if granted Outdoor Relief at all, is seldom given more than 2*s*. or 3*s*. a week, no consideration being given to the special needs of her condition.'[132] In some cases mothers were only given 1*s*. or 1*s*. 6*d*. for the child and nothing for themselves. Nor were relieving officers given any particular instructions to grant special food to pregnant women. After the birth of the infant no follow-up service was offered in the form of nursing or home helps.[133]

Preparation for Motherhood and Infant Rearing

Unlike voluntary bodies who were very active in educating mothers in diet, hygiene, and breast-feeding by the turn of the century, Poor Law authorities were slow to undertake such preventive measures. Partly this might have stemmed from the fact that much of it was already being undertaken by local authorities. Established under the Local Government Act of 1894, the borough councils had increasingly assumed some of the Guardians' former duties in registration of births and deaths, sanitation, and hospital provision.[134] Local councils soon became key figures in the provision of maternal and infant welfare, most notably in the form of milk supplies, infant welfare centres, and health visitors.[135] Editors of the Minority Report in 1909 were scandalized, however, that similar activities were not also being undertaken by Poor Law authorities.

In view of the fact that the mothers are, in the great majority of cases, extraordinarily ignorant on these points, it does not seem to us economical that so large an expenditure should annually be incurred from the Poor Rate in order to provide for the birth of infants, without any precautions being taken to prevent these infants from dying within a few days or weeks of birth. Nor do we find the Destitution Authorities in any part of the Kingdom taking any heed whatsoever of the conditions under which the 50,000 infants under five years of age, whom they have always on their books as Outdoor paupers, are being reared. The

---

131 Poplar, 6 Feb. 1907, 536 (Po BG/53).
132 Webbs, *Break-Up of the Poor Law*, 86.   133 Ibid.
134 Crowther, *Workhouse System*, 91.
135 Further information can be found in Ch. 6.

mothers may nurse their infants themselves, or may use the most insanitary bottles; they may feed their infants properly, or give them potatoes or red herrings; they may lock them up in a deserted room all day (since the Guardians make it necessary for the mothers to go out to work), or they may leave them (with dummy teats or 'comforters') with the most careless neighbours; they may overlay them in bed; they may even insure their little lives with one of the Industrial Insurance Companies, and so use some of the Guardians' Outdoor Relief money thus hideously to speculate in death without any warning or prohibition and without even any attention by the Destitution Authority, out of whose funds these infants are being maintained.[136]

Provision made by Poor Law authorities in this area was slightly improved with the passing of the Maternity and Child Welfare Act in 1918 which empowered local authorities to provide maternity and infant welfare services such as antenatal clinics. Like many voluntary hospitals, a number of Poor Law institutions began to provide their own antenatal clinics from the 1920s. In 1926 Bethnal Green Hospital made arrangements for their mothers to have antenatal check-ups. All applicants who sought to give birth in the maternity wards were advised to report to the sister at least three months before they expected to be confined. They were no longer expected to apply directly to the relieving officer.[137]

One of the prime objectives of the Act was to co-ordinate services and prevent overlapping.[138] By the 1920s it was common both for the Poor Law authorities to send their mothers to municipal antenatal clinics, and for the council to fund maternity beds within Poor Law hospitals. Although moves were made in Poplar to convert a room for antenatal work, they were still dependent on the council for most of its antenatal care.[139] This had its limitations. Any important antenatal treatment had to be obtained either from the patient's own doctor or from a suitable hospital.[140] The Local Government Act of 1929 finally enabled local councils to take over Poor Law infirmaries and their maternity services.

Use of Services by Jewish Mothers

With the increasing advances made in maternity provision as well as religious toleration within Poor Law institutions, what was the uptake of

---

[136] Webbs, *Break-Up of the Poor Law*, 87.
[137] Bethnal Green, 18 Mar. 1926, 56 (Be BG/163).
[138] N. Gebbie, 'Some Effects of the Local Government Act, 1929, or the Future of Maternity and Child Welfare', *Med. Offr.*, 1 Nov. 1930, 193.
[139] Poplar, 30 Dec. 1925, 290 (Po BG/72).
[140] Poplar, 27 July 1927, 112 (Po BG/74).

services by Jewish patients? Unfortunately no figures remain for how many Jewish mothers approached the parish for help during their confinement. None the less it would seem, from the evidence available on infirmary and workhouse provision as a whole, that they tried their best to avoid such care. Tables 5.8 and 5.9 indicate that a much smaller percentage of the total cases of Jews helped by the parish were in receipt of indoor relief than the general population. Indeed, as the tables show, Jewish aliens were much more likely to rely on outdoor relief (usually medical relief in their case) than on indoor relief. This was in complete contrast to the general population during this period. Given the restrictions being imposed on outdoor relief and the increasing emphasis on indoor relief in East London during this period the great number of Jews accepting outdoor relief is surprising.[141]

One explanation for the low number of Jews claiming indoor relief might have been the demographic structure of the Jewish population. The majority of claimants for indoor relief among the general population tended to be the elderly.[142] Indeed, in the last three decades of the nineteenth century there had been a substantial increase in the number of elderly who were institutionalized, a very large number of whom were women. The level of institutionalization of the elderly was also much greater in London than elsewhere.[143] With the passing of the Old Age Pensions Act in 1908 many of the elderly began to disappear from workhouse institutions. Between 1908 and 1912 the mean number of paupers in workhouses fell by nearly 25 per cent. None the less the old-age pensions were reserved for those people 'over 70 on low incomes and of

[141] For more information on the crusade against outdoor relief generally see K. Williams, *From Pauperism to Poverty* (London, 1981), 96–107, 128–35. In the context of East London see Ryan, 'Politics of Relief', 142–51. For the fall in total population using outdoor relief in these years see Crowther, *Workhouse System*, 60, fig. 1. See also figures for London compared with England and Wales in LCC, *London Statistics*, 20 (1909–10), 73.

[142] In the 1850s outdoor relief was not denied to the elderly. The workhouse was intended to serve those elderly whose destitution was assumed to be the result of improvidence. In the 1890s Charles Booth and the report of the Royal Commission on the Aged Poor estimated that of those aged 60–75, 88 out of every 1,000 were in the workhouse. Those who were older were even more likely to be in a workhouse (Crowther, *Workhouse System*, 42, 73). In 1903 Booth also calculated that over half the 487,000 in receipt of outrelief were over 60, with a greater proportion in rural areas. More than three-quarters of these elderly were women (C. Booth, *Poor Law Reform* (London, 1911), 24, 36–7). See also D. Thompson, 'Workhouse to Nursing Home: Residential Care of Elderly People in England Since 1840', *Ageing and Society*, 3 (1983), 43–70, 49, table 1.

[143] Thompson, 'Workhouse to Nursing Home', and 'The Welfare of the Elderly in the Past: A Family or Community Responsibility?', in M. Pelling and R. Smith (eds.), *Life, Death and the Elderly: Historical Perspectives* (London, 1991). See also the introduction, especially pp. 15–20.

TABLE 5.8. *Total number of Austrian, Russian, and Polish immigrants to whom Poor Law relief was granted by those East London unions particularly used by East European immigrants in 1909 and 1911*

Parish or union	Year	Total aliens	Total Austrian, Hungarian, Russian, and Polish	Austrian, Hungarian Russian, Polish as % of total
Bethnal Green	1909	170	146	86
	1911	200	178	89
	1912	145	128	88
	1913	132	102	77
City of London	1909	55	16	29
	1911	71	30	42
	1912	21	11	52
	1913	24	13	54
Mile End Old	1901–2	558	486	87
Town	1909	422	357	85
	1911	487	416	85
	1912	605	529	87
	1913	599	535	89
Poplar	1909	118	11	9
	1910	125	9	7
	1911	102	11	11
	1912	111	10	9
St George's-in-	1901–2	710	612	86
the-East	1909	1,530	1,257	82
	1911	991	791	80
	1912	601	528	88
	1913	448	352	79
Whitechapel	1901–2	669	549	82
	1909	900	706	78
	1911	649	505	78
	1912	536	427	80
	1913	585	511	87

Note: The majority of Austrian, Hungarian, Russian, and Polish immigrants who settled in East London were Jewish. A number of Germans (who could have been also Jewish) were confined in these institutions, but they have not been included in the statistics for this table. Figures exist for the years 1901–2, 1909, and 1911–13 only.

Sources: LCC, *London Statistics*, 21–4 (1910–13); *RC Alien Immigration*, PP 1903 IX pt. II, Apps. XXV and XXVI.

TABLE 5.9. *Percentage of total cases of aliens and general population receiving different forms of relief out of total relieved in East London unions, 1909–1911*

Parish or union	Year	Indoor Relief		Outdoor Relief		
		General Population %	Aliens %	Medical* Aliens %	Other	
					General Population %	Aliens %
Bethnal Green	1909	85	59	39	15	2
	1911	87	48	49	13	3
	1912	90	50	47	10	3
	1913	87	11	84	13	5
Mile End Old	1909	59	27	73	41	1
Town	1911	56	25	75	44	1
	1912	60	23	77	40	1
	1913	56	17	82	44	1
St George's-in-	1909	—	18	76	—	1
the-East	1911	88	19	75	12	5
	1912	90	23	69	11	2
	1913	89	29	70	15	2
Whitechapel	1909	95	38	54	5	2
	1911	97	44	50	3	2
	1912	96	47	44	4	3
	1913	97	56	74	3	1

Note: Figures only exist for aliens for 1909–13.

* No separate category is listed for the general population receiving outdoor medical relief; it appears as part of the total other outdoor relief.

Source: Based on figures from LCC, *London Statistics*, 21–4 (1910–13).

good moral character', and those who had specifically not received any poor relief. This limited the extent to which the pensions reached those who needed it.[144] The changing provision for the elderly, however, does not explain the very small numbers of Jews receiving indoor relief. Demographically, as Chapter 2 has shown, the Jewish population, particularly the immigrants, was a relatively young one in the early twentieth century.

[144] Indeed the elderly continued to form the majority of inmates of Poor Law institutions well into the 20th c. Crowther, *Workhouse System*, 59, 84, 110.

This meant that there were fewer potential elderly claimants for indoor relief among the Jewish population.

Part of the explanation for the relative absence of Jewish inmates applying for indoor relief and their larger numbers claiming medical relief lay in the policy pursued by the JBG.[145] The chief aim of the JBG was to provide relief where religious issues were at stake and aid could not be found elsewhere. Unlike indoor parish relief which limited religious observance and other cultural activities, outdoor, such as medical, relief permitted more freedom. The JBG therefore did all that it could to prevent their poor from having to accept indoor relief. Medical relief, however, was considered a lesser need and was not provided by the JBG after 1873.[146] Those who could not afford medical relief or gain charitable care were therefore forced to depend on the local union.

Records from the United Synagogue Visitation Committee show that the majority of Jews claiming indoor relief sought the shelter of the infirmary rather than the workhouse (see Table 5.10). Mile End seems to have had a higher number Jewish inmates in its workhouse than others. This may perhaps have been because its policies towards Jewish inmates were more liberal than others. In addition to this, casual labour and poverty were not as acute in Mile End, perhaps allowing the union greater freedom in their expenditure on ritual requirements for Jewish patients. Guardians in Mile End also tended to be more radical than other unions in East London.[147] Overall, however, even in Mile End Jews appeared to make much more use of the infirmary than of the workhouse.

Using sample years Gerry Black has shown that Jews made up a very small percentage of those who went into the infirmaries in the East End (see Table 5.11). Those less likely to have Jewish inmates included the City of London Infirmary (primarily catering for men after 1909), which was based in Bow where there were few Jews, and the Bethnal Green Infirmary which Jews would have been deterred from entering because it was initially attached to the workhouse. Religious observance in infirmaries might prove difficult, but in workhouses the rules were even stricter. The number of Jews housed in the Whitechapel Infirmary was

---

[145] For more information on the JBG and the welfare it provided see Ch. 3. See also L. Marks, ' "Dear Old Mother Levy's": The Jewish Maternity Home and Sick Room Helps Society, 1895–1939', *Soc. Hist. Med.* 3 (1990), 61–88, 74–6.

[146] JBG, *AR* (1879), 18; see also JBG, *ARs* (1873), 22; (1891), 10–11; and (1896), 18–19. See also Ch. 3, and Marks, 'Dear Old Mother Levy's', 74–5.

[147] Ryan has argued that the radical politics of Mile End which began in the 1880s remained constant up to 1914. She argues that Mile End was influential in shifting the other unions in East London to a greater political focus ('Politics of Relief', 139, 156–7).

TABLE 5.10. *Total Jewish inmates admitted over the year to various Poor Law institutions, distinguishing between workhouse and infirmary*

Union	Year	Infirmary/hospital inmates*	Workhouse inmates
Bethnal Green	1884	—	1
	1885	—	2
	1887	—	10
	1888	—	5
	1889	—	14
	1890	—	5
	1891	—	3
	1896	—	1
	1905	15	—
	1910	77	7
	1911	105	11
	1912	101	13
Mile End	1910	232	154
	1911	232	108
	1912	239	101
St George's-in-the-East	1901	89	—
	1905	103	53
	1910	223	35
	1911	232	51
	1912	179	2
Whitechapel	1905	148	10
	1910	413	15
	1911	377	17
	1912	375	6

* Bethnal Green established a separate hospital in 1900: before that sick patients were accommodated in the workhouse.

Source: United Synagogue, Visitation Committee, Minutes, 1902–14.

remarkably low given that it was based in an area with a heavy concentration of Jews, that it provided kosher food, and was noted for its good arrangements for Jewish women.[148] Of all the infirmaries the one in Mile End Old Town had the highest number of Jewish patients, although this

[148] The good treatment of Jewish women in the Whitechapel Infirmary was highlighted at a conference between delegates from the United Synagogue's Visitation Committee and JBG's Sanitary Committee in 1907 (Black, 'Health and Medical Care', 187–9).

TABLE 5.11. *Total number of Jewish patients compared to total number of in-patients in the various infirmaries in East London, 1899–1927*

Parish or union	Year	Total in-patients	Total Jews	% Jews
City of London	1899	1,045	31	2.96
	1900	848	19	2.24
	1901	1,028	16	1.55
	1904	1,909	18	0.94
	1908	2,370	23	0.97
	1913	1,564	38	2.42
Bethnal Green[1]	1902	2,183	23	1.05
	1910	2,903	90	3.10
	1915	2,392	80	3.34
	1916	2,117	97	4.58
	1917	2,061	101	4.90
	1918	1,663	89	5.35
St George's-in-the-East	1908	unknown	unknown	6
Whitechapel	1900	4,844	234	4.83
	1910	4,135	411	9.93
	1915	3,442	382	11.09
Mile End Old Town[2]	July–Dec. 1919	812	96	11.82
	1920	2,019	272	13.47
	1921	2,203	382	17.34
	1922	2,815	585	20.78
	1923	2,976	709	23.82
	Jan.–May 1924	1,407	353	25.08
	11 Dec. 1926–11 Dec. 1927	4,157	737	17.72

[1] taken from the admission and discharge registers.
[2] taken from the creed registers.
Source: Black, 'Health and Medical Care', 187–9, tables 4–7.

perhaps reflected the specific years in which the figures were recorded. After World War I infirmaries were more liberal in their religious provision and no longer possessed the same stigma, so that patients were less reluctant to enter them.

By 1929 maternity services provided by Poor Law authorities had improved greatly compared with the nineteenth century. Maternity cases were no longer mixed with the general poor and were now being looked after by trained midwives, nurses, and medical officers both on the district and in increasingly updated maternity wards. Women using these facilities no longer faced the same stigma as fifty years previously. The concern for maternal mortality during this period was reflected in an improvement in midwifery standards and preventive health care in many organizations dealing with mothers. When examined from the perspective of maternal mortality, particularly in the case of the low rates of puerperal fever achieved in the workhouses, it appears that Poor Law institutions offered mothers a level of medical expertise which was better than traditionally assumed, and helped to compensate for their social and economic deprivation. In the case of the infants, however, where environmental, social, and economic factors were vital for survival, workhouses offered much poorer sanitary and dietary conditions than those of infants in their own homes and this was reflected in the high rates of infant mortality in Poor Law institutions.

Accompanying the shifts in attitude towards helping mothers during their confinements, Poor Law institutions also became more liberal in their attitudes towards non-Anglican inmates. This was most clearly seen in their increasing religious dietary provision for Jews. Although statistics are minimal for the Jewish immigrants using the services, the data available suggest that they increasingly began to enter the Poor Law infirmaries as religious provision expanded and attitudes to non-Anglicans softened.

Whatever advances were made in the years 1870–1929, the maternity services provided by the Poor Law authorities continued to be inferior to those offered in voluntary institutions. Even in the hands of local government, these services could not hope to catch up with developments in the voluntary sector. Years of meagre funding had ensured that even under the council these services remained second-rate by comparison with the charitable institutions with their royal connections and royal patronage.[149] Staff in Poor Law infirmaries remained underpaid and their turnover was usually rapid, and medical equipment tended to be less advanced than that found in voluntary hospitals. In East London this contrasted starkly with the services of voluntary hospitals such as The London Hospital and the East End Maternity Home which, as Chapter 4 has shown, offered a wide range of services, including a large district midwifery service, an increasing number of maternity beds, and ante- and postnatal care. Both

[149] Crowther, *Workhouse System*; Flinn, 'Medical Services', 51, 55, 59; Smith, *People's Health*. See F. K. Prochaska, *Philanthropy and the Hospitals of London: The King's Fund, 1897–1990* (Oxford, 1992).

hospitals were cherished among East London residents and were known to have a dedicated staff.

Like other mothers, Jewish mothers, therefore, would have chosen wherever possible to obtain their midwifery care from the voluntary sector which seemed to be more advanced than that offered by the Poor Law and later the local government authorities. The relative absence of Jewish mothers in the Poor Law infirmaries might explain some of the lower rates of infant mortality found among the Jewish population. Indeed, as this chapter has shown, those infants who were born and stayed in Poor Law institutions tended to fare worse than those outside such institutions. Illegitimate infants tended to predominate among those infants cared for by Poor Law institutions. These infants usually had a higher rate of mortality than their legitimate counterparts. Yet, as Chapter 2 has shown, illegitimacy was rare among the Jewish population, which might also have resulted in fewer Jewish women using Poor Law institutions, thus keeping the risk of mortality among Jewish infants low.

6

Domiciliary and Dispensary Maternity Provision

MUCH of the care Jewish mothers in East London received before, during, and after childbirth was provided outside hospitals. Most charitable provision was available to mothers in their own homes and did not bind them to restrictions imposed on those confined within institutions. Nevertheless these services had their own demands which could be problematic for Jewish mothers. This chapter examines the forms of support which were available outside the hospitals in East London, and the interactions which Jewish patients had with these services.

Directories for East London charitable organizations between 1870 and 1939 indicate an enormous number of organizations working for the benefit of the mother and child, beyond what might perhaps be expected for such a poor area, and starting from a very early period. In his study of poverty in East London, Charles Booth revealed a complex network of district nursing organizations, dispensaries, and clinics providing medical care in the 1880s and 1890s.[1] Plentiful provision for the area continued well into the twentieth century. When members of the Carnegie Trust visited Stepney with the intention of establishing a large centre for maternity and child welfare, they declared that such a centre was not needed because the area was already so well catered for by voluntary and municipal bodies.[2]

By the early twentieth century maternity and child welfare was increasingly being financed by the state rather than the voluntary sector. This was reinforced by the Maternity and Child Welfare Act of 1918. Under this legislation local authorities were required to create specific committees for administering maternal and infant welfare. Local councils and voluntary institutions could also apply for grants to help provide paid midwives, health visitors, infant welfare centres, day

---

[1] C. Booth, *Life and Labour of the People in London*, ser. 1, *East London*, (1889), i. 127–9; Charles Booth Collection (BLPES): File A38, p. 4; File A32, p. 17; File 33, p. 43; File B181, pp. 105–7, 109. [2] Stepney MOH, *AR* (1930), 85.

nurseries, and milk and food for necessitous mothers and infants.[3] Implementation of the 1918 Act varied enormously between councils and regions. Some new schemes were developed under the Act, but many of those which did emerge stemmed from voluntary activities of the nineteenth century.[4]

Voluntary organizations, often supported by local government grants, continued to play a vital role in the provision of maternal and infant welfare well into the inter-war period. In East London, voluntary agencies retained a hold over maternal and child welfare services longer than in many other places.[5] By the 1920s, therefore, a complex network of maternal and child welfare schemes was being supplied by the local government and the voluntary sector. A number of these services overlapped in their aims and in their provision. Historians who have examined the social policies behind maternal and infant welfare services have stressed that in the late nineteenth and early twentieth centuries many of the services were directed towards the welfare of the infant and not the mother. By focusing on aggregate national data, these researchers seem to have underestimated the complexity of provision for mothers.[6] What emerges from a local study of East London is that services were more responsive to local needs. It would seem that while many policy-makers failed to appreciate the real needs of mothers, voluntary and municipal agencies in East London did make an effort to cater for mothers' requirements.[7] Although

[3] J. Lewis, *The Politics of Motherhood* (London, 1980), 34.

[4] Summers and Prochaska have demonstrated that many of the maternal and child welfare schemes of the late 19th and early 20th c. were rooted in the work undertaken by women philanthropists from the early 19th c. Their work has shown that recent historians of maternal and child welfare have tended to concentrate too narrowly on the contribution made by the male government and medical establishment which has denied the influence of female philanthropic workers active on the issue much earlier. See A. Summers, 'A Home from Home: Women's Philanthropic Work in the Nineteenth Century', in S. Burman (ed.), *Fit Work for Women* (London, 1979), 33; F. K. Prochaska, 'A Mother's Country: Mothers' Meetings and Family Welfare in Britain, 1850–1950', *Hist.* 74 (1989), 379–99, 393–4.

[5] Chief MOH, *AR* (1937). By contrast with East London, Woolwich, a borough in SE London where the Labour Party controlled the council from early on, had very few voluntary agencies. From 1906 Woolwich had municipal infant welfare centres, its first voluntary centre only appearing in 1914. See Woolwich MOH, *ARs* (1906–15).

[6] Lewis, *Politics of Motherhood*; A. Davin, 'Imperialism and Motherhood', *Hist. Workshop J.* 5 (1978), 9–65; and C. Dyhouse, 'Working-Class Mothers and Infant Mortality in England, 1895–1914', *J. Soc. Hist.* 12 (1979), 248–67.

[7] Many women's groups, such as the Women's Co-operative Guild, actively campaigned for the government to focus its efforts as much on the high levels of morbidity faced by women as on the rising levels of maternal morbidity in the 1920s and 1930s. While the government increasingly took measures to curb maternal mortality it did very little to tackle morbidity which many women felt should have as much priority (Lewis, *Politics of Motherhood*, 42–50).

much of the welfare was geared towards the health of the infant and child, it necessarily involved provision for the mother. The voluntary and municipal services could not eradicate the overwhelming poverty in the area, but the nursing care and social welfare they offered gave some support to mothers who otherwise had nothing.

Research on maternal and child welfare has centred on how the ideology of motherhood and the kind of models to which mothers were expected to conform shaped the services provided and the experience of mothers.[8] Few studies, however, have focused on the specific provision for childbirth. Many of the organizations examined in this chapter, such as midwifery charities, district nursing associations, and medical missions, while affected by the discussions promoted by policy-makers, provided a service which was different from child welfare schemes elsewhere. Maternal and child welfare is here explored for its contribution to provision for childbirth and the care of the infant up to the age of 1 year. During the inter-war period three major anxieties shaped official policy towards maternal and child welfare provision: (1) the continuing decline and social differential in the birth rate; (2) the persisting high maternal mortality; and (3) the need to replace the losses of the First World War.

This chapter examines the variety of services that were available to Jewish mothers in East London outside the hospitals and other institutions between 1870 and 1939. Jewish mothers appear to have made as much use of the amenities as did the general population, but their experience was different because of their immigrant and religious status. Central to the issue is whether the changes that occurred to maternal and child welfare in these years made the facilities more accessible to Jewish mothers. While many of the services available to Jewish mothers in the twentieth century were more secular in their orientation than they had been in the nineteenth century, some religious demarcations none the less remained. This chapter examines the extent to which this influenced the relationship between the organizers of these services and Jewish mothers, and how this altered over time.

[8] Peretz's research on Oxford, Tottenham, and Merthyr Tydfil, e.g., has explored how the attitudes promoted by the maternal and infant welfare movement and the marketing of products specifically geared to mothers and their infants affected the experience of motherhood during the 1920s and 1930s. In practice it was very difficult for mothers on low incomes to adhere to the advice given to them (E. P. Peretz, 'The Costs of Modern Motherhood to Low Income Families in Interwar Britain', in V. Fildes, L. Marks, and H. Marland (eds.), *Women and Children First: International Maternal and Infant Welfare, 1870–1945* (London, 1992)).

TABLE 6.1. *Number and place of deliveries undertaken by the Royal Maternity Charity, 1872–1891*

Year	Total deliveries	Deliveries in Eastern District		Deliveries in Western District	
		No.	%	No.	%
1872	3,666[1]	2,565	70	932	25
1873	3,220	2,331	72	889	28
1874	3,059[2]	2,126	69	737	24
1880	3,595	3,022	84	573	16
1882	2,999	2,522	84	477	16
1883	2,700	2,317	86	383	14
1885	3,331[3]	3,017	91	168	5
1886	4,000	3,580	90	420	11
1889	3,427	2,977	87	450	13
1890	3,325	2,811	85	514	15
1891	3,571	2,777	78	794	22

[1] Includes 169 deliveries in the Southern district.
[2] Includes 196 deliveries in the Southern district.
[3] Includes 146 deliveries not specified for district.

Source: RMC, *Minutes* (1872–91).

Types of Services Provided

An organization directly concerned with the care of the mother during her confinement was the Royal Maternity Charity (RMC). Established in 1757, the RMC supplied qualified midwives to the poor in their own homes within a one-mile radius of St Paul's.[9] Although its headquarters were not in East London, many of its cases were from Bethnal Green, Mile End, and Whitechapel. Indeed, as Table 6.1 shows, over two-thirds of its patients were from its Eastern district in the years 1872 to 1891.[10]

Numerous associations were active in caring for the mother and her infant after birth in East London, but this chapter focuses on four. Not all these agencies had their base in East London, but a great number of their patients were from that area. Firstly there was the Nurses of St John the Divine founded at St John's House in 1848, who first undertook

---

[9] J. Hall Davis, *Parturition and Its Difficulties* (London, 1865).
[10] RMC, Minutes, 1863.

work in East London with the cholera epidemic of 1866.[11] Secondly there were Mrs Ranyard's Bible Nurses, who were established in 1868 and continued to work in East London until 1918. They were among the earliest district nurses to have undergone some form of training in London, and the largest in number.[12] Two other nursing agencies active in this field were the East London District Nursing Society (ELNS) created in 1868,[13] and the Shoreditch and Bethnal Green Nursing Association (SBGNA), organized in 1888. Unlike the other two, the ELNS and the SBGNA had their headquarters in East London.[14] The ELNS was most active in areas with high concentrations of Jewish immigrants (see Map 6.1 showing the districts covered by the ELNS in the 1880s).[15] More primary sources remain for the ELNS and the Bible Nurses than for the other nursing associations.[16]

In addition to the RMC and various nursing associations, East London was inundated with medical missions. At various times during the period 1880 to 1939 at least nine medical missions operated within the East End. Some of the medical missions were:

---

[11] During the 1860s the St John the Divine Nurses were attached to the Wapping Infirmary (E. Ramsay, *East London Nursing Society, 1868–1968: A History of a Hundred Years* (London, 1968), 17–18). The nurses of St John played an important part in hospital work and the reforms taking place in hospital nursing. For more detailed study of the history behind the establishment of the St John the Divine Nurses see A. Summers, *Angels and Citizens* (London, 1988), 20; 'The Mysterious Demise of Sarah Gamp: The Domiciliary Nurse and her Detractors *c*.1830–1860', *Vict. Stud.* 32/3 (1989), 365–86, 379–80; and 'The Costs and Benefits of Caring: Nursing Charities *c*.1830–*c*.1860', in J. Barry and C. Jones (eds.), *Medicine and Charity Before the Welfare State* (London, 1991). See also F. Cartwright, *The Story of the Community of the Nursing Sisters of St John the Divine* (London, 1968).

[12] Between 1868 and 1874, 78 of Mrs Ranyard's nurses were trained at hospitals such as Guy's Hospital, Westminster Hospital, and The London Hospital. By 1898 Mrs Ranyard's nurses numbered between 80 and 90 in total (Ranyard Nurses, *ARs* (1881), 3, and (1898), 7). For further detail on these nurses see F. K. Prochaska, 'Body and Soul: Bible Nurses and the Poor in Victorian London', *Hist. Research*, 60/143 (1987), 336–48, 340; and F. Ducrocq, 'The London Biblewomen and Nurses Mission, 1857–1880: Class Relations/ Women's Relations', in B. J. Harris and J. K. McNamara (eds.), *Women and the Structure of Society* (Durham, NC, 1984). Ranyard Nurses, *ARs* (1898, 1916, 1918, and 1925).

[13] Until the 1880s the ELNS had only 3 private nurses and these had no formal hospital training. This contrasted with the Bible Nurses. See Prochaska, 'Body and Soul', 340.

[14] The SBGNA was formerly known as the Haggerston and Hoxton District Nursing Association.

[15] Ramsay, *ELNS*, 7–8; *ELNS*, *ARs* (1882), 3, and (1883), 3. The ELNS was sponsored by Mrs Stuart Wortley and Mrs Robert Wigram.

[16] Material on the Bible Nurses is kept among the papers relating to Mrs Ranyard's Mission at the GLRO. Papers for the ELNS are kept at THL, where there is also a handful of sources on other nursing associations.

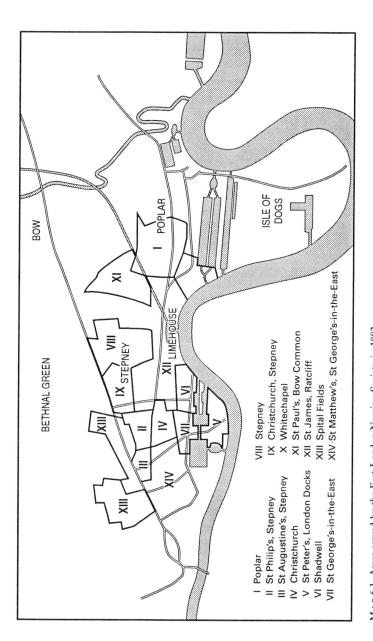

MAP 6.1. Areas served by the East London Nursing Society in 1882
Source: adapted from East London Nursing Society, Minutes (1882), THL, 441.

I   Poplar
II   St Philip's, Stepney
III St Augustine's, Stepney
IV   Christchurch
V   St Peter's, London Docks
VI   Shadwell
VII St George's-in-the-East
VIII Stepney
IX   Christchurch, Stepney
X   Whitechapel
XI   St Paul's, Bow Common
XII St James, Ratcliff
XIII Spital Fields
XIV St Matthew's, St George's-in-the-East

Medical missions in East London[17]

1. Mission Hall, Philpot Street (Medical Mission to the Jews).
2. Central Mission Hall (1891), 4 Goulstone Street (London Society for Promoting Christianity Among the Jews).
3. Gilhead Medical Mission (1878), Fournier Street (British Society for the Propagation of the Gospel among the Jews).
4. Barbican Mission to the Jews, 82 Whitechapel Road.
5. Bethnal Green Mission (1901), 305 Cambridge Road.
6. Bethesda Mission to the Jews, 262 Commercial Road.
7. All Saints' Medical Mission (1897), 31 Buxton Street.

Other missions working in the East End in 1898[18]

Sponsored by Church of England:

1. London Society for Promoting Christianity Amongst the Jews (1809)
2. East London Mission to the Jews (c.1875), 87 Commercial Road (medical)
3. East End Mission to the Jews (c.1880), 119 Leman Street (medical)
4. All Saints' Medical Mission (1897), Buxton Street

Affiliation unknown:

1. Mildmay Mission to the Jews (1876), 79 Mildmay Road, Philpot Street
2. Wild Olive Mission (1891), 4 Vine Street, Minories

Unsectarian:

1. Barbican Mission to the Jews (1879), 33 Finsbury Square, London, EC
2. Hebrew Christian Teaching to Israel (1894), 114 Whitechapel Road
3. London City Mission, 52 Alcombury Street
4. Whitechapel Medical Mission to the Jews (1900)

Most medical missions were no more than ten minutes walk away from the homes of the poor in the East End (see Map 6.2).[19] Few primary documents exist for the majority of these missions. More information remains for the All Saints' Dispensary (known as the All Saints' Out-Patient Hospital from 1907) established in 1897 and for the medical

---

[17] G. Black, 'Health and Medical Care of the Jewish Poor in the East End of London, 1880–1939', Ph.D. thesis (Leicester, 1987), 158.

[18] All Saints' Medical Mission, Minutes, 1898 (AJA).

[19] Black, 'Health and Medical Care', 158.

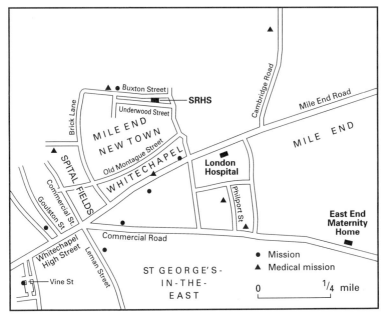

MAP 6.2. Missions and medical missions in the East End, 1898–1901
Source: All Saints' Medical Mission, Minutes (1898); G. Black, 'Health and Medical Care of the Jewish Poor in the East End of London, 1880–1939', Ph.D. thesis (Leicester, 1987), 158.

mission run by the London Society for Promoting Christianity Among the Jews (LSPCJ) from 1891.[20]

Maternity Work

The RMC played a key role in providing skilled midwifery care to the very poor within the East End. Horrified by the low standards of midwifery care available to mothers in lying-in institutions and from the parish, the charity aimed to supply trained midwives to work with the poor in their own homes under the supervision of a group of physicians.

[20] Correspondence and Papers relating to the All Saints' Hospital are held at AJA, University College London Library. In 1851 the Society of All Saints' of the Poor established a scheme to train nurses. Essentially an Anglican nursing order, they had close connections with UCH in London. They might also have had links with All Saints' Hospital in East London, but the connection is not mentioned in primary or secondary sources. For more information on the All Saints' nurses see S. W. F. Holloway, 'The All Saints' Sisterhood at University College Hospital, 1862–1899', *Med. Hist.* 3/1 (1959), 146–56. Sources for the LSPCJ mission are held in the Bodleian Library, Oxford.

TABLE 6.2. *Number and outcome of deliveries undertaken by the RMC, comparing rates of maternal mortality with the rest of England and Wales, 1867–1917*

Year	Royal Maternity Charity			England and Wales
	Deliveries	Maternal deaths	Maternal mortality rate (per 1,000)	Maternal mortality rate (per 1,000)
1867–70	14,052	26	1.85	—
1871–5	16,471	34	2.06	—
1876–80	16,209	51	3.14	—
1871–80	32,688	85	2.6	4.7
1881–5	12,226	37	3.02	—
1886–90	18,246	44	2.41	—
1891–5	19,961	34	1.70	5.49
1896–9	15,651	27	1.72	4.69
1902–4	10,236	14	1.36	4.27
1907	2,376	3	1.26	—
1909	2,351	5	2.13	—
1916–17	1,113	1	0.89	—

Source: RMC, Minutes (1867–1917); Registrar-General, *ARs of Births, Deaths and Marriages for England and Wales* (London, 1921), 78, table 42.

Any case of infection was inspected and midwives were expected to maintain strict standards of cleanliness.[21] By the late nineteenth century, as Table 6.1 shows, RMC midwives were attending on average over 3,000 cases a year, many of whom were in East London. The high quality of care that these midwives offered can be judged from the remarkably low rates of maternal mortality that they achieved in these years. In the years 1871–80 the overall rate of maternal mortality for England and Wales was 4.7, while the rate for the RMC was 2.6. Table 6.2 shows similarly low rates for the following years. Not only was maternal mortality low among the RMC, but the number of deaths from puerperal fever was also small.[22] Such low rates of maternal mortality among the RMC might be accounted for by the skill of the midwives as well as the fact that all the births took place in the patients' homes. Table 6.3 also indicates that, with the exception of the years during the First World War, very few of

[21] After 1883 all pupil midwives trained by the charity had to pass the exam set by the London Obstetrical Society (RMC, *AR* (1883), 101).   [22] See Ch. 5, n. 64.

TABLE 6.3. *Number of deliveries undertaken by the RMC and cases to which a doctor was called*

Year	Deliveries	Doctor attended	
		No.	%
1867–70	14,052	354	2.5
1871–5	16,471	493	2.9
1876–80	16,209	641	3.9
1881–5	12,226	712	5.8
1886–90	18,246	515	2.8
1891–5	19,961	472	2.4
1896–9	15,651	413	2.6
1902–4	10,236	156	1.5
1907	2,376	143	6.0
1909	2,351	191	8.2
1916–17	1,113	148	13.3

Source: RMC, Minutes (1867–1917).

the births were attended by doctors for emergencies, which suggests a high level of expertise among the RMC midwives.

The absence of national aggregate statistics on neonatal mortality before the early twentieth century makes it difficult to compare the rates found for the RMC patients with the rest of England and Wales. Tables 6.4 and 6.5, however, indicate that the RMC achieved good records. In 1907 the rate of neonatal mortality registered for the RMC was 15.9 per 1,000 births, while for England and Wales it was 40.7. The low rate of neonatal mortality was also found for other years (see Table 6.4). As Chapters 2 and 5 have already pointed out, the historical determinants of neonatal mortality are hard to define, but can be linked to birth injury due to bad maternity care. The small number of neonatal deaths found for the RMC would therefore suggest, as in the case of maternal mortality, that the charity offered a good standard of care. Unfortunately no comparison can be made for the rate of stillbirths among the RMC patients as listed in Table 6.4, as the Registrar-General did not record stillbirths as a separate category until 1926.[23]

By contrast with the RMC, midwifery work constituted a very small

[23] In 1927 the rate of stillbirths for England and Wales was 40 per 1,000 total births (live and still). See Registrar-General, *AR* (1940), 6, table C.

TABLE 6.4. *Rates of neonatal mortality and stillbirths among cases by the RMC, 1867–1917*

Year	Deliveries	Neonatal deaths	Neonatal mortality rate (per 1,000)	Stillbirth deaths	Stillbirth mortality rate (per 1,000)
1867–70	14,052	58	4.12	446	31.7
1871–5	16,471	68	4.12	475	28.8
1876–80	16,209	75	4.63	599	36.9
1881–5	12,226	43	3.52	493	40.3
1886–90	18,246	94	5.15	510	27.9
1891–5	19,961	78	3.9	537	26.9
1896–9	15,651	101	6.45	378	24.1
1902–4	10,236	58	5.7	198	19.3
1907	2,376	38	15.9	84	35.35
1909	2,351	37	15.7	85	36.15
1916–17	1,113	13	11.7	—	—

Source: RMC, Minutes (1867–1917).

TABLE 6.5. *Rates of neonatal mortality among cases attended by the RMC and the overall rates for England and Wales*

Year	RMC	England and Wales
1907	15.9	40.7
1909	15.7	40.3
1916	12.8	36.9
1917	10.16	37.1

Source: RMC, Minutes (1867–1917); Registrar-General, *ARs of Births, Deaths and Marriages for England and Wales* (London, 1938–9), 21, table 9.

part of the care offered by the medical missions. Indeed, many of the medical missions were reluctant to provide midwifery care because of the fierce competition they faced from the maternity work of the voluntary hospitals in the area. This is illustrated in the case of the history of the midwifery service attatched to the All Saints' Medical Mission. In 1905, All Saints' Hospital, with the financial help of one lady patron, began to provide a certified midwife for some patients.[24] The number using the

[24] All Saints' Hospital, *AR* (1905), 8.

service grew rapidly, eighty-two women being delivered in the first ten months of providing the service, seventeen of whom were first-time confinements.[25] Despite the increasing number of midwifery cases undertaken by the mission's midwife, her services were terminated in 1907. During her time at the mission she delivered 104 cases and was reported to have 'done much to raise the sanitary conditions and self-respect of the people'. Her job ended as a result of the competition imposed by the decision of London Hospital in 1907 to extend its midwifery services through the introduction of maternity nurses working on the district free of charge.[26]

By contrast with the medical missions, the nursing associations saw their services as complementary to those offered by the hospitals. Rather than attempting to provide midwifery care, their aim was to help in the general nursing of maternity cases. In the late nineteenth century Mrs Ranyard's nurses looked after the greatest number of maternity cases (see Table 6.6). The society forbade its nurses to act as midwives, but all its nurses were expected to have a certificate in monthly nursing from a lying-in hospital together with a hospital and district nurse training.[27] Confinement cases could only be cared for 'under a doctor's direction'. Each nurse was trained in 'scrupulous cleanliness' and the use of antisepsis.[28] In certain districts the nurses were set apart for obstetric and monthly work only, collaborating with maternity departments of specific hospitals such as Charing Cross Hospital and St Thomas's Hospital.[29] The maternity branch of Mrs Ranyard's nurses was reported to be very popular in the late 1890s, but by 1914 they had diminished in number and continued to do so during the years of World War I (see Table 6.6).[30]

---

[25] Although there had been 'several anxious cases owing to insanitary homes, privation and inadequate accommodation' all the cases were reported to have 'done well' (All Saints' Hospital, *AR* (1906), 10–12).

[26] All Saints' Hospital, *AR* (1907), 8–9. One other mission which seems to have provided a maternity service was Mildmay Mission Hospital, but this service was for private patients. One Jewish woman remembered giving birth there in the 1930s, for which she paid £2 5s. She chose to go there because it was easily accessible (Jewish Women's League, interviewed by L. Marks, London, 9 May 1990, tape). More information concerning the maternity nurses provided by London Hospital appears in Ch. 4.

[27] Ranyard Nurses, *AR* (1898), 7.

[28] The Ranyard Mission argued that the work carried out by their nurses protected mothers from 'the carelessness and ignorance of well-meaning neighbours' (Ranyard Nurses, *AR* (1898), 10; *The Nursing Branch of the Bible Women and Nurses*, booklet for nurses (n.d.), 8 (GLRO file: A/RNY/162)).   [29] Ranyard Nurses, *AR* (1906), 25.

[30] How many of the maternity cases cared for by Mrs Ranyard's nurses were in the East End is not known, except that very few were taken in the later years when the organization was no longer working in the heart of the area.

TABLE 6.6. *Percentage of maternity work undertaken by different district nursing associations, 1885–1937*

Year	Ranyard Nurses		ELNS		St Johns Nurses		SBGNA	
	Total maternity cases	% of all cases	Total maternity cases	% of all cases	Total maternity cases	% of all cases	Total maternity cases	% of all cases
1885–90	—	—	682	5	—	—	—	—
1891–5	—	—	658	3	—	—	—	—
1896–1900	—	—	999	4	—	—	—	—
1901–5	5,858	15	689	3	—	—	—	—
1906–10	5,125*	12*	634	3	—	—	—	—
1911	1,035	12	108	3	—	—	—	—
1912	802	9	164	4	—	—	—	—
1913	—	—	177	3	—	—	—	—
1914	807	7	160	3	—	—	—	—
1915	756	6	145	3	—	—	—	—
1916	669	6	128	3	—	—	—	—
1917	493	5	68	3	480	12	—	—
1918	310	3	80	2	461	12	—	—
1919	395	4	157	2	—	—	—	—
1920	542	5	176	5	—	—	42	0.76

Year								
1921	—	—	153	5	675	21	—	—
1922	—	—	131	4	387	27	—	—
1923	126	3	—	—	—	—	—	—
1924	128	1	34	3	521	27	—	—
1925	—	—	—	—	—	—	—	—
1926	—	—	—	—	—	—	—	—
1927	—	—	24	1	—	—	—	—
1928	126	1	10	0.3	—	—	—	—
1929	—	—	8	0.3	—	—	97	1.7
1930	—	—	17	0.5	—	—	94	1.2
1931	—	—	17	0.6	—	—	75	1.2
1932	—	—	—	—	—	—	74	8.4
1933	—	—	—	—	—	—	83	28
1934	—	—	—	—	—	—	86	10
1935	—	—	—	—	—	—	83	8.2
1936	—	—	—	—	—	—	76	9.4
1937	—	—	—	—	—	—	71	10.2

* Figures for years 1907–12.

Source: ARs for Mrs Ranyard Nurses, ELNS, St Johns Nurses, and SBGNA.

After the war more maternity cases were being cared for by the nurses of St John than by the other associations (see Table 6.6). The nurses of St John had a long tradition of maternity work, beginning with their involvement in the maternity ward in King's College Hospital in 1864. Later they established their own maternity home in Chelsea in 1876 where they trained midwives.[31] From their earliest days in Poplar the nurses provided midwifery care on a large scale.[32] Between 1917 and 1918 they covered a total of 8,108 cases, of whom 941 or 12 per cent were midwifery cases. The number of midwife cases had risen to 1,062 out of a total of 6,842 cases, or 16 per cent of the total in the years 1920 and 1921. In addition to this they catered for ante- and postnatal cases, but these only formed about 1.7 per cent of the cases in 1921 and 1922.[33]

Maternity cases formed a very small proportion of the total patients cared for by the ELNS (see Table 6.6). Nevertheless, the Association had close ties with the East End Maternity Home (EEMH) and London Hospital, who referred maternity cases to them. The SBGNA also appears to have taken on maternity work, but the only figures available concern the inter-war period. In 1921 the SBGNA cared for a total of thirty-three mothers, paying on average thirteen visits to each of the mothers. By 1929 the number of mothers helped was fifty-two.[34]

While the majority of maternity work carried out by the nursing agencies was not concerned specifically with midwifery, some of the associations did provide midwives. Unlike independent, untrained midwives who found it much more difficult to continue their practice with the tightening regulation of midwives after 1902, midwives supplied by district nursing associations conformed more to the legislative standards and continued their work in the early twentieth century. Some of the associations increased their midwifery provision in the inter-war years. By 1938 the ELNS was 'entirely responsible for full-time midwifery for

[31] Florence Nightingale was very interested in this home. See 'The Community of Nursing Sisters of St John the Divine', Centenary Pamphlet of St John's Nurses (1948).
[32] 'The Community of Nursing Sisters of St John the Divine', 8; St John the Divine Nurses, *Appeals*, 1933–8; *East End News*, 16 Nov. 1934. Unfortunately the number of midwifery cases looked after by the nurses of St John is unavailable aside from the years 1917–24.
[33] St John the Divine Nurses' Association, *ARs* (1917–24). For fuller figures see L. Marks, 'Irish and Jewish Women's Experience of Childbirth and Infant Care in East London, 1870–1939: The Responses of Host Society and Immigrant Communities to Medical Welfare Needs', 340, table 8.4.
[34] Bethnal Green MOH, *ARs* (1921–9). Fuller figures appear in Marks, 'Irish and Jewish Women's Experience of Childbirth', 340, table 8.5.

the Stepney area', and was working in conjunction with, and receiving funding from, the Council.[35] In the same year the nurses of St John established a school for midwives in conjunction with the Royal College of St Katherine.[36]

Much of the funding of the district nursing associations by the borough councils reflected the increasing municipal provision for maternity care. Councils not only paid for district nursing associations to undertake some of their maternity cases, but also made subscriptions to maternity hospitals to maintain beds for local authority cases.[37] Such provision, however, was not free to the patient. Indeed, as Table 6.7 shows, in the case of Stepney patients were charged for beds in public hospitals (originally Poor Law institutions). The charge varied according to the family income and how many children a woman already had. It is not known how many mothers in East London were helped in this way, nor the extent to which the scale of charges reflected the real incomes of the families living in East London in these years.

In addition to funding district nursing associations, a number of borough councils also developed their own midwifery services. Neither Stepney nor Poplar had a borough midwifery scheme. Poplar expected its necessitous patients instead to claim back fees they had paid for their maternity care.[38] By contrast Bethnal Green began to provide a borough midwifery service from 1924. As in the case of maternity beds in hospitals, the fees charged for the midwifery service were dependent on the family's income and access to maternity benefit (see Table 6.8).[39] Table 6.9 shows the number of cases and visits Bethnal Green's borough midwives undertook. Out of the total births in the borough the midwife only

---

[35] 'Superintendent's Report', in ELNS, Minutes, Apr. 1938, 11. In 1937 the ELNS appointed a maternity nurse to care for maternity cases in its own home (Minutes, May 1937, 146).

[36] 'The Community of Nursing Sisters of St John the Divine'.

[37] Many of the maternity cases paid for by Stepney council to go into the EEMH included those who had surnames common to the Irish and the Jewish population (Stepney MCW Committee, Minutes, 1919–39).

[38] Poplar MOH, 'Maternal Mortality', in Stepney MCW Committee, Minutes, 18 June 1935.

[39] In 1926 the council had to lower the fees because of the free midwifery services being provided by The London Hospital which were great competition for its midwifery service. The free midwifery service offered by The London Hospital had also forced the All Saints' Medical Mission to close its midwifery service (see above). Private midwives and other hospitals such as the EEMH also found it difficult to compete with the free service of The London Hospital and continually complained that it was undercutting the livelihood of private midwives (Bethnal Green, 'Public Health Surveys', 3 June 1925; 7 Jan. 1926 (PRO file: MH 52/156)).

TABLE 6.7. *Scale of charges set by Stepney Council to mothers for maternity treatment in the special maternity wards of Whitechapel, St George's-in-the-East, and Mile End Hospitals, 1929*

Family income after deducting rent, insurance, and other charges		Charges to patient per case		
		Eligible for single maternity benefit and not more than 1 child	Eligible for double or single maternity benefit	Ineligible
			Add £1 in each case	Deduct £1 in each case
Below £2	5s per week			
Above £2	5s and not above £2 7s	£3		
£2 6s	8s	£3 1s		
£2 8s	9s	£3 2s		
£2 9s	10s	£3 3s		
£2 10s	11s	£3 4s		
£2 11s	12s	£3 6s		
£2 12s	13s	£3 8s		
£2 13s	14s	£3 10s		
£2 14s	15s	£3 12s		
£2 15s	16s	£3 14s		
£2 16s	17s	£3 16s		
£2 17s	18s	£3 18s		
£2 18s	19s	£4		
£2 19s	£3	£4 2s		
		£4 4s		

Source: Stepney MCW Committee, Minutes, 1 Oct. 1929, 218 (THL, 1086).

TABLE 6.8. *Midwifery fees charged for the Bethnal Green Borough Midwifery Service according to number in family and income, 1924*

No in family	\	Fees charged for midwifery services													
Family income →	4s to 4s 11d	5s to 5s 11d	6s to 6s 11d	7s to 7s 11d	8s to 8s 11d	9s to 9s 11d	10s to 12s 5d	12s 6d to 14s 1d	15s to 17s 5d	17s 6d to 19s 11d	20s to 22s 5d	22s 6d to 24s 11d	25s to 29s 11d	30s to 34s 11d	35s and over
1	—	—	—	—	—	—	(2s 6d)	(3s)	(4s)	(5s)	(6s)	(7s 6d)	(10s)	(12s 6d)	(15s)
2	1s 6d (3s)	2s (3s 6d)	2s 6d (4s)	3s (4s 6d)	3s 6d (5s)	4s (6s)	6s (8s 6d)	7s 6d (10s)	10s (12s 6d)	12s 6d (15s)	15s (18s)	17s 6d	20s (25s)	22s 6d (30s)	25s
3	1s 6d	2s 6d	3s	3s 6d	4s	4s 6d	7s 6d	10s	12s 6d	15s	18s	21s	25s	25s	—
4	2s	3s	3s 6d	4s	4s 6d	5s	10s	12s 6d	15s	18s	21s	25s	25s	—	—
5	2s 6d	3s 6d	4s	4s 6d	5s	5s 6d	12s 6d	15s	18s	21s	25s	25s	—	—	—
6	3s	4s	4s 6d	5s	5s 6d	6s	15s	18s	21s	25s	25s	—	—	—	—
7	3s 6d	4s 6d	5s	5s 6d	6s	6s 6d	18s	21s	25s	25s	—	—	—	—	—
8	4s	5s	5s 6d	6s	6s 6d	7s	21s	25s	25s	—	—	—	—	—	—
9	4s 6d	5s 6d	6s	6s 6d	7s	7s 6d	25s	25s	—	—	—	—	—	—	—
10	5s	6s	6s 6d	7s	7s 6d	8s	25s	—	—	—	—	—	—	—	—

Notes: Income scale is subject to addition in respect of maternity benefit if any. The numbers in brackets are for the first confinements.

* Family income was usually calculated per head with deductions made for travel expenses and money accepted for lodgers.

Source: Bethnal Green, 'Public Health Survey', 1924 (PRO file MH 52/156).

TABLE 6.9. *Cases and visits undertaken by the borough midwifery service in Bethnal Green, 1925–1937*

Year	Total births in Bethnal Green	Borough Midwife Cases		Visits by borough midwife	Bookings by borough midwife
		No. undertaken by borough midwife	% of total births		
1925	2,630	24	0.91	—	—
1926	2,501	138	5.5	1,020	—
1927	2,353	114	4.8	1,122	—
1929	2,064	120	5.8	1,490	—
1930	1,955	149	7.6	1,720	—
1935	1,438	97	6.7	975	133
1937	1,258	75	6.0	—	—

Source: Bethnal Green MOH, *ARs*; Registrar-General, *ARs of Births, Deaths and Marriages for England and Wales* (1925–1937).

catered for a small handful of patients, never exceeding more than 7.6 per cent of the total births in the borough.

The prime motive behind the midwifery service offered by Bethnal Green council was to provide a service for necessitous mothers who could not afford to provide their own care.[40] Indeed many midwives could not afford to practise in Bethnal Green because of the shortage of patients who could pay enough for them to make a decent living. By 1917 the average midwife charge in London was either '12s. 6d. for first births and 10s. for all subsequent ones, or 15s. for first births, in which case 12s. 6d. was the normal fee thereafter'. By the 1930s midwife fees were usually 35s. for a first birth and 40s. for subsequent ones. Doctors' charges were much higher than this. In 1917 the average doctor's fee was between 1½ and 2 guineas. By 1936 this had risen to £3 for the first birth and £2 for multiparous patients.[41] Bethnal Green council estimated that less than a third of the mothers in the area could afford to hire private doctors or

[40] Often the only form of midwifery help a necessitous mother could acquire was provided by the Board of Guardians, but very few mothers appear to have asked for such care in Bethnal Green, for in 1923 out of a total 645 births only 21 mothers sought maternity care under the auspice of the Poor Law (Bethnal Green, 'Public Health Survey', 4 Apr. 1924 (PRO file: MH 52/156)). See also Ch. 5 for more detail on the maternity care provided by Poor Law institutions.

[41] Lewis, *Politics of Motherhood*, 141. For fees charged by midwives in earlier years see Ch. 3.

midwives in 1924. Most mothers had to rely on charitable midwifery care. At least a third of the mothers from Bethnal Green were attended by medical and midwifery students provided by teaching institutions such as The London Hospital. This does not seem to have had an adverse effect on maternal mortality in the area, but members of the council objected to the women being used as 'teaching material'. Regarding this situation as unsatisfactory, the Council provided midwives at its own expense without backing or financial help from the Ministry of Health.[42]

Nursing Care for Mothers during Illness

Aside from providing help for mothers in the days immediately following a birth, district nursing associations and medical missions offered nursing care to those with ailments during pregnancy or in the months after the delivery. Some of the mothers on the district they cared for also suffered complications from abortions and miscarriages. They nursed the mothers alongside surgical and fever patients, as well as dispensing medicines.[43] As with midwifery, nursing services offered by district nursing associations continued after the Maternal and Child Welfare Act of 1918. No specific municipal nursing association was established in East London in the inter-war period, and councils depended on the existence of voluntary provision.[44]

The nursing care provided by the district nursing associations and medical missions offered a vital service to many mothers. Women who had many children and were poor often had symptoms which some medical professionals, and the women themselves, attributed to childbirth.[45] The extent to which women were plagued by illness is shown by the number of women seen by the ELNS. Over half the cases nursed by the ELNS during the 1880s were women, some of whom were helped

[42] Bethnal Green, 'Public Health Survey', 4 Apr. 1924 (PRO file: MH 52/156). Similar complaints were not voiced in Poplar or Stepney.

[43] While nursing associations had some clinics, a greater amount of their time was spent in caring for patients in their own homes. Most medical missions provided their services through a clinic, but home visits to patients were also made. All Saints' Hospital boasted an extensive follow-up service for their patients, which they claimed to be superior to many medical institutions in London (All Saints' Hospital, *AR* (1908), 7–8). See also Black, 'Health and Medical Care', 164–5.

[44] See e.g. Poplar, 'Public Health Survey' (1930), app. 12 (PRO file: MH 66/372).

[45] See e.g. letters from mothers published in 1915 by the Women's Co-operative Guild, which revealed that large numbers of women suffered complications from childbirth (M. Llewellyn Davies, *Maternity: Letters from Working Women* (London, 1915; repr. 1984).

TABLE 6.10. *Number of women cared for by the ELNS, 1884–1926*

Year	Total cases	Women	
		Total	% of total cases
1884–5	5,213	3,043	58
1886–90	14,795	6,793	46
1891–5	17,525	8,763	50
1896–1900	25,594	11,540	45
1901–5	23,650	10,957	46
1906–10	20,666	9,391	45
1911–15	22,178	8,260	37
1916–20	17,656	5,312	30
1921–6	24,171	7,217	30

Source: ELNS, *ARs* (1884–1926).

after a miscarriage or needed care for a breast abscess.[46] Women continued to dominate the figures in the years up to 1925 (see Table 6.10). Nationally, married women who were lucky enough to have insurance were shown to have much higher rates of sickness than men in the years 1911, 1921, and 1931.[47] In 1939 a national survey of 1,250 working-class wives found that only 31 per cent were in good health, 22.3 per cent were categorized as 'indifferent', 15.2 per cent were listed as 'bad', and 31.2 per cent as 'very grave'. The women were reported to have a large range of debilitating illnesses. Their conditions included prolapsed wombs, anaemia, gynaecological disorders, swollen ankles, toothache, and varicose veins.[48]

A great number of women also had medical complaints arising from abortion. Between 1928 and 1930 the Registrar-General reported a rise of 21 per cent in the number of abortions.[49] In 1936 the British Medical Association estimated that between 16 and 20 per cent of all pregnancies ended in abortion, making the annual number of abortions between 110,000 and 150,000; 50 per cent of these were believed to be illegal abortions. Many of the abortifacients women could purchase through advertisements

---

[46] ELNS, *AR* (1884).   [47] Lewis, *Politics of Motherhood*, 43–4.

[48] M. Spring Rice, *Working-Class Wives* (London, 1939; repr. 1981), 28–9. Unaccounted for are 0.3%.

[49] J. Emanuel, 'The Politics of Maternity in Manchester, 1919–1939: A Study From Within a Continuing Campaign', M.Sc. thesis (Manchester, 1982), 63.

were ineffective, but many contained poisonous ingredients such as lead. Some resorted to hot baths or falling down stairs, or, in the last resort, to an abortionist. The consequences could often be disastrous, but it is not known how many abortions resulted in illness or death. Women frequently concealed from doctors the complications they suffered following abortion, presenting their ailments instead as general illness.[50]

Preventive Work and Social Welfare

By the early twentieth century all the organizations were undertaking preventive work. Much of this was rooted in the schemes devised by health visitors in the late nineteenth century, which in turn owed much to the health visiting schemes of lady missionaries, such as Mrs Ranyard's Bible Nurses.[51] Preventive work undertaken by the voluntary and municipal agencies largely constituted advice and not treatment, which severely limited the influence they had on the mother's health.[52] Classes on infant care, home nursing, cooking, and sewing were offered at institutions such as the Stepney School for Mothers.[53]

All organizations, including the RMC, provided some form of social welfare for their patients, either through mothers' meetings or through their nurses. Nurses could obtain certain necessities such as food, clothing, and baby-linen for their patients from a samaritan fund.[54] Medical missions dispensed milk, coal, bread, cash, and toys, as well as hospital letters, to their patients.[55] The relief given by these agencies made little

[50] 'The Abortion Report', *Br. Med. J.* 17 June 1939, 1248–51, 1248; A. McClaren, *Birth Control in Nineteenth-Century England* (London, 1978), 232–40; Lewis, *Politics of Motherhood*, 17; E. Roberts, *A Woman's Place: An Oral History of Working-Class Women 1890–1940* (Oxford, 1984), 97–100; I. Loudon 'Deaths in Childbed from the Eighteenth Century to 1935', *Med. Hist.* 30/1 (1986), 1–41, 27.

[51] Summers, 'A Home from Home', 39, 43, 45, 51–7 and Prochaska, 'Body and Soul', 342–4. For more information on the development of health visiting and its work see C. Davies, 'The Health Visitor as Mother's Friend: A Woman's Place in Public Health, 1900–1914', *Soc. Hist. Med.* 1/1 (1988), 39–59.

[52] *MH Memorandum 13/MCW*, in Stepney MCW Committee, Minutes, 24 Feb. 1920. Infant welfare centres concentrated on providing advice so that they would not be perceived as competitors against general practitioners working in the field. Lewis assumes that they had no ambitions to be competitors when this might not have been the case (Lewis, *Politics of Motherhood*, 102–3, 109). [53] Stepney MOH, *AR* (1912), 55.

[54] *The Nursing Branch of the Bible Women and Nurses*, booklet for future nurses (n.d.), 15; 'Report of the Sub-Committee on Nursing', ELNS, Minutes, Dec. 1894 (THL file: 442); RMC, *AR* (1883).

[55] Black, 'Health and Medical Care', 169. See also All Saints' Medical Mission, Minutes; Barbican Mission to the Jews, *ARs* (1882, 1938) (GLRO file: A/FWA/C/D128/1); East End Mission, Correspondence and Papers, 1917–36 (GLRO file: A/FWA/C/D163/1).

impact on the poverty of the area as a whole, but for some it must have been a means of supplementing a tiny income.[56]

Religious Orientation of the Services Provided

All these organizations aimed to provide charitable medical services for the poor in their own homes, but their motives for doing so varied. While the RMC saw itself as a purely unsectarian charity,[57] most of the nursing associations were influenced by the religious zeal directed towards the prevention of the general decline in religious devotion which seemed to be pervading the nation in the nineteenth century.[58] Nothing is known about the religious attitude of the SBGNA, but the others had some religious principles behind their creation.

Nurses supplied by Mrs Ranyard had an explicitly evangelical outlook.[59] Originally drawn from women formerly employed as 'Bible Women',[60] Mrs Ranyard's nurses were expected to be devout Christians who would

[56] Just before World War I the Fabian Women's Group called on the state to improve living standards and welfare provision to lighten the burden of motherhood. Their study of mothers in Lambeth between 1909 and 1913 showed even respectable hard-working mothers could not survive on the meagre incomes brought home by their husbands. One of the conclusions of the study was that 'any weighing centre, school for mothers, or baby clinic which does exist is fighting the results of bad housing, insufficient food, and miserable clothing—evils which no medical treatment can cure. Such evils would be put an end to by the State grant' (M. Pember Reeves, *Round About a Pound a Week* (London, 1913; repr. 1984), 229).

[57] In 1871 it cautioned one of its midwives for promoting 'spiritualist views', and requested she be 'careful not to allow her principles and views to interfere with the proper discharge of her duties to patients' (RMC, Minutes, 31 Jan. 1871, 404). The case came before the committee because several complaints had been made and a subscriber had withdrawn his funds on the allegation that the midwife, Mrs Ayers, had let her 'spiritualist views' prejudice her in her work (RMC, Minutes, 10 Jan. 1871, 401). The text is unclear in what was meant by 'spiritualist views', but it probably implied that Mrs Ayers was trying to convert patients to spiritualism.

[58] M. E. Baly, *A History of the Queen's Nursing Institute 1887–1987* (London, 1987). For a good discussion on the ways in which religious zeal influenced philanthropy in general, see Summers, 'A Home from Home', 35–7, and 'The Costs and Benefits of Caring'.

[59] The model on which Mrs Ranyard based her nurses was the nursing sisterhoods of the Roman Catholic and High Church. See *Missing Link* (magazine published by the mission) (1868), 34 (GLRO file: A/RNY/104).

[60] Bible Women were Protestant women whose duty was to visit the poor in their own homes, sell them Bibles in instalments, and educate them in the principles of Christianity and in domestic affairs. Prochaska has argued that the Bible Women were the first kind of district visitor. He has also stressed that many of the aims of Mrs Ranyard's mission later influenced other organizations such as the Charity Organization Society and social-work pioneers like Octavia Hill (Prochaska, 'Body and Soul', 337).

promote a spiritual message with their practical duties.[61] Nurses, it was argued, had more opportunities than the minister of religion to encourage the sinner to reform. As the organization's instructions revealed,

Remember those moments are given to the Nurse far more frequently than to the Minister. However indefatigably he visits he can never, perhaps, find the doors of the soul flung so wide open as she does, during those tremendous moments when she is ministering to the body, in bending over the man struck down, or the mother amid her children.[62]

A similar message was promoted by the medical missions whose prime purpose was to gain converts.[63] Missionary work among the sick was seen as particularly productive as outlined by the Bishop of Stepney, who stated that 'sick persons were more susceptible to spiritual influences and the knowledge put into their mind at such a time might afterwards lead to good results'.[64] Medical work was seen as only the beginning of a proselytizing process, as the East Mission stated in 1912, 'The sole aim of our medical work is to lead these people from Judaism to the light of the Gospel, and to heal the disease of the soul through curing the sickness of the body . . . Hundreds owe their conversion to the Providence which, working through their sickness, brought them to the Medical Mission.'[65] Similarly in 1913 the Barbican Mission reported, 'The Medical Mission continues to fulfil its very useful purpose . . . The essential missionary side of the enterprise is always kept uppermost.'[66]

The spiritual ministrations of the Bible Nurses were focused towards patients of all religious persuasions, including Catholics and Jews.[67] Medical

---

[61] *Missing Link* (1868), 218, and (1870), 161–2; Ranyard Nurses, *AR* (1898), 11; Prochaska, 'Body and Soul', 340. While many of the early nurses were drawn from the Bible Women, in later years nurses were recruited from the mothers' meetings run by the mission. Ideally the nurses were drawn from single women aged 25–35, or from women whose children had died, or were at school. In 1904 the Society 'jealously preserved' its 'Christian constitution', arguing that it would do so as long as there was 'no religious disability' attached to municipal or hospital training or appointments (Ranyard Nurses, *AR* (1906), 24).

[62] Ranyard Nurses Jubilee Publication (1889), 33 (GLRO file: A/RNY/91).

[63] United Synagogue, Mission Committee, *Report of the Executive Committee* (c.1912), 51 (CRO file: 907). See also All Saints' Hospital, *ARs.*

[64] Speech made by the Bishop on opening a medical mission to the Jews in Old Saints' Parish, Buxton Street, in 1896 (*ELO*, 24 Oct. 1896).

[65] *Report of the East End Mission* (1912), 10, 15, cited in United Synagogue Committee Mission Committee, *Report of the Executive Committee*, 14–15. See also All Saints' Hospital, *AR* (1907), 4.

[66] *Immanuel's Witness* (Magazine of the Barbican Mission), Mar. 1913, 7, cited in United Synagogue, Mission Committee, *Report of the Executive Committee*, 15.

[67] Special instruction was given on how to approach Catholic constituents and how the Bible should be read to them (*Missing Link* (1868)).

missions, however, the majority of them established during the peak of the Jewish immigration, were primarily directed at Jews. The names of the missions also confirmed that they concentrated their attention on the Jewish population. While the Bible Nurses read prayers in the homes of the sick, patients who visited medical mission dispensaries were expected to attend religious services and to listen to biblical sermons before a doctor cared for them. The Medical Mission in Philpot Street sometimes locked its doors once the patients were inside to prevent escape from prayers.[68] One Jewish doctor in East London remembered the 'tragic-comic scenes' presented by the 'poor [Jewish] women with their squalling children in their arms, sitting on bare benches, dumbly suffering but studiously deaf to the 30 minutes harangue from the Missionary which was an essential prerequisite of treatment.'[69] Missions such as the All Saints' Medical Mission (known as the All Saints' Outpatient Hospital from 1907), which was milder in its proselytization, nevertheless promoted Christian literature in Hebrew, Yiddish, and English among their patients.[70]

Medical missionaries tended to see Jewish women as more accessible than the men, who were at work all day, and saw medical relief as the easiest means of contact.[71] Sister Steen, of the Barbican Medical Mission to the Jews, argued that young mothers were particularly good clients in so far as they often heeded the mission's religious teachings when they came for help and advice. Their infants were also thought to be good targets for conversion.[72] In 1905 the All Saints' Medical Mission provided a midwifery service for the first time, and this was specifically aimed at immigrant women. The mission pictured such a service as 'a great boon, not only to the English mothers, but more especially to the poor Polish and Russian Jewish mothers, who, in a strange land, have often to undergo great privations, and submit to much pain and suffering

[68] United Synagogue, Mission Committee, *Report of the Executive Committee*, 14, 27.

[69] R. Salaman, 'The Helmsman Takes Charge' (Memoirs), unpublished MS (n.d.), 36. A similar impression was conveyed by Revd J. F. Stern of the East London Synagogue to the United Synagogue conference in 1926 (CRO file: 957).

[70] Report of Parochial Mission to the Jews (PMJ), 1897–Apr. 1898, in All Saints' Medical Mission, Minutes, 35. The All Saints' Mission changed its name from being a dispensary to an out-patients' hospital because of the large number of surgical and medical patients it was now receiving (All Saints' Hospital, *AR* (1907), 4).

[71] C. Bermant, *Point of Arrival* (London, 1975), 217; All Saints' Hospital, *AR* (1905), 6; LSPCJ, *AR* (1896), 15.

[72] *Immanuel's Witness*, June 1938, in Barbican Mission to the Jews, *49th AR* (1937–8), 38 (GLRO archive: A/FWA/C/D128/1). Similarly, workers from the Ranyard Mission reported that while Catholics did not like to attend meetings 'for fear of the priest', they were 'very willing to hear the Bible read in their houses' ('Report from Goswell Road Mission', *Missing Link* (1870), 300 (GLRO file: A/RNY/106)).

from unqualified ministrations, which are especially aggravated by their terrible ignorance of sanitary arrangements.'[73] It argued that its maternity branch brought the mission into 'much more cordial relations with Jewish mothers, especially those from Russia and Poland' who had previously associated Christianity with persecution.

The degree to which the nurses of the Ranyard Mission and other medical missions were successful in transforming the souls of their patients is difficult to judge. One worker for the dispensary of the Barbican Mission to the Jews who sang and played Hebrew melodies with a Christian message, argued that, 'The Hebrew melody generally touches Jewish emotions, and the words of the Christian message bring the consoling comfort of Christ to the Jewish heart. The patients listen gladly, and some have been attracted to come to the other meetings and classes.'[74] Similarly in 1901 the All Saints' Medical Mission reported that its dispensary had brought a 'very great blessing to the poor people' and had 'undoubtedly' done 'a great deal towards breaking down the feeling of suspicion existing between the English and the Jews'.[75] Nevertheless it is doubtful whether many Jewish patients were converted through the work of the medical missions. Even Sister Steen reported that while patients were willing to see a doctor, they were 'very reticent' about 'being visited' or discussing religion.[76] Missionaries were aware that their patients might be converting for insincere reasons, as one Mission stressed in 1898:

Every care should be taken to obviate the possibility of Jews attaching themselves to the Christian Church for merely mercenary reasons, and that while being ready to assist Jews, as well as other parishioners, with such advantages as are provided by well managed Clubs, Institutes, Reading rooms, Sick Dispensaries, etc., the Church should absolutely discountenance the association of relief from the first to last without attendance on religious services.[77]

Despite these reservations the LSPCJ argued that the work of its medical mission was 'very effective and telling'. In the years 1809–1900 the total number of Jews baptized in London by the missionaries of the LSPCJ was 2,022, making an average of twenty-two baptisms a year. How many remained converts is unknown.[78]

By contrast with the medical missions, the nursing associations, with

[73] All Saints' Hospital, *AR* (1905), 8.　　[74] *Immanuel's Witness*, June, 1938, 41.
[75] 'PMJ at Home and Abroad', *AR* (1901), in All Saints' Medical Mission, Minutes. All Saints' Medical Mission was under the auspices of the PMJ.
[76] *Immanuel's Witness*, June 1938, 38.
[77] East London Jewish Fund Pamphlet (1898), in All Saint's Mission, Minutes, 9.
[78] W. T. Gidney, *The History of the London Society for Promoting Christianity Among the Jews, 1809–1908* (London, 1908), 533.

the notable exception of Mrs Ranyard's nurses, were not openly evangelical. The Nursing Sisters of St John the Divine were the first Anglican nursing sisterhood in England,[79] but those who joined its orders were not expected to take religious vows.[80] Similarly, while the ELNS aimed for its nurses to have a 'good influence' in 'gently' persuading its patients 'to come to Church', its spiritual message was not overt.[81] In 1909 the ELNS was accused of attempting to 'proselytize' nonconformist patients, but Father Murphy commented that he never heard anything but praise from his Catholic constituents about its work.[82] Appreciation was also expressed by the Jewish community and Jewish patients over the years.[83]

Interaction between Jewish Patients and the Providers

Little is known about the interaction between Jewish patients and organizations like the Nurses of St John or the SBGNA, but evidence suggests that the other organizations, particularly the RMC and ELNS, had frequent dealings with Jewish patients. The latter agencies especially had strong links with the Jewish community. Members of the established Anglo-Jewish community sat on the board of governors and took prominent roles in the running of each organization. The Jewish Board of Guardians also subscribed to both associations on a regular basis.[84] Each agency appears to have filled a vital gap in services for the Jewish poor as well as the community around them.

While no statistics remain of the number of Jewish patients cared for by the RMC and ELNS, it is clear that they formed a large proportion of their clientele. Both agencies were sensitive to the needs of Jewish patients who were unable to speak English. In 1896 the Charity employed four Jewish midwives who could speak Yiddish to cater specially for their Jewish patients. Similarly the ELNS hired a Yiddish-speaking Jewish nurse in 1906, sponsored and directed by the JBG.[85] Given the good provision made by the RMC and the ELNS for Jewish patients and their

---

[79] Robert Bentley Todd, professor of the medical department at King's College Hospital, was motivated to establish the nursing sisterhood because of a belief that more religious discipline would transform abysmal nursing standards (Cartwright, *The Story of the Community of the Nursing Sisters of St John the Divine*).

[80] Partly as a precaution against nurses being accused of bringing high church views into hospital wards.   [81] ELNS, *AR* (1885), 13.

[82] See Ramsay, *ELNS*, 12; *ELO*, 14 Jan. 1911, 2; and 11 Feb. 1911.

[83] See e.g. ELNS, *AR* (1890), 6 and (1901), 10; *JC*, 18 May 1906, 9.

[84] The RMC was receiving a subscription from the JBG from 1880 and the ELNS from 1906 (RMC, Minutes, 29 Jan. 1880; *JC*, 18 May 1906, 9; ELNS *AR* (1906)).

[85] *JC*, 7 Feb. 1896, 15; 18 May 1906, 9.

non-proselytizing approach it is not surprising that many Jewish patients sought their services.

What is more puzzling is that many Jewish patients used the facilities provided by the medical missions whose evangelical message was hard to ignore. The attraction of the medical missions was that they provided medical care free or at a minimal economic cost.[86] The Goulston Street Mission charged patients 1*d.*, plus an additional 1*d.* if they received a bottle of medicine. Many Jews also had a high regard for the skills of the missions' medical staff.[87] All Saints' Medical Mission received a large proportion of Jews into its clinics.[88] In its first year at least three-quarters of its patients were Jewish. The mission claimed that it had treated at least 16 per cent of the total Jewish parishioners in their area.[89] Returns from the Mission for the period October 1897 to April 1899, showed that of the total 4,594 attendances, 2,861, or 62 per cent, were Jewish. Table 6.11 shows that the proportion of Jewish patients continued to be high. In 1921 the dispensary was forced to close its doors due to lack of funds, but during its 25 years of existence 51,254 attendances had been made, an average of almost 2,847 a year, of whom three-quarters had been Jewish.[90] It is not known how many of the women delivered by the dispensary's midwife were Jewish, but the mission reported that many Russian and Polish mothers were asking for midwifery care under its auspices. According to the mission, Jewish mothers had commented that the mission's midwife was 'much more sympathetic than the Jewish midwives'.[91]

The high level of Jewish attendance at such missions caused grave anxiety for many Jews over the years.[92] Repeated calls were made for the

[86] See interview with Dr Ian Gordon, who visited the Gilhead Medical Mission, Fournier Street, as a child (in Black, 'Health and Medical Care', 168). This was also stressed by the United Synagogue's Mission Committee, *Executive Committee Report* (*c.*1912), 15.

[87] United Synagogue, Mission Committee, ibid. 15, 26; B. Aronovitch, *Give It Time* (London, 1974), 116; Black, 'Health and Medical Care' (1987), 168.

[88] Black has argued that the All Saints' Mission had a gentler approach than most medical missions in East London ('Health and Medical Care', 166).

[89] 'Report of PMJ', 1897–Apr. 1898, All Saints' Medical Mission, Minutes, 35.

[90] 'All Saints' Hospital, *AR* (1921), 5. My search through the *ARs* of the hospital has revealed a greater number of attendances over the years than Black has calculated. His total came to 44,438 ('Health and Medical Care', 167).

[91] 'All Saints' Hospital, *AR* (1906), 6.

[92] Continual letters appeared in *JC* and over the years a number of investigations were made by the established community into the impact medical missions were having on Jewish immigrants. The first investigation arose in 1879 with the termination of medical relief by the JBG and was later followed up in 1896 when calls were made for it to reconsider its decision. In 1905 another enquiry was made by the United Synagogue's East End Committee, which concluded that nothing could be done 'to counteract the steps taken by the Missionaries'. As late as 1926 the United Synagogue mounted an additional

TABLE 6.11. *Total number of Jews treated by the All Saints' Dispensary, Buxton Street, 1897–1921*

Year	Attendances			Cases		
	Total	Jewish patients	Jews as % of total	Total	Jewish patients	Jews as % of total
1896–7	3,882	2,372	61	1,180	—	—
1896–1900	10,000	7,000	70	—	—	—
1899	6,000	4,000	67	—	—	—
1903	—	—		2,400	—	—
1904	2,776	—	—	1,038	841	81
1905	3,311	—	—	1,376	922	67
1906	2,597	—	—	1,348	1,072	79
1907	3,560	—	—	1,544	—	—
1908	3,290	1,013	31	—	—	—
1909	—	—	—	1,786	1,462	82
1910	3,651	—	—	1,768	—	—
1911	3,159	—	—	1,725	1,406	82
1912	3,000	—	—	1,328	—	—
1913	2,610	1,740	67	—	984*	—
1914	2,304	—	—	1,196	—	—
1915	2,538	1,851	73	—	—	—
1916	2,467	1,812	74	—	—	—
1917	1,858	1,424	77	845	—	—
1918	1,487	1,086	73	698	—	—
1920	1,187	994	84	—	—	—
1921	1,459	1,079	74	—	—	—
1896–1921	51,254	17,999	—	18,235	6,687	—

* New cases.

Source: All Saints' Hospital, *ARs* (1896–1921).

JBG to provide more medical services such as a free dispensary to reduce the attraction of those run by missionaries. Some urged the founding of the London Jewish Hospital as an answer to the problem. Others regarded the work of the missionaries as self-defeating.[93] Despite the fears of many Jews, particularly those of the more established Anglo-Jewish

conference on the issue, which again surmised that no steps could be taken against the missionaries and the Jewish patients' use of their clinics. The matter was brought up yet again in 1933 in a letter to the *JC* (Black, 'Health and Medical Care', 172–6).

[93] *JC*, 6 Nov. 1896, 16; 20 Nov. 1896; Black, 'Health and Medical Care', 172–3.

élite, the large proportion of Jewish patients attending the medical missions suggests that they did not mind the proselytizing activities. In addition to obtaining skilled medical attention cheaply, patients received more individual attention at a medical mission than in a big hospital such as The London Hospital, where an average of thirty seconds was spent on each patient after hours of waiting.[94] Medical missions also did not expect their patients to undergo searching questions from a parochial medical officer or a Lady Almoner. In general the atmosphere of medical missions was more congenial. 'The dispensaries were small institutions; the doctors were less busy, and not inclined to hurry. They gave time for general conversation and personal sympathy. They made enquiries after relatives, and the patients were encouraged to come again. None of the general hospitals or public dispensaries could be carried on in this way.'[95] Medical missions were also within walking distance of the patients' homes, were open at convenient times, and made an effort to provide staff who spoke Yiddish.[96]

Changing Structure of Provision

By the turn of the century, maternal and child welfare facilities had begun to increase with the growing state concern for infant mortality. State provision of such services, however, remained minimal before World War I. While local councils were in charge of the notification of births and were beginning to employ health visitors, the voluntary sector, as with midwifery and nursing, continued to dominate the field.[97] In 1902 and 1908 a committee of Stepney Council called for the employment of health visitors by the Council, but were instead forced to turn to the financial assistance of a private benefactor and the Local Government

---

[94] Black, 'Health and Medical Care', 164–5.

[95] Some contemporaries suggested that Jews had a more nervous disposition than most patients and were therefore more likely to make a series of visits to doctors and hospitals, making the mission one more institution to visit in their rounds (Black, 'Health and Medical Care', 169). [96] Black, 'Health and Medical Care', 169.

[97] The majority of infant welfare centres in Britain before the First World War were run by voluntary groups. Two societies most involved in the work were the National Conference on Infant Mortality, founded in 1906 (in 1912 became the National Association for the Promotion of the Welfare of Children under School Age) and the Association of Infant Consultations and Schools for Mothers, established in 1911 (became the Association of Infant Welfare and Maternity Centres in 1930). See Lewis, *Politics of Motherhood*, 33–4. See also P. Thane, 'Genre et protection sociale: La Protection maternelle et infantile en Grande-Bretagne, 1860–1918', *Genèses*, 6 (1991), 73–97.

Board for funding.[98] Just before World War I a larger proportion of the infants visited in the boroughs of Stepney and Poplar were visited by health visitors appointed by the voluntary agencies. In 1914 the Stepney Medical Officer of Health argued that voluntary societies undertook the greater part of the work in the borough and were especially active in the provision and maintenance of the schools for mothers.[99] The visits paid by the voluntary health visitor accounted for 70 per cent of the total visits paid to infants in the borough of Poplar in 1914.[100]

During the war years government and local authority sponsorship of services increased greatly. Maternal and infant welfare work expanded after 1915 when 50 per cent grants were made available to local authorities for the support of infant welfare centres.[101] After 1915 all births were also to be notified to councils, so that arrangements could be made for a health visitor to visit the infant and encourage the mother to attend clinics. In Stepney in the years 1914 to 1915 the ratio of babies visited by the municipal health visitors rose from 32 to 41 per cent of all the babies visited.[102] None the less, although the outbreak of war signalled a growing tendency towards municipal provision, voluntary agencies continued to dominate the scene. By 1916 thirty-five local authorities were running infant welfare centres in England, but 160 centres were still organized by branches of voluntary societies.[103] Voluntary bodies remained dominant in the provision of such services in East London. While the percentage of infants visited by voluntary health visitors dropped from 68 to 59 per cent between 1914 and 1915, they were still visiting the majority of infants.[104]

The Maternal and Child Welfare Act of 1918 reaffirmed the national

---

[98] Only in 1910 did Stepney Council begin to employ its own health visitor. By contrast health visitors were appointed by Bethnal Green Council in 1906 and by Poplar in 1908. Like voluntary health visitors, those appointed by the boroughs were expected to visit the homes of the poor and to advise mothers on breast-feeding, matters of home hygiene, how they should manage their health during pregnancy, care for and clothe their infants, and notify births. See Stepney MOH, *ARs* (1902), 85; (1910), 38; (1913), 65–7.

[99] Stepney MOH, *AR* (1914), 54–5. Voluntary organizations providing infant welfare centres and health visitors included the St George's-in-the-East Infant Welfare Association (established 1909), the Stepney Mothers' and Babies' Welcome (established 1910) and the SRHS (established 1895, see Ch. 5). In Poplar similar work was being undertaken by the Poplar Infant Welfare Care Association and the Royal College of St Katherine (Poplar MOH, *AR* (1914), 27).

[100] Poplar Public Health Committee, Minutes, 1912–14.

[101] Lewis, *Politics of Motherhood*, 96.

[102] Stepney MOH, *ARs* (1914), 55 and (1915), 25.

[103] Lewis, *Politics of Motherhood*, 34.

[104] Stepney MOH, *ARs* (1914), 55, and (1915), 25.

commitment to maternal and child welfare, but its provision was not comprehensive and was implemented unevenly. In many places, like Poplar and Stepney, voluntary associations remained the backbone of the maternal and infant welfare services into the inter-war years.[105] Indeed their presence might have acted as a brake to municipal provision in the area. After 1920 the Ministry of Health was willing to pay at least half the expenditure of these voluntary organizations.[106] Tables 6.12 to 6.15 indicate that voluntary services continued to supply the majority of the maternal and child welfare facilities in Stepney and Poplar in the interwar years. In 1933 voluntary associations in Stepney were supplying more health visitors, and running more infant welfare centres, antenatal clinics, and day nurseries than the Council (Table 6.12). Similarly, as Table 6.13 shows, most of the ante- and postnatal visits in Poplar were carried out by voluntary health visitors in the years until 1935.

Boroughs not only varied in the degree to which voluntary and municipal bodies dominated the provision of maternal and infant welfare, but also in the charges they set for such services. A Population Investigation Committee in the late 1930s, and a study undertaken by a social researcher from Southampton University in 1939, revealed a wide variation between authorities in deciding who was eligible for free treatment under the maternal and child welfare schemes. This not only included the provision of milk and dinners, but also midwifery and convalescent

---

[105] In 1921 Poplar Labour Council was sent to gaol for spending too much of its rates on relief of the local poor. Known as Poplarism, this provoked an ardent debate about the legitimacy of over-spending rates on poor relief in the 1920s and 1930s. Poplar's policy on public relief did not extend into maternity and child welfare. Voluntary organizations continued to run the bulk of the services in the area, and some voluntary schemes for infant welfare in Poplar, such as those run by Sylvia Pankhurst and Muriel and Doris Lester, were more radical than others. Pankhurst and the Lester sisters saw their infant welfare measures as part of broader 'radical and emancipatory political project which did not keep women in the home'. For more information concerning the politics of Poplar and the activities of Pankhurst and the Lester sisters, see G. Rose, 'Locality, Politics and Culture: Poplar in the 1920s', Ph.D. thesis (London, 1988), 28–32; and 'The Struggle for Political Democracy: Emancipation, Gender and Geography', *Society and Space: Environment and Planning*, 8/4 (1990), 395–408.

[106] Letter from MH to Stepney MCW Committee, 12 Nov. 1920, in Stepney MCW Committee, Minutes, 12 Oct. 1926, 228. See also Lewis, *Politics of Motherhood*, 96. While many Councils were happy to see the continuation of voluntary agencies in the provision of maternal and infant welfare, some opposed using voluntary workers instead of trained professionals. In 1925 the Stepney MCW Committee argued that while voluntary visitors were very useful they were no substitute for trained health visitors who had experience in child welfare nursing, sanitation, and, in many cases, midwifery. Instead the voluntary workers could be used to make informal visits to mothers in their home and arrange for convalescent or dental treatment or some form of social welfare (Stepney MCW Committee, Minutes, 8 Dec. 1925).

TABLE 6.12. *Number of facilities run by voluntary and municipal bodies in Stepney in 1933*

	Council	Voluntary Association
Health visitors employed by	11	15
Infant welfare centres provided by	7	9
Antenatal clinics run by	1	3
Day nurseries run by	—	5

Source: Stepney MOH, *AR* (1933).

treatment for mothers and infants.[107] Just as Peretz has shown in the cases of Oxfordshire, Tottenham, and Merthyr Tydfil, the scales set in East London widely differed between each authority as well as between services. Tables 6.7 and 6.8 as well as Tables 6.14 and 6.15 show the different charges Stepney and Bethnal Green set for milk supplies, midwifery fees, and the treatment of maternity cases in hospitals and in convalescent homes. No figures remain on how this affected cases in reality, but in 1929 and 1930 approximately half the mothers supplied by maternity outfits in Bethnal Green were not charged, and only a quarter were expected to pay the full price.[108]

Such variations were reflected not only in the different charges but also in the variety of expenditure set by each council for maternal and infant welfare work. Table 6.16 shows how the expenditures of Stepney and Poplar compared with other councils in 1922–3. This table indicates that of the total estimate for expenditure on maternal and child welfare work, the sums spent by Stepney were much larger than in many other places. This might be accounted for by the large population the council had to serve. Such an explanation, however, does not hold for Poplar, where the population was much smaller but the estimated budget comparatively high. In Poplar the high estimates might have been connected with the radical politics of the council, as demonstrated by its public relief policies during these years. Other boroughs which had comparably high estimates for this type of work were areas with large populations and with reputations for progressive maternal and child welfare provision from voluntary and council bodies, such as Shoreditch, St Pancras, and Woolwich. In all

---

[107] Peretz, 'Costs of Modern Motherhood', 266–8.

[108] Bethnal Green, 'Public Health Survey' 1931, (PRO file: MH 66/311). For full details on the number helped, see Marks, 'Irish and Jewish Women's Experience of Childbirth', 344, table 8.17.

TABLE 6.13. *Number and percentage of ante- and postnatal visits paid by municipal and voluntary health visitors in Poplar*

Year	Public Health Department				Royal College of St Katherine (voluntary)				Combined total
	Antenatal	Postnatal	Total visits	% of all visits in borough	Antenatal	Postnatal	Total visits	% of all visits in borough	
1914	594	1,714	2,308	34	1,234	3,318	4,552	66	6,860
1925	1,509	1,497	3,006	42	2,193	1,888	4,081	58	7,087
1935	2,643	1,072	3,715	51	2,531	1,040	3,571	49	7,286

Source: Poplar, *ARs* (1914–35).

TABLE 6.14. *Stepney Council charges to mothers for convalescent treatment, 1924*

No. in family	Scale of income per head after deducting rent	
	Fee 5s. per week	Fee 10s. per week
1	13s.	15s.
2	10s. 6d.	12s. 6d.
3	8s. 6d.	10s.
4	7s. 6d.	8s. 6d.
5	7s.	8s.
6	6s. 6d.	7s. 6d.

Source: Stepney MCW Committee, Minutes (3 June 1924).

cases the total expenditure approved by the Ministry of Health was below that set by the councils.

The Influence of the Changing Structure on the Experience of Jewish Mothers

The hold retained by voluntary societies over maternal and child welfare services in East London affected the access Jewish mothers and their infants had to these services and their experience of them. By the early twentieth century, while many of the medical missions continued to combine evangelical work with their care, much of the religious orientation of the other nursing associations had diminished. Government sponsorship of voluntary organizations after World War I reinforced the emphasis on secular services.

Although voluntary agencies retained much of their independence after 1918, their reliance on government funding made them subject to greater scrutiny than before. Many were forced to accede to demands made of them by the maternal and child welfare committees. In addition to this many of the prominent members of the committees set up in East London under the Maternal and Child Welfare Act were Jewish, such as Alice Model, who had an interest in safeguarding the denominational interests of their respective communities. This was reinforced by the strong Jewish representation on borough councils, particularly in Stepney where Labour Jewish councillors initiated some of the more progressive

TABLE 6.15. *Different scales set by Stepney and Bethnal Green Councils and the Ministry of Health for the provision of milk, 1922 and 1929*

No. in family	1922				1929	
	MH suggested scale		Stepney Council's Scale		Bethnal Green Council's scale approved by MH	
	Free	Half cost	Free	Half Cost	Free	Half cost
1	13*s*.	15*s*.	16*s*.	18*s*.	14*s*.	16*s*.
2	10*s*. 6*d*.	12*s*. 6*d*.	13*s*.	14*s*. 6*d*.	12*s*.	14*s*.
3	8*s*. 6*d*.	10*s*.	10*s*. 6*d*.	11*s*. 6*d*.	10*s*.	12*s*.
4	7*s*. 6*d*.	8*s*. 6*d*.	9*s*. 6*d*.	10*s*. 6*d*.	9*s*.	10*s*.
5	7*s*.	8*s*.	8*s*.	9*s*. 6*d*.	8*s*.	9*s*.
6	6*s*. 6*d*.	7*s*. 6*d*.	8*s*.	9*s*.	7*s*.	8*s*.
7	—	—	7*s*. 6*d*.	8*s*. 6*d*.	—	—
8	—	—	7*s*.	8*s*.	—	—
9	—	—	6*s*. 6*d*.	7*s*. 6*d*.	—	—
10	—	—	6*s*.	7*s*.	—	—
11	—	—	5*s*. 6*d*.	6*s*. 6*d*.	—	—
12	—	—	5*s*.	6*s*.	—	—
13	—	—	4*s*. 6*d*.	5*s*. 6*d*.	—	—

Notes: All charges were calculated once rent had been deducted and were assessed per head. The difference in the scales set by the MH and Stepney Council remained more or less the same. A similar table appeared in 1927. Note that both Bethnal Green and Stepney set a higher income under which the mothers were eligible.

Source: Stepney, MCW Committee, Minutes (10 Oct. 1922), 130–1; Bethnal Green, 'Public Health Survey', 1930–1 (PRO file: MH 66/311).

measures taken by the council in the 1920s.[109] Oscar Tobin, for instance, the first Labour chairman of Stepney Council's Public Health and Maternity Committee, was Jewish. Under him infant welfare work was greatly enlarged in the borough and an extensive milk distribution scheme for

[109] With the exception of the council elections in 1922, the Labour Party held the majority of seats in Stepney from 1919, many seats being held by Jews. The Mile End branch of the Labour Party, e.g., was practically all Jewish. For more information on the politics of the Jewish population in East London in the inter-war years and their representation on the council, see E. R. Smith, 'Jews and Politics in the East End of London, 1918–1939', in D. Cesarani (ed.), *The Making of Modern Anglo-Jewry* (Oxford, 1990), 150–3; and 'East End Jews in Politics, 1918–1939: A Study in Class and Ethnicity', Ph.D. thesis (Leicester, 1990), 81–2.

TABLE 6.16. *Amount spent on maternal and child welfare work undertaken by councils in London in relation to population size and number of infants under 5 years old, 1922–3*

Borough	Population	Children < 5 yrs., 1921	IMR	Total est. for MCW work (£)	Est. for provision of milk and dinners (£)	Received MH approval	
						Total expenditure on MCW (£)	Total expenditure on milk and dinners (£)
East London:							
Poplar	154,100	14,610	83	16,303	11,400	7,638	2,735
Shoreditch	105,200	9,203	114	19,078	13,085	6,458	2,500
Stepney	249,738	24,835	89	21,090	12,000	12,600	4,180
Elsewhere in London:							
Chelsea	64,290	3,335	78	2,782	750	2,520	750
Deptford	113,500	—	88	4,058	1,000	—	—
Hackney	224,200	15,566	64	6,626	2,700[1]	6,626	2,700
Hampstead	86,890	4,889	88	3,270	300	3,070	300
Fulham	160,000	10,756	—	7,100	1,000	7,100	1,000
Kensington	175,686	11,572	110	4,030	1,000	3,970	1,000
St Pancras	212,900	14,235	76	15,795	3,000	14,850	1,343
Southwark	184,388	15,101	90	7,736	3,000	3,844[2]	1,343
Woolwich	135,307	13,021	62	13,318	5,700	8,182	1,700

[1] No dinners.
[2] Amount received.

Source: Summary of replies received by Shoreditch Borough Council for the Financial Year 1922–3 to assess the provision of milk supplies. In Stepney Maternity and Child Welfare Committee, Minutes (12 June 1922) 75.

babies and nursing mothers was established, costing nearly £15,000 a year. Such measures were not always greeted with enthusiasm by other Jewish councillors of different political persuasions, who may have resented the financial burden this put on ratepayers.[110]

None the less, despite the trend towards secularization, as well as the increasing Jewish representation on maternal and child welfare committees, certain difficulties remained. Many of the services provided in East London were still divided along denominational lines. A number of the maternal and infant welfare clinics provided by the local council were held in halls leased from religious institutions. In Stepney, although Labour councillors were keen to see that all the borough's residents were treated equally, in reality the facilities were clearly demarcated between the Jewish community and other, non-Jewish, agencies, and distinctions were made as to who would serve Jewish patients.[111] This could cause problems for Jewish mothers. In 1925 the Dame Colet Maternity and Child Welfare Centre, a voluntary organization, was reprimanded by the Stepney Maternity and Child Welfare Committee for its treatment of Jewish cases. The centre provided for poor Jews but refused to do so for wealthier ones. The centre contended that in its experience 'a number of Jewish mothers' who attended its clinics 'lived in the less poor streets' and were therefore in a better position to purchase foods at retail prices than others who could only afford to buy the food as supplied by the centre at cost price. No distinction was made for the social status of non-Jewish patients.[112] Jewish mothers were also refused treatment by Stepney School for Mothers in 1926 and a municipal maternity and child welfare centre in 1936.[113]

While such policies of these organizations might have stemmed from anti-Semitism, particularly in the case of the Dame Colet Centre, this was not the entire picture.[114] Rather, it reflected the way in which

---

[110] *JC*, 25 Nov. 1921, 18, *ELA*, 26 Nov. 1921, 3; See also Smith, 'East End Jews', 84, 88.

[111] Stepney Borough Council Minutes, 20, 29 Mar. 1920; 26 Apr. 1920. See also Smith, 'East End Jews', 85. The absence of Maternity and Child Welfare Committee Minutes for Poplar and Bethnal Green have made it difficult to establish how widespread these incidents were.

[112] Stepney MCW Committee, Minutes, 10 Feb. 1925, 483; 19 May 1925, 24.

[113] Stepney MCW Committee, Minutes, 12 Jan. 1926, 109; 18 Oct. 1938, 225–6.

[114] Some perceptible discrimination against Jews in the 1920s more clearly arose in the educational and housing policies pursued by the LCC. In 1920 the LCC ruled that only children of British-born subjects were entitled to their educational scholarships, which excluded many Jewish children whose parents could not be naturalized. Similar restrictions were imposed on LCC accommodation, and Jews often could not get the full Unemployment Benefit. See Smith, 'East End Jews', 241–3. See also Ch. 3, nn. 54–5.

maternal and infant welfare services were structured generally. Jewish patients were considered a separate category by the council and voluntary organizations because of the abundance of Jewish services in the area. Even before World War I a very high number of health visitors were employed by Jewish voluntary societies to visit Jewish infants, accounting for over a quarter of the total infants visited in the area. This continued into the inter-war years.[115] By 1919 voluntary maternity and infant welfare clinics were being held in sixteen different centres in Stepney, alongside five antenatal clinics and eight crèches. See Map 6.3 for the location of the various maternal and infant welfare services in 1919. The abundance of such provision stemmed partly from the increased maternal and child welfare activity during the war. In the years that followed the war, however, the number of maternal and infant welfare clinics declined. By 1929 there were only nine maternity and infant welfare centres and four crèches. In all these services Jewish agencies played an important role. Four of the nine maternal and infant welfare centres in 1929, for instance, were Jewish.[116] While all the maternal and infant welfare centres in the borough were voluntary, they were intricately connected with the council's services and received grants from the MH and later the LGB.[117] Jewish mothers who attended Stepney's municipal antenatal clinic in Limehouse were usually referred 'to their own particular hospitals'.[118]

Such a separation of Jewish patients from others also reflected the problems Jews continued to face as an ethnic and religious minority. Just as it was important for Jewish mothers to have sympathetic health professionals caring for them during childbirth, so it was in the months after the event. A large proportion of the work carried out by maternal and infant welfare centres was concerned with feeding and diet. For Jewish mothers it was important that the food provided by the centres and the advice about what to do within their homes accorded with the Jewish dietary laws. Given that instruction was a vital component of the work undertaken by such centres it was also important to have people who could communicate with those Jewish mothers who did not understand

---

[115] It is not known how many of these health visitors were Jewish. Originating out of the tradition of lady visitors (often ladies of the leisured class), health visiting was not accorded the same disdain as midwifery or nursing was in the Jewish community. For more information on Jewish lady visitors see M. Steiner, 'Philanthropic Activity and Organization in the Manchester Jewish Community, 1867–1914', MA thesis (Manchester, 1974), 105–10.

[116] Stepney MOH, *AR*, (1919, 1929); Stepney MCW Committee, Minutes, 12 Jan. 1926, 109. [117] Stepney MCW Committee, Minutes, 24 Feb. 1920.

[118] Stepney 'Public Health Survey', app. D (b), 1932, p. xi (PRO file: MH 66/391).

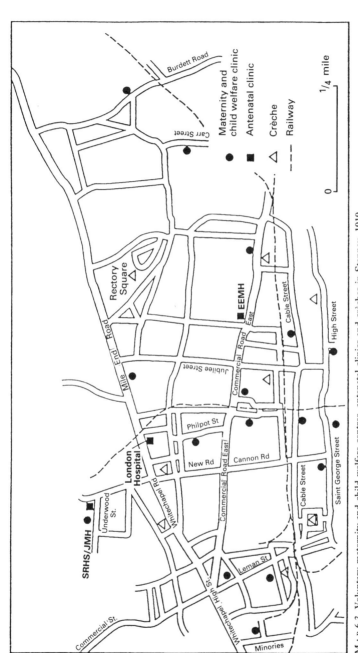

MAP 6.3. Voluntary maternity and child welfare centres, antenatal clinics and crèches in Stepney, 1919

Source: Stepney MOH, *AR* (1919).

English. As Alice Model argued in 1926, it was 'highly desirable that Jewish mothers should attend only Jewish centres owing to the difference in customs, language and dietary laws to those obtaining [*sic*] to the Christian centres'.[119]

Jews were not the only ethnic-religious minority to have their own facilities in Stepney. Many of the infant welfare centres and crèches in East London in the inter-war years were being run by Catholic organizations, catering for Catholics, primarily the descendants of the Irish immigrants who had arrived in the mid-nineteenth century. Like the Jews, the Irish-Catholics in Stepney also had a prominent position in the council chamber. Indeed, 'The Jews and the Irish both assumed, in proportion to their numbers, a far greater role in local politics than the native English population. Throughout the interwar period, approximately one-third of the sixty Stepney councillors were Jewish; one third were Irish and the remaining third native English.'[120] This ethnic-religious composition of the council chamber proved particularly important in the struggle for birth-control provision in the area, which showed that while the religious orientation of many medical services had diminished greatly since the nineteenth century, religion remained a potent force in shaping the provision of certain types of services.

Birth-control was a contentious issue for many, whatever their denomination or class, during the 1920s and 1930s.[121] While the Lambeth Conference of Anglican Bishops and many medical practitioners, among others, condemned the use of birth-control, the Catholic Church was one of the strongest opponents on the issue.[122] During the 1920s opposition to

[119] Stepney MCW Committee, Minutes, 12 Jan. 1926, 109.

[120] Smith, 'East End Jews', 99.

[121] Many advocates of birth-control during the early 20th c. were eugenicists who belonged to the Malthusian League. Linked to arguments of physical degeneracy, which saw the middle-class being swamped by the high birth rate amongst the 'unhealthy' working-class, much of the efforts of the Malthusian League were aimed at the working-class who they claimed could eliminate poverty by limiting their families. While some (male) socialists opposed birth-control because of the emphasis given to it by the Malthusian League, working-class women's groups and the Workers' Birth Control Group, established in 1924, were vital proponents in the struggle for access to birth-control. Some women, however, including members of the Labour Party, opposed birth-control on the grounds that it would subject women to their husbands even more (Lewis, *Women in England, 1870–1950* (Brighton, (1984; 1986), 32; and *Politics of Motherhood*, 196–200; McClaren, *Birth Control*, 61, 215–18. For a fuller discussion on the conflict over birth-control within the Labour Party see C. Collins, 'Women and Labour Politics in Britain, 1893–1932', Ph.D. thesis (London, 1991), 281–90.

[122] Dr Halliday Sutherland, a doctor, was the chief Catholic opponent to Marie Stopes. Encouraged by the Catholic Truth Society he published a book on the Catholic view of birth-control, to which Marie Stopes took exception, leading her to sue for libel in 1923.

birth-control was repeatedly voiced in national and local Catholic news-papers.[123] Fearing that public institutions were about to be given public money to offer birth-control advice, the Catholic community, with the support of Catholic residents in East London, sent a circular to the Ministry of Health in 1925 calling on them not to do so.[124]

Not all those living in the borough, however, were Catholic, nor were they all opposed to the provision of birth-control. Indeed the struggle over birth-control in Stepney reflected some of the very real ethnic-religious tension within the borough. Whenever birth-control came up as a subject in the Council Chamber, voting was divided along 'ethno-religious lines with Jewish councillors in firm opposition to Irish-Catholic councillors'.[125] In 1927 a voluntary birth-control clinic was established in Stepney, promoting a heated discussion within the Council Chamber. Some councillors, such as Miriam Moses, who was also a prominent Jewish communal leader, called for municipal provision of contraceptive information for poor mothers, arguing that they should have it available in the same way as rich people. None the less, while Miriam Moses saw this as an issue which should not be determined by a question of religion, those who opposed municipal provision regarded birth-control as a sub-ject which should not even be discussed by the council.[126] The strength of such opposition within the council and in the borough can be meas-ured by the resolution that was passed in 1929, which forbade any council workers to provide information on birth-control, arguing that the practice was not only 'probably illegal' and against the public policy of the Min-istry of Health, but also 'highly offensive to the religious beliefs and conscientious opinions of many inhabitants of the borough'.[127] Yet while the resolution in 1929 showed the council to have a certain consideration

Letters of support for Dr Sutherland from the Catholic establishment can be found in the Westminster Diocese Archive, file Bo 5/59. See also R. Hall (ed.), *Dear Dr Stopes: Sex in the 1920s* (London, 1978; 1981), 59; and *Marie Stopes: A Biography* (London, 1978), 193, 197–241; B. Brookes, *Abortion in England, 1900–1967* (Oxford, 1988), 63.

[123] *Magazine of the Sacred Heart* (parish magazine of St Mary and St Michael Church, Commercial Road), Sept. 1925, pp. v–vi; *The Tablet*, 9 Apr. 1921, 475; 5 Aug. 1922, 187; 28 Oct. 1922, 579; 29 Nov. 1924, 701; 13 Dec. 1924, 812–13.

[124] *Magazine of the Sacred Heart*, Sept. 1925, pp. v–vi. This contrasted with the repeated calls that were being made by women at the Labour Party Annual Conferences in 1925, 1926, and 1927 for the provision of birth-control information through local authority clinics (Lewis, *Women in England*, 20).

[125] For more information on the battles between Jewish and Irish councillors as well as in the East End generally, see Smith, 'East End Jews', 91, 229–33.

[126] Stepney MCW Committee, Minutes, 15 Mar. 1927, 308.

[127] Ibid. 19 Feb. 1929, 63.

of the residents it was serving, this changed in 1931 when the council accepted the Ministry of Health's new ruling that contraceptive information should be made available through maternal and child welfare centres to those women for whom childbearing would be dangerous.[128] In contrast to the Irish-Catholic councillors, all the Jewish councillors of whatever political party supported this resolution.[129] Ethnic-religious identity therefore remained an important factor in shaping the politics behind the provision of maternal and infant welfare facilities into the 1930s.

Services Provided under the New Structure

Many of the services offered under the Maternal and Child Welfare Act of 1918 originated from provision made in the late nineteenth century. This was most clearly the case in the supply of nutritional needs, which was vital to mothers in East London, who were often undernourished. Studies showed that mothers often stinted themselves for the benefit of their husband and children, and frequently had the worst diet in the family. While most men had some meat in their diet, women subsisted on bread and tea. Just before the First World War, family budgets in Lambeth showed that women had a third of the amount men could spend on food on a daily basis. On average, women had $2^1/_2d.$ while men had $6d.$[130]

From early on in their history, district nursing associations and medical missions supplied nourishment to their necessitous patients. By the early twentieth century some free milk was distributed by voluntary milk depots, most of which was directed towards the infant. Charitable organizations such as the Stepney Babies' Welcome and the Stepney Invalid Kitchen established in 1910 also supplied dinners to necessitous women after the child was born on the recommendation of the health visitor.[131] During World War I and afterwards local authorities began to supply such meals to necessitous pregnant and nursing mothers. Cups of tea and biscuits were also provided at maternal and infant welfare clinics.[132] Jewish

---

[128] Ibid. 14 Apr. 1931, 38.

[129] *ELA*, 9 July 1932, 6; Stepney Borough Council, Minutes, 31, 29 Apr. 1931. Not all in the Jewish community condoned birth-control, and like many Anglican churchmen, the Chief Rabbi opposed birth-control in the 1920s. Increasing state support of birth-control, however, seems to have overridden such objections by the 1930s.

[130] B. S. Rowntree, *Poverty: A Study of Town Life* (London, 1901), 54–5; D. Oddy, 'Working-Class Diets in Late Nineteenth-Century Britain', *Econ. Hist. Rev.* 23 (1970), 314–23, 321; Pember Reeves, *Round About A Pound A Week*, 140.

[131] Stepney MOH, *AR* (1910), 39, 43.

[132] Lewis, *Politics of Motherhood*, 72–3. One health visitor from Poplar in 1915 commented that the cup of tea was often a major incentive conducing women to come to the clinics (Poplar Public Health Committee, Minutes, 9 Feb. 1915, 80).

mothers, as poor as the other mothers in the area, made as much use of this service as the rest of the population. Surnames common to the Jewish population repeatedly appeared in the applicant lists in the minutes of the Stepney Maternity and Child Welfare Committee. Charges were made for this service and assessed according to a family's income.

Table 6.16 reveals that in 1922–3 the provision of milk and dinners constituted at least half the estimated budget for maternal and infant welfare in Poplar and Stepney. In 1921 the Ministry of Health was forced to cut its expenditure to mothers and infants in the interests of national economy. Accordingly local authorities were ordered to limit the amount of free milk they were providing.[133] Milk and food bills between 1919 and 1920 had amounted to 17.3 per cent of the total maternal and child welfare budgets allotted to local authorities, but by 1929–30 this had declined to 13.4 per cent.[134] Like many others, Bethnal Green, Poplar, and Stepney councils, together with many Labour women's organizations consistently opposed the limits required for the provision of free services.[135]

In addition to nutritional aid, by the 1920s dental care was included in many of the facilities offered by maternal and infant welfare centres. Such provision had already been made by medical missions from the early twentieth century. Charitable dental services, whether provided by a medical mission or a maternal and infant welfare centre, were a blessing for many given that a large proportion of mothers suffered poor teeth as a result of their insubstantial diets and because dental care was expensive.

As previous chapters have already shown, antenatal care also became an increasingly important component in maternal and infant welfare services in the inter-war period. Arrangements for antenatal provision varied greatly between boroughs.[136] Between 1919 and 1922 Stepney had one of the lowest rates of maternal mortality in London, which some attributed to the good antenatal provision in the area.[137] Apart from the antenatal

---

[133] Stepney MCW Committee, Minutes, 10 Oct. 1922, 130–1. Concern over the quality of milk and the spread of tuberculosis was also used by government officials to withhold distribution. See L. Bryder, *Below the Magic Mountain: A Social History of Tuberculosis in Twentieth-Century Britain* (Oxford, 1988), 17–18, 133–8.

[134] Lewis, *Politics of Motherhood*, 173.

[135] Stepney MCW Committee, Minutes, 10 Oct. 1922, 131–2; and 2 Oct. 1928, 46; *The Labour Woman*, Nov. 1921, 171.

[136] One of the earliest councils to provide municipal antenatal care was Hampstead in 1917. Three years earlier antenatal services were set up in Kensington, but these were initiated by voluntary agencies. See Hampstead MOH, *AR* (1917), 33–4; 'Report of the Work of Infant Welfare in the Borough of Kensington', 24 July 1914 (PRO file MH48/164). See also Acting MOH Report for Kensington, 5 July 1916, and Kensington MOH Report submitted to the Medical Sub-Committee, 30 Jan. 1917 (PRO file MH 48/164).

[137] Stepney MCW Committee, Minutes, 15 July 1924, 418–20.

clinics provided by the hospitals as outlined in Chapter 4, local authorities were also active in dispensing antenatal care. In 1920 Bethnal Green founded its first antenatal clinic. Councils also provided funds for voluntary organizations to supplement its antenatal work. Three antenatal clinics began to be run in Poplar by the voluntary organizations in 1919. By 1928 Stepney had four voluntary antenatal clinics and one municipal one.[138] In 1935 a questionnaire filled in by health visitors for the Stepney Medical Officer of Health revealed that of the 3,118 mothers confined for that year, 2,737 or 93 per cent had received antenatal care. This was high given that 88 per cent of all the women giving birth in Stepney for that year were said to have responded to the questionnaire. Indeed, when compared to other boroughs in London this was extremely high. The closest to Stepney was Kensington, where 85 per cent of all mothers attended antenatal clinics in 1934. By contrast just over 50 per cent of the mothers in Hampstead and Woolwich received such attention.[139] While no statistics remain for Poplar or Bethnal Green, Table 6.13 shows that between 1914 and 1935 the number of antenatal visits undertaken by health visitors appointed by Poplar Council and voluntary agencies increased.

Apart from medical attention before birth, mothers also needed other kinds of support during and after their confinements. Many mothers experienced much mental anguish in trying to keep a family together when ill or about to give birth.[140] District nursing associations did much for the mother in her own home, but the fear that their work might be associated with domestic labour limited the amount of chores they undertook within the home.[141] Local councils were also slow to provide home helps, and such provision was dependent on the policy of individual councils.

Poplar Council did not provide any home helps. Stepney Council, however, attempted to employ home helps as early as the 1920s, but the

---

[138] Poplar Public Health Committee, Minutes, 8 Apr. 1919, 221; Stepney MCW Committee, Minutes, 2 Oct. 1928.

[139] Hampstead MOH, *AR* (1932), 41; Kensington MOH, *AR* (1934), 10; (1937), 10; Woolwich MOH, *AR* (1931–7); Kensington Council, Minutes, 28 July 1931, 343; Stepney MCW Committee, Minutes, 16 Jan. 1935 (THL file 1088).

[140] Dr Eden from Charing Cross Hospital, Ranyard Nurses, *AR* (1906), 28 (GLRO file: A/RNY/18). In 1883 the RMC appealed to their governors not to inconvenience their patients by requiring them to make too many personal applications as this often meant husbands lost time from work, or caused women to neglect their families in order to make the journey (RMC, *AR* (1883), 48).

[141] Baly, *History of Queen's Nursing Institute*, 157. This is also discussed at length in Ch. 3, in connection with the home helps provided by SRHS.

plans were dropped when difficulties arose over the engagement of suitable candidates and the lack of backing from the Ministry of Health.[142] Prior to 1935 when the first municipal home help was appointed by Stepney Council to care for special cases, neighbours or district nursing associations such as the ELNS and Sisters of St John were considered better candidates for undertaking such work than the Council. Some mothers in Stepney could apply for a grant to cover the expenses of a home help.[143]

Bethnal Green Council had a more positive policy than Stepney, or Poplar which provided no home helps at all. In 1928 the Bethnal Green Council established a panel of four home helps and by 1935 was supplying eighteen home helps for 163 mothers. Such work undoubtedly helped some, as one letter to the Bethnal Green Council indicated.

I consider it my duty to express my keen appreciation of the timely and needed help given by your Centre in the after effects of my wife's confinement . . . may I add that the services rendered by Mrs —— have exceeded all expectations. Nothing has been a trouble to her. She has been a genuine mother to the children . . . and remarkably clean.[144]

The percentage of births covered by the municipal home help in Bethnal Green increased steadily from 1928, rising to just over 15 per cent of the total births in 1937. While initially mothers seemed to have carried most of the cost of this service, by the 1930s the council was financially covering for a substantial number of the cases (see Table 6.17).

In addition to help within the home, arrangements were also made from early on for mothers to be sent to convalescent homes. For instance, Tower Hamlets Mission enabled mothers to go on day excursions to the countryside or for two weeks' holiday to the seaside. Every summer the mission took 250 women on such day excursions and 300 to the seaside for a fortnight.[145] Similarly Mrs Ranyard's nurses helped their patients to go to a convalescent home. Table 6.18 shows that women made up the greatest number of patients helped by the organization in this way. In later years comparable provision was made by the local authorities. As

---

[142] Stepney MOH, *AR* (1920), 16; Stepney 'Public Health Survey', 1932, 5 (PRO file: MH 66/392); Poplar MOH, 'Report', 26 Nov. 1919 (PRO file: MH52/202); Stepney MCW Committee, Minutes, 30 Aug. 1920, 203.

[143] Stepney MCW Committee, Minutes, 11 May 1920, 148; 15 Oct. 1935; 11 Feb. 1936.

[144] Bethnal Green MOH, *AR* (1935), 45.

[145] The date of these activities is unspecified; Tower Hamlets Mission, 'Documents/Key Files', 1875–1933 (GLRO file: A/FWA/C/D57/2).

TABLE 6.17. Mothers aided by the Bethnal Green home helps scheme, 1928–1938

Year	Home helps			Total cases	% of total births in Bethnal Green	Total cases paying	% of cases paying
	On panel	Temporary	Total				
1928	4	—	4	14	0.65	12	86
1929	8	—	8	65	3.15	44	68
1930	8	6	14	165	8.44	134	81
1935	12	6	18	163	11.33	67	41
1936	12	6	18	172	13.10	61	35
1937	12	6	18	190	15.10	61	32
1938	10	14	24	186	14.13	69	37

Source: Bethnal Green MOH, *ARs* (1928–38).

TABLE 6.18. *Number of women, men, and children sent to the convalescent home by Ranyard Nurses, 1897–1916*

Year	Total cases	Women		Men		Children	
		Total	% of total cases	Total	% of total cases	Total	% of total cases
1897–8, 1901	937	679	72	142	15	116	12
1903–5	822	633	77	115	14	74	9
1907–10	1,552	1,104	71	275	18	173	11
1911–16	2,037	1,490	73	392	19	155	8

Source: Ranyard Nurses, *ARs* (1897–1916).

Table 6.14 reveals for Stepney, patients helped in this way were charged according to their income.

Jewish mothers had recourse to a wide variety of domiciliary and dispensary services outside voluntary and Poor Law institutions in the event of pregnancy and childbirth. Access to the care provided by these agencies was freely available to Jewish mothers in the same way as access to voluntary hospitals and Poor Law maternity provision. None the less, their experience of these facilities was influenced by ethnic and religious considerations which changed over time. During the late nineteenth century domiciliary and dispensary services had a comparable religious orientation to voluntary hospitals and Poor Law institutions. By the early twentieth century however, with the exception of medical missions whose emphasis continued to be one of proselytization, these organizations were more aware of the religious and cultural needs of their non-Anglican patients. This coincided with an increasing secularization of medical services as a whole; a trend which was accentuated by the expansion in municipal provision. The new municipal services were less religiously orientated than their predecessors, reflecting the shift in attitudes towards religion and medical care. Medical discoveries in pain relief offered new answers and began to displace the importance of religious solace.[146]

Municipal expansion, however, was gradual, and voluntary institutions, now partly funded by the state, continued to be strong in East London throughout the inter-war period. This both helped and hindered

[146] For more thoughts on this subject see Prochaska, 'Body and Soul', 336, 347.

Jewish patients. It gave communal Jewish agencies active in maternal and child welfare more financial security and interaction with the wider community, but demarcations were retained as to who should be treated by which organizations. Jewish mothers no longer feared being converted, but their care was still divided between different agencies which were divided along religious lines for practical reasons. Similarly, ethnic-religious considerations continued to shape the provision and character of the services provided, as testified by the struggle over birth-control.

Bibliography

The works listed are restricted to those which have been mentioned in the text together with a selection of sources which provide a general history of immigration as well as the history of childbirth and maternal and infant welfare services.

AJA	Anglo Jewish Archives
Bodleian	Bodleian Library, Oxford
BL	British Library
BLPES	British Library of Political and Economic Sciences
CRO	Chief Rabbi's Office Archive, also known as United Synagogue's Archive
GLRO	Greater London Record Office
JWB	Jewish Welfare Board Archive
LH	London Hospital Archive
Mocatta	Mocatta Library, University College, London University (Most of this collection has now been moved to Parkes Library, Southampton University)
PRO	Public Record Office
St Barts	St Bartholomew's Hospital Archive
SA	Salvation Army Archive
THL	Tower Hamlets Local History Library and Archive.

MANUSCRIPT SOURCES

Note: Most of the archival collection previously at Mocatta Library, University College, London, has been moved to Parkes Library, Southampton University.

Hospitals

British Hospital for Mothers and Babies. Woolwich (GLRO)
Midwifery School Register, 1911–19 (H14/BMB/C1/1/1).
Chicago Lying-in Hospital (North-Western Memorial Hospital Archives)
Annual Reports (1895–34)
Case books (1895–34)

City of London Maternity Hospital (GLRO)
Annual Reports (1841–1940).
District Case Books, 1915–35.

Matron's Case Book, 1872–8; 1923–6; 1928–30; 1933–6; 1938–41.
Out-patients Admission Registers, 1875–1935.

East End Maternity Hospital (LH)
Annual Reports (1910–39).
Maternity Registers, 1884–1935.
Minutes, 1943 (S 591).

East London Hospital for Children and Dispensary for Women (LH)
Managing Committee, later Board of Management, and Annual Meetings of the
  Court of Governors, Minutes, 1 Jan. 1868–4 Jan. 1870.
  Scrapbook, 1901–14.

London Hospital
LH:
Annual Reports (1875–1939).
Blue File Committee, Minutes (LM/5/22), 1905, Circumcision (LM/5/27),
  1906.
House Committee, Minutes, 1917.
Green and White Charities Registers, numbers 80, 81, 86.
Marie Celeste Lying-In Wards:
  In-Patient Registers, 1905–35.
  District Registers, 1905–35.
Maternity Registers of the Medical Students, 1885–1935.

Holland, E., 'Report of External Maternity District and on the Urgent Need of
  Reforming the Work of Students Thereon', Apr. 1919 (LH/A/17/35).
THL:
Marie Celeste Samaritan Society, *Annual Reports* (1937, 1938).
Morris, E. W. (House Governor), 'Report of a Visit to the District Maternity
  Charity with Miss Nicholls, District Midwife', 19 Dec. 1922. Also in *London
  Hospital Illustrated* (1933), 10–11.

London Jewish Hospital (LH)
House Committee, Minutes, 1934–6
New York Lying-in Hospital (New York Hospital-Cornell Medical Center Medical
  Archives)
Annual Reports 1890–1932
Birth Registers 1890–1932

Salvation Army Mothers Hospital
SA:
Annual Reports (1911–47).
Case Books: girls' statements, 1886–8.

District Notes (from 1930s), City and Hackney, some from Dagenham Management Council, Minutes, 1914–23.
Medical Records, 1890–1910.
Midwife Case Notes, 1929–42.
Newspaper Clippings File on Salvation Army Mothers' Hospital.
Salvation Army Mothers' Hospital, Minutes, 1914–22.

St Bart's:
Admission Registers, 1915, 1925, 1935.
Medical Reports, 1924–30.

Nursing Associations

East London Nursing Society (THL)
Minutes, 1877–1939; *Annual Reports* (1880–1939).

Mrs Ranyards Nurses (GLRO)
Annual Reports (1898–1935); Papers; *The Nursing Branch of the Bible Women and Nurses*, Booklet for Future Nurses (n.d., file A/RNY).

St John the Divine Nursing Association (THL)
Annual Reports (1917–18), (1921–2); St John the Nurses, *Appeals*, 1933–8; St John the Divine's Nurses, The Community of Nursing Sisters of St John the Divine' Centenary Pamphlet (1948).

Shoreditch and Bethnal Green District Nursing Association (THL)
Annual Reports (1927–39).

Other Welfare and Health Organizations

Stepney Association for Rescue and Protection Work amongst Children (THL)
Annual Reports (1933–4).

Stepney Infant Welfare Centre and Babies' Nursing Home (THL)
Annual Reports (1926–7).

The Voluntary Maternity and Child Welfare Centres of Bethnal Green (THL)
Annual Report (1918–19).

Medical Missions:
All Saints' Medical Mission (AJA)
Minutes, Correspondence, Papers, and *Annual Reports* (1897–1921).

Barbican Mission to the Jews (GLRO)
Immanuel's Witness.
49th AR (1937–8) file A/FWA/C/D128/1.

London Society for Promoting Christianity Amongst the Jews (Bodl.)
Annual Report (1896).

Public Health Committees and Organizations

THL:

Stepney Maternity and Child Welfare Committee, Minutes, 1919–39.
Poplar Health Committee, Minutes, 1901–39.

Kensington Local History Library:

Kensington Council Committee, Minutes, 1902–39.

MOH, *Annual Reports* (THL and GLRO):

Bethnal Green (1871), (1873–1939).
Hampstead (1902–39).
Kensington (1902–39).
Poplar (1870–87), (1890–1938).
Stepney (1870–1938).
Woolwich (1902–39).

Government Papers (PRO)

MH *Public Health Administration and Services Files*

MH48/164 ('Report of the Infant Welfare in the Borough of Kensington', and Kensington Public Health Report).
MH 48/166 (Stepney MOH Report and Public Analyst 1901–19).
MH 52/31 (Local Government Act 1929, Maternity and Child Welfare Scheme for Payments to Voluntary Associations).
MH 52/55 (Maternity Homes Byelaws).
MH 52/156–7 (Bethnal Green Borough Council: Maternity and Child Welfare: Midwifery 1924–31).
MH 52/191 (Poplar Borough Council: Maternity and Child Welfare 1924–6).
MH 52/198*a–b* (Shoreditch Borough Council: Model Welfare Centre, Birth-Control Clinic).
MH 52/202–4 (Stepney Borough Council: Maternity and Child Welfare: Home Helps and Maternity Helps, School for Mothers, Jewish Maternity Home; 1920–1935).

MH 66 *Public Health Surveys*

MH 66/311–13 (Bethnal Green: Public Health Survey, Appendices, Correspondence 1930–2).
MH 66/339–42 (Hackney: Public Health Survey, Appendices, Correspondence 1933–7, MOH *Annual Report* (1937)).
MH 66/371–3 (Poplar: Public Health Survey, Appendices, Correspondence 1930–4).
MH 66/381–4 (Shoreditch: Public Health Survey, Appendices, Correspondence 1930–3, MOH Report 1937)).

MH 66/391–3 (Stepney: Public Health Survey, Appendices, Correspondence 1932–4).

MH 66/1081 (Public Health Surveys: Chelsea to Hackney, 1932–5).

MH 66/1083 (Public Health Surveys: Lambeth to Shoreditch, 1931–5).

MH 79/346 (Interdepartmental Committee on Milk Consumption, 30 Jan. 1936).

Home Office Files (HO 45)

1909–10 Effect of the Old Age Pensions Act on Applications for Naturalization, 154320 (10537).

1912–13 Applicants for Naturalization and their Knowledge of English, 226279 (10687).

1917–19 Ministry of Health Bill, 1919, Suggested Transfer of Certain Home Office Powers and Duties, 337412 (10841).

Deputation from the Jewish Community to the Home Office, 374355 (11068).

Friendly Societies Files

FS 1/461/2219, FS 1/444/1818, FS 1/476/2830, FS 1/465/2321, FS 1/465/2324, FS 1/487/3872, FS 1/488/3973, FS 3/2115, 2116, FS 4/29, FS 7/5/194, FS15/443, FS 15/995, FS 15/999, FS 16/57, 58.

Board of Guardians (GLRO)

Bethnal Green

Bethnal Green Hospital Committee, Minutes, 1903–29.

Board of Guardians, Minutes, 1846–72, 1876–7, 1879–80, 1884–5.

Orders of Removal to Other Unions, 1843–79.

Out Letters to Ministry of Health, 1920–1930.

Palatine Infirmary Committee, Minutes, 1896–1903.

Register of Orders of Removal from and to Other Unions, 1879–1901.

Triennial Reports, 1894–1912.

Waterloo House and Infirmary, Minutes, 1895–1929.

St George's-in-the-East Union

Board of Guardians, Minutes, 1870–1924.

Bromley House's Register of Births, 1866–1923.

House Committee, Minutes, 1909.

Infirmary Committee, Minutes, 1914–15.

Infirmary's Religious Creed Register, 1868–76.

Poplar Union

Board of Guardians, Minutes, 1870–1929.

Deputation to the Ministry of Health, 1924.

Financial and Statistical Statements, *Annual Report* (1900).

Whitechapel Union

Board of Guardians, Minutes, 1869–1926.

Committees, Minutes, 1879–1922.

Correspondence with the Local Government Board and Ministry of Health, 1874–1924.

Charity Organization Society (GLRO)

Annual Reports (1913–39).

Charity files containing correspondence and reports:

Barbican Mission to the Jews, *Annual Reports* (A/FWA/C/D/128/1).

East End Mission, 1917–36 (A/FWA/C/D/163/1).

East London Hospital for Children and Dispensary for Women, (A/FWA/C/D50).

Homes of Hope, 1873–98 (A/FWA/C/D23/1–5).

Little Sisters of the Assumption, 1885–1957 (A/FWA/143/2).

Providence Night Refuge, 1872–1947 (A/FWA/C/D49/1–4).

St Pelagia's Homes, 1895–1956 (A/FWA/D245/1).

Tower Hamlets Mission, 1875–1933 (A/FWA/C/D57/1–4).

Correspondence Files (A/FWA/C/C9/1 and A/FW/C/C12/1).

Council and District Committees, *Annual Reports* (1918–19).

Council, Minutes, 1908–13.

Medical Advisory Committee Minutes, 1915–20.

King's Fund Papers (GLRO)

Report on CLMH (A/KE/246/9; 514/6; 538/18; 735/39; 738/44).

Report on EEMH (A/KE/248/1).

Report on the Jewish Maternity Hospital and Bearstead Memorial Hospital (JMH) (A/KE/250/9; 520/7; 538/4; 735/51, 738/70).

Report on London Hospital (A/KE/252/1; 282; 522/4; 540/1; 545/18; 551; 731/6; 733/9; 737/8; 738/39).

Personal Papers

Charles Booth Collection, Files A24, A32, A33, A38, B181, B209 (BLPES).

Lady Battersea: Papers (BL) Add. MSS 47909–14.

Margaret Mead Papers: Projects in Contemporary Cultures, 1933–77, Columbia University Research in Contemporary Cultures Files (Library of Congress, Washington, DC, Manuscripts Division), files G44–53.

Redcliffe Salaman: Scientific and personal papers; includes Memoirs, 'The Helmsman Takes Charge' (Cambridge University Library).

Catholic Community

Little Sisters of the Assumption, also known as Nursing Sisters of the Poor (NSP archives: 34 Chepstow Villas, London, W11)

Album: Photos of the Bow Convent.

Fifty Years in the Harvest Field (Booklet for the Golden Jubilee of the Sisters' Arrival in England, June 1880–1930).

Lists of lectures by priests and laymen to Brothers' Meetings.

Notes on the Background to the Order.

Patient Notes from Little Sisters of the Assumption based in Notting Hill, 1886–7, 1916, 1918, 1920, 1922.

Transcripts of letters from Dr S. Alexander, 19 Feb. 1891; Dr R. Wheeler 2 Feb. 1892; and Dr D. Taylor, Christmas 1896.

Unpublished letters to L. Marks from Sister M.L. (archivist), 21 June 1988; Nov. *c.*1988.

Yearly Reports of Patient Statistics, 1904–7.

Little Company of Mary

Extract of the *History of Little Guardians' Home in St John's Wood* (n.d. and n.p.).

Unpublished letter to L. Marks from Provincial Superior (Ealing), 31 May 1988.

Unpublished letter to L. Marks from Sister E.M. (Nottingham), 26 June 1988.

Providence (Row) Night Refuge and Shelter (Archives: Crispin St., London, E1)

Notes from Providence Row (n.d., no author).

Providence Row, *Annual Report* (1987).

Providence (Row) Night Refuge and Home, 'Providence Row, 1860–1960', pamphlet (London, n.d.)

Sisters of Mercy, 'Sisters of Mercy: 1858–1977', pamphlet (London, n.d.)

Settlement of the Holy Child

THL:

Annual Reports (1931–2, 1962/3).

Archives of the Convent of the Holy Child, Mayfield, East Sussex:

Letter from Connie Sherwin to the Settlement, 3 May 1948.

Settlement, Minutes, 1913–47.

The Mayfield Review, 1913–36 (Box: B 36c).

Westminster Diocese Archive

Files:

Abortion (Hi. 2/2 1935–7).

Birth Control: Stopes *v.* Bourne *et al.* (Bo. 1/13, 1931–2; Bo. 5/59; Hi. 2/16).

Catholic Nurses Guild (Hi. 2/95).

Catholic Parents Association (Bo. 1/188).

Catholic Womens League (Bo. 1/30, 1906–12; Bo. 5/906; Hi. 2/34).

Catholic Womens' League (Bo. 1/30; Bo. 5/70 (b), 1924–31; Hi. 2/34).
Convents (with laundries, Bo. 1/94).
Crusade of Rescue (Homes for Destitute Catholic Children) (Bo. 1/46, 1920–3; Hi. 2/59, 1930–40).
Divorce (Bo. 1/12; Hi. 2/67).
Hackney (Bo. 1/92).
Hanwell (Bo. 1/92).
Hospitals (Bo. 1/63, 1905–31; Hi. 2/114–115; chaplains; Hi. 2/116; statistics: Hi. 2/190A).
Irish (Bo. 1/72, 94; Bo. 5/70 ab – Irish affairs).
Marriage, Divorce, and Birth-Control (Bo. 1/12).

Jewish Community Sources:

Catalogue of the Anglo-Jewish Historical Exhibition (London, 1888) (Mocatta).

Material relating to Synagogues (CRO)
Files:
General A–C 1899–1911, Misc. A–F 1916–23, Misc. F–I 1916–23, Misc. M–P, 1916–23, Misc. P–R, 1916–23, Misc. S–T, 1916–23, Misc. U–Z, 1916–23.
Mission Committee (file 957).
United Synagogue Council, Minutes, 1880–1902.
United Synagogue, Mission Committee, *Report of the Executive Committee* (*c.*1912) (file 907).
United Synagogue, Visitation Committee, Minutes, 1871–1914.
Visitation Committee (file 674A).
Welfare Committee (file 673).

Jewish Association for the Protection of Girls and Women
JWB:
Annual Reports, 1887–1939.
Council, Minutes, 1917–33.
General Committee of Jewish Ladies' Society, Minutes, 1896–1903.
General Committee, Minutes, 1900–1.
General Purposes Committee, Minutes, 1928–32.
Minutes, 1885–7; 1896–1903.
Montefiore House, General Committee, Minutes, 1922; School Register (no. B. 7)
Sarah Pyke House, Committee, Minutes, 1904–10, 1937–46.

New York Public Library:

Jewish International Conference on the Traffic in Girls and Women, *Official Report* (London 1910).

Jewish Board of Guardians for the Relief of the Poor
JWB:

Emigration Canvassing Committees, Minutes, 1908–9.
Executive, Minutes, 1869–1912.
Health Committee, Minutes, 1911–22.
Sanitary Committee, Minutes, 1885–1911.

Mocatta:

Annual Reports (1870–1939).
Jewish Board of Guardians, Presidential Address, AGM, 22 Mar. 1937 (box file
   pamphlet BA 28 COH).

Jewish Day Nursery (material kept by Mrs C. Rantzen)
Annual Reports (1897–1943).
Minutes, 1936.

Jewish Friendly Societies (Mocatta)
Association of Jewish Friendly Societies, *Annual Reports*, (1918–38).
Achei Brith and Shield of Abraham Friendly Societies, *Annual Reports*, (1927–40).

Jewish Infant Welfare Centre (THL)
Annual Reports (18th 1934–5), (22nd, 1938–9).

Jewish Mothers' Welcome and Infant Welfare Centre (THL)
Annual Report, (1932–3).

Poor Jews' Temporary Shelter (Mocatta)
Annual Reports, (1924, 1930–1, 1937, 1939).

Sick Room Helps Society and Jewish Maternity Hospital
THL:
Newspaper cutting of Queen Mary's Visit to the East End, 1916 (file O71.1).
Annual Report (1936).

Mocatta:
Annual Report (1937).

PRO:
Annual Report (1931) in Stepney Borough Council, 'Public Health Report', 1925–
   9 (file MH55/203–304)

Union of Jewish Women (Mocatta and AJA)
Annual Reports (1903–38).

Executive Committee, Minutes, 1902–8 (file AJ 26/B. 1); 1902–10 (file AJ 26/B. 2). General Committee, Minutes, 1902–15 (file AJ 26/A. 1–2).

Unpublished letters to L. Marks concerning the Jewish Maternity Home (deposited at The London Museum of Jewish Life)

Mrs M.B., London, 10 Nov. 1987.*
Mr S.B., London, 5 Nov. 1987; 19 Nov. 1987.q*
Mrs G.C., Middlesex, 11 Nov. 1987.*
Mrs M.S.C., Essex, 1 Nov. 1987; 16 Nov. 1987; 23 Nov. 1987.*
Mrs S.C., London, 11 Nov. 1987; 19 Nov. 1987.*
Mrs A.T.F., Cardiff, 30 Oct. 1987.*
Mrs H.G., West Sussex, 20 Nov. 1987.q*
Mrs M.S.G., London, 2 Nov. 1987.*
Mrs R.G., London, 10 Feb. 1988.
Miss T.G., London, 6 Nov. 1987; 19 Nov. 1987;q 1 Feb. 1988.i*
Mr M.K., London, 30 Oct. 1987.*
Mrs R.K., Essex, 11 Nov. 1987.*
Mrs B.L., Cambridge, 26 Dec. 1987.
Mrs L.L., London, 17 Nov. 1987.*
Mrs M.L., London, Nov. 1987.
Mrs S.L., London, 1 Nov. 1987.*
Mrs E.M., Galilee, Israel, 4 Dec. 1987; 18 Jan. 1988.q
Mrs E.P., London, Nov. 1987 (3 letters, last letterq)
Mrs R., London, Nov. 1987; 12 Nov. 1987.q*
Mrs S.R., London, 12 Nov. 1987.*
Mrs A.S., London, 1 Nov. 1987.i*
Mrs T., Essex, 18 Nov. 1987; 10 Dec. 1987.q*
Mrs I.T., London, 31 Oct. 1987; 13 Nov. 1987.*
Ms B.J.T, Hertfordshire, 8 Dec. 1987.
Mrs M.V., Hertfordshire, 13 Nov. 1987; 26 Nov. 1987.*
Mrs E.Y., London, 5 Nov. 1987; 11 Nov. 1987.*
Mrs W., London, 31 Nov. 1987.i

All letters were answered with a questionnaire.

* Letters which have been typed as excerpts.
q Letter with answers to questionnaire.
i Interviewed.

ORAL MATERIAL

Interview tapes and transcripts of L. Marks (deposited at The London Museum of Jewish Life and the National Sound Archive)

All interviews occurred in London unless stated otherwise.

Mrs A.E., 5 May 1987 (tape).

Mrs A.S., 13 Dec. 1987 (transcript).

Mrs B.L., 28 Oct. 1987 (notes).

Dr C., 15 Dec. 1987 (notes).

Jewish Day Club, 14 Dec. 1987 (notes).

Mrs D.G., 27 Sept. 1987 (transcript).

Miss D.J., 21 Dec. 1987 (tape).

Mrs E.C., 13 Jan. 1988 (transcript).

Mrs F.M., 2 June 1987 (tape).

Kingshold Day Centre, 17 Nov. 1987 (tape).

Mrs K.B., 4 Nov. 1988 (notes).

Jewish Women's League, 9 May 1990 (tape).

Miss M.B., 7 July 1987 (transcript).

Mr M.F., 2 June 1987 (transcript).

Mrs N.A., 10 June 1987 (transcript).

Miss P.G., 25 Oct. 1987 (tape).

Mrs R.C., 28 Oct. 1987 (tape).

Mrs R.W., 29 Sept. 1987 (tape).

Dr S.S., 7 July 1987 (tape).

Sisters of Charity, 14 Dec. 1987 (notes).

Sister E.M. (NSP), Nottingham, 11 Nov. 1988 (notes).

Sister P., Sister of Mercy, 9 Dec. 1987 (transcript).

Stepney Day Settlement Club, 28 Oct. 1987 (tape).

Miss T.G., 22 Jan. 1988 (transcript).

Mrs W., 8 Dec. 1987 (notes).

Mrs R.W.F., 6 May 1992 (notes).

Age Exchange Theatre Trust

Jewish: Tapes for *From Stepney Green to Golders Green* (London, 1987); especially North London Progressive Synagogue Ladies' Guild Association (4 Mar. 1987), and Mrs F.E.

Irish: Miss C.P., Mr M.B., Miss J.B., Miss B.H.

Jerry White Interview Transcripts (for *Rothschild Buildings: Life in an East End Tenetment Block* (London, 1980))

Discussion at Stepney Jewish Club (T 7:16).

Mrs A. (T 7:07/1–3; 9; 13; 30; 32)   Mrs L. (T 37/1–2).

Mrs A.K. (T 7.15).   Mrs L.B. (T 7 02/1–2).

Mrs B.A.   Miss M. (T 44; 45).

Mr D. (T 7:11/1–2).   Mr M.A. (T 7.8).

Miss E. (T 7:12/1–2; 14).   Mr M.D.

Mrs F.   Mrs M.H.

Miss F.P. (T 7:04/1–2).   Mrs M.L. (T 7:33/1–2; 36/1–2).

Mrs G. (T 7:31).

Miss H. ('I' 7:25/1–2; 28/1–2).

Mr and Mrs Harris.

Mrs J. (T 7:18; 19; 22/1–2; 27; 40).

Mr J.B. (T 7:34/1–2, 43).

Mr J.C.

Mr I.R. (T 7:1R, 2R).

Mrs K. (T 7:20/1–2; 21, 41).

Mr R. (T 7:23/1–2; 24/1–3; 26/1–2; 29; 42).

Mr R.L.

Miss R.W. (T 7.10).

Miss S.M. (T 7:17 1–2).

Mr V. (7:5).

Mrs Y. (T 35/1–2).

Museum of Jewish Life in London

T 51; T 64 (transcript); T 93; T 80; T 74; T 69; T 60; T 11.

PARLIAMENTARY PAPERS

Royal Commission on the Poor Laws in Ireland: The State of the Irish Poor in Great Britain, PP 1836 XXXIV, Appendices G and H.

House of Lords Select Committee on Poor Law Relief. PP 1888 XV, Proceedings, Evidence, Appendices.

House of Lords Select Committee on the Sweating System, Report and Minutes of Evidence, 1 Aug. 1888; ii. 20 Dec. 1888; iii. 24 May 1889; iv. 17 Aug. 1889; v. Appendix and Proceedings, 1890 (SP 1888 XX, XXI; 1889 XIII, XIV; 1890 XVII, 257).

House of Commons Select Committee on Alien Immigration, Report and Minutes of Evidence, i. 27 July 1888; ii. 8 Aug. 1889 (SP 1888 XI, 419; 1889 X, 265).

Royal Commission on Alien Immigration, PP 1903 IX pts. I and II (Cd. 1741; Cd. 1742; Cd. 1743) Report, Minutes of Evidence, Appendix.

Report of the Interdepartmental Committee on Physical Deterioration, PP 1904 XXXII (Cd. 2175; Cd. 2210), Minutes of Evidence, Appendix.

Royal Commission on the Poor Law and Relief of Distress, PP 1909, Reports, Minutes of Evidence, and Appendix (SP 1909 XXXVII (Cd. 4499); XXXIX (Cd. 4625); (Cd. 4626); (Cd. 4626); XL (Cd. 4684); XLI (Cd. 4835); XLII (Cd. 4850); XLIII (Cd. 4653), (Cd. 4690); XLIV (Cd. 4795), (Cd. 4890), (Cd. 4632); XLV (Cd. 4631).

Report from the Select Committee on Midwives Registration, PP 1890 XVII.

Report from the Select Committee on Midwives Registration, PP 1892 XIV 1, Minutes of Evidence (Cd. 6841).

Report on the Select Committee on Midwives Registration, PP 1893–4 XIII, Proceedings of the Committee and Minutes of Evidence (Cd. 6891).

Bill to Secure Better Training of Midwives and to Regulate their Practice, PP 1900 III (8), 507; (150), 517.

Midwives Act Committee, PP 1909 XXXIII (Cd. 4822; Cd. 4823), Minutes of Evidence. *Reports from Commissioners, Inspectors and Others on the Working of the Midwives Act*: Central Midwives Board, *Reports*, SP 1909 XXXIII (Cd. 4507; Cd. 4725); 1911 XXXV (Cd. 5505); 1912–13 XL (Cd. 6061); 1913 XXXIV (Cd. 6755); 1914 XLI (Cd. 7304); 1914–16 XXVII (Cd. 7784); 1914–16 XXVII (Cd. 8142); 1916 XIII (Cd. 8408); 1919 XXV (Cmd. 17).

Bill to Make Further and Better Provision with Respect to Feeble-Minded and Other Mentally Defective Persons, PP 1912–13 (213) III, pt. II.

Maternity and Child Welfare Act, PP 1918 (10) II, 251.

Local Government Board Annual Reports of Commissioners, PP 1879–1919 (SP 1880 XXVI; 1881 XLVI; 1882 XXX; 1883 XXVIII; 1884 XXXVIII; 1885 XXXII; 1886 XXXI; 1887 XXXII; 1888 XLIX; 1889 XXXV, 193; 1890 XXXIII; 1890–1 XXXIII; 1892 XXXVIII; 1893–4 XLIII; 1894 XXXVIII; 1895 L; 1896 XXXVI; 1897 XXXVI; 1898 XXXIX; 1899 XXXVII; 1900 XXXIII; 1901 XXV; 1902 XXXV; 1903 XXIV; 1904 XXV; 1905 XXXI; 1906 XXXV; 1907 XXVI; 1908 XXX; 1909, pt. 1 XXVIII, pt. 2 XXIX; 1910 XXXVIII; 1911 XXXI; 1912–13 XXXV; 1913 XXXI; 1914 XXXVIII; 1915 XII, 511; 1916 XIII; 1917–18 XVI, 131; 1918 XI, 229; 1919 XXIV, 379).

NEWSPAPERS AND PERIODICALS

All the World, Salvation Army newspaper.

British Medical Journal.

Catholic Directory.

Charity Organisation Review.

Di Tsukunft, The Future, Yiddish newspaper.

The Deliverer, Salvation Army newspaper.

East London Advertiser.

East End News.

East London Observer.

Immanuel's Witness, magazine of the Barbican Mission (GLRO file: A/FWA/ C/D128/1).

Jewish Chronicle.

Jewish World.

Jewish Year Book.

The Labour Woman.

The Lancet.

League of London Hospital Nurses Review, 1–8 (1932–9) (THL and LH).

London Hospital Illustrated (1933–6) journal put out by London Hospital (THL and LH).

Magazine of the Sacred Heart (1906–40), parish magazines of St Mary and St Michael Catholic Church, Commercial Road, (THL).

The Medical Officer.

The Missing Link Magazine (1868–1900), Mrs Ranyard's Nurses' Magazine (GLRO).

Onward (1924–40), journal of the CLMH, (GLRO).
Public Health.
The Tablet.
The War Cry, Salvation Army journal.

OCCASIONAL OFFICIAL PAPERS AND PRINTED REPORTS

Interdepartmental Committee on Abortion, 'The Abortion Report', *British Medical Journal*, 17 (June 1939), 1248–51.

LCC, *London Statistics* (London, 1889–1939).

MH, *42nd Annual Report on Infant and Child Mortality* (HMSO, 1913).

MH, *Memorandum: Maternity Hospitals and Homes* (HMSO, 1920).

MH, *Final Report of Departmental Committee on Maternal Mortality and Morbidity* (HMSO, 1932).

MH, Reports on Public Health and Medical Subjects, 68, 'High Maternal Mortality in Certain Areas', by Janet Campbell (HMSO, 1932).

MH, *Report of the Inter-Departmental Committee on Abortion* (HMSO, 1939).

Registrar-General, *Annual Reports of Births, Deaths and Marriages for England and Wales* (London, 1870–1939).

Registrar-General, *Decennial Supplement of Births, Deaths and Marriages for England and Wales* (London, 1870–1939).

Registrar-General, *Quarterly Returns of Births and Deaths for England and Wales* (London, 1880–1910).

UNPUBLISHED THESES

Black, G., 'Health and Medical Care of the Jewish Poor in the East End of London, 1880–1939', Ph.D. thesis, Leicester, 1987.

Collins, C., 'Women and Labour Politics in Britain, 1893–1932', Ph.D. thesis, London, 1991.

Cutting, R., 'The Jewish Contribution to the Suffrage Movement', BA thesis, Anglia Polytechnic, 1988.

Emanuel, J., 'The Politics of Maternity in Manchester, 1919–1939: A Study from Within a Continuing Campaign', M.Sc. thesis, Manchester, 1982.

Feldman, D. M., 'Immigrants and Workers, Englishmen and Jews: The Immigrant to the East End of London, 1880–1906', Ph.D. thesis, Cambridge, 1985.

Gillespie, J. A., 'Economic Change in the East End of London during the 1920s', Ph.D. thesis, Cambridge, 1984.

Higginbotham, A. R., 'The Unmarried Mother and Her Child in Victorian London, 1834–1914', Ph.D. thesis, Indianapolis, 1985.

Koven, S., 'Culture and Poverty: The London Settlement House Movement, 1870–1914', Ph.D. thesis, Harvard University, Cambridge, Mass. 1987.

Livshin, R., 'Aspects of the Acculturation of the Children of Immigrant Jews in Manchester, 1890–1930', M.Ed. thesis, Manchester, 1982.

Marks, L., 'Irish and Jewish Women's Experience of Childbirth and Infant Care in East London, 1870–1939: The Responses of Host Society and Immigrant Communities to Medical Welfare Needs', D.Phil. thesis, Oxford, 1990.

O'Connor, A., 'Child Murderess and Dead Child Traditions: A Comparative Study', Ph.D. thesis, University College, Dublin, 1987.

Peretz, E. P., 'Local Authority Maternal and Child Welfare Services in England and Wales, 1919–1939: A Comparative Study of Three Local Areas', Ph.D. thesis, Middlesex University, 1992.

Rose, G., 'Locality, Politics and Culture: Poplar in the 1920s', Ph.D. thesis, Queen Mary College, London University, 1988.

Ross, E. M., 'Women and Poor Law Administration, 1857–1909', MA thesis, London, 1956.

Smith, E. R., 'East End Jews in Politics 1918–1939', A Study in Class and Ethnicity, Ph.D. thesis, Leicester, 1990.

Steiner, M., 'Philanthropic Activity and Organisation in the Manchester Jewish Community, 1867–1914', MA thesis, Manchester, 1974.

Tananbaum, S., 'Generations of Change: The Anglicization of Russian Jewish Women in London, 1880–1939', Ph.D. thesis, Brandeis University, 1990.

Wilkinson, A. M., 'The Beginnings of Disease Control in London: The Work of the Medical Officers of Health in Three Parishes, 1856–1900', D.Phil. thesis, Oxford, 1981.

Williams, N., 'Infant and Child Mortality in Urban Areas of Nineteenth-Century England and Wales: A Record Linkage Study', Ph.D. thesis, Liverpool, 1989.

Other Unpublished Works

O'Shea, F., 'Community, Poverty and Criminality Among the Irish in East London, 1850–1914', unpublished paper submitted to Department of History and Civilization, European University Institute, Florence, June 1988.

Pappenheim, B., 'Jewish Women in Religious Life', read at Women's Congress at Munich, 1912 (Museum of Jewish Life, file 66, 1987).

PUBLISHED SOURCES

(Place of publication London unless stated otherwise)

Before 1939

ABBOTT, G., 'The Midwife in Chicago', *Am. J. Sociol.* 20/5 (1915), 684–99.

ADLER, H., 'Jewish Life and Labour', in H. Llewellyn Smith, *The New Survey of London Life and Labour* (1934), vi.

ASHBY, H. J., *Infant Mortality* (Cambridge, 1915).

Association of Infant Welfare and Maternity Centres, *Report on Enquiry on Existing Ante Natal Centres* (1925).

Association of Infant Welfare and Maternity Centres, *Talks on Health* (1929).

BAKER, J. S., 'Schools for Midwives', *Am. J. Obstet. and Diseases for Women and Children*, 65 (1912), 256–70, (repr. in J. B. Litoff, *The American Midwife Debate: A Sourcebook on its Modern Origins* (Westport, Conn. 1986).

BANISTER, J., *England Under the Jews*, 3rd edn. (1907).

BATTERSEA, C., *Reminiscences* (1922).

BELL, F., *At the Works* (1907; repr. 1985).

BILLINGS, J. S., 'Vital Statistics of the Jews in the United States', in *Census Bulletin*, 19 (Washington, DC, 30 Dec. 1890) 3–23.

BOOTH, C., *Life and Labour of the People in London: East London*, i. 2nd edn. (1889); ser. 1, *Poverty*, 4 vols. (1902); ser. 2, *Industry*, 5 vols. (1895–7); ser. 3, *Religious Influences*, 7 vols. (1895–7); *Notes on Social Influences and Conclusion*, final vol. (1902).

—— *Poor Law Reform* (1911).

BOOTH, W., *In Darkest England* (1890).

BOSANQUET, H., *Rich and Poor* (New York, 1896).

BRACKENBURY, H., 'Maternity in Its Sociological Aspects', *Soc. Serv. Rev.* 18/5 (Mar. 1937), 37–47.

CHADWICK, E., *Report on the Sanitary Condition of the Labouring Population of Great Britain*, with an introduction by M. W. Flinn (1842; repr. Edinburgh, 1965).

CLARKE, J. H. (ed.), *England Under the Heel of the Jew* (1918).

CROWELL, E. S., 'The Midwives of New York' (*c*.1915), repr. in J. B. Litoff, *The American Midwife Debate: A Sourcebook on its Modern Origins* (Westport, Conn. 1986).

DENVIR, J. *The Irish in Britain* (1897).

FISHBERG, M., 'Health and Sanitation of the Immigrant Jewish Population of New York', *The Menorah*, 33/2 (Aug. 1902), 158–90.

—— *The Jews: A Study of Race and Environment* (London and New York, 1911).

FRANKLIN, C., *Caroline Franklin, 1863–1935: An Appreciation* (book printed and written by friends for private circulation, 1936—copy held at BL (1086 cc.15)).

GEBBIE, N., 'Some Effects of the Local Government Act, 1929, or The Future of Maternity and Child Welfare', *Med. Offr.*, 1 Nov. 1930, 193.

GIDNEY, W. T., *The History of the London Society for Promoting Christianity Among the Jews, 1809–1908* (1908).

GOLDING, L., *Magnolia Street* (London, 1932).

HALL DAVIS, J., *Parturition and Its Difficulties* (London, 1865).

HARDY, G., 'Workhouse Death-Rate in Childbirth', *J. Stat. Soc.* 30 (1867), 171–3.

HART, E., 'The Mosaic Code of Sanitation', *Sanitary Rec.* 1 (1877), 183.

HEINRICK, H., *A Survey of the Irish in England* (1872; repr. with intro. by A. O'Day, 1990).

HOLLINGSHEAD, J., *Ragged London in 1861* (1861; repr. with intro. by A. S. Wohl, 1986).

HOPE, E. W., 'Observations on Autumnal Diarrhoea in Cities', in *Publ. Health* (July 1899), 660–5.

HOPE, E. W., and CAMPBELL, J., *Report on the Physical Welfare of Mothers and Children: England and Wales* (1917), i and ii.

HURRY, J. B., *District Nursing on a Provident Basis* (1898).

Infant Mortality Committee, 'Report of the Infant Committee', *Trans. Obstet. Soc.* 13 (1870), 132–49.

—— 'Concluding Report of Infant Mortality Committee', *Trans. Obstet. Soc.* 14 (1871), 388–93.

LANE-CLAYPON, J., *The Child Welfare Movement* (1920).

LEROY, A., *History of the Little Sisters of the Poor* (1906).

Little Company of Mary, *A Short Account of the Foundress of the Little Company of Mary*, with an intro. by B. Williamson (Rome, 1927).

LLEWELLYN DAVIES, M., *Maternity: Letters from Working Women* (1915; repr. with intro. by Gloden Dallas, 1984).

LLEWELLYN SMITH, H., *The New Survey of London*, 9 vols. (1930–5).

LONDON, J., *The People of the Abyss* (1903).

MCLEARY, G. F., *The Early History of the Infant Welfare Movement* (1933).

——— *The Maternity and Child Welfare Movement* (1935).

MARTINDALE, C. C., *The Foundress of the Sisters of the Assumption* (1936).

MAYHEW, H., *London Labour and the London Poor*, (1851; repr. 1964), i.

MELLANBY, E., 'Accessory Food Factors (Vitamines) in the Feeding of Infants', *The Lancet* (17 Apr. 1920), 856–64.

MOORE, G., *Esther Waters* (1894).

MOUAT, F. J., 'Notes on Statistics of Childbirth in Lying-In Wards of Workhouse Infirmaries of England and Wales for ten years, 1871–1880', *Trans. Internat. Med. Cong.* 4 (1881), 392–94.

MUNRO KERR, J. M., *Maternal Mortality and Morbidity* (Edinburgh, 1933).

NEWMAN, G., *Infant Welfare: A Social Problem* (1906).

NEWSHOLME, A., *Fifty Years in Public Health* (1935).

NIGHTINGALE, F., *Introductory Notes on Lying-In Hospitals* (1876).

OXLEY, W. H. F., 'Prophylaxis in Midwifery', *Med. Offr.*, 25 Aug. 1928, 79–81.

PEARSON, K., and MOUL, M., 'The Problem of Alien Immigration into Great Britain' *Ann. Eug.* 11 (1925), 5–127.

PEMBER REEVES, M., *Round About a Pound a Week* (1913; repr. with intro. by S. Alexander, 1984).

RAMSBOTHAM, 'The Eastern District of the Royal Maternity Charity', *Lond. Med. Gaz.*, NS 2 (1843–4), 619–25.

ROSENBAUM, S., 'A Contribution to the Study of Vital and Other Statistics of the Jews in the United Kingdom', *J. Roy. Stat. Soc.* 68 (1905), 526–56.

ROWNTREE, B. S., *Poverty: A Study of Town Life* (1901).

RUPPIN, A., *The Jews of Today* (1913).

RUSSELL, C., and LEWIS, H. S., *The Jew in London* (1901), with intro. by Canon Barnett.

SALAMAN, R., 'Anglo-Jewish Vital Statistics', *JC Supplements*, 26 Aug., 29 July, and 27 May 1921.

Society for the Holy Child of Jesus, *The Life of Cornelia Connelly* (1922).

SPRING RICE, M., *Working-Class Wives* (1939; repr. with intro. by B. Wootton, 1981).

STALLARD, J. H., *London Pauperism among Jews and Christians: An Inquiry into the Principles and Practice of Outdoor Relief in the Metropolis* (1867).

STEELE, F. M., *The Convents of Great Britain* (1902; 1925).

——*Monasteries and Religious Houses of Great Britain and Ireland* (1903).

SUMNER, M. S., 'Hospital Visits', in A. A. Leith (ed.), *Every Girl's Annual, Extra Supplement* (1887).

TAUSSIG, F., *Abortion, Spontaneous and Induced: Medical and Social Aspects*, National Committee on Maternal Health (1936).

TWINING, L., *Workhouses and Pauperism* (1898).

WALD, L., *The House on Henry Street* (New York 1915; repr., 1971).

WEBB, B., *My Apprenticeship* (1926; repr. 1971).

WEBB, S., and WEBB, B. (eds.), *The Break-Up of the Poor Law: Being Part One of the Minority Report of the Poor Law Commission* (1909).

WHITELEGGE, B. A., and NEWMAN, G., *Hygiene and Public Health* (1905).

WILLIAMS, W., *Deaths in Childbed* (1904).

WOODBURY, R. M., *Causal Factors in Infant Mortality: A Statistical Study Based on Investigations in Eight Cities* (Washington, 1925).

After 1939

ABEL-SMITH, B., *The Hospitals* (1964).

ADELSTEIN, A. M., and MARMOT, M. G., 'The Health of Migrants in England and Wales: Causes of Death', in J. K. Cruickshank and D. G. Beevers (eds.), *Ethnic Factors in Health and Disease* (1989).

ALDERMAN, G., *The Federation of Synagogues, 1887–1987* (1987).

——*London Jewry and London Politics* (1989).

ALEXANDER, S., 'Women's Work in Nineteenth Century London: A Study of the Years 1820–50', in E. Whitelegg *et al.* (eds.), *The Changing Experience of Women* (Oxford, 1982).

ALEXANDER, S., DAVIN, A., and HOSTETTLER, E., 'Labouring Women: A Reply to Eric Hobsbawm', *Hist. Workshop J.* (1979), 174–82.

ALEXANDER, Z., 'Let it Lie upon the Table: The Status of Black Women's Biography in the UK', *Gender and Hist.* 2/1 (1990), 22–34.

ANSON, P. F., *The Religious Orders and Congregations of Great Britain and Ireland* (1949).

ARONOVITCH, B., *Give it Time* (1974).

AZEN KRAUSE, C., *Grandmothers, Mothers and Daughters: Oral Histories of Three Generations of Ethnic American Women* (Cambridge, Mass. 1991).

BALARAJAN, R., and BOTTING, B., 'Perinatal Mortality in England and Wales: Variations by Mother's Country of Birth, 1982–1985', *Health Trends,* 21 (1989), 79–84.

BALLARD, L. M., ' "Just Whatever They Had Handy"': Aspects of Childbirth and Early Childcare in Northern Ireland, Prior to 1948', *Ulster Folklife,* 31 (1985), 59–72.

BALY, M. E., *A History of the Queen's Nursing Institute, 1887–1987* (1987).

BANKS, J. A., *Prosperity and Parenthood* (1956).

BARON, S., *Jews Under the Tsars and Soviets* (New York, 1964; 1973).

BAUM, C., HYMAN, P., and MICHEL, S., *The Jewish Woman in America* (New York, 1976).

BAYOR, R. H., *Neighbours in Conflict: The Irish, Germans, Jews, and Italians of New York City 1929–1941* (Chicago, 1988).

BERMAN, S., 'The Status of Women in Halakhic Judaism', in E. Koltun, *The Jewish Woman: New Perspectives* (New York, 1976).

BERMANT, C., *The Cousinhood: The Anglo-Jewish Gentry* (1971).

——*Point of Arrival* (1975).

BIALE, R., *Women and Jewish Law: An Exploration of Women's Issues in Halakhic Sources* (New York, 1984).

BLACK, E., *The Social Politics of Anglo-Jewry, 1880–1920* (Oxford, 1988).

BOCK, G., and THANE, P. (eds.), *Maternity and Gender Policies: Women and the Rise of European Welfare States, 1880–1950* (1991).

BODNAR, J., *The Transplanted: A History of Immigrants in Urban America* (Indianapolis, 1985).

BOLSTER, E., *The Sisters of Mercy in the Crimean War* (Cork, 1964).

BORST, C. G., 'The Training and Practice of Midwives: A Wisconsin Study', *Bull. Hist. Med.* 62 (1988), 606–27.

——'Wisconsin's Midwives as Working Women: Immigrant Midwives and the Limits of a Traditional Occupation, 1870–1920', *J. Am. Ethnic Hist.* (1989), 24–49.

BRÄNDSTRÖM, A., 'The Impact of Female Labour Conditions on Infant Mortality: A Case Study of the Parishes of Nedertorneå and Jokkmokk, 1800–1896', *Soc. Hist. Med.* 1/3 (1988), 329–58.

BRISTOW, E. J., *Vice and Vigilance* (Dublin, 1977).

——*Prostitution and Prejudice: The Jewish Fight against White Slavery, 1870–1939* (Oxford, 1983).

BROOKES, B., 'Women and Reproduction', in J. Lewis (ed.), *Labour and Love: Women's Experience of Home and Family, 1850–1940* (Oxford, 1986).

——*Abortion in England, 1900–1967* (1988).

BRYDER, L., 'The First World War: Healthy or Hungry?', *Hist. Workshop J.* 24 (1987), 141–57.

——*Below the Magic Mountain: A Social History of Tuberculosis in Twentieth Century Britain* (Oxford, 1988).

BUCKMAN, J., *Immigrants and the Class Struggle: The Jewish Immigrant in Leeds, 1880–1914* (Manchester, 1983).

——'Alien Working-Class Response: The Leeds Jewish Tailors, 1880–1914', in K. Lunn (ed.), *Hosts, Immigrants and Minorities: Historical Responses to New-comers in British Society, 1870–1914* (Folkestone, 1980).

BULMER, M., *The Social Basis of Community Care* (1987).

BULMER, M., BALES, K., and KISH SKLAR, K. (eds.), *The Social Survey in Historical Perspective* (Cambridge, 1991).

BURMAN, R., 'The Jewish Woman as the Breadwinner: The Changing Value of Women's World in a Manchester Immigrants Community', *Oral Hist.* 10/2 (1982), 27–39.

——'Growing up in Manchester Jewry: the Story of Clara Weingard', *Oral Hist.* 12/1 (1984), 56–63.

——' "She Looketh Well to the Ways of Her Household": the Changing Role of Jewish Women in Religious Life, *c.*1800–1930', in G. Malmgreen (ed.), *Religion in the Lives of English Women, 1760–1930* (1986).

——'Jewish Women and the Household Economy in Manchester, *c.*1890–1920', in D. Cesarani (ed.), *The Making of Modern Anglo-Jewry* (Oxford, 1990).

BURMAN, S. (ed.), *Fit Work for Women* (1979).

BURNET, J. R., and PALMER, H., *'Coming Canadians': An Introduction to a History of Canada's Peoples* (Toronto, 1988).

CALDWELL, J. C., 'Cultural and Social Factors Influencing Mortality Levels in Developing Countries', in S. H. Preston (ed.), *Annals of the American Academy of Political and Social Science: World Population: Approaching the Year 2000* (London and New Delhi, 1990).

——'Major New Evidence on Health Transition and its Interpretation', *Health Transition Review*, 1/2 (1991), 221–9.

CAMPBELL, R., and MACFARLANE, A., *Where to be Born? The Debate and the Evidence* (Oxford, 1987).

CAMPION, M., *Place of Springs: The Story of the First 100 Years of the Province of the Maternal Heart (English Province) at Little Company of Mary* (Liverpool, 1977).

CARROLL, M. G., *Father Pernet, Little Sister of the Assumption* pamphlet (1955).

——*Swallows of the Garret* (Cork, 1952).

CARTWRIGHT, F., *The Story of the Community of the Nursing Sisters of St John the Divine* (1968).

CESARANI, D. (ed.), *The Making of Modern Anglo-Jewry* (Oxford, 1990).

CHAMBERLAIN, M., *Old Wives' Tales* (1981).

CHAMBERLAIN, M., and RICHARDSON, R., 'Life and Death', *Oral Hist.* 10/1 (1983), 31–43.

CHENEY, R. A., 'Seasonal Aspects of Infant and Childhood Mortality: Philadelphia, 1865–1920', *J. Interdisc. Hist.* 14 (1984), 561–85.

CHRIST, C., 'Victorian Masculinity and the Angel in the House', in M. Vicinus (ed.), *A Widening Sphere* (Indianapolis, 1972).

City and Hackney Health Authority, 'The Mother's Hospital', in *The City and Hackney Health Authority Newsletter*, 12 (May 1986), 1.

CLARK KENNEDY, A. E., *The London: A Study in the Voluntary Hospital System*, 2 vols. (1963).

CLEAR, C., *Nuns in Nineteenth-Century Ireland* (Dublin, 1987).

——'The Limits of Female Autonomy: Nuns in Nineteenth-Century Ireland', in M. Luddy and C. Murphy (eds.), *Women Surviving: Studies in Irish Women's History in the Nineteenth and Twentieth Centuries* (Dublin, 1990).

COHEN, S., 'Anti-Semitism, Immigration Controls and the Welfare State', in *Critical Social Policy*, 13 (1985), 73–92.

COLLINS, K., *Go and Learn: The International Story of Jews and Medicine in Scotland* (Aberdeen, 1988).

CONDRAN, G. A., and KRAMAROW, E. A., 'Child Mortality among Jewish Immigrants to the United States', *J. Interdisc. Hist.* 22/2 (1991), 223–54.

CONNOLLY, G., 'Irish and Catholic: Myth or Reality? Another Sort of Irish and the Renewal of the Clerical Profession among Catholics in England, 1791–1918', in R. Swift and S. Gilley (eds.), *The Irish in Victorian Britain* (1985).

COOTER, R., *In the Name of the Child: Health and Welfare, 1880–1940* (1992).

CORRSIN, S. D., *Warsaw Before the First World War: Poles and Jews in the Third City of the Russian Empire, 1880–1914* (New York, 1989).

CROWTHER, M. A., *The Workhouse System, 1834–1929* (1981).

——'Paupers or Patients? Obstacles to Professionalization in the Poor Law Medical Service Before 1914', *J. Hist. Med.* 39 (1984), 33–54.

CURTIS, S. E., and OGDEN, P. E., 'Bangladeshis in London, a Challenge to Welfare', *Revue européenne des migrations internationales*, 2/3 (1986), 135–49.

DAVIDOFF, L., 'The Separation of Home and Work? Landladies and Lodgers in Nineteenth and Twentieth Century England', in S. Burman (ed.), *Fit Work For Women* (1979).

DAVIDOFF, L., and HALL, C., *Family Fortunes* (1987).

DAVIES, C. (ed.). *Rewriting Nursing History* (1980).

——'The Health Visitor as Mother's Friend: A Woman's Place in Public Health, 1900–1914', *Soc. Hist. Med.* 11 (1988), 39–59.

DAVIN, A., 'Imperialism and Motherhood', *Hist. Workshop J.* 5 (1978), 9–66.

DAVIS, G., 'Little Irelands', in R. Swift and S. Gilley (eds.), *The Irish in Britain* (1989).

DECLERCQ, E. R., 'The Nature and Style of Practice of Immigrant Midwives in Early Twentieth-Century Massachusetts,' *J. Soc. Hist.* 19 (1985), 113–29.

DELAMONT, S., and DUFFIN, L. (eds.), *The Nineteenth-Century Woman: Her Cultural and Physical World* (1978).

DIGBY, A., *Pauper Palaces* (1978).

DINER, H., *Erin's Daughters in America: Irish Immigrant Women in the Nineteenth Century* (Baltimore, 1983).

DONNISON, J., *Midwives and Medical Men: A History of the Struggle for the Control of Childbirth* (1977; repr., 1988).

DOUGHERTY, P., *Mother Mary Potter: Foundress of the Little Company of Mary, 1847–1913* (1961).

DRACHMAN, V. G., 'The Loomis Trial: Social Mores and Obstetrics in the Mid-Nineteenth Century', in J. W. Leavitt (ed.), *Women and Health in America* (Madison, Wis., 1984).

DRIVER, F., 'The Historical Geography of the Workhouse System in England and Wales, 1834–1883', *J. Hist. Geog.* 153 (1989), 267–86.

DUCROCQ, F., 'The London Biblewomen and Nurses Mission, 1857–1880: Class Relations/Women's Relations', in B. J. Harris and J. K. McNamara (eds.), *Women and the Structure of Society* (Durham, NC, 1984).

DUFFIN, L., 'The Conspicuous Consumptive: Woman as an Invalid', in S. Delamont and L. Duffin (eds.), *The Nineteenth-Century Woman: Her Cultural and Physical World* (1978).

DWORK, D., 'Health Conditions of Immigrant Jews on the Lower East Side of New York, 1880–1914', *Med. Hist.* 25/1 (1981), 1–40.

——*War is Good for Babies and Other Young Children: A History of the Infant and Child Welfare Movement, 1898–1918* (1987).

DYE, N. S., 'Modern Obstetrics and Working-Class Women: The New York Midwife Dispensary, 1890–1920', *J. Soc. Hist.* 20 (1987), 549–64.

DYHOUSE, C., 'Working-Class Mothers and Infant Mortality in England, 1895–1914', *J. Soc. Hist.* 12 (1979), 248–67.

DYOS, H. J., and WOLFF, M. (eds.), *The Victorian City: Images and Reality*, 2 vols. (1973).

ENDELMAN, T. M., *The Jews of Georgian England, 1714–1830* (Philadelphia, 1979).

——'Communal Solidarity among the Jewish Élite of Victorian London', *Vict. Stud.* 28/3 (1985), 491–526.

——*Radical Assimilation in English Jewish History, 1656–1945* (Indianapolis, 1990).

EWBANK, D. C., and PRESTON, S. H., 'Personal Behaviour and the Decline in Infant and Child Mortality: The United States, 1900–1930', in J. Caldwell *et al.*, *What We Know about Health Transition: The Cultural, Social and Behavioural Determinants of Health* (Canberra, 1990), i.

EWEN, E., *Immigrant Women in the Land of Dollars: Life and Culture on the Lower East Side, 1890–1925* (New York, 1985).

FAIRBANKS, J., *Booth's Boots: Social Service Beginnings in the Salvation Army* (1983).

FEHENEY, J. M., 'Delinquency among Irish Catholic Children in Victorian London', *Irish Hist. Stud.* 13/92 (1983), 319–29.

FELDMAN, D. M., 'Historical Review: "There was an Englishman, an Irishman and a Jew . . .": Immigrants and Minorities in Britain', *Hist. J.* 26/1 (1983), 185–99.

—— 'The Importance of Being English: Jewish Immigration and the Decay of Liberal England', in D. Feldman and G. Stedman Jones (eds.), *Metropolis London: Histories and Representations Since 1800* (1989).

FIELDING, S., *The Church and the People: Catholics and their Church in Britain, c.1880–1939'* (Coventry, 1988).

FILDES, V., 'Breastfeeding in London, 1905–1919', *J. Biosoc. Sci.* 24 (1992), 53–74.

—— 'Breastfeeding Practices during Industrialization, 1800–1919', in F. T. Falkner (ed.), *Infant and Child Nutrition Worldwide: Issues–Perspectives* (Miami, 1991).

FINESTEIN, I., 'Jewish Emancipationists in Victorian England: Self-Imposed Limits to Assimilation', in J. Frankel and S. J. Zipperstein (eds.), *Assimilation and Community: The Jews in Nineteenth-Century Europe* (Cambridge, 1992).

FINNEGAN, F., 'The Irish in York', in R. Swift and S. Gilley (eds.), *The Irish in the Victorian City* (1985).

FISHMAN, W. J., *East End Jewish Radicals, 1875–1914* (1975).

—— *East London, 1888* (1988).

FISSELL, M. E., 'The "Sick and Drooping Poor", in Eighteenth-Century Bristol and its Region', *Soc. Hist. Med.* 2/1 (1989), 35–58.

FITZPATRICK, D., 'A Peculiar Tramping People: The Irish in Britain, 1801–70', in W. E. Vaughan (ed.), *A New History of Ireland* (Oxford, 1989), v.

—— 'A Curious Middle Place: The Irish in Britain, 1871–1921', in R. Swift and S. Gilley (eds.), *The Irish in Britain* (1989).

FLINN, M. W., 'Medical Services Under the New Poor Law', in D. Fraser (ed.), *The New Poor Law in the Nineteenth Century* (1976).

FOX, E., 'The Jewish Maternity Home and Sick Room Helps Society, 1895–1939: A Reply to Lara Marks', *Soc. Hist. Med.* 4/1 (1991), 117–22.

—— 'Powers of Life and Death: Aspects of Maternal Welfare in England and Wales Between the Wars', *Med. Hist.* 35 (1991), 328–52.

FRASER, D., *The New Poor Law in the Nineteenth Century* (1976).

FRIEDMAN, A., 'Midwifery: Legal or Illegal? A Case Study of an Accused, 1905', in C. Maggs (ed.), *Nursing History: The State of The Art* (1987).

FUCHS, R. G., and PAGE MOGH, L., 'Pregnant, Single and Far From Home: Migrant Women in Nineteenth-Century Paris', *Am. Hist. Rev.* 95/4 (1990), 1007–31.

GAINER, B., *The Alien Invasion: The Origins of the Aliens Act of 1905* (1972).

GARRARD, J. A., *The English and Immigration: A Comparative Study of the Jewish Influx, 1880–1910* (Oxford, 1971).

GARTNER, L. P., *The Jewish Immigrant in England: 1870–1914* (1960; 1973).

—— 'Anglo-Jewry and the Jewish International Traffic in Prostitution, 1885–1914', *Am. Jewish Stud. Rev.* 7–8 (1982–3), 129–78.

GILLESPIE, J. A., 'Poplarism and Proletarianism: Unemployment and Labour Politics in London, 1918–1934', in D. Feldman and G. Stedman Jones (eds.), *Metropolis London: Histories and Representation Since 1800* (1989).

GILLEY, S. W., 'Protestant London, No Popery and the Irish Poor, 1830–1860', *Recusant Hist.* 104 (1969), 210–30.

—— 'The Roman Catholic Mission to the Irish in London', *Recusant Hist.* 103 (1969–70), 123–45.

—— 'The Catholic Faith of the Irish Slums: London, 1840–1870', in H. J. Dyos and M. Wolff (eds.), *The Victorian City: Images and Reality*, 2 (1973).

—— 'English Attitudes to the Irish in England, 1789–1900', in C. Holmes (ed.), *Immigrants and Minorities in British Society* (1978).

—— 'Irish Catholicism in Britain, 1880–1939', in S. Fielding (ed.), *The Church and the People: Catholics and their Church in Britain, c.1880–1939* (Coventry, 1988).

GITELMAN, Z. Y., *Jewish Nationality and Soviet Policies* (Princeton, NJ, 1972).

—— *A Century of Ambivalence: The Jews of Russia and the Soviet Union, 1881 to the Present* (New York, 1987).

GITTINS, D., 'Married Life and Birth Control Between the Wars', *Soc. Hist.* 3/2 (1975), 53–64.

—— 'Women's Work and Family Size Between the Wars', *Oral Hist.* 5 (1977), 84–100.

—— *Fair Sex, Family Size and Structure, 1900–1939* (1982).

GLASMAN, J., 'Assimilation by Design: London Synagogues in the Nineteenth Century', in T. Kushner (ed.), *The Jewish Heritage in British History: Englishness and Jewishness* (1992).

GLENN, S., *Daughters of the Shtetl: Life and Labour in the Immigrant Generation* (Ithaca, NY, 1990).

GORDON KUZMACK, L., *Woman's Cause: The Jewish Woman's Movement in England and the United States, 1881–1933* (Columbus, Oh., 1990).

GRAHAM, N., 'The Epidemiology of Acute Respiratory Infections in Children and Adults: A Global Perspective', *Epidemiol. Rev.* 12 (1990), 149–78.

Great Britain Committee on Medical Aspects of Food Policy, *Present Day Practice in Infant Feeding: Third Report* (1988).

GREENBERG, B., *On Women and Judaism* (Philadelphia, 1981).

GREENBERG, L., *The Jews in Russia*, ii. *The Struggle for Emancipation, 1881–1917* (1951).

GWYNN, R., *The Huguenot Heritage* (1985).

HALL, R., *Marie Stopes: A Biography* (1978).

—— (ed.), *'Dear Dr Stopes': Sex in the 1920s* (1978; 1981).

HARDY, A., 'Rickets and the Rest: Diet, Infectious Disease and the Late Victorian Child', *Soc. Hist. Med.* 5/3 (1992).

—— *The Epidemic Streets: Infectious Disease and the Rise of Preventive Medicine, 1856–1900* (Oxford, 1993).

HENNOCK, E. P., 'Poverty and Social Theory in England: The Experience of the Eighteen-Eighties.', *Soc. Hist.* 1 (1976), 67–91.

—— 'Concepts of Poverty in the British Social Surveys from Charles Booth to Arthur Bowley', in M. Bulmer, K. Bales, and K. Kish Sklar (eds.), *The Social Survey in Historical Perspective* (Cambridge, 1991).

HERSCHEL, S. (ed.), *On Being a Jewish Feminist* (New York, 1985).

HEWITT, M., *Wives and Mothers in Victorian Industry* (1958).

HIGGINBOTHAM, A. R., 'Respectable Sinners: Salvation Army Rescue Work with Unmarried Mothers, 1884–1914', in G. Malmgreen (ed.), *Religion in the Lives of English Women, 1760–1930* (1986).

——' "Sin of the Age": Infanticide and Illegitimacy in Victorian London', *Vict. Stud.* 32/3 (1989), 319–38.

HODGKINSON, R. G., *The Origins of the National Health Service* (1966).

HOLLOWAY, S. W. F., 'The All Saints' Sisterhood at University College Hospital, 1862–1899', *Med. Hist.* 3/1 (1959), 146–56.

HOLMES, C., (ed.), *Immigrants and Minorities in British Society* (1978).

——*Anti-Semitism in British Society, 1876–1939* (1979).

——*John Bull's Island: Immigration and British Society, 1871–1971* (1988).

HYMAN, P., 'The Other Half: Women in the Jewish Tradition', in E. Koltun (ed.), *The Jewish Woman: New Perspectives* (New York, 1976).

ILLINGWORTH, J., *et al.*, 'Diminution in Energy, Expenditure During Lactation', *Br. Med. J.* 292 (15 Feb 1986), 437–41.

INGLIS, K. S., *Churches and the Working-Classes in Victorian England* (1963).

Irish in Britain History Centre, *The History of the Irish in Britain: A Bibliography* (1986).

JACKSON, J. A., *The Irish in Britain* (1963).

——'The Irish in East London', *East London Papers*, 6/2 (1963), 105–19.

JACKSON, P., 'Women in Nineteenth Century Irish Emigration', *Internat. Migration Rev.* 18/4 (1984), 1004–45.

JAKOBOVITS, I., Chief Rabbi, 'Jewish Medical Ethics', printed pamphlet from St Paul's Lecture, 23 Nov. 1976.

JALLAND, P., *Women, Marriage and Politics* (Oxford, 1986).

JONES, C., 'Sisters of Charity and the Ailing Poor', *Soc. Hist. Med.* 2/3 (1989), 339–48.

JONES, E., and EYLES, J., *An Introduction to Social Geography* (Oxford, 1977; 1979).

KAPLAN, M. A., 'Gender and Jewish History in Imperial Germany', in J. Frankel and S. J. Zipperstein (eds.), *Assimilation and Community: The Jews in Nineteenth-Century Europe* (Cambridge, 1992).

KATZ, D. S., *Philo-Semitism and the Readmission of the Jews to England, 1603–1635* (1982).

——'The Jews of England and 1688', in O. P. Grell *et al.* (eds.), *From Persecution to Toleration* (Oxford, 1991), 217–49.

KENNEDY, P., and NICHOLLS, A. J. (eds.), *Nationalist and Racialist Movements in Britain and Germany Before 1914* (1981).

KENNEDY, R., *The Irish: Emigration, Marriage and Fertility* (1973).

KIERNAN, V. G., 'Britons Old and New', in C. Holmes (ed.), *Immigrants and Minorities in British Society* (1978).

KIRK, N., 'Ethnicity, Class and Popular Toryism, 1850–1870', in K. Lunn (ed.), *Hosts, Immigrants and Minorities: Historical Responses to Newcomers in British Society, 1870–1914* (Folkestone, 1980).

KIRKWOOD, K., HERBERTSON, M. A., and PARKES, A. S., 'Biosocial Aspects of Ethnic Minorities', in D. A. Coleman (ed.), *Demography of Immigrants and Minority Groups in the UK: Proceedings of the 18th Annual Symposium of the Eugenics Society*, London, 1981 (1982).

KLIER, J. D., 'Russian Jewry on the Eve of the Pogroms', in J. D. Klier and S. Lambroza (eds.), *Pogroms: Anti-Jewish Violence in Modern Russian History* (Cambridge, 1992).

KLIER, J. D., and LAMBROZA, S. (eds.), *Pogroms: Anti-Jewish Violence in Modern Russian History* (Cambridge, 1992).

KNIGHT, P., 'Women and Abortion in Victorian and Edwardian England', *Hist. Workshop J.* 4 (1977), 37–81.

KOBRIN, F. E., 'The American Midwife Controversy: A Crisis of Professionalization', *Bull. Hist. Med.* 40 (1966), 350–63.

KOLTUN, E. (ed.), *The Jewish Woman: New Perspectives* (New York, 1976).

KOSMIN, B. A., 'Nuptiality and Fertility Patterns of British Jewry, 1850–1980: An Immigrant Transition?', in D. A Coleman, *Demography of Immigrants and Minority Groups in the UK: Proceedings of the 18th Annual Symposium of the Eugenics Society*, London, 1981 (1982).

KOVEN, S., and MICHEL, S., 'Womanly Duties: Maternalist Politics and the Origins of Welfare States in France, Germany, Great Britain, and the United States', *Am. Hist. Rev.* 95/4 (1990), 1076–1108.

KUNITZ, S., 'Review of *Fatal Years*', *Health Transition Review*, 1/2 (1991), 233–5.

KUSHNER, T., 'An Alien Occupation: Jewish Refugees and Domestic Service in Britain, 1933–1948', in W. E. Mosse *et al.* (eds.), *Second Chance: Two Centuries of German-Speaking Jews in the United Kingdom* (Tübingen, 1991), 555–78.

——(ed.), *The Jewish Heritage in British History* (1992).

KRAUT, A. M., *The Huddled Masses: The Immigrant in American Society, 1880–1920* (Arlington Heights Ill., 1986).

——'Healers and Strangers: Immigrant Attitudes Toward the Physician in America: A Relationship in Historical Perspective', *J. Am. Med. Ass.* 263/13 (1990), 1087–11.

LADD-TAYLOR, M., *Raising a Baby the Government Way: Mothers' Letters to the Children's Bureau, 1912–1932* (New Brunswick, NJ, 1986).

——' "Grannies" and "Spinsters": Midwife Training Under the Sheppard-Towner Act', *J. Soc. Hist.* 22 (1988), 255–75.

LAMPHERE, L., *From Working Daughters to Working Mothers: Immigrant Women in a New England Industrial Community* (Ithaca, NY, 1987).

LEAVITT, J. W., 'Birthing and Anaesthesia: The Debate over Twilight Sleep', in J. W. Leavitt (ed.), *Women and Health in America* (Madison, Wis. 1984).

——(ed.), *Women and Health in America* (Madison, Wis. 1984).

——' "Down to Death's Door": Women's Perceptions of Childbirth in America', in J. W. Leavitt (ed.), *Women and Health in America* (Madison, Wis. 1984).

——*Brought to Bed: A History of Childbearing in America, 1750–1950* (Oxford, 1986).

——'Joseph DeLee and the Practice of Preventive Obstetrics', *Am. J. Publ. Health*, 7810 (1988), 1353–9.

LEBZELTER, G. C., 'Anti-Semitism: A Focal Point for the British Radical Right', in P. Kennedy and A. J. Nicholls (eds.), *Nationalist and Radical Movements in Britain and Germany Before 1914* (1981).

LECHTIG, A., *et al.*, 'Effect of Maternal Nutrition on Infant Mortality', in W. H. Moseley (ed.), *Nutrition and Human Reproduction* (New York and London, 1977).

LEE, A., 'Aspects of the Working-Class Response to the Jews in Britain, 1880–1914', in K. Lunn (ed.), *Hosts, Immigrants and Minorities: Historical Responses to Newcomers in British Society* (Folkestone, 1980).

LEE, C. H., 'Regional Inequalities in Infant Mortality in Britain, 1861–1971: Patterns and Hypotheses', *Popul. Stud.* 45 (1991), 55–65.

LEE, R., 'Uneven Zenith: Towards a Geography of the High Period of Municipal Medicine in England and Wales', *J. Hist. Geog.* 14/3 (1988), 260–80.

LEES, L. H., 'Patterns of Lower Class Life: Irish Slum Communities in Nineteenth Century London', in S. Thernstrom and R. Sennett (eds.), *Nineteenth-Century Cities* (New Haven, Conn. 1969).

——'Mid-Victorian Migration and the Irish Family Economy', *Vict. Stud.* 20/1 (1976), 25–43.

——*Exiles of Erin: Irish Migrants in Victorian London* (Manchester, 1979).

LEES, L. H., and MODELL, J., 'The Irish Countryman Urbanized: A Comparative Perspective on the Famine Migration', *J. Urban Hist.* 3/4 (1977), 387–90.

LENNON, M., MCADAM, M., O'BRIEN, J. (eds.), *Across the Water: Irish Women's Lives in Britain* (1988).

LEON, A., *The Jewish Question: A Marxist Interpretation* (1950), translated by E. Germain, with intro. by N. Weinstock (New York, 1970).

LEVENTHAL, J. M., *et al.*, 'Does Breastfeeding Protect Against Infections in Infants Less than 3 Months of Age?', *Pediatrics*, 78 (5 Nov. 1986), 896–903.

LEVY, A. B., *East End Story* (*c.*1949).

LEWIS, J., 'The Ideology and Politics of Birth Control in Inter-War England', *Women's Studies International Quarterly*, 2 (1979), 33–48.

——*The Politics of Motherhood: Child and Maternal Welfare in England, 1900–1939* (1980).

——'The Social History of Social Policy: Infant Welfare in Edwardian England', *J. Soc. Pol.* 9 (1980), 463–86.

——*Women in England, 1870–1950* (Brighton, 1984; 1986).

——'Introduction: Reconstructing Women's Experience of Home and Family', in J. Lewis (ed.), *Labour and Love: Women's Experience of Home and Family, 1850–1940* (Oxford, 1986).

——(ed.), *Labour and Love: Women's Experience of Home and Family, 1850–1940* (Oxford, 1986).

—— 'The Working-Class Wife and Mother and State Intervention, 1870–1918', in J. Lewis (ed.) *Labour and Love: Women's Experience of Home and Family, 1850–1940* (Oxford, 1986), 99–120.

—— 'Mothers and Maternity Policies in the Twentieth Century', in J. Garcia, R. Kilpatrick, and M. Richards (eds.), *The Politics of Maternity Care: Services for Childbearing Women in Twentieth-Century Britain* (Oxford, 1990).

—— 'Models of Equality for Women: The Case of State Support for Children in Twentieth-Century Britain', in G. Bock and P. Thane (eds.), *Maternity and Gender Policies: Women and the Rise of European Welfare States, 1880s–1950s* (1991).

LIPMAN, V. D., *Social History of the Jews in England, 1850–1950* (1954).

——*A Century of Social Service, 1859–1959: The Jewish Board of Guardians* (1959).

—— 'Age of Emancipation', in V. D. Lipman (ed.), *Three Centuries of Anglo-Jewish History* (Cambridge, 1961).

——*A History of the Jews in Britain Since 1858* (Leicester, 1990).

LITOFF, J. B., *American Midwives: 1860 to the Present* (Westport, Conn., 1978).

—— (ed.), *The American Midwife Debate: A Sourcebook of its Modern Origins* (Westport, Conn., 1986).

LODGE, M., 'Aspects of Infant Welfare in Coventry, 1900–1940', in B. Lancaster and T. Mason (eds.), *Life and Labour in a Twentieth-Century City: The Experience of Coventry* (Coventry, 1986).

LOUDON, I. S. L., 'Historical Importance of Outpatients', in *Br. Med. J.* 1 (1978) 974–7.

—— 'Deaths in Childbed from the Eighteenth Century to 1935', *Med. Hist.* 30/1 (1986), 1–41.

—— 'Obstetric Care, Social Class and Maternal Mortality', *Br. Med. J.* 2 (1986), 606–8.

—— 'Puerperal Fever, the Streptoccus and the Sulphonamides, 1911–1945', *Br. Med. J.* 2 (1987), 485–90.

—— 'Maternal Mortality, 1880–1950: Some Regional and International Comparisons', *Soc. Hist. Med.* 1/2 (1988), 183–228.

—— 'Some Historical Aspects of Toxaemia Pregnancy: A Review', *Br. J. Obstet. & Gynaecol.* 98 (1991), 853–8.

—— 'On Maternal and Infant Mortality, 1900–1960', *Soc. Hist. Med.* 4/1 (1991), 29–74.

—— 'Some International Features of Maternal Mortality, 1880–1950', in V. Fildes, L. Marks, and H. Marland (eds.), *Women and Children First: International Maternal and Infant Welfare, 1870–1945* (1992).

——*Death in Childbirth: An International Study of Maternal Care and Maternal Mortality, 1800–1950* (Oxford, 1992).

LOVELL, J., *Stevedores and Dockers: A Study of Trade-Unionism in the Port of London, 1870–1914* (1969).

Lowe, W. J., 'The Lancashire Irish and the Catholic Church, 1846–1871: The Social Dimension', *Irish Hist. Stud.* 20/77 (1966), 129–55.

—— 'The Outcast Irish in the British Victorian City: Problems and Perspectives', *Irish Hist. Stud.* 25/99 (1987), 264–76.

Lunn, K., 'Political Anti-Semitism before 1914', in K. Lunn and R. Thurlow (eds.), *British Fascism or the Radical Right in Inter-War Britain* (1976).

—— (ed.), *Hosts, Immigrants and Minorities: Historical Responses to Newcomers in British Society* (Folkestone, 1980).

Lunn, K., and Thurlow, R. (eds.), *British Fascism: Essays on the Radical Right in Inter-War Britain* (1978).

McClaren, A., *Birth Control in Nineteenth-Century England* (1978).

McCleary, G. F., *The Development of British Maternity and Child Welfare Services* (1945).

McEwan, M., *Health Visiting* (1950).

Macnicol, J., *Family Allowances* (1981).

Macfarlane, A., 'Statistics and Policy-Making in the Maternity Services', *Midwifery* (1985), 150–61.

Macfarlane, A., and Mugford, M., *Birth Counts. Statistics of Pregnancy and Childbirth*, 2 vols. (1984).

Maggs, C., 'Nurse Recruitment to Four Provincial Hospitals, 1881–1921', in C. Davies (ed.), *Rewriting Nursing History* (1980).

Mahler, H., 'The Safe Motherhood Initiative: A Call to Action' in *The Lancet*, (21 Mar. 1987), 668–70.

Malmgreen, G. (ed.), *Religion in the Lives of English Women, 1760–1930* (1986).

Mamdani, M., and Ross, D., 'Review Article: Vitamin A Supplementation and Child Survival: Magic Bullet or False Hope?', *Health Policy and Planning*, 4 (1989), 273–94.

Marcus, J. R., *Community and Sick Care in the German Ghetto* (Cincinatti, 1947).

Marks, L., 'Review of *Bread Givers* by Anzia Yezierska', *Shifra*, 3 and 4 (1986), 42–3.

—— 'The Experience of Jewish Prostitutes and Jewish Women in the East End of London at the Turn of the Century', *The Jewish Quarterly*, 34/2 (126) (1987), 6–10.

—— ' "Dear Old Mother Levy's": The Jewish Maternity Home and Sick Room Helps Society, 1895–1939', *Soc. Hist. Med.* 3/1 (1990), 61–88.

—— 'Working Wives and Working Mothers: A Comparative Study of Irish and East European Jewish Married Women's Work and Motherhood in East London, 1870–1914', in the Polytechnic of North London Irish Studies Centre, *Occasional Papers Series*, 2 (1990).

—— 'Ethnicity, Religion and Healthcare', *Soc. Hist. Med.* 4/1 (1991), 123–8.

—— 'Carers and Servers of the Jewish Community: The Marginalized Heritage of Jewish Women in Britain', in T. Kushner (ed.), *The Jewish Heritage in British History* (1992).

—— 'Mothers, Babies and Hospitals: "The London" and The Provision of Maternity Care in East London, 1870–1939', in V. Fildes, L. Marks, and H. Marland (eds.), *Women and Children First: International Maternal and Infant Welfare, 1870–1945* (1992).

—— ' "The Luckless Waifs and Strays of Humanity": Irish and Jewish Immigrant Unwed Mothers in London, 1870–1939', *Twentieth Cent. Br. Hist.* 3/2 (1992), 113–37.

—— 'Medical Care for Pauper Mothers and Their Infants: Poor Law Provision and Local Demand in East London, 1870–1929', *Econ. Hist. Rev.* 46/3 (1993).

—— 'Race, Class and Gender: The Experience of Jewish Prostitutes and other Jewish Women in the East End of London at the Turn of the Century', in J. Grant (ed.) *Silent Voices* (forthcoming).

MARLAND, H., *Medicine and Society in Wakefield and Huddersfield* (Cambridge, 1987).

—— 'A Pioneer in Infant Welfare: The Huddersfield Scheme, 1903–1920', *Soc. Hist. Med.* 6/1 (1993), 25–50.

MECKEL, R. A., *Save the Babies: American Public Health Reform and the Prevention of Infant Mortality, 1850–1929* (Baltimore and London, 1990).

MILLER, K. A., *Emigrants and Exiles: Ireland and the Irish Exodus to North America* (Oxford, 1988).

MILLWARD, P., 'The Stockport Riots of 1852: A Study of Anti-Catholic and Anti-Irish Sentiment', in R. Swift and S. Gilley (eds.), *The Irish in Victorian Britain* (1985).

MITCHELL, B. R., *European Historical Statistics, 1750–1975* (Cambridge, 1980).

—— *British Historical Statistics* (Cambridge, 1988).

MOORE, M. J., 'Social Work and Social Welfare: The Organisation of Philanthropic Resources in Britain, 1900–1914', *J. Br. Stud.* 16 (1977), 85–104.

MORLEY, R., *et al.*, 'Mother's Choice to Provide Breast Milk and the Developmental Outcome', *Archives of Disease in Childhood*, 63 (1988), 1382–5.

MOSCUCCI, O., *The Science of Woman: Gynaecology and Gender in England, 1800–1929* (Cambridge, 1990), 185–7.

MOSELEY, W. H., *Nutrition and Human Reproduction* (New York and London, 1977).

MUNRO KERR, J. M., JOHNSTONE, R. W., and PHILLIPS, M. H. (eds.), *Historical Review of British Obstetrics and Gynaecology, 1800–1950* (Edinburgh, 1954).

MURPHY-LAWLESS, J., 'The Silencing of Women in Childbirth or Let's Hear it From Bartholomew and the Boys', *Women's Internat. Forum*, 11 (1988), 293–9.

OAKLEY, A., 'Wisewoman and Medicine Man: Changes in the Management of Childbirth', in J. Mitchell and A. Oakley (eds.), *The Rights and Wrongs of Women* (London, 1976; 1979).

—— *Women Confined: Towards a Sociology of Childbirth* (Oxford, 1980).

—— *The Captured Womb: A History of the Medical Care of Pregnant Women* (Oxford, 1984).

O'CONNOR, A., 'Listening to Tradition', in L. Steiner-Scott, *Personally Speaking: Women's Thoughts on Women's Issues* (Dublin, 1985).

ODDY, D., 'Working-Class Diets in Late Nineteenth-Century Britain', *Econ. Hist. Rev.*, 2nd ser. 23 (1970), 314–23.

ORBACH, A., 'The Development of the Russian Jewish Community, 1881–1903', in J. D. Klier and S. Lambroza (eds.), *Pogroms: Anti-Jewish Violence in Modern Russian History* (Cambridge, 1992).

O'TUATHAIGH, M. G. A., 'The Irish In Nineteenth-Century Britain: Problems of Integration', in R. Swift and S. Gilley (eds.), *The Irish in the Victorian City* (1985).

PAMUK, E. R., 'Social Class Inequality in Infant Mortality in England and Wales from 1921 to 1980', *Eur. J. Popul.* 4 (1988), 1–21.

PELLING, M., and SMITH, R. (eds.), *Life, Death and the Elderly: Historical Perspectives* (1991).

PERETZ, E. P., 'The Professionalization of Childcare', *Oral Hist.* 17/1 (1989), 22–8.

——'A Maternity Service for England and Wales: Local Authority Maternity Care in the Inter-war Period in Oxfordshire and Tottenham', in J. Garcia, R. Kilpatrick, and M. Richards (eds.), *The Politics of Maternity Care: Services for Childbearing Women in Twentieth-Century Britain* (Oxford, 1990).

——'Regional Variations in Maternal and Child Welfare Between the Wars: Merthyr Tydfil, Oxfordshire and Tottenham', in D. Foster and P. Swan (eds.), *Essays in Regional Local History* (Hull, 1992).

——'The Costs of Modern Motherhood to Low-Income Families in Interwar Britain', in V. Fildes, L. Marks, and H. Marland (eds.), *Women and Children First: International Maternal and Infant Welfare, 1870–1945* (1992).

——'Infant Welfare in Oxford between the Wars', in R. Whiting (ed.), *Oxford and Its People* (Manchester, 1992).

PHOENIX, A., 'Black Women and Maternity Services', in J. Garcia, R. Kilpatrick, and M. Richards (eds.), *The Politics of Maternity Care: Services for Childbearing Women in Twentieth-Century Britain* (Oxford, 1990).

POLLINS, H., *Economic History of the Jews in England* (1982).

PRAIS, S. J., and SCHMOOL, M., 'Statistics of Milah and the Jewish Birth Rate in Britain', *Jewish J. Sociol.* 11/1 (1970), 187–93.

PRESTON, S. H., and HAINES, M. R., *Fatal Years: Child Mortality in Late Nineteenth-Century America* (Princeton, NJ, 1991).

——'Response to Comments on *Fatal Years*', *Health Transition Review*, 1/2 (1991), 240–4.

PROCHASKA, F. K., *Women and Philanthropy in Nineteenth-Century England* (Oxford, 1980).

——'Body and Soul: Bible Nurses and the Poor in Victorian London', *Hist. Research*, 60/143 (1987), 336–48.

——*The Voluntary Impulse: Philanthropy in Modern Britain* (1988).

306 *Bibliography*

——'A Mother's Country: Mothers' Meetings and Family Welfare in Britain, 1850–1950', *Hist.* 74 (1989), 379–99.

——*Philanthropy and the Hospitals of London: The King's Fund, 1897–1990* (Oxford, 1992).

QUIROGA, V. A. M., *Poor Mothers and Babies: A Social History of Childbirth and Child Care Hospitals in Nineteenth-Century New York City* (New York, 1989).

RAMSAY, E., *East London Nursing Society, 1868–1968: A History of a Hundred Years* (1968).

RICHARDSON, R., *Death, Dissection and the Destitute* (1988; 1989).

RICHARDSON, R., and HURWITZ, B., 'Joseph Rogers and the Reform of Workhouse Medicine', *Br. Med. J.* (16 Dec. 1989), 1507–10.

RIVETT., G., *The Development of the London Hospital System* (1986).

ROBERTS, E., 'Working-Class Standards of Living in Barrow and Lancaster, 1890–1914', in P. Thane (ed.), *Essays in Social History* (Oxford, 1986).

——*A Woman's Place: An Oral History of Working-Class Women, 1890–1940* (Oxford, 1984; 1986).

ROBERTS, R., *The Classic Slum* (1971; 1977).

ROSE, G., 'The Struggle for Political Democracy: Emancipation, Gender and Geography', *Society and Space: Environment and Planning*, 8/4 (1990), 395–408.

ROSE, L., *The Massacre of the Innocents: Infanticide in Britain, 1800–1939* (1986).

ROSE, M., 'Settlement, Removal and the New Poor Law', in D. Fraser (ed.), *The New Poor Law in the Nineteenth Century* (1976).

ROSENBERG, D., *Facing up to Anti-Semitism: How Jews in Britain Countered the Threats of the 1930s* (1985).

ROSENFIELD, A., and MAINE, D., 'Maternal Mortality—A Neglected Tragedy: Where is the M in MCH?', *The Lancet* (13 July 1985), 83–5.

ROSS, E., ' "Fierce Questions and Taunts": Married Life in Working-Class London, 1870–1914', *Fem. Stud.* 8/3 (1982), 575–602.

——'Women's Neighbourhood Sharing in London before World War One', *Hist. Workshop J.* 15 (1983), 4–27.

——'Labour and Love: Rediscovering London's Working-Class Mothers, 1870–1918', in J. Lewis (ed.), *Labour and Love: Women's Experience of Home and Family, 1850–1940* (Oxford, 1986).

ROTH, C., *History of the Jews in England*, 3rd edn. (Oxford, 1964).

ROWBOTHAM, S., *Hidden from History: 300 Years of Women's Oppression and the Fight Against It* (1973).

RYAN, P. A., ' "Poplarism", 1894–1930', in P. Thane (ed.), *The Origins of British Social Policy* (1978).

——'Politics and Relief: East London Unions in the Late Nineteenth and Early Twentieth Centuries', in M. E. Rose (ed.), *The Poor and the City; The English Poor Law in its Urban Context, 1834–1914* (Leicester, 1985).

RYAN JOHANSSON, S., 'Sex and Death in Victorian England', in M. Vicinus (ed.), *A Widening Sphere* (Indianapolis, 1977).

SAMUEL, R., 'The Roman Catholic Church and the Irish Poor', in R. Swift and S. Gilley (eds.), *The Irish in Victorian Britain* (1985).

SCHMELZ, U. O., *Infant and Early Childhood Mortality among Jews of the Diaspora* (Jerusalem, 1971).

SCHOFIELD, R., 'Did Mothers Really Die? Three Centuries of Maternal Mortality in "The World We have Lost" ', in R. Smith, L. Bonfield, and K. Wrightson (eds.), *The World We Have Gained* (Oxford, 1987).

SCHOLTEN, C. M., ' "On the Importance of the Obstetric Art": Changing Customs of Childbirth in America, 1760–1825', in J. W. Leavitt (ed.), *Women and Health in America* (Madison, Wis., 1984).

SCOTT, J., and TILLY, L. A., 'Women's Work and the Family in Nineteenth-Century Europe', in C. E. Rosenberg (ed.), *The Family in History* (Philadelphia, 1975).

SCOTT, J. W., 'Gender: A Useful Category of Historical Analysis', *Am. Hist. Rev.* (1986), 1053–75.

——Gender and the Politics of History (New York, 1988).

SCOTT SMITH, D., 'Mortality Differentials Before the Health Transition', *Health Transition Rev.* 1/2 (1991), 235–7.

SEARLE, G. R., *The Quest for Efficiency, 1899–1914* (Oxford, 1971).

SELAVAN, I., 'Bobba Hannah, Midwife', *Am. J. Nursing*, 73, pt. 4 (1973), 681–3.

SEMMEL, B., *Imperialism and Social Reform* (1960).

SESSIONS RUGH, S., 'Being Born in Chicago', *Chicago History*, 15/4 (1986–7), 4–21.

SHLOMOWITZ, R., and McDONALD, J., 'Babies at Risk on Immigrant Voyages to Australia in the Nineteenth Century', *Econ. Hist. Rev.* 44/1 (1991), 86–101.

SILBER, J., 'Some Demographic Characteristics of the Jewish Population in Russia at the End of the Nineteenth Century', *Jewish Soc. Stud.* 5 (1980), 269–80.

SINGER, I., *Of a World That is No More* (trans. J. Singer, 1970).

SMITH, E. R., 'Jews and Politics in the East End of London, 1918–1939', in D. Cesarani (ed.), *The Making of Modern Anglo-Jewry* (Oxford, 1990).

SMITH, F. B., *The People's Health, 1830–1910* (1979).

SOLOWAY, R., 'Counting the Degenerates: The Statistics of Race Deterioration in Edwardian England', *J. Contemp. Hist.* 17/1 (1982), 137–64.

STAHL WEINBERG, S., *The World of Our Mothers: The Lives of Jewish Immigrant Women* (Durham, NC, 1988).

STEDMAN JONES, G., *Outcast London: A Study in the Relationship Between Classes in Victorian Society* (1971; 1984).

SUMMERS, A., 'A Home from Home: Women's Philanthropic Work in the Nineteenth Century', in Burman, S. (ed.), *Fit Work for Women* (1979).

——Angels and Citizens: British Women as Military Nurses, 1854–1914 (1988).

——'The Mysterious Demise of Sarah Gamp: The Domiciliary Nurse and her Detractors, c.1830–1860', *Vict. Stud.* 32/3 (1989), 365–86.

——'The Costs and Benefits of Caring: Nursing Charities, c.1830–c.1860', in

J. Barry and C. Jones (eds.), *Medicine and Charity Before the Welfare State* (1991).

SWIFT, R., and GILLEY, S. (eds.), *The Irish in the Victorian City* (1985).

——(eds.), *The Irish in Britain, 1815–1939* (1989).

SZRETER, S., 'The Importance of Social Intervention in Britain's Mortality Decline, *c.*1850–1914: A Reinterpretation of the Role of Public Health', *Soc. Hist. Med.* 1/1 (1988), 1–39.

TEITELBAUM, M. S., 'Male and Female Components of Perinatal Mortality: International Trends, 1901–1963', *Demography*, 8 (1971), 541–8.

THANE, P., 'Women and the Poor Law in Victorian and Edwardian England', *Hist. Workshop J.* 6 (1978), 29–51.

——(ed.), *The Origins of British Social Policy* (1978).

——*The Foundations of the Welfare State* (1982).

——'The Working Class and State "Welfare" in Britain, 1880–1914', *Hist. J.* 27/4 (1984), 877–900.

——'Government and Society in England and Wales, 1750–1914', in F. M. L. Thompson (ed.), *Cambridge Social History of Britain, iii. Social Agencies and Institutions* (Cambridge, 1990).

——'Genre et protection sociale: La Protection maternelle et infantile en Grande-Bretagne, 1860–1918', *Genèses*, 6 (1991), 73–97.

——'Visions of Gender in the Making of the British Welfare State: The Case of Women in the British Labour Party and Social Policy, 1906–1945', in G. Bock and P. Thane (eds.), *Maternity and Gender Policies: Women and the Rise of the European Welfare States, 1880s–1950s* (1991).

——'Women in the British Labour Party and the Construction of State Welfare, 1906–1945', in S. Koven and S. Michel (eds.), *Mothers of the New World* (1993).

THÉRÈSE, M., *Cornelia Connelly: A Study in Fidelity* (1963).

THOMPSON, B., 'Infant Mortality in Nineteenth-Century Bradford', in R. Woods, and J. Woodward (eds.), *Urban Diseases and Mortality in Nineteenth Century England* (1984).

THOMPSON, P., *Socialists, Liberals and Labour: The Struggle for London, 1885–1914* (1967).

——'Voices from Within', H. J. Dyos and M. Wolff (eds.), *The Victorian City: Images and Reality* (1973), i.

——*The Edwardians* (1975).

THOMSON, D., 'Workhouse to Nursing Home: Residential Care of Elderly People in England Since 1840', *Ageing and Society*, 3 (1983), 43–70.

——'The Decline of Social Security: Falling State Support for the Elderly since Early Victorian Times', *Ageing and Society*, 4 (1984), 451–82.

——'The Welfare of the Elderly in the Past: A Family or Community Responsibility?', in M. Pelling and R. Smith (eds.), *Life, Death and the Elderly: Historical Perspectives* (1991).

THURLOW, R. C., 'Satan and Sambo: The Image of the Immigrant in English

Racial Populist Thought Since the First World War', in K. Lunn (ed.), *Hosts, Immigrants and Minorities: Historical Responses to Newcomers in British Society, 1870–1914* (Folkestone, 1980).

TITMUSS, R. M., *Birth, Poverty and Wealth: A Study of Infant Mortality* (1943).

TRANTER, N. L., *Population and Society, 1750–1940* (1985).

VICINUS, M., *Independent Women: Work and Community for Single Women, 1850–1920* (1985).

VINCENT, D., *Literacy and Popular Culture: England, 1750–1914* (Cambridge, 1989)

WALKOWITZ, J., *Prostitution and Victorian Society* (Cambridge, 1981).

—— 'Jack the Ripper and the Myth of Male Violence', *Fem. Stud.* 8/3 (1982), 543–75.

WALL, R., 'Infant Mortality in the 1890s', *Loc. Popul. Stud.* 17 (1976), 48–50.

WALLER, P., *Town, City and Nation* (Oxford, 1983).

WARREN, K. S., 'McKeown's Mistake', *Health Transition Review*, 1/2 (1991), 229–33.

WATERMAN, R., *A Family of Shopkeepers* (1973).

WATERS, M. C., *Ethnic Options: Choosing Identities in America* (Los Angeles, 1990).

WATERSON, P. A., 'The Role of the Environment in the Decline of Infant Mortality: An Analysis of the 1911 Census of England and Wales', in *J. Biosoc. Sci.* 18 (1986), 457–70.

WEATHERFORD, D., *Foreign and Female, Immigrant Women in America, 1840–1930* (New York, 1986).

WEBSTER, C., 'Healthy or Hungry Thirties?', *Hist. Workshop J.* 13 (1982), 110–29.

—— 'Health, Welfare and Unemployment During the Depression', *P&P* 109 (1985), 204–30.

WEINDLING, P., 'The Contribution of Central European Jews to Medical Science and Practice in Britain, 1930s–1950s', in W. E. Mosse *et al.* (eds.), *Second Chance: Two Centuries of German-Speaking Jews in the United Kingdom* (Tübingen, 1991), 243–54.

WEINER, D. B., 'The Brothers of Charity and the Mentally Ill in Pre-Revolutionary France', *Soc. Hist. Med.* 2/3 (1989), 321–39.

WHITE, J., *Rothschild Buildings: Life in an East End Tenement Block, 1887–1920* (1980).

WHITEHEAD, E. W., *A Form of Catholic Action: The Little Sisters of the Assumption* (1947).

WHITELEGG, E., *et al.* (eds.), *The Changing Experience of Women* (Oxford, 1982).

WILLIAMS, B., *The Making of Manchester Jewry, 1740–1875* (Manchester, 1976; 1985).

—— 'The Beginnings of Jewish Trade-Unionism in Manchester, 1889–1891', in Lunn, K. (ed.), *Hosts, Immigrants and Minorities: Historical Responses to Newcomers in British Society* (Folkestone, 1980).

—— 'The Anti-Semitism of Tolerance: Middle-Class Manchester and the Jews, 1870–1900', in A. J. Kidd and K. W. Roberts (eds.), *City, Class and Culture: Studies of Social Policy in Victorian Manchester* (Manchester, 1985).

——' "East and West": Class and Community in Manchester Jewry, 1850–1914', in D. Cesarani (ed.), *The Making of Modern Anglo-Jewry* (Oxford, 1990).

WILLIAMS, K., *From Pauperism to Poverty* (1981).

WILLIAMS, N., 'Death in its Season: Class, Environment and the Mortality of Infants in Nineteenth-Century Sheffield', *Soc. Hist. Med.* 5/1 (1992), 71–94.

WILLMONT, P., and YOUNG, M., *Family and Kinship in East London* (1957; 1967).

WINTER, J. M., 'Infant Mortality and Maternal Mortality and Public Health in Britain in the 1930s', *J. Eur. Econ. Hist.* 8 (1979), 439–62.

——'The Decline of Mortality in Britain, 1870–1950', in T. Barker and M. Drake (eds.), *Population and Society in Britain, 1850–1980* (1982).

——'Aspects of the Impact of the First World War on Infant Mortality in Britain', *J. Eur. Econ.* Hist. 11 (1982), 713–38.

——'Unemployment, Nutrition and Infant Mortality in Britain, 1920–1950', in J. M. Winter (ed.), *The Working Class in Modern British History* (Cambridge, 1983), 232–305.

——*The Great War and the British People* (1986).

WISCHNITZER, M., *To Dwell in Safety: The Story of Jewish Migrations Since 1800* (Philadelphia, 1948).

WOHL, A. S., *Endangered Lives: Public Health in Victorian Britain* (1983; 1984).

WOODS, R. I., WATTERSON, P. A., and WOODWARD, J. H., 'The Causes of Rapid Infant Mortality Decline in England and Wales, 1861–1921', pt. 1, *Popul. Stud.* 42 (1988), 343–66.

——'The Causes of Rapid Infant Mortality Decline in England and Wales, 1861–1921', pt. 2, *Popul. Stud.* 43 (1989), 113–32.

WOODS, R., and WOODWARD, J., 'Mortality, Poverty and the Environment', in R. Woods and J. Woodward (eds.), *Urban Diseases and Mortality in Nineteenth Century England* (1984).

WOODWARD, J. H., *To Do the Sick No Harm: A Study of the British Voluntary Hospital System to 1875* (1974).

WRAY, J. D., 'Maternal Nutrition, Breastfeeding and Infant Survival', in W. H. Moseley (ed.), *Nutrition and Human Reproduction* (New York and London, 1977).

WRIGLEY, E. A., *Population and History* (1969; 1973).

YEZIERSKA, A., *Bread Givers* (1984).

ZBOROWSKI, M., and HERZOG, E., *Life is with People: The Culture of the Shtetl* (New York, 1952, with intro. by M. Mead).

Index